German Crime Dramas from Network Television to Netflix

German Crime Dramas from Network Television to Netflix

Sunka Simon

BLOOMSBURY ACADEMIC
NEW YORK • LONDON • OXFORD • NEW DELHI • SYDNEY

BLOOMSBURY ACADEMIC
Bloomsbury Publishing Inc
1385 Broadway, New York, NY 10018, USA
50 Bedford Square, London, WC1B 3DP, UK
29 Earlsfort Terrace, Dublin 2, Ireland

BLOOMSBURY, BLOOMSBURY ACADEMIC and the Diana logo are trademarks of
Bloomsbury Publishing Plc

First published in the United States of America 2023
Paperback edition published 2024

Copyright © Sunka Simon, 2023

For legal purposes the Acknowledgments on pp. ix–x constitute an extension
of this copyright page.

Cover design: Eleanor Rose
Cover image: Still from *Dark* © Netflix / Collection Christophel / ArenaPAL

All rights reserved. No part of this publication may be reproduced or transmitted
in any form or by any means, electronic or mechanical, including photocopying,
recording, or any information storage or retrieval system, without prior
permission in writing from the publishers.

Bloomsbury Publishing Inc does not have any control over, or responsibility for, any
third-party websites referred to or in this book. All internet addresses given in this
book were correct at the time of going to press. The author and publisher regret any
inconvenience caused if addresses have changed or sites have ceased to exist,
but can accept no responsibility for any such changes.

A catalog record for this book is available from the Library of Congress.

ISBN: HB: 978-1-5013-6872-1
PB: 978-1-5013-7049-6
ePDF: 978-1-5013-6870-7
eBook: 978-1-5013-6871-4

Typeset by Deanta Global Publishing Services, Chennai, India

To find out more about our authors and books visit www.bloomsbury.com and
sign up for our newsletters.

CONTENTS

List of Figures viii
Acknowledgments ix

Introduction 1
   Screening Globally, Watching Locally 6
   The Long Life of Crime: Lessons for Post-Network Television 12
   Program Guide 18

PART ONE Network Television

1 History and Format of the Crime Series *Tatort* (*Crime Scene*) (ARD, 1970–) 27
   Innovating within the Tried and True 30
   Intersections of National, Regional, and Local Viewing 34
   Tatort Tourism 36
   "Close to Reality" 39

2 Following the Flow: The National News, Regional Crimes, and Global Literacy 41

3 *Tatort* Hamburg (NDR) 48
   "Rechnen Sie mit dem Schlimmsten!" ("Worst-Case Scenario," dir. Peter-Schulze Rohr; NDR, September 24, 1972) 49
   "Voll auf Hass" ("Committed to Hate," dir. Bernd Schadewald; NDR, November 8, 1987) 62
   "Auf der Sonnenseite" ("On the Sunny Side," dir. Richard Huber; NDR, October 26, 2008) 73

4 *Tatort* Berlin (SFB/RBB) 86

Berlin in the Crosshairs of Films and Television 86
"Keine Tricks, Herr Bülow" ("No Tricks, Mr. Bülow," dir. Jürgen Roland; RBB/SFB, May 28, 1989) 89
"Berlin, beste Lage" ("Berlin, Top Location," dir. Matti Geschonneck; RBB, January 10, 1993) 103
"Eine ehrliche Haut" ("An Honest Skin/Man," dir. Ralph Bohn; RBB, January 4, 2004) 114

5 *Tatort* Dresden and Leipzig (NDR/MDR) 127

"Taxi nach Leipzig" ("Taxi to Leipzig," dir. Peter-Schulze Rohr; NDR, November 29, 1970) 130
"Jetzt und Alles" ("Now and Everything," dir. Bernd Böhlich; MDR, July 31, 1994) 148
"Todesstrafe" ("Death Penalty," dir. Patrick Winczewski; MDR, May 25, 2008) 162

Conclusion 177

Regions and/as Mediascapes 179

PART TWO Netflix

1 Introduction 183

Converging on Crime 183
Netflix and the German Mediascape 186
From *Berlin Alexanderplatz* (1980) to *Babylon Berlin* (Netflix/Sky/ARD, 2017–) 193
Fernsehfilm, Limited Series, and Period Drama 197
Unofficial US Format Adaptations and Cultural Authenticity 200
Transnational Casting and Production Practices 202

2 Crime Time: *Dark* (Netflix, 2017–20) 204

Dark Synopsis 206
Transmedia Families 207
Time-Shifting as a Post-Network Formal and Narrative Device 213
Experimenting with Television: The Bunker/Children's Room 220
The Modular Architecture of Post-Network Original Language Crime Dramas 230

3 Relational Memory: *Perfume* (Netflix, 2018) 257
   Switching Channels: Domestic Rivals on Netflix 257
   Waxing Nostalgic: *Perfume*, Postmemory, and Restorative Nostalgia 265
   Peripheral Adjacencies: Welcome to Fargo, Germany 268
   Relational Memory and Micro Flows in Transmedia Television 271
   Abandoned Futures and Ruined Pasts 277

4 Watching National German Television on Netflix: *Dogs of Berlin* (Netflix, 2018–) 283
   Dogs of Berlin Synopsis and Narration 283
   Reproducing the East as Homeland 289
   Violent Crime as Authentication Factor 292
   "Kaiserwarte": Surveilling Bodies in Motion 295
   Transmedia Migration as White Male Privilege 299
   The Illusion of Liveness: Watching Soccer with Neo-Nazis 302

Conclusion 312

Bibliography 317
Index 325

FIGURES

1. String wall in *Dark* from a fan site investigating family connections 216
2. Ulrich and Katharina as their 1986 teenage versions in *Dark*, Season 1 (Netflix, 2017) 219
3–4. Children's/bunker room, *Dark*, Season 1 (Netflix, 2017) 221
5–6. Jonas (2052) and Jonas (2019) in *Dark*, Season 1 (Netflix, 2017); Raider/Twix Candy Bar (1986/2022) 231
7–8. Locations: Reinfelder Schule, Berlin (2019); Heisenberg Gymnasium (Hamburg, 2021) 238

ACKNOWLEDGMENTS

The beginnings of this book go back to 2010, when my partner, our six-year-old son, and I spent a semester in Hamburg. Mike worked on his own book, Sander enrolled in first grade at my old elementary school, and I immersed myself in the substantial *Tatort*-related holdings of the *Norddeutscher Rundfunk* (NDR, Northern German Broadcasting) archive. The archivists at the NDR allowed me access to in-house memos and ARD yearbooks, and with their help, I collected all print and digital reception on each episode of *Tatort* I had selected for the study. Without their generosity, analyzing the television flow between *Tagesschau*, *Tatort*, and each premiere's critical reception would not have been possible. My first sincere thank you thus goes to the NDR.

The generous sabbatical support of my institution, Swarthmore College, made it possible to devote crucial focused time to this involved interdisciplinary German Media Studies project. After serving four years as Associate Provost, the time off was essential. My dear colleague and friend Carina Yervasi gave vital feedback on the book proposal, stabilized me in moments of panic, and always allowed me to share my enthusiasm. Our cross-cultural dialogues and joint teaching and research initiatives have been an immense source of inspiration and joy to me over the years. *Merci beaucoup*! At different stages, my departmental colleagues Patricia White and Bob Rehak graciously and instrumentally supported the project and connected endeavors. I value your input and collegiality. Without the rigorous, collaborative learning alongside students in my many TV classes over the years, this book could not have been written.

Katie Gallof, Stephanie Grace-Petinos, the copyeditors at Bloomsbury, as well as the anonymous peer reviewers: Thank you for making this book better through your informed and thoughtful suggestions.

Throughout the book's development, my parents, Eva and Dieter, and my sister, Siska, have been energetic correspondents, stimulating dialogue partners, and big-hearted hosts. For many years, prior to *DasErste.de*, my father made sure that I had access to *Tatort* by taping the show for me. *Danke*! And if it had not been for my mother, who showed an interest in and prompted conversations about our lives and projects until her final week, writing would have been a lonelier process. I deeply miss her and our invigorating talks.

And finally, to my small family, Mike and Sander: I am grateful for you. During our Covid-induced reclusiveness, we sustained each other, and—watched and debated television shows together. What do a seventeen-year-old Twitch streamer, a historian, and a German media studies scholar have in common? Engaged viewership across network, cable, and internet: *Blackish* (2014–22) and the remake of the *Wonder Years* on ABC (2021–), CW's *Legacies* (2018–), *Lucifer* (2016–21) and *After Life* on Netflix (2019–22), and Mark Rober on YouTube. Thank you to the inspired writers, creators, producers, and actors for forging interpersonal connections through episodic and long-arc storytelling, and to media-makers, readers, and fellow crime drama fans for spending time with me tracking the genre's paths from network television to Netflix.

Introduction

Deutschland '83–'89 (AMC/Sundance/Fremantle/RTL, 2015–21) is an East/West German spy-thriller series taking place in the years before and immediately after unification in 1989. It was also the first German television drama that aired on an American television channel before it was broadcast in Germany. Its 1980s storyline allows AMC to revisit its own cable-era past (October 1, 1984), while double-agent protagonist Martin Rauch's (Jonas Nay) code-switching mimics transnational television during convergence. His fate rests in his ability to give a convincing performance to all sides. The actor and his character need to represent 1980s East German realities believably to diegetic and non-diegetic East and West German audiences and engagingly to viewers across the globe while combining that German specificity with the serial format lessons German writers and producers learned from imported American television over the past thirty years. In the third installment of the series (*Deutschland '89*), in a further twist of media reflexivity, Martin begins working for the Americans, as are German television writers and directors involved in coproduction deals with the Comcast-owned Sky Deutschland, AMC, HBO, or Netflix.

The show's internal border-crossings reflect on the history of German television to serve both sides of the Iron Curtain until 1989. During that time, most East Germans could illicitly access West German networks' offerings which were dominated by US films and series. By contrast, most US viewers first discovered German-made television through AMC and Netflix. It is ironic that the private capitalist media system with its incompatible technology and lack of multilinguistic access—and *not* communism—prevented US viewers from accessing East and West German television narratives until 2015.

Instead of acknowledging the complexity of the factors contributive to this lopsided television exchange and, as a result, the US knowledge gap about German television history, trade journals and news media covering the success of German-language original shows in the convergence era instead profess their disdain for German television history. Seventy years of domestic television production is summed up as "peculiar" at best or "very boring, stiff, didactic—very German, very narrow-minded" at worst.[1] In all likelihood, those delivering these sweeping assessments never saw more than a sample episode, since domestic series were not subtitled unless sold abroad. But as Jason Mittell and Ethan Thompson put it: "To understand TV, you need to watch TV." And they poignantly continue: "some types of television require particular viewing practices to really understand them, such as long-term viewing of serials and series, or the contextualized viewing of remakes or historically nostalgic programming."[2] This book promises to deliver on both.

Lack of quality is not the reason why it took so long for the United States to start buying and binging German series. A grab bag of the good and bad arguably defines television as a medium. In contrast to West Germans' broad access to US television series from *Baywatch* to *Mad Men*, even the most critically acclaimed domestic German productions did not make it across the Atlantic. While New German Cinema productions were shown at US festivals, fans and critics had trouble accessing the television projects by some of the movement's directors. Nevertheless, some of Germany's crime dramas were successfully sold as television films (*Fernsehfilm*) or as seasonal packages across Europe, the Middle East, and Asia (*Derrick, Tatort, Bella Block*). With its arrival on AMC in 2015, the *Deutschland* series thus symbolically reunited a divided Germany with one of its allies at the very moment that that postwar allegiance would begin a fragile phase with Trump's election. *Deutschland '83* crossed the Atlantic and breached a previously impenetrable screen for domestically produced television. On its heels came the crime-fantasy-horror hybrid *Dark* (2017–20), the first multi-season German series to reach a broader US and global audience on Netflix.

After a significant rise in new subscriptions through the early global pandemic (2019–20), the bifurcation of streaming platforms increased competition, while economic uncertainties forced many cross-platform viewers to become cost-conscious. This in turn has led streamers to reassess their practice of making an entire season accessible at once. In the 2021 season, Disney Plus's *The Mandelorian* and in the 2022 season, Amazon's *Marvelous Mrs. Maisel* were released on a weekly basis. The streamers have thus returned to network protocols in order to keep viewers from binging and dumping subscriptions within the free trial period. As it is adapting to these new circumstances, Netflix has so far been reluctant

---

[1] Adam Lusher, "Deutschland 83. Scandinavian TV Takes a Back Seat as New Show Ushers in Golden Age for German TV Dramas," *The Independent*, May 15, 2015, https://www.independent.co.uk/arts-entertainment/tv/news/deutschland-83-scandinavian-tv-takes-backseat-new-show-ushers-golden-age-german-tv-dramas-10254241.html (accessed November 18, 2020).
[2] Ethan Thompson and Jason Mittell, "Introduction," in *How to Watch Television*, ed. Ethan Thompson and Jason Mittell (New York: New York University Press, 2013), 7.

to invest in extended runs for new shows (limiting even successful series to two or three seasons), to function as a reliable delivery vehicle of US television classics, and to subtite and stream canonical foreign-language shows originally produced for home markets. This book contends that long-running domestically produced television shows that succeeded in interacting with and competing against imported US formats along with globally circulating popular culture content can offer vital instruction for emergent media. Repeatedly and creatively having had to adapt to industry and technology changes to weather crisis moments, long-running network crime dramas bear crucial information and inspiration for producers and executives, and for creative teams and program directors.

As American-based global conglomerates seek to attract and retain subscribers at home and abroad, a culturally specific approach to German television, dedicated to the intersection between television text, medium-specific aesthetics, and mediascape, can contribute significantly not only to research but also to industry. Yet the majority of contemporary television research and theory published in German remains untranslated, even though the field of television studies has developed significantly in Germany since the 1980s. By connecting media studies and German studies, this book aims to bridge the resulting gaps. It approaches German television crime dramas with an eye toward uncovering the continuities with and departures from media-specific network exhibition strategies by taking into account the role of television flow, internal segmentation, aesthetic patterns, and narrative formats.

The longevity of a particular series sets television studies apart from film studies, if only by the impossibility of achieving conclusive and finite coverage. Jason Mittell developed five principles of cultural genre analysis for television: paying attention to the particular attributes of the medium, negotiating between specificity and generality, composing discursive genealogies, understanding genre as cultural practice, and situating genres within larger systems of power.[3] In analyzing a series like *Tatort* (ARD, *Crime Scene* 1970–) that celebrated its fifty-year anniversary in 2020, my approach follows Mittell's in combining a medium-reflexive historical lens with a commitment to contextualize cultural specificity without decreasing the importance of the individual television text itself. Instead of reducing episodes to their plotlines and character representations or ascribing them to a production goal or phase of the network, this book takes them seriously as media texts that speak to, reflect, and contribute to social, technological, epistemological, and aesthetic situatedness. Exploring situatedness becomes

---

[3] Jason Mittell, "A Cultural Approach to Television Genre Theory," in *Thinking Outside the Box*, ed. Gary Edgerton and Brian Rose (Lexington: University of Kentucky, 2005), 37–64, here 55–9.

even more important in the case of original language productions, the majority of which were unavailable to non-English speakers during the network era and continue to be inaccessible as streamers prefer to produce, coproduce, or license new original language content. But rather than condensing a complexly unfolding geopolitical moment to a kernel of accepted knowledge after the fact as a backward glance on history is wont to perform, the book's cultural media studies approach seeks to recapture the precarious and messy positionality of a televisual moment in the flow of time and space. The aim is not to provide a grand narrative of postwar German television history—for that there are critical books by Wulf Kansteiner, among others[4]—but to read the episodes situationally, in their media moment. How crime dramas construct, represent, and reflect on their situatedness—during the network, cable/satellite, and the streaming era—discusses the very "reference points and stuff of conversations" that David Morley imagines as the creative communal effect of watching global and/as regional television at a specific juncture.[5]

Analyzing the confluence of regional, national, and global intertextual and paratextual concepts and movements, and how these not only become material in topicality or character ranges but find expression in the formal language of both genre and medium, sheds light on the continuities between network and Netflix eras—and how, in turn, television, in its varying materializations as a player in national, transnational, and global industries, shapes how viewers conceive of their situatedness, what counts as and feels like local, national, and global. A 2013 study of cross-platform media migration within and between national communities, between diasporic communities and their home- and host-lands, analyzed how network, satellite, and streaming television effected the paths of integration (e.g., how British network television is shaping what signifies as "local" for many Irish viewers). Its authors remind us to stay aware of the multi-nodal connections between geopolitical relations, transnational existences, mobility, and media use across platforms: "Media use is inflected with personal history and biographical reflection, particularly for people whose experience of movement and mobility involves the accretion of relationships and connections stretched and mediated in space and time."[6] A crime drama that has been on air on national television for over fifty years participates in and shapes the accumulation of relationalities differently than a three-season crime drama on Netflix. In an era of cross-platform mobility that fosters

---

[4] Wulf Kansteiner, *In Pursuit of German Memory: History, Television and Politics after Auschwitz* (Columbus: Ohio University Press, 2006).
[5] David Morley, *Family Television: Cultural Power and Domestic Leisure* (London: Routledge reprint, 2005), 11.
[6] A. Kerr, R. King O Riain, and G. Titley, "Transnational Media Networks and the 'Migration Nation,'" in *Migrations: Ireland in a Global World*, ed. M. Gilmartin and Allen White (Manchester: Manchester University Press, 2013), 98–114, here 99.

global circulation and comingling of domestically produced television it becomes even more important to explore how crime dramas contribute to the imaginary of "German/y."

The first part of the book centers on the ARD network's flagship series *Tatort*, whose big tent concept is closely interwoven with the federal structure of its public network, currently comprised of nine regional broadcast stations. The stalwart show's concept predates the regional spin-off format of its namesake, the popular US media franchise *CSI* (CBS 2000–15), by thirty years. The German concept integrates rotating regional contributions under one program umbrella, which has implications for how it represents the connections between the local, regional, national, and how it responds to the challenges of global television. Aided by adhering to a stringent windowing since the 1970s (Sunday night at 8:15 p.m.), each participating region produces its own episodes that are folded into a weekly rotation that gets screened on the national broadcaster, over the years occasionally even featuring contributions from Austrian and Swiss affiliates ORF and SRG/SSR. Through *Tatort*, national German television has thus facilitated its regions' image-productions and (self)representations since 1970. From production model to reception and PR strategies, the back-and-forth transition between local and global discourses and representations necessitated and fostered a consistent dialogue between different audience demographics, between different identity configurations and allegiances.

Tatort's substantial episode archive encompassing three major mediascape changes makes the negotiation process between the geopolitical layers and their changing (self)representations visible. At the same time, the show's long-term survival depended on its intertextual dialogue with the development of the television crime drama writ large. While the rotation between different regional teams has limited seriality to character backstories and chemistry, rather than larger conspiratorial plotlines, for example, the program structure has accentuated differences in point of view through directing styles, casting and acting, location-based politics and social milieu, pacing and aesthetics. To understand this concept more fully, the first part analyzes three episodes from three contributing *Tatort* regions, whose premiere dates fall into network, privatization, and convergence eras. Close readings of each episode are contextualized by the specific history, casting, and style of the region's contributions, Sunday evening's ritualized televisual flow between national news and crime drama as well as critical and viewer engagement with actors, narration, and aesthetics. Every episode analysis assesses media reflexivity as the show's format adapts to each mediascape change while keeping the co-construction of local, regional, national, and global concepts in focus.

Paying close attention to how *Tatort* has successfully navigated the multiple mediascape changes bears lessons for current and future production and exhibition engagements with streaming platforms, the focus of the second part of the book. The book reevaluates *Tatort*'s regional diversification strategy as a crossover model for the streaming era. How the weekly change in cast, location, and tone is contained by general adherence to the format brand that makes each regional episode a recognizable *Tatort* episode, for example, finds its current equivalent in a limited series concept like Netflix's trans-European chamber-drama *Criminal* (Germany/France/UK/Spain). The book's second part explores how post-2017 German crime dramas (*Babylon Berlin*, *Dark*, *Perfume*, *Criminal*, and *Dogs of Berlin*) rework culturally specific formal and narrative conventions for global circulation on Netflix.

After outlining the continuation and departure from established network practices in the case of *Babylon Berlin* on Netflix, each chapter of the second part is devoted to one post-network crime drama and concentrates on the dynamic interplay between serial televisual textuality and the adaptation processes caused and demanded by globally circulated original language television. While the second part takes into consideration the first seasons of each Netflix show (seven to twelve episodes each), it continues the approach of placing close readings of televisual aesthetics in conversation with genre-based narrative strategies and the (self)representation of geopolitical themes and identities.

This introduction lays the groundwork for the historical, cultural, textual, and formal exploration of the German crime drama as evidence of a continuity-driven success story from network to post-network eras of television. The first section centers on television as a medium that triangulates between local, regional, national, and global positionalities and flows of information. A historical exploration of the centrality of the crime genre for postwar German literary and visual cultures follows. Post 2017, German crime dramas showcase the emergence of domestically produced projects as globally circulated television on Netflix. In foregrounding the genre's contribution to the construction and representation of regional, national, and global concepts, the introduction maps the book's path through the intertwined history of German television and the crime drama.

Screening Globally, Watching Locally

In his 1986 path-breaking study of London-based low- to mid-income white families and their network television viewing habits, David Morley claimed that

> television is being used purposefully by family members to construct the occasions of their interactions, and to construct the context within which they can interact. It is being used to provide the reference points, the ground, the material, the stuff of conversation.[7]

---

[7] Morley, *Family Television*, 11.

In *Making Room for TV* (1992), Lynn Spigel investigated how the television set in the postwar American family room "became a focus for debates on family life, gender roles, and the uses of domestic space."[8] What both studies have in common is the insistence on television as a nodal point of mediated interaction and cocreation. Both authors describe how network television represents positionalities and debates as much as it forms them, how viewing thrives on television's capacity to format the construction of gender, racial, ethnic, class, and local/global patterns as a mixture of encoding and decoding patterns outlined in Stuart Hall's three modes of reading: preferred, negotiated, and oppositional. Hall maintained that television interrupted the presumed transparency of the sender-message-receiver model because

> [t]he televisual practice takes "objective" (that is, systemic) responsibility precisely for the relations which disparate signs contract with one another in any discursive instance, and thus continually rearranges, delimits and prescribes into what "awareness of one's total environment" these items are arranged.[9]

According to Hall, televisual practice constructs patterns of reception that are "not 'natural' but the product of an articulation between two distinct moments."[10] Following from this, specific televisual practices create and resituate viewer positionalities along a spectrum of identity formation/confirmation through flow-based intertextualities.

Hall's approach thus revised the previously dominant approach toward the effects of television expressed by the cultivation hypothesis (e.g., George Gerbner, 1969), which argued that viewers' perceptions of and interactions with "social reality" adopt the representational qualities accorded to "life and society" on and from television.[11] Along these lines, Joan K. Bleicher contended that "television produces and transmits collective social and cultural myths" that its narrative models became normative for everyday life.[12] If one takes Morley's, Spigel's, and Hall's approaches to television to indicate a multidirectional construction process, any orthodox take on the cultivation hypothesis becomes questionable. Instead, it would be more productive to think of mediated reception as a set of perception

---

[8]Lynn Spigel, *Making Room for TV: Television and the Family Ideal in Postwar America* (Chicago: University of Chicago Press, 1992) back cover.
[9]Stuart Hall, "Encoding/Decoding," in *The Cultural Studies Reader*, ed. Simon During (London/New York: Routledge, 1993), 507–17, here 514.
[10]Ibid., 516.
[11]George Gerbner, "Toward 'Cultural Indicators': The Analysis of Mass Mediated Public Message Systems," *AVCR* 17 (1969): 137–48.
[12]Joan Kristin Bleicher, *Fernsehen als Mythos* (Opladen: Westdeutscher Verlag, 1999). All translations from primary and secondary sources are the author's own.

layers through which viewers filter and frame situations, texts, constructs of community and self, and through which their relationships with and the shape of institutionally, geopolitically, economically, and familially organized units are continuously both reworked and reinforced.

While Netflix's interface illustrates these permeable and constantly realigning intersections between individual, local, regional, national, and global flows of information and viewer positions, a dynamic interplay between them already existed on television during the network era, albeit to a different degree, utilizing different pathways. Netflix's attention to "customization" is a very effective part of the neoliberal ideology that equates consumer choice with free expression, agency, and democracy, hailing the rearranging of the building blocks of one's user interface as "watching TV your way." Yet, anyone's Netflix profile and usage is bound by the technological-ideological apparatus, by algorithms, a combination of public and private infrastructures, including those constructed by hard- and software, by the interests of Netflix as an exceedingly vertically integrated business (coproducing, purchasing, licensing, adapting, and distributing films, television, video games, and web series around the world), by its US-centric philosophy of leisure and entertainment, by its ad agencies, and so on.[13] As Ramon Lobato and others have shown, delivering Netflix in the serviced regions of the globe is a change-prone enterprise that interconnects local, regional, national, global aspects in differently weighted configurations. But Netflix's creators, producers, and its users are also feeding back into the system when they seek to fine-tune or even hack the platform's notifications and suggestions. Liking *Dark*, for example, yields *Dogs of Berlin* and *Perfume*, both German productions, but also Nordic noir series like *Darkwind* and *The Break*. This extrapolation on the basis of collected viewer data from the site assumes a commonality between geopolitical (a specific region and its cultural products) and media-specific categories (liking a specific TV genre). Thus, while the national and regional might not be foregrounded in the same way as during the broadcast era, the lingering power of geopolitical identity concepts is still formatively enshrined in television selection and viewing processes.

The result of Netflix's algorithms forges a historical, formal, and cultural connection within a concept like "crime drama." While users have the power to include crime dramas as a favorite pastime or not, making it part of the filter through which the system reads them, they have only limited power to change the category of "crime drama." This process visualizes socially dominant assumptions that fuse media-preferences to geopolitical constructs, precisely those reception filters that make Morley's, Spigel's and

---

[13]Ramon Lobato, *Netflix Nations: The Geography of Digital Distribution* (New York: NYU Press, 2019), 100–5.

Hall's arguments about the multidirectionality of television so valuable. Seeing these assumptions and filters applied is likely to have an effect on choice in turn, standardizing even further what counts as "crime drama" or as globalized or culturally specific and regional.

In addition, we need to consider that Netflix changes its thumbnails based on viewer preferences, essentially working as personalized clickbait. Instead of one DVD-type cover for each show or film for all users, each viewer gets an image selected by a category-based algorithm aggregating viewer preferences for genres, subgenres, and actors: if you watched a lot of crime dramas and your viewing habits reveal a preference for strong female leads, you will likely get a shot from a female protagonist on the show.[14] Netflix not only narrowcasts according to genre preference and assumed geopolitical allegiances (Germany to Scandinavia) but also mirrors and reinstalls genre alongside identity categories (race, gender, and sexuality), even if viewers resisted being labeled by watching globally and intersectionally across borders of many kinds: genres, genders, races, sexualities, languages, and nationalities. Since streaming platforms count on and brand themselves through global reach, accessibility, and outlook, Catherine Johnson's work has shown how important it is to peel back the data-driven rhetoric and analyze infrastructure design along with actual program content, genre formats, and viewing practices crisscrossing between domestic, international, network, and post-network modes.[15]

There are many mediated reception layers, differing in technology, format, duration, and aural-visual intensity by medium and by individual/social group during any given day. Television is but one of them and often not alone. Mobile phones, social media, and internet surfing have made substantial gains on the reception share of television, whether it happens on a separate or the same screen, whether it is on or off. However, as research into cross-platform mobility between television and social media has revealed, what is communicated via second screens on cell phones or computers often concerns what audiovisual content one is watching on the television set or on one's favorite mobile device.[16]

What makes long-running television series special, regardless of the screen on which one is watching them, is the durable and reliable familiarity they gain and assume for the regular viewer, becoming installed as a social ritual. Streamers have developed their own viewing rituals. Watching virtually with friends is increasingly made possible with the help of connected features provided by third parties or the networks and platforms themselves (e.g.,

---

[14] Dany Roth, "The Secret behind Netflix's Personalized Thumbnails," *Looper*, November 8, 2020, https://www.looper.com/274997/the-secret-behind-netflixs-personalized-thumbnails/ (accessed December 15, 2020).
[15] Catherine Johnson, *Online TV* (New York: Routledge, 2019).
[16] See studies by Henry Jenkins, Jonathan Gray, Matt Hills, Rebecca Wanzo, among others.

Disney+ has an integrated party-watch app, daserste.de has the *Mediathek*). The Covid-19 stay-at-home orders have brought into the spotlight the continuity of and need for ritualistic and shared viewing experiences via Zoom, Discord, or FaceTime. These rituals might differ by mode and degree from those of the mythologized oedipal families in the heyday of broadcast television, but the notion that post-network viewing has done away with television as a social ritual outside of what passes as event television should be similarly passé as the notion that television is dead.[17]

As a network crime drama that is referred to as a national treasure, *Tatort* (*Crime Scene*, ARD, 1970–) has achieved and retained its status as a weekly social ritual in Germany, at home with family members or with friends and strangers in a local bar. The immediate postwar generation might watch it religiously network-style once a week, while boomers might binge their favorite regional detective team from a themed DVD box set, when the mood strikes. Millennials might select specific or missed episodes on daserste.de, and a cross-section of viewers catch it Sunday night at their local watering hole. Of course, a growing portion of the population does all of the above or some of the above, depending on whether they watch alone or with others, are at home or on the road. And yet, a fate *Tatort* shares with other high-quality domestically produced television content is that it is not well known outside of Germany.[18]

Convergence, watching domestic and global content time-shifted on the same and across different platforms, highlights the fluctuating concepts of the local, regional, national, and global. While German network viewers became well-versed in appropriating the abundance of foreign television imports through the standardized practice of synchronization, by comparison, their US counterparts had little exposure to different national productions during the big tent era of television. That changed during the cable/satellite era, but only for US viewers actively seeking out that niche-based content. Multi-platform viewing with subtitles and different audio language tracks has broadened this access, putting a plethora of shows on a spectrum from culturally specific and accented to those configured for global consumption within easy reach for a trial episode.

As these domestically produced shows circulate on Netflix, they are also reshaping affective and mnemonic paths along the global-local spectrum. In her study of metaphysical media, Emily Edwards argues that "film and television (...) suspend the flow of historical time for audiences, removing

---

[17]See Amanda D. Lotz, "Preface to the Second Edition," in *The Television Will be Revolutionized* (New York: NYU Press, 2014), xiii.

[18]Susanne Eichner, "Crime Scene Germany: Regionalism, Audiences, and the German Public Broadcasting System," in *European Television Crime Drama and Beyond*, ed. Kim Toft Hansen, Steven Peacock, and Sue Turnbull (London: Routledge, 2018), 173–92.

them from linear time and projecting them into the mythic, archaic moment."[19] What are the connections between this "mythic, archaic moment," televisual flow, the different mediascapes, the crime genre, and forms of identity formation (gender, race, class, sexuality, nationality, and ethnicity)? What is the continuing appeal of crime dramas on network television, if not the serial looking and therefore continuous deferral of change, conversion, and death? How are we to understand that a cancelled show produces affect akin to symptoms of mourning in its fans? And how did binge-watching in the early Netflix era relate to not wanting to let go, to be suspended in that "mythic, archaic time"? Dominik Maeder, who explores the connection between seriality and death through the lens of psychoanalysis, contends that "seriality is to be defined as an epistemological form that creates a specific procedural order of (self-)awareness" allowing for the differentiated but continuous narrativization of repetitions and following from this that "the subject of psychoanalysis first arrives at its representation in the serial mode."[20] This follows Judith Butler's emphasis on reiteration as the process by which gender is codified and naturalized. Maeder's addition allows us to see that dichotomic patterns of psychosocial anxieties reveal themselves and constitute the subject in polysemically coded restatements of traumatic and pleasurable dreams and memories.

If network television is all about the glance, not the gaze, as John Ellis argued, then this is the furtive and reassurance-seeking glance that seeks to be anchored in one's own existence and wills the reiteration of future reassuring looks.[21] But the very look is a sign of the anxiety and the knowledge, however repressed, that the look might, someday, encounter a dark screen. One's own and society's demise therefore becomes synonymous with the rupture of televisual flow. Most apocalyptic scenarios depicted in fiction, film, and television mark society's transition from normalcy to apocalypse with the blinking out of one public service television signal after another, while short-wave radio, letters, and oral reports accompany the atomistic time after. In the imagination, the end of civilization becomes synonymous with a retrogression of media.[22]

Tatort's televisual crime scenes have guaranteed a continuity of that glance—and all identity constructs interwoven with that look—for over half a century, even for people not watching the show ("Is that still on? Yes,

---

[19] Emily D. Edwards, *Metaphysical Media: The Occult Experience in Popular Culture* (Carbondale: Southern Illinois University Press, 2005), 27.
[20] Dominik Maeder, "Das serielle Subjekt: Eine Skizze zur Poetologie des Serial Dramas," in *Transnationale Serienkultur. Theorie, Aesthetik, Narration und Rezeption neuer Fernsehserien*, ed. Susanne Eichner, Lothar Mikos, Rainer Winter (Wiesbaden: Springer, 2013), 87–102, here 95.
[21] John Ellis, *Visible Fictions: Cinema, Television, Video* (1992) (London: Routledge, 2000).
[22] Just to name three recent ones here: Emily St. John Mandel's novel *Station 11* (2014), the film *How It Ends* (dir. David M. Rosenthal, 2018), and the TV series *Revolution* (NBC, 2012–14).

it's still on!"). Its fixed installation in the television schedule anchors rapid changes in the medium, in the industry, and in viewers' lives, letting them therapeutically rehearse for and engage with impermanence, whether they do so cynically via Twitter, exasperatedly yelling at the screen as a long-term opinionated fan, vegging on the couch, or seriously in dialogue with the topic of the episode. A steady flow of Sunday evening *Tatort* episodes accompanied viewers from the Cold War through domestic terrorism, social upheavals, the constitution of the European Union, economic and political turbulations, (re)unification, demographic changes, and major mediascape revolutions (privatization in the late 1980s and the internet decade of the 1990s that spawned the current convergence). When the fabric of the nation frayed, boundaries blurred, cultural markers shifted, and social rituals dissolved or changed irreversibly, *Tatort*'s format and schedule loyalty guaranteed that there would always be another chance to look. The unchanged 1970s title sequence, which features an extreme close-up of a pair of eyes returning the viewer's look, makes this explicit. At the start of *Tatort*, the apparatus looks into its medium's and the country's future while anchoring the viewer amid temporal and televisual flow.

A long-running network television series is thus an ideal place to investigate the connections between geopolitical concepts, medium specificity, the crime genre, and identity formation. Examining the history and development of the German crime drama as a genre in literary and visual fiction will situate the rise of *Tatort* on network television and explain the resurgence of German crime dramas on Netflix, and it will illuminate how the *Krimi*'s cultural significance is always in dialogue with aspects of its generic aesthetics.

The Long Life of Crime: Lessons for Post-Network Television

> It was and is the mission of crime stories to tell fairy tales that nevertheless harbor the entire bitter and problematic reality of life in the 20th century. That's what makes them worth reading.[23] (Helmut Heissenbüttel)

Rapid urban development at the end of the nineteenth century in Germany caused drastic social and political changes for the young nation's self-understanding as historically defined by its regional and "rural" identities. Anxieties about urban modernity find expression in films such as *Wo ist Coletti* (dir. Max Mack, 1913), *M—eine Stadt sucht einen Mörder* (dir. Fritz Lang, 1931), *Berlin Alexanderplatz* (dir. Phil Jutzi, 1931), and *Emil und*

---

[23]Karl Unger, "Kritisch-liberale Bullen am Tatort Gesellschaft," *Konkret*, February 1982, 34.

die Detektive (dir. Gerhard Lamprecht, 1931). Crime, gender constructs, and the specter of nationalism dominate the representational expression of this anxiety. In Alfred Döblin's *Berlin Alexanderplatz* (1929) and Irmgard Keun's *Das kunstseidene Mädchen* (1932) the act of walking and looking through the metropolis of Berlin turns into deciphering a never-ending flow of information and stimulation. Protagonists are at turns anxious of losing themselves to or eager to merge with it. As Franz Biberkopf experiences, the city spits him out after each attempt at immersion, leaving him a different person at each turn. Doris costumes herself and performs short-lived roles in the lives of men but eventually, even the long-sought offer of marriage and respectability cannot convince her to uncouple from her love affair with the city and its reflection of herself. As Björn Bollhöfer argues, "the imagined landscape of the city has become a filmic landscape."[24] He continues: "[t]he crime story sets the city in scene as a riddle, as a dangerous and fascinating network of social and spatial relationships that require decoding."[25] I would argue that unlike the longer duration of a film with its three arcs of beginning, middle, and end, both Weimar-era novels demonstrate a penchant for a concatenation of episodic narrative segments necessitating the characters' reinventions of themselves, which deliver montage-like scenes pushed out of a continuous, amorphous vertical and horizontal urban flow. Genres mingle: commercial ads merge with internal thoughts, gossip in the street, and political slogans. Both novels famously have an open ending. Franz falls in line with marching boots indicating the march of history toward war; Doris just disappears into city life. Series and seriality meet each other in the narration systems of these modern city novels and create an interrelationship that is spectacularly suited to audiovisual storytelling, envisioning a system of narration that would become prevalent in a medium then in its very infancy: television.

Films that project the urban topography by means of an early car chase (as in *Emil*) or a manhunt with handheld lanterns through cavernous dark factory floors (as in *M*) symbolically code urban places as flight corridors of labyrinthine proportions and implications. These visual flights also structure urban space by means of a precarious duality of hunter and hunted, perpetrator and victim, in which, from the very beginning, the roles might easily revert (as in *M*). Bollhöfer again: "Film and television ascribe meanings to spaces and create geographies that enter everyday reality."[26] This "fictional social reality" (John Fiske) existed then as it exists now in constant negotiations with a viewer's lived social reality.[27] And as a medium,

---

[24] Björn Bollhöfer, *Geographien des Fernsehens: Der Kölner Tatort als mediale Verortung kultureller Praktiken* (Köln: Transcript, 2007), 18.
[25] Ibid., 165.
[26] Ibid., 19.
[27] John Fiske, *Understanding Popular Culture*, 2nd ed. (New York: Routledge, 2011).

not only does television integrate itself much more seamlessly into the rhythm of everyday life, it also shares the domestic and private sphere of its consumers while bringing the public sphere indoors. Spatial codifications, such as identifying crime with urban spaces, progressively reappropriate one another the more frequent cross-comparisons between fictional and nonfictional environments become, taking up intertwined residues in the viewer's memories. Underscored contrasts between city and village might reinforce the codified naturalization of dichotomies such as "safe" and "unsafe," "moral" and "immoral," and assign these values affect-laden spatial properties in the forms of *Heimat* versus metropolis. Thus, from the beginning of the twentieth century, the duality of city versus small town/country has been read through the lens of crime, unilaterally channeling anxieties caused by social change through the vertical and horizontal labyrinthine directionality of urban spaces. This codification is successful when the topographical properties of social values are reproduced even when crime is absent in the urban text or present in the rural text. Spatial metaphors begin to refer to nonspatial attributes and vice versa.[28] This is the textual and representational interstice that *Tatort* navigates and in which it resides.

In addition to a topographical epistemology that inscribes "space as a formal constant,"[29] crime stories and thrillers like *Tatort* have long been the focus of narratological research because they, like no other genre, mimic the process of reading and combine it with a phenomenological analysis of textual and contextual traces while appealing to the hunger for spectacle in mass audiences. From the beginning of their literary history, writers like E. A. Poe have not only composed crime fiction but also included genre-theoretical reflections as part of the fictional text. Their astute observations on the workings of the analytical mind have in turn found fans in German literary, sociological, and philosophical scholars, for example, Karl Marx, Walter Benjamin, Helmut Heissenbüttel, Horst Bosetzky. While the tradition of crime stories hails from British and American literary culture, *Krimis* were a significant part of the postwar German culture industry for their remarkable suitability to social critique, their interest in "revealing secrets," and their ability to delve into questions of guilt without seeming overtly invested in Holocaust remembrance.[30]

Here, it is helpful to apply Thomas Elsaesser's exploration of "parapraxis" (based on the Freudian *Fehlleistung* he translates as "performed failure")

---

[28]Bollhöfer, *Geographien des Fernsehens*, 132.
[29]Ibid., 114.
[30]Richard Albrecht, "Literarische Unterhaltung als politische Aufklärung. Der neue deutsche Kriminalroman in der Bundesrepublik der 70er Jahre. Ein literatur-gesellschaftlicher Nekrolog," *Recherches Germaniques* 14 (1984): 119–43, here 122.

to the *Krimi* genre.³¹ Elsaesser is interested in "absence as presence," specifically the absence of the Holocaust in New German Cinema, and he defines parapraxis as "a kind of effort, a kind of persistence, usually one with unexpected or unwanted results, including typical reversals or displacements in time and space." The "Holocaust as media-event in the 1990s and beyond," he continues, "partakes in mourning work but in a way that makes compulsive iteration symptomatic for its in-completion" (Elsasser 410–11). German *Krimis* and television crime dramas make apparent the "compulsive iteration" of a displaced mourning work through their ritualized forms of reception, and their investment in probing the fragility and validity of democratic laws along with the ethical compass of German state representatives. *Krimis* enabled postwar authors and initiated their readers into seeking to understand and analyze systemic violence facilitated by state-sponsored ideologies in the German past and present, in the European context, and in the world at large.

One of Germany's most popular *Krimi* and *Tatort* authors, Michael Molsner explains his own interest in the genre in 1978, in the aftermath of the tumultuous events of the terror of Munich (1972) and domestic terrorism (1977): "I selected the crime form because the thriller especially unsparingly questions the sources of violence as an expression of hierarchical power (...) as if violence were an anxiety-provoking normalcy of our daily life."³² In 1982, Karl Unger uttered the suspicion that for West German crime authors, "social critique is more important than the story."³³ Horst Bosetzky added that German crime fiction is something special, "because [it] takes place in Germany and works on German problems."³⁴ In that same year, Molsner underscored that he believed the genre to be the most adequate form to describe "Europe's conjoining societies."³⁵ Their thoughts make apparent the *Krimi*'s simultaneous ability to express culturally specific developments while pointing to the genre's ability to serve an important function on a medium-reflexive and transnational level.

Dealing with perpetrators and victims, individual or collective murders stemming from personal, economic, and political motivations, raises questions about Germany's role in Europe, past and present, about the sources and consequences of fascism and the Holocaust for the individual

---

³¹Thomas Elsaesser, "New German Cinema and History: The Case of Alexander Kluge," in *The German Cinema Book*, ed. Tim Bergfelder, Erica Carter, Deniz Göktürk, and Claudia Sandberg (London: BFI, 2020), 408–17, here 410–11.
³²Michael Molsner, "Die Obszönität der Fakten: Möglichkeiten des deutschen Kriminalromans," *Kürbiskern* 4 (1978): 64–72, here 71.
³³Unger, "Kritisch-liberale Bullen am Tatort Gesellschaft."
³⁴Ibid., 35.
³⁵Michael Molsner, *Die Trivialität der Träume*, 9–10, as quoted in Albrecht, "Literarische Unterhaltung als politische Aufklärung," 131.

and society. Horst Bosetzky is adamant that he does *not* want his *Krimis* to support "fascist thought patterns" (*faschistische Denkmuster*).[36] At the same time, *Krimi* author Richard Hey points directly to the gray area of the perpetrator/victim axis, when he reads it as a continuum to foreground the existential tension: "Even as a crime story reader, victims interest me more than perpetrators, and perpetrators only in so far as they are victims at the same time."[37] Hey's continuum emphasizes the nurture over nature argument accepted as the dominant sociological concept in the 1970s. Perhaps with Lang's *M* in mind, Fred Beinersdorfer adds more problematically: "There are perpetrators who are simply victims, who could not act otherwise."[38] If one connects this social-critical inventory of crime fiction from the 1960s to the 1980s to the notion that "Germans are hooked on murders," one arrives at Karl Marx's conundrum that "[a] criminal produces crime (. . .) The criminal produces an impression, partly moral, partly tragic, as the case may be, and thus offers the movement of moral and aesthetic feelings of the audience a 'service.'"[39]

Ingrid Brück interprets this appeal of crime fiction in the German context as a service to complex democracy at work: "Something legal can be illegitimate, something illegal can be acknowledged to be legitimate from a differentiated moral perspective—the crime drama as a social-political television game: Part Two of Democratization."[40] Horst Bosetzky shares Brück's assessment; he considers the *Krimi* "a part of democratization" and a "personal means of resistance."[41] These testimonies to the social-political function of domestically produced *Krimis* would allocate to crime fiction a relatively generous share of what German historian Konrad Jarausch and others attest has turned into sociopolitically successful memory and memorialization work in postwar Germany.[42]

Despite Richard Albrecht's attempt to constitute a necrology of German crime fiction after the 1970s, the *Krimi* genre continues to provide important "services" to its audience.[43] In retrospect, it is fair to insist that crime fiction

---

[36]-ky quoted in Erhard Schütz, ed., *Zur Aktualität des Kriminalromans* (München: Fink, 1978), 78.
[37]Richard Hey, "Über das langsame Verfertigen von Mördern beim Beschreiben ihrer Opfer" (Seminar Lecture, University of Regensburg, October 8–10, 1976), 4–11.
[38]Quoted by Waltraud Berle, "Tatort Bundesrepublik," *Vorwärts*, January 8, 1983.
[39]Karl Marx, *Theorien über den Mehrwert*, Volume 1.
[40]Ingrid Brück, "Krimigeschichte(n). Zur Entwicklung des deutschen Fernsehkrimis," in *Fernsehforschung in Deutschland. Themen - Akteure - Methoden*, ed. Walter Klingler et alii (Baden-Baden: Nomos, 1999), 407.
[41]Quoted by Berle, "Tatort Bundesrepublik."
[42]Konrad Jarausch and Michael Geyer, *Shattered Past: Reconstructing German Histories* (Princeton: Princeton University Press, 2003).
[43]Albrecht, "Literarische Unterhaltung als politische Aufklärung," 119.

and dramas became *the* genre to initiate a return to German-run productions on German television screens. In the words of Knut Hickethier:

> The success of the first domestic television crime productions shows already early on that many spectators harbored a desire to connect to habitual orientation points when entertaining themselves with crime stories. While casting German actors [in US narrative formats] often still sufficed to reach viewers in the late 1950s and early 1960s (. . .) in the following years those domestically produced crime series that were spatially and culturally adapted to German conditions increasingly proved successful.[44]

Exploring the role crime fiction played in establishing, maintaining, and interrogating a topographically mapped epistemology, for the process of historical and political self-reflection, will unearth the causes for the immense success of domestically produced television crime dramas like *Stahlnetz* (ARD, 1958–68, 1999–2003), *Der Kommissar* (ZDF, 1969–76), *Tatort* (ARD, 1970–), *Polizeiruf 110* (DFF, 1971–90; ARD, 1990–), *Derrick* (ZDF, 1974–98), *SOKO* Munich (ZDF, 1978–2020, with several regional spin-offs since 2001), *Bella Block* (ZDF, 1994–2018), *Der Dicke/Die Kanzlei* (ARD, 2005–12), series that have managed to compete with and outperform US-made prime-time crime dramas on German television.[45] Along with long-running German soaps (*Lindenstraße*, ARD, 1985–2020, and *Gute Zeiten, Schlechte Zeiten*, RTL, 1992–), crime dramas represent, model, format, theorize, and react to a significant domestic turn in the oft-labeled "Americanized" popular German culture.[46] And now, Netflix's original German crime dramas are not only exporting that successful domestic product category to heretofore unreachable television audiences (the United States in particular), but they are also screening the nation to online viewers domestically and to other European countries, continuing rather than breaking with a trend. The question that bears closer scrutiny is how German crime dramas on Netflix continue, rework, or halt the parapraxis of displacement Elsaesser constituted for German films from the 1960s to today. If serial crime narratives play a part in stabilizing postwar German and European democracies, at what costs does this stabilization

---

[44] Knut Hickethier, *Geschichte des deutschen Fernsehens* (Stuttgart: J.B. Metzler, 1998), 237.
[45] Christian Pundt establishes *Stahlnetz*'s enduring legacy for the genre (1958–68). He argues that the early series' "varied detectives and localities [made] the narration of crime stories with changing local color possible." *Mord beim NDR. Tatort mit Manfred Krug und Charles Brauer* (Münster: LIOT, 2002), 15.
[46] See Uta Poiger, *Jazz, Rock and Rebels: Cold War Politics and American Culture in a Divided Germany* (Oakland: University of California Press, 2000), and Agnes Mueller, ed., *German Pop Culture: How "American" Is It?* (Ann Arbor: University of Michigan Press, 2004).

occur, what regional, national, and global constructs of Germany, and who/what is German does it develop in the process, how and why?

Program Guide

This book is focused on the productive interplay between episodic televisual texts, their culturally specific production contexts, their viewer engagement practices, and critical television studies. Each chapter approaches the crime drama format and television text at its center with an eye toward uncovering the intersections between media-specific network and post-network exhibition strategies, television flow and internal segmentation, aesthetic patterns, and narrative formats.

I would ask readers expecting an encyclopedic overview of German crime dramas or an investigation into the genre of the television crime drama more generally to turn to the thoroughly indispensable contributions by Luca Barra and Massimo Scaglioni (*A European Television Fiction Renaissance*, 2020), Kim Toft Hansen, Steven Peacock, and Sue Turnbull (*European Television Crime Drama and Beyond*, 2018), Andreas Sudmann's 2017 work on serial televisual aesthetics, Sue Turnbull (*TV Crime Drama*, 2014), Katharina Hall (*Crime Fiction in Germany. Der Krimi*, 2016), Thomas Kniesche (*Contemporary German Crime Fiction. A Companion*, 2019) as well as the works cited, without whose crucial contributions this book would have been impossible.

Part One—Watching *Tatort* since 1970

> *Tatort* is possibly the greatest, longest-running and most revealing project about contemporary German history that popular culture has to offer, as such it could probably only be developed at a strange network like the ARD. (*Der Spiegel*, November 25, 2000)[47]

> [In 2016, in Germany] [t]he favorite genres of television series are comedy (sitcom, satire etc.), action (superheroes, adventure etc.) as well as international crime dramas and science fiction and fantasy. (. . .) With the weekly German crime drama *Tatort*, only one German series is represented in the Top-10. Among viewers of German and European crime series, 16% of the interviewed stated they watched every episode of the cult series revolving around different *Tatort* investigators' cases. (statista.de)[48]

---

[47] *Der Spiegel*, November 25, 2000.
[48] The study is based on a 2016 representative sampling of over one thousand viewers. "Statistiken zu Fernsehserien," *statista.de*, August 28, 2020, https://de.statista.com/themen/2069/fernsehserien/ (accessed November 23, 2020).

Tatort is television history, yet outside of Germany and German expats, hardly anyone has heard of it. According to statista.de, among a total of 38.5 million television households by 2020, the average number of viewers of the crime series *Tatort* between 1999 and 2019 was 8.28 million. For some popular regional teams of the show, for example, episodes from Münster, *Tatort* reached an average of over twelve million viewers.[49] Just fifteen years ago, a research project like this would have been almost impossible. Personal VHS tapes were then the only accessible archive but required the use of a region-free or PAL VCR in the United States. Releases of bundled episodes on DVD in the 2010s still required a region-free DVD player. None of these DVDs featured English subtitles. Domestic German television going back to the network era thus remained problematically inaccessible and as a result uninteresting to English-only critics and scholars, not to mention the broader US public. In the case of *Tatort*, Susanne Eichner additionally points to the regional format's weddedness to the "peculiar broadcasting structure of the German federal system" and a longstanding reception habit "that cuts through all milieux" and across generations that make *Tatort* a German success story but have so far limited the series' global circulation:

> Since the introduction of dual broadcasting in Germany in the 1980s, giving public and commercial free-to-air television equal standing, ratings for television programmes have decreased. This development was further intensified with the diversification of television caused by the introduction of satellite broadcasting, and later by digitalisation processes. Blockbuster hits became the realm of major live events such as sport competitions or major entertainment events. Fictional formats clearly did not target a broad, mass market, but specific audiences with specific genre preferences. *Tatort*, with its noticeable success, seems to contradict these developments. In fact, the series has become *the* success story of German television, being cited repeatedly as one of the last bright stars of national broadcast television, bringing together families and friends each Sunday evening, and providing a topic for discussion during the following week. Although this is a unique success story, this phenomenon has gone more or less unnoticed by the international community.[50]

Susanne Eichner's and Michelle Mattson's articles sought to bridge the knowledge gap but had limited space to dig deeper into the intersections between cultural and media-specificity, formal language, and televisual

---

[49]Ibid.
[50]Eichner, "Crime Scene Germany," here 189 and 175. Michelle Mattson, "*Tatort*: The Generation of Public Identity in a German Crime Series," *New German Critique* 78 (Fall 1999): 161–81.

textuality. This book makes a more sustained engagement with the show possible and hopes to introduce English-language crime drama viewers and scholars to not only the reasons for *Tatort*'s domestic success but also its legacy and lessons for the streaming era. Since *Tatort*'s longevity requires a long-term scholarly and viewer investment that most readers won't be able or willing to match, my approach seeks to recast the original televisual moment and connect it to the current one, not to nostalgically reproduce it but to reflect its time and medial space alongside its dialogue with the sociopolitical situation and the medium's possibilities and limitations at the time. The aim of the first part of the book is to read the network crime drama *within* its rapidly changing broadcast environment. In theorizing and analyzing a network series' format as well as specific episodes across multiple decades, it is consequently fundamentally important to pay attention to how genre conventions, media practices, geopolitics, and television's medium specificity co-constructed one another.

Coined by Raymond Williams in 1974, "television flow" is "the defining characteristic of broadcasting, simultaneously as a technology and as a cultural form."[51] Raymond Williams started his chapter on television flow by regaling readers with his personal observations from a late night of television viewing in a Florida hotel room in the early 1970s. Williams discovered that the medium was comprised of more than its program segments in the very moment that he situated himself as an English scholar/viewer on a stateside visit. The cross-cultural contrast of presentation and programming fueled his critical muse. His work was not only taken seriously but became foundational for medium-specific television studies. For television studies, it matters where, what, when, and how Williams watched. Precisely because DVDs and streaming content rarely capture the television flow and instead feature single episodes or YouTube snippets, long-term experience with and knowledge of network television and the cable era in Germany and the United States matters.

In the *Tatort* chapters, I therefore situate the premiere broadcast of each episode within the context of its immediate lead-in neighbor, the nightly news program. Research on the *Tagesschau* themes and how they intersect with the episodes thus aims to build a scaffolding to facilitate an awareness of the sociohistorical, cultural, and political Now. Because the ARD has retained the same window and program pairing since the show's inception, the linear adjacency has formed a specific reception habitus for both programs and influenced the German crime drama's format itself. It also contributed significantly to regional and national identity formations that emerged in dialogue with global discourses. Paying attention to the flow allows for a triangulation between generic code-switching, perceptions, and

---

[51] Raymond Williams, *Television. Technology and Cultural Form* (London: Routledge, 1974), 86.

representations of the global, the national, and the regional, and between the medium, text, and audience.

Thus, while scholars like Eichner have repeatedly emphasized the "national cultural specificity" of *Tatort* and other network German crime dramas as limitations to its global dissemination, I argue that its format's dialogue with the news, and its drive for sustained social relevancy, has resulted in a series of formal experiments and adjustments that have built an archive of medium-reflexive textuality that not only bears traces of each and every mediascape change but also advice on how to survive them.

My positionality as a viewer of *Tatort* growing up in Hamburg, West Germany, in part one of this book is thus a reflected aspect of the study and in dialogue with my current position as a German-American academic viewer of Netflix in part two this book. This geopolitical range, while privileged Western European, also partakes in the synchronicity of different spectatorship modes that the regionally organized, nationally broadcast, and/or globally circulated programs in both parts produce and shape. My familiarity with the three regions of the *Tatort* franchise—Hamburg, Berlin, Dresden and Leipzig—lies on a spectrum that in turn matches, exceeds, or falls short of respective local to global contingents of the domestic and international audience. Further, my selection of regions in part one of the book neither pretends to be all-inclusive nor does it aim to provide a summary of all regional constructs. I refer anyone interested in the other regions and their changing detective teams over the years to existing in-depth studies in the bibliography. My study of the three selected regions aims at understanding how the produced regionalism intersects with the genre on television during the three key periods of the medium's transformation.

Part Two—Watching German Crime Dramas on Netflix since 2017

Stuart Hall's preferred, negotiated, and oppositional reading modes do occur not only within a given set of dominant cultural practices but also across cultures. The burst of discovery for viewers excited about accessing original language content on Netflix should be recognized as a continuity of television practices for most of the world outside of the United States, rather than a new frontier in broad- and narrowcasting. Postwar West German networks imported the majority of their fictional content from the United States and the United Kingdom with dialogue synchronized in German. The East German network DFF (Deutscher Fernsehfunk) imported content from its Eastern European allies along with supposedly "unbiased" entertainment offerings from the West. And most East Germans took advantage of being able to receive West German television. While dubbing facilitated cultural appropriation of non-German content in both cases, switching between dominant structural, ideological, narrative, and aesthetic approaches trained German network viewers to deal with code-switching, to read themselves into and out of character profiles, settings, and plotlines not representing what they experienced in their daily lives. A disconnect remained and frequently brought viewers face to face with the Lacanian mirror of mis/recognition, especially poignant in the German-German encounters on television, but also noticeable in the adoption of the Western for reworking the loss of tribal belonging in both Germanies. Viewers accepted or denied this disconnect to see themselves represented allegorically or aspirationally, or they watched oppositionally with intent or in constant negotiation by default. With the exception of daytime television and commercial interruptions which did not take root in West Germany until privatization in the mid-1980s, West German viewers still shared a large archive of postwar network television history with their counterparts in the United States while becoming eager consumers of the increasing fare of domestic productions and streaming offers.

While cross-cultural negotiations of television practices remain a well-rehearsed daily habit for German viewers, whether on network or Netflix, this is a new phenomenon for English-only speakers in the United States, especially those that did not frequent Latin-American, French-Canadian or Asian-American cable or satellite channels. The result is a different conceptualization, creative representation, and reception-based interweaving of regional, national, and global discourses in television practices and in learned modes of reception and comprehension. It is important to acknowledge that German and US television audiences started in different positions at the beginning of the streaming era. For American viewers, the world suddenly opened up and turned the subtitled Korean-produced *Squid Game* into the water-cooler success of summer 2021, an unprecedented feat in US television history. For Germans who had just entered the successful phase of domestic television productions, adding multiple seasons of serial self-representations to the global screen was a boon on the one hand but a double-edged sword on the other hand. Spending German broadcast fees and subsidies for coproductions that are stuck behind a pay-wall on an American-owned subscription service remains a hard sell.

In addition, having to tweak the format to go global while attracting German viewers with a larger homegrown library on Netflix becomes an artistic and ideological challenge. One quick example based on online viewer comments: while US viewers appreciative of gross comedies and teen drama who followed the social media grapevine to watch the German-language crime-dramedy *How to Sell Drugs Online (Fast)* (Netflix, 2019–20) ended up being pleasantly surprised that Germans could do humor (Rotten Tomatoes gives it a score of 89 percent), and younger German viewers highlighted its innovative editing features (for which the show won a Bambi, equivalent of an Emmy), older German viewers accustomed to high-quality television dramas from the United States recoiled: "When one compares Maximilian

Mundt [who plays protagonist Moritz] with Bryan Cranston [lead in AMC's *Breaking Bad*], galaxies, not worlds lie between them."[52] Thus, even though Germany-based Netflix users remain eager for German-language originals on the platform, streamers need to carefully calibrate their small German-language libraries to maximize attracting new while sustaining its existing German subscriber base, which remains one of the highest in Europe.

Consequently, the second part of the book examines continuities and discontinuities in television practices as they pertain to or are carried by the genre of the crime drama. It explores the diverse crime drama formats, production, and reception modes that forged a path for future domestic German-language series on global streaming platforms. While each of these shows brings their own sets of approaches and strategies to the television convergence era, all of them are informed by entrenched network crime drama formats along with the pervasiveness of literary adaptations in the German mediascape, the critical success of cinema/television coproductions dating back to the 1970s, especially in the form of limited series, and the perennial popularity of period and heritage dramas.

To situate the shows' departures from national network television within their many continuities, the second part highlights the connections between R. W. Fassbinder's *Berlin Alexanderplatz* (Bavaria/RAI/WDR, 1980) and *Babylon Berlin* (Sky1/ARD/Netflix, 2017). The flagship-character of *Babylon Berlin* (going into its fourth season at the time of writing) is especially interesting because it premiered on the global subscription-based platform and has had a delayed domestic run on the public network ARD, the same network that is responsible for *Tatort*. Analyzing its production and distribution flow, its director and cast portfolios, I show what cultural and media-specific aspects set it up to become a successful cross-platform crime drama.

Following this snapshot of confluences in the case of the cinematic heritage crime drama *Babylon Berlin*, I turn to a closer textual reading of three post-network crime dramas. Rather than interpreting each show using the same critical inventory, how each approaches the genre and how its representational model situates it differently along the local/global spectrum necessitate an analytical nimbleness that these shows also demand from their diverse global audiences. As the first domestically produced original German-language television series for Netflix, *Dark* (2017–20) offers a hybrid crime format that merges elements of horror, science fiction, fantasy, and mystery. It had a successful three-season run that ended in the summer of 2020. Key aspects for *Dark*'s analysis had to consist of the drama's substantial cross-platform fan engagement that fed off of its intentional narrative complexity

---

[52]https://www.moviepilot.de/serie/how-to-sell-drugs-online-fast/kritik (accessed February 20, 2022).

and the intertextual interweaving of cultural specificity and global popular culture readability.

The transmedia adaptation of Patrick Süskind's novel and 2006 film (directed by Tom Tykwer and produced by Bernd Eichinger), *Perfume* (2018) was coproduced by the ZDF and its online affiliate ZDFneo. The show's single season brought domestic inter-network competition to the streaming giant. Its saturated look at the 1990s in numerous flashback segments and the camera's voyeuristic gaze structure express formal and narrative choices that demand closer attention, especially considering this crime drama's focus on gender and sexuality. *Perfume*'s narrative structure also employs a micro-flow segmentation that intersects with binge-watching. I discuss how this narrational strategy produces a relational memory relay for a conservative German imaginary in tune with its network's history, organizational structure, and its director's previous television oeuvre.

Dogs of Berlin (2018–19) presents yet another production and format model of the German crime drama on Netflix. Unlike *Dark* or *Perfume*, *Dogs of Berlin* was produced by Syrreal Entertainment, showrunner Christian Alvart's own production company based in Berlin. *Dogs* and *Dark* are private domestic-global ventures, whereas the two other crime dramas are public-private coproductions. In the final section, I explore how and why *Dogs of Berlin* follows *Tatort*'s traditional network-based crime drama protocols more than the other two shows, and I discuss where and why it departs from the calibrated, even if ultimately system-confirming, political self-reflexivity that has been the trademark of the German crime drama culture so far.

PART ONE

Network Television

1

History and Format of the Crime Series *Tatort* (*Crime Scene*) (ARD, 1970–)

The series *Tatort* is Germany's longest-running television crime drama, encompassing five crucial decades and numerous locations.[1] When Netflix began its global reach in 2010, the network staple *Tatort* was still the most popular crime series on German television. About 7.10 million viewers watched the first-run episodes of the show in its standard Sunday night slot at 8:15 p.m. This represents a market share of 20.6 percent.[2] For its unrivaled longevity alone, *Tatort* is a bottomless resource of Germany's relationship with history and memory. Holger Wacker and Almut Oetjen emphasize "that *Tatort* not only wrote television history but also a piece of contemporary history."[3] Knut Hickethier, one of Germany's most prominent media scholar summarizes the importance of the crime genre on German television as follows: "Through its broad dissemination the crime film [*sic*]

---

[1] "Der *Tatort* ist die älteste Krimireihe im deutschen Fernsehen. Der erste *Tatort* 'Taxi nach Leipzig' (NDR) wurde am 29. November 1970 ausgestrahlt. Im Mai wird die 700. Folge im Ersten gezeigt. Während der 'Tatort' zu Beginn nur einmal monatlich auf Sendung ging, ermitteln die Kommissare heute bis zu vier Mal im Monat. In 2008 werden 34 neue 'Tatorte' zu sehen sein, immer sonntags um 20.15 Uhr," http://www.daserste.de/tatort/beitrag_dyn~uid,5tcmwk8npmvi6hxv~cm.asp (accessed September 7, 2010).
[2] "Nach wie vor ist der 'Tatort' die meistgesehene Krimireihe im deutschen Fernsehen. Im Schnitt hat jeder Bundesbürger 14 Tatorte gesehen. Die Erstausstrahlungen des *Tatorts* auf dem Sendeplatz am Sonntagabend um 20:15 Uhr im Ersten verfolgten 2007 durchschnittlich 7,10 Millionen Zuschauer, das entspricht einem Marktanteil von 20,6 Prozent." Ibid.
[3] Holger Wacker and Almut Oetjen, *Tatort: Das grosse Buch für Fans* (Berlin: Schwarzkopf und Schwarzkopf, 2002), 2.

has formed our perception of the world, our understanding of society in an unconscious manner unlike any other fictional genre."[4]

As John Ellis cautions: "TV is persistent in working over history for us, yet at the same time it cuts us off from our history" because it happens in the perpetual Now, its programming oriented toward the current event but not the contextual framework of the event.[5] Thus, my tasks in this book are to contextualize the "perception of the world" represented in *Tatort* and as *Tatort* while analyzing how and why the show has configured self-representation through the lens of the crime drama. If Hickethier is correct, the way its program bible has approached regional, national, and global issues has "unconsciously" intersected with Germany's relationship to itself, its history, its understanding of itself as a society and as a nation especially because its representational matrix has set a course for and withstood each major televisual reconfiguration (network, cable/satellite, internet).

Because *Tatort* is a flagship product of the ARD, *Das Erste* (*Deutsche Fernsehen*), journalists and scholars have highlighted *Tatort* as "a high-quality European alternative" to US American imports.[6] As such, it is important to consider the ninety-minute drama's place within and for the "German turn" within popular German culture. Since the 1970s, the three public networks, and since the 1980s also their cable rivals, have increasingly invested in domestic and local productions.[7] Since its conception, one of the overarching foundational aspects of *Tatort* has been the regional, (con)federal element, indicating that this regionalism is directly linked to a growing self-definition of Germany within a Europe concerned about the dominance of US exports and other forms of perceived global cultural imperialism. That the regional is conceptualized and functionalized as resistance to the appeal of the global is not a new concept, yet it remains to be shown on a case-by-case basis how this resistance or appeal is structured, what aesthetic models it employs, and how it layers over already existing, already globalized structures.

The network ARD, one of Germany's original two networks and itself the umbrella network of nine regional stations (SFB/RBB—Sender Freies Berlin/Rundfunk Berlin-Brandenburg, WDR—Westdeutscher Rundfunk,

---

[4]Knut Hickethier, "Einleitung," in *Filmgenres: Kriminalfilm*, ed. Knut Hickethier und Katja Schuhmann (Stuttgart: Reclam, 2005), 38.
[5]John Ellis, *Visible Fictions: Cinema, Television, Video*, 1992 ed. (London: Routledge, 2000), 17.
[6]Daniel Süss, *Der Fernsehkrimi, sein Autor und der jugendliche Zuschauer* (Bern: Huber, 1994), 67.
[7]Sara Mously summarizes the existing media studies scholarship on this issue: "die Tendenz einer verstärkten Zuwendung zu nationalen und regionalen Produktionen zeichnet sich seit den siebziger Jahren ab. (. . .) Vor allem öffentlich-rechtliche Sender reagieren auf die steigende Zuschauerpräferenz für heimische Medienprodukte, indem sie vermehrt lokal produzierte Serien in der Hauptsendezeit platzieren." *Heimat im Fernsehen* (Saarbrücken: VDM Verlag, 2007), 13–14.

SR—Saarländischer Rundfunk, SWR—Südwestrundfunk, BR—Bayrischer Rundfunk, MDR—Mitteldeutscher Rundfunk, HR—Hessischer Rundfunk, RB—Radio Bremen, and NDR—Norddeutscher Rundfunk), is explicitly marketing the regionalism of its format structure:

> The ARD as the organization of German broadcasting stations is specifically committed to the concept of federalism and the support of the regions. The 19 detective teams from *Tatort* and *Polizeiruf 110* contribute to this concept in an entertaining and successful way.[8]

In this quote, the inclusion of the only East German crime drama outlasting the fall of the wall—*Polizeiruf 110* (911 Emergency)—underscores the ARD's commitment not only to an ongoing North-South but also to a critical West-East dialogue.

Tatort's regional production and broadcasting structure combine separate regional industrial interests, politics, and social customs with a national crime drama template, so that each detective team subseries provides both adherence to and variations on the genre format and the national standard. Each regional team is associated with and represents major and minor urban areas as well as greater regional affiliations. Each regional network produces two to four episodes annually. These episodes get placed into the nationally broadcast *Tatort* lineup, which alternates premieres and reruns between regions every Sunday night. Concretely, if one Sunday features a Münster *Tatort*, the next Sunday it could be Hamburg, Köln, or Leipzig.

In 1970, this (de)centralized structure projected the federal structure of the new democracy to the nation while adhering to an entrenched region-based understanding of the nation that dates to pre-1871 but found renewed currency during the Third Reich. The 1940 film *Wunschkonzert* (Eduard von Borsody), for example, featured soldiers from different regions vying to get their music choices to air on the national request concert broadcast, cementing a tribal concept of the nation well within the *völkisch* ideology of the time. After 1989, the regional structure of the broadcast network facilitated an early integration of the five East German states (the MDR began contributing episodes with East German inspector Ehrlicher in 1992),[9] its contribution to structural and symbolic unification enhanced by ARD's continuation of the East German series *Polizeiruf 110* (DFF, 1971–89; ARD, 1990–), a show that Alan Cornell calls "the sole survivor of GDR

---

[8]Süss, ibid.
[9]Wilma Harzenetter, *Der Held Schimanski in den Tatort-Folgen des WDR* (Alfeld: Coppi, 1996), 4–5.

television for adult audiences."[10] Already on October 28, 1990, the WDR (Westdeutscher Rundfunk, FRG station) and DFF (Deutscher Fernsehfunk, GDR station) coproduced the crossover episode "Unter Brüdern" ("Among Brothers") in which *Polizeiruf 110*'s cast and storylines united with *Tatort*'s to solve an art smuggling case across the border.[11] With this crossover episode, the GDR product was successfully folded into the ARD's lineup, keeping loyal East German viewers from abandoning the network for satellite alternatives while rebranding the defunct national entity as a region.

The 1990 crossover episode reprised *Tatort*'s first broadcasted episode from 1970. In it, Hamburg's inspector Trimmel took a "Taxi nach Leipzig" ("Taxi to Leipzig") to pursue a lead involving a dead child discovered at a West German border station. But taking a taxi across the Iron Curtain on official police business was not possible in 1970. That type of special operation would have had to be negotiated at top levels. As we shall see in a closer look at this episode, *Tatort* insists on solving the impasse through interpersonal and professional connections that forge a path toward interregional bonding, without letting the situation blow up into national political theater. The latter of course belies the fact that viewers on both sides of the wall were inspired to connect regional to national discourse, speculating about unification "among brothers," which was, as we saw, the very title *Tatort* gave its first post 1989 joint East (*Polizeiruf 110*) and West (*Tatort*) episode.

The interconnectedness between the network's and the format's pliable regional franchise structure distinguishes *Tatort* in production and reception from other broadcast crime dramas that are filmed in situ with a set ensemble cast, like *Der Kommissar*, *Derrick*, *Der Alte*, or *Bella Block*. Even ZDF's only comparable program, the 1978 conceived *SOKO* (Special Investigation Unit), whose forty-year run ended in 2020, differs from *Tatort* in taking place in Munich and having some of the longest reigning investigators in German television history (e.g., Wilfried Klaus as Horst Schickl, 1978–2008), even though it has since loosely adopted the *Tatort* format by featuring several city spin-offs over the years (Wismar, Kitzbühl, Postdam, Hamburg).

Innovating within the Tried and True

Since its inception, as soon as the regional format asserted and proved itself, *Tatort* producers have been very conscious of and diligent about the

---

[10] Alan Cornell, "Series, Location, and Change: National Reunification as Reflected in German Television Detective Series," in *Crime Scenes: Detective Narratives in European Culture since 1945*, ed. Anne Mullen and Eimar O'Beirne (Amsterdam: Rodopi, 2000), 5–6.
[11] Ibid.

delicate balance of format retention, brand recognition, and innovation. The typical format can be accurately captured in two minutes, wonderfully parodied by Walulis on YouTube,[12] consisting of the following segments and subsegments: the crime-scene banter, the different character profiles of the detectives to create tension and comic relief, soap opera elements, and different professional/emotional approaches, showcasing the city/region in interspersed transitory scenes between committed crimes, inspections, interviews, headquarter meetings, and everyday domestic life, mining a socially relevant topic by unraveling power hierarchies and connections, pursuing a false lead before landing on the correct one, and, whenever possible and plausible, a chase scene.

With these built-in narrative segment redundancies, *Tatort* "forged connections between multiple series and maintained those connections over time" facilitating an easy dis- or reattachment even as "foreground[ed] narrative existents (characters and settings)" were exchanged, when investigator teams and their regional locations left or joined the franchise.[13] While Sarah Kozloff's argument for the importance of existents for network television and its complicated task to retain loyal viewers while onboarding new viewers mid-stream holds true for a series of one, the *Tatort* world comprised of regional mini-series stretched this golden rule from the beginning. By rotating its teams and regions on a weekly basis, it socialized viewers to accept a well-crafted package of internal brand differentiation amid format retention. This very structure, getting viewers to either compartmentalize or indulge in the offered paratextual and intertextual hyperdiegesis, set it up not just to survive both mediascape changes but also to thrive within and through them. *Tatort* is thus a rarity in that it has sustained what Derek Johnson calls "world-building energies" on a national level for half a century so far.[14]

The format's simplicity is combined with the finesse of not only reflecting or reacting to but co-constructing sociopolitical realities. Generally, *Tatort* producers and directors who have innovated within the tried and true have won out in the long term over those seeking a more radical transformation of the format.[15] Continuity and stability are most obvious in the decision to

---

[12]Philip Walulis, "Der typische *Tatort* in 123 Sekunden." *Walulis sieht fern*, https://www.youtube.com/watch?v=9QENcN-srE0 (accessed May 18, 2020).
[13]Sarah Kozloff invoked by Derek Johnson in "Spin-Offs, Crossovers, and World-building 'Energies,'" in *Reading Contemporary Serial Television Universes. A Narrative Ecosystem Framework*, ed. Paola Brembilla and Ilaria A. De Pascalis (New York: Routledge, 2018), 74–92, here 78–9.
[14]When Derek Johnson argues that "no one of these world-building energies used in the late-network area could create a cohesive, hyperdiegetic world indefinitely," it proves that US scholars might benefit from transnational television studies to expand their archives. Ibid., 89.
[15]The Hamburg *Tatort* has been embroiled in a debate on this very issue since Krug and Brauer took their leave in 2001. First, the NDR flirted with an undercover cop format, which I discuss

retain the same title sequence over fifty years.¹⁶ Suggestions of meddling with the sequence have not been met favorably by the court of public opinion, even for a *bonafide* German movie star.¹⁷ As proof of its audial iconicity, the score has made an appearance on the phones of characters in other cop shows and films, thereby bestowing on *Tatort* a privileged access to the Real while at the same time building a richly layered intertextual fictional world. Since it made an appearance as the lead character's cell phone ring tone on the crime comedy series *Tatortreiniger/Crime Scene Cleaner* (NDR, 2011–18), which was successfully exported around the globe, it is entirely possible that *Tatort*'s theme score is the only trace of the longest-running German crime drama that has reached a broader global audience.

If the steadfast unchanging title sequence demonstrates ARD's conservativism toward the crime drama format, the segmentation variety of cold opens, titles, and credits tells a more flexible story. Thus, innovation and experimentation are tied to the reproduction of the reliably familiar within the internal segmentation of a seventy-five to ninety-minute episode, the windowing of the premiere broadcast (Sundays at 8:15 p.m.), and the variation between regions and their leading detectives, who differ not only by age, gender, ethnicity, and character psychology but also by their approach to the genre (more comedic, stoic, paranoid, hectic, or more dramatic).¹⁸

Thus, while adhering to general genre parameters, the *Tatort* format has the ability to switch between narration types that reposition the viewer from week to week and tweak the internal segmentation flow from case to case. Sometimes, investigative efforts on the part of detectives and viewers involve overcoming both the built-in limitations to knowledge about a case and the subjective blind spots in the interpretation process of the clues leading to the sources of crime and guilt. Other times, the culprit is known from the beginning, and viewers get involved in a search for psychological, economic, political, pathological, or intersectional motivations along with the detectives or in competition with them. In the majority of episodes utilizing one of these variable narration models, the individual or groups committing a crime are embedded in larger power structures signaling broader institutional failures (of the state, of the medical system, of the family unit, etc.). In addition,

---

in the Hamburg section, then, Christian Alvart and Til Schweiger teamed up to integrate more US-style action into each episode. While Schweiger has so far stayed on as Tschiller after Alvart stepped down, the format is being readjusted to a slower speed at the time of writing.

¹⁶See Eike Wenzel, ed., *Ermittlungen in Sachen Tatort* (Berlin: Bertz, 2000), 8–9.

¹⁷Sha/dpa, "Til Schweiger will *Tatort* Vorspann kippen," *Der Spiegel*, March 30, 2012, https://www.spiegel.de/kultur/tv/til-schweiger-tatort-vorspann-abschaffen-a-824765.html (accessed January 7, 2021).

¹⁸For example, the two annual episodes of the Münster team portrayed by actors Axel Prahl (Thiel) and Jan Josef Liefers (Boerne) (WDR, 2002–) have a comedic bent, while Martin Wuttke (Andreas Keppler) on the Leipzig team (MDR, 2008–15) configured the detective with a psychosocially darker side.

Tatort's team rotation, each with their own approaches to investigative work and operating within different local and regional contexts, modifies the genre from week to week and keeps the viewer on their toes.

On the casting side, there is hardly a German actor who has not starred in at least one *Tatort* episode at some time in their career. The show's longevity, on the national and often also on regional level,[19] thus caters to not only showcasing fresh talent but also populating the small screen with known and beloved fan favorites from German and international blockbusters. A case in point would be the pairing of well-pedigreed German actor Til Schweiger (as Nick Tschiller) and relative newcomer Fahri Yardim (as Yalcin Gümer). Due to his highly rated performance on the Hamburg team in *Tatort*, Yardim was rehired by his *Tatort* director and *Dogs of Berlin* showrunner, Christian Alvart, as one of the male leads on his Netflix crime drama. And since *Tatort* is better known to more people in Germany than one-off films or most US productions, the characters they have played there will always forge a connection between the two environments. One famous example is the crossover between *Tatort* and *Game of Thrones* (HBO, 2011–19). Since airings of the two shows and her performances coincided between 2011 and 2014, German viewers will have read Sibel Kekilli's performance as Tyrion Lannister's lover Shae with her fourteen-episode stint as Klaus Borowski's partner Sarah Brandt in *Tatort* in mind and vice versa. Some will additionally remember her from Fatih Akin's international success *Head-On* (2005). As Kekilli's international success shows, *Tatort* has been a laboratory for talent throughout its running time (e.g., Nastassja Kinski, Sabine Sinjen, Götz George, Mathieu Carrière, Manfred Krug, Axel Prahl, Ulrich Tukur, Sibel Kekilli, Til Schweiger, Simone Thomalla).[20] This also goes for directing credits. Even though experienced longtime associate directors of the regional stations or the ARD direct the majority of episodes, *Tatort* has functioned as a testing ground for film and television directors. Both established and budding German film directors directed episodes of *Tatort* before or as they became known in German and international cinema circles (e.g., Wolfgang Petersen, Oliver Hirschbiegel, Dominik Graf, Angelina Maccarone). The show even hosted Samuel Fuller as guest director for the 1973 episode "Tote Taube in der Beethovenstraße" (Dead Dove in Beethoven Street).

Linguistically, the *Tatort* concept relies on standard German spoken by all major protagonists and antagonists. The exceptions are episodes contributed by the Austrian ÖRF, its Swiss companion station SF, and, for a while, by the Bavarian station BR. Regional, ethnic, and class-related accents manifest

---

[19]Some regional detective teams stay together for ten or more years producing two to four episodes annually, while others change more frequently. This depends partially on reception and ratings, but also on actor availability.
[20]Kekilli's photo graces the second edition of the academic staple *The German Cinema Book* (London: BFI: 2020).

themselves mainly through minor characters, policemen and policewomen walking the local beat, witnesses and suspects, and occasional performances by character actors.[21] While Björn Bollhöfer is correct that this treatment of dialect variations from standard German marginalizes the importance of dialect for the show's believability and authenticity mandate, the use of standard German produces a linguistic space that is representative of Germany's self-understanding as ruled by a broad educational middle-class synonymous with the nation's *Leitkulturträger*. Speaking and understanding German has become one of the overriding concerns through which multicultural integration and migration have been nationally appraised since 1989, catapulted to public attention and reaching hysteric proportions during Thilo Sarrazin's promotion of his problematic book *Deutschland schafft sich ab* (August 2010).[22] Through the centrality of the mostly standard German-speaking detectives as identification figures, the *Leitkultur* concept, expounded by Sarrazin to include not only cultural or educational but also genetic-biological predeterminations, ties the national to the regional and marks each regionally produced episode audibly as German because of its shared standard middle-class idiom. Standardization trumps nuanced differentiation and anchors a sought-after sense of shared social and communal normality, a normality which is increasingly perceived to be endangered as evidenced in the platforms of populist politicians and their party (Alternative für Deutschland, AFD).

Intersections of National, Regional, and Local Viewing

A Hamburg viewer can understand and enjoy the Leipzig *Tatort* episodes for or despite its Saxon *Lokalkolorit*, while the local viewer brings familiarity with the area to the viewing process. Thus, while home-turf authenticity is part of the appeal of *Tatort*'s multiregional format, this should not be confused with audience preferences. As Sara Mously justly points out in the interpretation of her failure to prove a correlation of viewers' identification with their local origin and preferential selection for locally matching *Tatort*

---

[21] In his intensive study of Kölner *Tatort* productions, Björn Bollhöfer also observes that "Nebenfiguren bringen eine lokale Färbung in die Handlung und verorten so die Geschichte," which he attributes to the show's intention to mark "eine Kluft zwischen Klein- und Bildungsbürgertum." He calls this variation from standard German in *Tatort* a "paradoxe Situation." *Geographien des Fernsehens*, 141–2.

[22] See Thilo Sarrazin in "Mögen Sie keine Türken, Herr Sarrazin?" *Die Welt*, August 29, 2010, http://www.welt.de/politik/deutschland/article9255898/Moegen-Sie-keine-Tuerken-Herr-Sarrazin.html (accessed October 22, 2010).

episodes: "Here, the viewer does not let go but rather analyzes the local references of the film: Are places and spaces authentically and realistically represented? Is the local reproduced in a subjectively "true" sense and not exaggerated cliché-style?"[23] Thus, due to the higher knowledge and expectation of subjectively constructed authentic referentiality in the case of one's residence, local reference can but does not have to be a factor in the preferential selection of and specifically the positive evaluation of a locally produced *Tatort* episode. What seems to matter more, especially since German viewers are practiced global-local code-switchers, is the affinity for the crime genre and the *Tatort* franchise, that an episode makes a believable connection to regional constructs as such and that the actors on the detective team sponsor fan-based viewing habits.[24]

The topic of regional authenticity is often debated on the ARD *Tatort* fan sites, specifically with regard to actors playing detectives assigned to a specific region yet not hailing from that region themselves (e.g., the East-Berliner Manfred Krug playing Paul Stoever in Hamburg). The ARD has so far voted against an authenticity mandate for its actors and characters. Nevertheless, producers are quite happy to cast actors with a matching regional background highlighting the match of actor and character biography on their website daserste.de.[25] Stressing professional mobility over local/regional background structurally intersects with the "ethnic turn," when producers strategically introduced Croatian transplant Miroslav Nemec as Ivo Batic to the Munich *Tatort* in the war-torn 1990s, then Turkish-German Mehmet Kurtulus as undercover agent Cenk Batu in Hamburg as a local in 2008. Both are presented as and represent models of successful migration and integration, not the least because of their command of standard German. It makes Batu even more believable to his mixed audience that he speaks Turkish with a German accent. That *Tatort*'s linguistic and casting practices, even if not always successfully, attempt to stay attuned to progressing cultural and political sensibilities on race and gender is further evidenced by the network's selection of Sibel Kekilli to play Sarah Brandt in the Kieler *Tatort* in 2010. Kekilli called her casting a "Ritterschlag" (knighthood) not only because of the show's cultural leverage but also because the character was, for once, not based on her Turkish-German background.[26] What gender-race-class-sexuality representation issues remain will be explored in more detail in the individual episode analyses.

---

[23] Mously, "die Tendenz einer verstärkten Zuwendung," 143.
[24] Ibid., 136.
[25] Simone Thomalla, cast as inspector Eva Saalfeld, is a case in point. Her beginning in 2006 was hailed as a "return to her roots." http://www.daserste.de/tatort/teams.asp?iid=4 (accessed September 22, 2010).
[26] "Sibel Kekilli: *Tatort* Rolle ist Ritterschlag," https://www.focus.de/kultur/kino_tv/medien-sibel-kekilli-tatort-rolle-ist-ritterschlag_aid_540479.html (accessed March 5, 2019).

Tatort Tourism

The standardization of high German with well-dosed sprinkles of dialect along with its photo-album journey through Germany's city- and landscapes have played into *Tatort*'s contribution to and extension of the national tourism industry. In his analysis of the East-West episodes *Quartett in Leipzig* and *Rückspiel*, Björn Bollhöfer contests: "In this way, the movements through the cities equal guided tours for tourists that do not leave out any sites."[27] Fans and producers refer to this phenomenon as "*Tatort*-Tourismus."[28] What is narratively functionalized in these episodes has entered into a lively and increasingly self-engendering dialogue with its extradiegetic referents, tying textual representation to film production, promotion, and geopolitical orientation. The rapid exchange of information by mobile devices has led to the leaking of location shoots and to a town's utilization of the shoot as a regional publicity stunt. More and more, a location shoot is seen as verification of the existence and economically viable "player-status" of a town or region in a medially interconnected world, in which the mediated projection of the town constructs and confirms its regional and global identity *as* a media-region: "The current *Tatort*-shoot confirms that the region is really a 'TV-Region.'"[29]

But the term also refers to specifically organized city-tours based on *Tatort*. This has become a profitable business in Münster.[30] As *Tatort* episodes move around within the German borders from state to state every Sunday, so does the viewer, who is increasingly familiar with the locations as the domestic tourism industry has grown exponentially due to unification, economic as well as temporal constraints, the Covid-19 pandemic, and the aging of the overall population.[31] Since employed Germans have a minimum of four weeks' vacation per year, often amounting to six weeks and more, one-third to one-half of this time is increasingly devoted to domestic travel.

---

[27]Bollhöfer, *Geographien des Fernsehens*, 160.
[28]See, for example, the announcement of a May 2010 shooting date for the town Wittlich, http://www.volksfreund.de/totallokal/wittlich/aktuell/Heute-in-der-Wittlicher-Zeitung-aufm-Wittlich-Lautzenhausen-Tatort-Krimi-Lena-Odenthal-Ulrike-Folkerts;art8137,2403353 (accessed September 13, 2010).
[29]On August 9, 2010, Werner Nuding (Obmann TVB Hall-Wattens) confirms this in "Letzter Drehtag für Mitterer-*Tatort*: Region Hall-Wattens positioniert sich als Top-Location für Film & Fernsehen," http://www.tourismuspresse.at/presseaussendung/TPT_20100809_TPT0002 (accessed September 13, 2010).
[30]Touristikarrangements *Tatort*: Münster, http://www.muenster.de/stadt/tourismus/arrangements_tatort.html (accessed September 13, 2010). This service provides a sightseeing tour of the town through the eyes of *Tatort* episodes.
[31]"ARD Interview zur Demografie-Debatte," April 14–21, 2007, http://www.ard.de/zukunft/kinder-sind-zukunft/kinder-brauchen-familie/demografie/-/id=520622/nid=520622/did=540860/zizx50/index.html (accessed September 22, 2010).

After the "anywhere but here" international tourism waves of the 1970s and 1980s, rediscovering German destinations has attained a solid following since the 1990s and might well grow even more due to lingering coronavirus mutations.[32]

J. Vogt goes so far as to call *Tatort*'s regional structure "Landeskunde als Thriller" ("geopolitical studies as thriller").[33] Mark Terkessidis explains that:

> the crime series develops an image of the cities. And this image is highly significant in the context of location rivalry ("Standortkonkurrenz"). (. . .) *Tatort* represents the German cities as consumable backdrop, as tourist picture, in which the specificity of the place, its authenticity, is guaranteed precisely through the cliché.[34]

Because local specificity and subsequent potential nonlocal viewer alienation are reconfigured through the reiterative use of geopolitical and social clichés in the series, so that one's own city "can re-appear as foreign in a suspenseful way," *Tatort* can utilize the media-specificity of television to its fullest extent. Through its format continuity since the early 1970s, weekly viewers are invited to participate in reading the mostly urban spaces, the murder scenes, and solving the crimes. The regular *Tatort* viewer thus functions as stand-in for another city's guest inspector.[35] This mechanism initiates viewers into an authorial discourse of control. The initial hesitation of encountering the unknown can thus more easily give way to a desire to "inspect" the location. Taking a trip becomes an inspection of a new place, to see whether it merits the energy and money spent. One inspects what works, what does not, what meets advertised expectations, what does not. All of this is measured against a perceived norm: a measuring stick derived of a contested intersection of presumed local, regional, and national essentialisms. Spotting a flaw or highlighting a deficiency is an affect-laden activity like one fan's hate-binging a trending reality show with friends or another fan's disgruntled investment in narrative complexity or a detective finding a clue to a buried body.

The hotel business has turned this kind of attitude into an advertising bonanza: "Go on a forensic quest with Hilton, (. . .) discover the *Tatort*

---

[32]Marketed as "Kurz-Nah-Weg" (Short-Close-Away), the German tourism industry website touts Germany's cultural, natural, culinary, and wellness wonders to its domestic customers. http://www.kurz-nah-weg.de/ (accessed October 14, 2010).
[33]Jochen Vogt, *Medien Morde: Krimis intermedial* (München: Fink, 2005), 117.
[34]Mark Terkessidis, "Die Heimatflüsterer," *Der Tatort: Der Mord zum Sonntag, DU* 779 (2007): 25.
[35]As Gunther Witte discusses in *25 Jahre Tatort: Eine Dokumentation* (ARD Publikation, 1995) the producers originally wanted to dramaturgically intersect the different locations by having one guest inspector from another city work together with a local detective in each episode, a concept soon seen as too "artificial."

cities: Berlin, Cologne, Munich on your own."[36] Hilton here cleverly manufactures the idea of discovering a crime-scene city "on one's own," relying on and strengthening the pitch to German tourists to become an independent metropolitan by staying in one of their German houses. The pocket Polyglott guide, theme-based on *Tatort* as "Wissenswertes im Visier" (Focus on What's Worth Knowing) and glued onto my *Tatort*-Leipzig DVD box, introduces the eager viewer and potential traveler to the five major cities of the franchise—Berlin, Hamburg, Köln, Leipzig, München—reissuing them as dominant tourist sites. The flaunted "Spurensuche" (forensic quest) of the brochure thus re-bundles the intersectional, tangential relationship of center and periphery of most *Tatort* episodes.[37]

Precisely because *Tatort* sites oscillate between worn-out clichés and off-beat unexpected locations, often nonidentical with typical local tourist attractions, and some takes are even filmed off-site due to economic and legal restrictions,[38] searching for shooting locations of a certain episode of *Tatort* has become a national pastime. What would otherwise only be accessible through local friends or relatives builds on and, in turn, increases the constructed familiarity of successful television serials.

This type of television-sponsored domestic tourism can coincide with "seeing the sites" but also often diverges from the centralized geography of the tourist industry and thus constructs an/other path from and to German identity formation: "The more *Tatort* dedicates itself to the *Heimat*, the less this *Heimat* has anything to do with the actual characteristics of a specific place."[39] As Terkessidis insists, *Tatort* underscored the notion of *Heimat* at a time that "the German city changed drastically" and the first wave of migrant laborers set in.[40] From the first episode onward, anxieties over race and gender play co-constitutive roles in the construction of *Heimat*, and these anxieties excavate their historical counterparts in German anti-Semitism and xenophobia. Seeing a German city through *Tatort* reveals a mediated German geopolitics that claims its link to regional and national *Heimat* constructs precisely through that concept's historical development as an "imagined community" (Benedict Anderson) and then polices the urban messiness of its materializations.[41] What types of pathways to and through the actual and imaginary geopolitical spaces *Tatort* paves, how this

---

[36] "Begeben Sie sich mit Hilton auf Spurensuche, (...) entdecken Sie auf eigene Faust die *Tatort*-Städte: Berlin, Köln, München." Hilton.de/minibreaks (accessed September 21, 2010).
[37] Polyglott Sonderausgabe für Walt Disney Studios Home Entertainment (September 2009).
[38] See Bollhöfer about the increase in "Motivimporte" in the case of the Köln production, 187.
[39] Terkessidis, "Die Heimatflüsterer," 26.
[40] Ibid., 27.
[41] Benedict Anderson, *Imagined Communities: Reflections on the Origin and Spread of Nationalism* (London: Verso, 1983).

mediation process functions, and how it is aesthetically packaged will be the focus of the detailed episode analysis in the following chapters.

"Close to Reality"

"*Tatort* Inventor," former ARD program coordinator Gunther Witte, explains the three foundational columns of the *Tatort* concept: "In first place: The focus is the detective. Then, the Regional, and the third big column was: 'Tatort' has to tell stories that are possible, imaginable and close to reality."[42] With over 1,000 episodes in 2019 and "no end in sight,"[43] similar to Jack Webb's "realism" concept for *Dragnet* (NBC,1951–59 and 1967–70), *Tatort* has not only consciously and subconsciously tackled red-hot regional and national sociopolitical issues, it also keeps revisiting them from multiple regional, ethnic, racial, and gendered angles at different temporal intersections, providing the viewer with a diversified, polysemic representational matrix while ensuring formal continuity. According to John Ellis, this medium specificity of broadcast TV produces three ideology effects through its "obsessional repetition of certain definitions and areas of concern, and the neglect of others," "the creation of specific areas or modalities of meanings, the generic patterns of thought," and finally "the way [the medium] place[s] the spectator in particular attitudes to events, creating a particular stance towards or view upon events."[44]

For *Tatort*, this is doubly true, since it has for half a century immediately been following the ritually watched other flagship production of the ARD: its nightly news program *Tagesschau*. Given that the official *Tatort* format calls for scripts grounded in "possible, imaginable" stories matched to a realism based on the representations of regional specificity, interest, and events, it should be asked what traces the programming sequence has left in each episode of *Tatort*, how the *Tagesschau*'s varying reality modes fueled how creators modulated their scripts, and how the conjoint viewing habits co-construct meaning, not just for the episode as text but also for the intersections between geopolitical positions each screening creates.

For example, Felix Mitterer wrote the 2009 episode "Baum der Erlösung" (Tree of Absolution) based on the "Minaret Debate of Telfs" (Austria), which revolved around the 2005 building permit of a twenty-meter-high minaret for the Eyup-Sultan congregation in the small Alpine village of

---

[42]"An erster Stelle: Im Mittelpunkt steht der Kommissar. Dann eben die Regionalität, und die dritte große Säule war: Der 'Tatort' muss Geschichten erzählen, die möglich, vorstellbar und realitätsnah sind." Interview with Gunther Witte, *Neue Osnabrücker Zeitung*, April 9, 2010, http://www.noz.de/deutschland-und-welt/politik/37932867/tatort-erfinder-gunther-witte-ist-ein-fan-der-muenster-krimis (accessed September 8, 2010).
[43]Witte, *25 Jahre Tatort*.
[44]Ellis, *Visible Fictions*, 16.

Telfs. The Austrian broadcast station ORF showed the 2009 *Tatort* episode as part of an integration-themed evening program geared toward enhancing cross-cultural understanding.[45] Michelle Mattson demonstrates that *Tatort*'s central focus on a current political issue does not mean that it is represented accurately or in its complexity nor that it educates its viewers to think critically. She reveals how tension between different positions often leads to a "conciliatory stance" that neutralizes the political thrust rather than allow it to percolate through public discourse.[46] In addition to Mattson's caution, Nico Carpentier applies Ernesto Laclau and Chantal Mouffe's 1985 discourse theory on subject positions within hegemonic systems to television studies. Carpentier makes clear that the mix of reality-based and fictional content on television constructs a medium-specific propensity to articulate *and* discursify historical events through the projection of "ordinary lives."[47] Therefore, special attention will have to be devoted to the textuality and aesthetics of each episode and how its representation of the sociopolitical climate intersects with the preceding *Tagesschau* and positions subjects (actors, characters, journalists, viewers) as social actors *as well as* within a certain hegemonic imaginary.

---

[45]"Schimpf-und Hasstiraden in Telfs," *Der Standard*, January 2, 2009, http://derstandard.at/1229975367449?sap=2&_pid=11633742 (accessed September 8, 2010).

[46]Michelle Mattson, "*Tatort*: The Generation of Public Identity in a German Crime Series," *New German Critique* 78 (Fall 1999): 161–81, here 181.

[47]Nico Carpentier, "Reality Television's Construction of Ordinary People," in *A Companion to Reality Television*, ed. Laurie Ouellette (New York: Wiley, 2014), 346.

2

Following the Flow

The National News, Regional Crimes, and Global Literacy

To follow television flow, Raymond Williams's cornerstone characteristic of network television as such, means unearthing partially obscured archival layers of dialogicity between production, narrative and formal integration, and reception of adjacent and competing programs within the broadcast window of a show's premiere. Unlike cursory glances from summarized insights gained by hindsight, a media-archaeological approach to the televisual network moment makes the triangulation between the historical Real, its mediated documentation, and the fictional Real visible. As Jane Feuer posited for her study of *Television and Reaganism*, "to correlate a shift in dominant narrative form of (. . .) network television with a shift in sensibilities outside the text" requires extensive research into the intertextual segmentation of Sunday evening's TV flow.[1] To take flow seriously, *Tatort*'s case has to be read through its immediate precursor, ARD's flagship evening news program, *Die Tagesschau*. The flow between the two segments in the Sunday evening ARD lineup has been cemented to construct a weekend viewing ritual that has prevailed despite social and media-related changes.

Each episode is interwoven with current national and global events through its format's insistence on the proximity to the historical Real and its place in the evening television flow. By following the evening news program, *Die Tagesschau*, Sunday night's crime drama connects nonfiction and fiction through a tableau of shared topics and representational reality modes that link not simply the content but often also the semiotic code of meaning construction. The public television news montage of global,

---

[1] Jane Feuer, *Seeing through the Eighties: Television and Reaganism* (Durham: Duke University, 1995), 129.

national, regional segments crafted for counterweighted political delivery introduces an intertextual associative mode of meaning construction that might not always produce content equivalencies but constructs a mnemonic and semiotic path through the reception and understanding of *Tatort* textuality. This linkage is specific to network television. Rather than dealing with different flow pairings every day (TikTok, YouTube) or different pairings for substantially different demographics (cable/satellite television), the constancy of the paired flow for a major sector of the population has had the potential to lay down specific reception and comprehension patterns between 1970 and the convergence era, patterns that for a significant portion of the generations born between the 1930s and 1970s continue to this day.

Relying on Erving Goffman's theory of framing (1974), criminologists Andrew J. Baranauskas and Kevin M. Drakulich used empirical methods to update prevalent notions about "media construction of crime" in 2018. They argue that consistency of framing and viewing habits drive believability, and that "the framing of crime by the media is more likely to resonate with media consumers if it reflects their local context."[2]

> By using two nationally representative surveys matched with contextual data, we identify two forms of media consumption that seem important to understandings of crime: local television news and TV crime dramas. (. . .) Television news viewers are also more likely to support tougher crime policies. Importantly, context matters: The influence of television news and crime dramas on perceptions of crime is strongest among White respondents who live near larger numbers of Black neighbors. (Ibid., 679)

While their US-based results do not completely map onto the German context due to differences in network television structure, demographics, and reception patterns, their study points toward the potential of the long-term *Tagesschau/Tatort* package for framing global events in terms of local and regional crime stories and vice versa. This will have to be kept in mind for the episode analyses, while maintaining a critical distance to the cultivation hypothesis.

David Morley emphasizes the work of Ovar Löfgren on Swedish network-era media to explain the effects of regularity. Löfgren describes how regularity informs "the fragments of cultural memory" that make up "the invisible information structure" of belonging and identity formation.[3]

---

[2] Andrew J. Baranauskas and Kevin M. Drakulich, "Media Construction of Crime Revisited: Media Types, Consumer Contexts, and Frames of Crime and Justice," *Criminology* 56, no. 4 (2018): 679–714. 682 and 679, respectively.

[3] Ovar Löfgren, "The Nation as Home or Motel?" (University of Lund, 1995) quoted by David Morley, "At Home with Television," in *Television after TV*, ed. Lynn Spigel and Jan Olsson (Durham: Duke University Press, 2004), 311.

Morley goes on to caution against assuming that diasporic community members within Germany are not included in or consciously withdrawing from these identity-forging paths and reminds us of the research on Turkish-German media practices by Kevin Robins, who found a hybrid both/and strategy, a "commuting migration" between Turkish language satellite, internet, and domestic network offerings in the host country.[4] How this media migration is in turn ignored or employed strategically by the ARD and within *Tatort*'s narrative ecosystem will have to be investigated in the flow and text-based analyses of each episode.

I am not the first to follow the flow of critical and viewer engagement between *Die Tagesschau* and *Tatort*. That honor goes to *Die Zeit*, Germany's premiere weekly magazine, when it published an article on December 4, 1970, that discusses the first *Tatort* episode "Taxi nach Leipzig" from November 29, 1970, in the context of the *Tagesschau* that preceded it. The author not only analyzes the conservative opposition's attack against then chancellor Willy Brandt's contract negotiations with Poland and the GDR (*Ostverträge*), which they term a "Stalingrad of German politics" and "an escalation of the Cold War," but he also reads the politicians' appearance on the *Tagesschau* as a performance, and he uses the crime drama that follows as a didactic corrective to their "Functionary-Metaphoricity." In *Tatort*, he says, a Hamburg detective shares cognac from a bottle with his Eastern colleague: "Let your heart speak, colleague, only bad men shoot in East and West, there where high German or Saxony dialect is spoken (. . .) There are commonalities, my man, that no barbed wire fence or wall will ever destroy."[5] This first flow analysis accentuates the importance of the intertextual dialogue between *Tagesschau* and *Tatort* that is established on a weekly basis and has continued uninterrupted from the network era in 1970 to today for a large percentage of the population.

Tagesschau introduced a daily screening regimen altering the private, temporal, and spatial evening flow of middle-class German households. During the network era, *Tagesschau* held the largest market share of television news programs. Even in 2019, it garnered an average of 9.8 million viewers per airing which ranked it the number one evening news program on German television. Considering the current media saturation and the 24/7 news cycle, this represents a significant retention of broadcast viewing rituals among German viewers.[6] James Carey and Klaus Beck distinguish ritualized viewing from mere media habitus. Ritual viewers schedule their lives to accommodate viewing. They do it as an expression of

---

[4]Kevin Robins, "Negotiating Spaces: Turkish Transnational Media," in *Media and Migration*, ed. Russell King and Nancy Wood (London: Routledge, 2001). Quoted by Morley 314.
[5]Momos, "Vom Kalten Krieg," *Die Zeit*, December 4, 1970.
[6]Bernhard Weidenbach, for *Statista*, April 8, 2020, https://de.statista.com/statistik/daten/studie/182978/umfrage/reichweite-der-tagesschau-seit-1992/ (accessed May 18, 2020).

and participating in a community, whether they watch alone or not. What content they schedule to watch is given more weight in their lives and in relation to other mediated and unmediated content. The thus integrated media content becomes "synreferential" with their social identity, their perception of reality. As the data shows, a large number of ritual viewers enter into *Tatort* from their already formulaically structured reception of the news. The pairing of *Tagesschau* and *Tatort*, at its height in the network era but continuing through privatization and media convergence, thus continuously creates "participation in a communally derived, synreferential construction of reality (meaning)."[7] With its cast of long-serving anchors (Köpke, Wieben, Veigel) staying on air for over twenty years at a time, "in its ritualistic character, the *Tagesschau* is probably the most steadfast thing one can get in unsteady times (. . .). It structures the New and integrates it into the Old."[8] Given that German networks to this day emphasize world news to a much higher degree than their US counterparts, the lack of control that viewers might feel when exposed to daily news dominated by the United States, Russia, and China is managed by the reliable format and the mix of familiarity with and respect for the main anchor's authority.

Audio and visual hooks are a mainstay of the opening shot of the 1970 and 2015 *Tagesschau*. Both feature the iconic gong-sound that has been calling viewers to the screen since December 26, 1952. Considering that German theaters, supermarkets, and high schools commonly utilize a gong signal to alert patrons and students to the beginning of the next segment in their programs or to make a special announcement, the audio trigger connects educational, economic, and entertainment sectors of society. The gong hails viewers of *Tagesschau* as subjects of interconnected institutions of local, regional, and national power (Louis Althusser). Given the longevity of the daily and weekend ritual of watching *Tagesschau*, the unchanged gong combined with the unchanged *Tatort* title sequence are capable of delivering an almost Pavlovian response in viewers and those within earshot.

In addition to the discursive intersections between institutions of power laid bare by the hailing effect of both shows' sound cues, the regional format of *Tatort* is directly linked to the national and international news. The temporal flow of the progressing evening program meets the spatial flow between geopolitical concepts, demonstrating the porousness not only of the national, regional, and global but also of the four reality modes Jeremy Butler sees as constitutional of televisuality (observational, expository,

---

[7] James W. Carey, "A Cultural Approach to Communication," in *Communication as Culture* (New York: Routledge, 2009), 11–28. Klaus Beck, *Medien und die soziale Konstruktion von Zeit* (Wiesbaden: Springer, 1994), 289.
[8] Fritz Wolf, "Die Tagesschau," in *Flimmerkiste*, ed. Nina Schindler (Hildesheim: Gerstenberg, 1999), 52–3.

participatory, and reflexive).⁹ Reality modes shift within the internal segmentation of the evening news: field reporters documenting an unfolding crisis might utilize the observational mode; summoned experts make arguments in an expository style, breaking the fourth wall; street interviews model the participatory mode; anchors might poke fun at a studio mishap or the foregrounded cameras might reveal the apparatus at work in a reflexive mode. This flow between reality modes situates viewers in different positions vis-à-vis the historical Real, media consumption, and subjectivity, including its global, national, regional, and local identity markers. The shifting modes reposition viewers and reconceptualize the historical world as much as their relationship to its representation. As the reality modes reconceptualize the historical Real formally and affectively, the push and pull in their different ontological formats carry over into watching *Tatort* at 8:15 p.m. Add to this the newsworthy timeliness *Tatort* founder Gunther Witte desired for his concept, and one program might be perceived as an extension of the other, especially when a *Tagesschau* segment airs as part of *Tatort* (to double down on the reality effect of the show) or a *Tatort* segment airs as part of the *Tagesschau* (e.g., celebrating the show's anniversary, the entrance or exit of a *Tatort* actor),

On Sunday evening, viewers might not immediately process the disconcerting content from the daily news, but they move from one formally stable segment to another. While viewers have to look outside into the world during *Tagesschau* and adapt to what they see, the extreme close-up of a pair of eyes in *Tatort*'s title sequence redirects this gaze. The surveilling subject's eyes—a dragnet emanating from one pupil—are now under surveillance. As the "techno-tele-media-apparatus" (as Derrida calls television, combining its technology, industry, distribution, and epistemological contraption) returns the look, it destabilizes the binary of world/home questioning "the naturalness and givenness of territorialized 'national belonging.'"¹⁰ While a viewer's main desire may be to "switch off" the impending and increasingly complex global crises and focus instead on a more concrete, supposedly manageable local/regional nemesis with certain closure at the end of the evening, what is local, regional, or global has become tenuous at best. Neither narrative closure nor the embodied representations of geopolitically scaled crimes (e.g., *Tatort* Hamburg vs. Manila) can contain the local-global intersections that the show and the flow thrive on. As the weekly team closes the local case, national and global forces keep intersecting with regional conflicts to produce new enigmas. While giving special attention to the

---

⁹Jeremy Butler, *Television: Visual Storytelling and Screen Culture* (New York: Routledge, 2018), 92.
¹⁰David Morley, "At Home with TV," in *Television after TV*, ed. Lynn Spigel and Jan Olsson (Raleigh: Duke University Press, 2004), 305.

textuality and aesthetics of each *Tatort* episode itself, critically reestablishing and analyzing the intersegmental flow between *Tagesschau* and *Tatort* can offer valuable insights into the drama's relationship to the sociopolitical climate and its representation through what Fritz Wolf terms an "ideological order."[11]

In addition, it is wise to reconsider Jürgen Habermas's insistence on the role of writing and reading for establishing the German public sphere as the rise of bourgeois emancipation in the late eighteenth century laid the groundwork for the project of modernity. Too often, visual media-makers and critics forget that viewers are also readers, especially in the German case. What viewers and critics read and write about shows, and what gets published in local, regional, and national print media, should not be ignored. Their public contributions are, similar to Henry Jenkins's television fans who become authors or textual poachers, part of the flow.[12] And similar to web-based fan engagement that falls on a spectrum from indie fanfic to officially licensed and maintained fan sites, the networks have always been eager to reclaim and redirect that flow for their own benefit.

One illustrative example is critics' and viewers' enthusiastic response to ARD's clever approach to the 2020 *Tatort Sommerpause* (production pause) made worse by the Covid-19 epidemic. Instead of resigning itself to the loss of viewers and aggravating loyal fans, the network combined the off-season with its fifty-year *Tatort* celebration, adding Friday evenings to the menu for reruns of classic *Tatort* episodes.[13] To quell worries of cancellation, *Berliner Morgenpost* provided a list of the lengths of different production pauses, proving that they had been a regular feature of the television calendar since 1996. This list not only demonstrated the interconnected active engagement between traditional print news media, online journalism, and dedicated viewers but also restored a sense of normalcy to the pandemic. It assured viewers anxious about the disruption of their regular lives that television routines were there to stay. Since new production was postponed until September 2020, the network asked viewers to vote for their fifty favorite episodes from the last twenty-five years to rerun on Sunday evenings until then. And digital and print newspapers followed suit by providing readers and viewers with historical context and behind-the-scenes expositions of each viewer-selected episode.[14]

The media saturation of sightings, rumors, scandals, and reviews surrounding *Tatort* productions can be located not separate from but on a continuous

---

[11] Fritz Wolf, "Die Tagesschau," 53.
[12] Henry Jenkins, *Textual Poachers: Television Fans and Participatory Culture* (New York: Routledge, 1992).
[13] *Die Zeit*, May 11, 2020, https://www.zeit.de/news/2020-05/11/jubilaeumsjahr-bringt-tatort-fans-laengste-sommerpause (accessed August 12, 2020).
[14] *Die Berliner Morgenpost*, July 24, 2020, https://www.morgenpost.de/kultur/tv/article229093337/Tatort-Aussergewoehnlich-lange-Sommerpause-2020.html (accessed August 12, 2020).

spectrum with today's social media blitz around a show or episode drop on Netflix or any broadcast, cable, or prime network, especially when one considers Germans' voracious print readership. Despite the challenges of privatization and digital media beginning in the mid-1980s, the following quotes from a 2009 and a 2014/15 market analysis make clear that print media has had a special place in Germany and is still very much a contender in the internet era:

> Germany's newspaper publishing world is the largest in Europe. Seven out of ten Germans over the age of 14 read a daily paper regularly, choosing between 351 different papers with a total circulation of 19.9 million copies. (2009)[15]
>
> In 2014, German newspapers reach 67.4% of the German speaking population over 14 with their print editions (. . .) Broken down: daily papers reach 63.2%, weekly newspapers 2.3% and Sunday editions 15.6%. Web based services of the publishers are popular reaching a reliable 43.9% of internet users (30.9 Million Unique Users). In addition, 9.6 million users utilize smartphone- or tablet apps to inform themselves about the local, national or international news. (2015)[16]

To contextualize and follow the flow, I pair the reading of each *Tatort* premiere with an assessment of the main topics covered in its immediate precursor, that evening's *Tagesschau*.[17] Subsequently, since the flow extends to post-viewing engagement with the show, I will analyze key critical and viewer reactions from print media for the network era and from online media for more recent episodes. Following the flow will highlight recurring patterns that establish both codified approaches to sociopolitical topics and corresponding televisual formats. These patterns will facilitate an assessment of network and post-network crime dramas. This method has the additional benefit of critically evaluating Henry Jenkins's post-network approach to engaged viewership, because the connection between the shifting reality modes within and between *Tagesschau* and *Tatort* will reveal how network viewers make use of their agency as fans and citizens as they participate in the public sphere.

---

[15] Anja Pasquay, "Die deutsche Zeitungslandschaft. Entwicklungen und Perspektiven," 2009, https://www.bdzv.de/fileadmin/bdzv_hauptseite/markttrends_daten/wirtschaftliche_lage/2010/assets/3_Pasquay_Zeitungslandschaft_mAbb.pdf (accessed June 1, 2020).
[16] Anja Pasquay, "Gedruckt oder auf dem Display—Deutschland liest Zeitung," 2015, https://www.bdzv.de/fileadmin/bdzv_hauptseite/markttrends_daten/Reichweiten/Pasquay_Reichweiten.pdf (accessed June 1, 2020).
[17] In most cases, I had access to the actual *Tagesschau* episode before *Tatort* premieres. Where I was not successful in locating a full episode, I resorted to the ARDs *Mediathek* news archive, including month-by-month reviews, *Tagesschau* retrospectives, YouTube.de's collective video library, and my research in NDR's Studio Hamburg archive.

3

Tatort Hamburg (NDR)

From this North German port metropolis, the second largest German city and self-identified media center of former West Germany, I will analyze three episodes, the first with inspector Paul Trimmel (Walter Richter) from 1972, the second with detectives Paul Stoever (Manfred Krug) and Peter Brockmöller (Charles Brauer) from 1987, and the third with Cenk Batu (Mehmet Kurtulus) from 2008. These episodes from Hamburg provide a cross-section of personnel, narratological, thematic, aesthetic, and *Tatort*-typical format developments while allowing for an interpretation of sociohistorical and political interactions between the medium, the format, and constructs of local, regional, national, and global spaces and identities.

When Christian Pundt complains to Studio Hamburg producer Kerstin Ramcke "that Hamburg has become somewhat of a cliché. (. . .) Everyone lives with a view of the harbor or at least a Fleet," she counters with the viewers' expectations: "Of course people expect that a bit from a *Tatort* that comes out of Hamburg, that's why we like to do that."[1] This exchange points to the rebound effect of television's relationship to realism, a schematics Thomas Radewagen argues "is accepted as reality and returns as a reality mandate for TV crime dramas to the network."[2] What national and international audiences might find typical for Hamburg, its grandiose reconstructed city hall and square, the seven church spires, including St. Michaelis and the ruin-memorial St. Nikolai, the two Alster lakes, Jungfernstieg and Landungsbrücken, Reeperbahn (the red light district), and the new harbor city with the Elbe Philharmonic Hall, is centrifugally

---

[1]Christian Pundt, "Interview with Kerstin Ramcke," November 24, 1999. *Mord beim NDR Tatort mit Manfred Krug und Charles Brauer* (Münster: LIT, 2002), 145.
[2]Thomas Radewagen, *Ein deutscher Fernsehbulle: Trimmel—der "Tatort"-Star und seine Mediengenese; eine vergleichende Untersuchung von Werremeiers Kriminal-Romanen und "Tatort"-Drehbüchern* (Berlin: Preprints zur Medienwissenschaft, 1985), 104.

condensed in the domestic specificity of Hamburg as "the Venice of the North" due to its many waterways, channels, and bridges or as a "riesiges Bumslokal" (a gigantic brothel).[3] Pundt does not analyze why the 1990s *Tatort* episodes with Stoever/Brockmöller overtly rely on the "water view" aspect of the metropolis, when previous *Tatorts* did not, or why some directors, if they showed water access, seemed to prefer the industrial side of the harbor. Why do the new Batu episodes alternate between the local flair of the Elbe beach, container-harbor industrial romanticism, and views from the Elbe ferries but eschew the "Fleet" views so privileged during the Stoever era? How do these site preferences situate class, race/ethnicity, gender, and regional interests and vice versa? What drives the repositioning, and how does it interact with the medium and genre conventions in each case?

"Rechnen Sie mit dem Schlimmsten!" ("Worst-Case Scenario," dir. Peter-Schulze Rohr; NDR, September 24, 1972)

Tagesschau Synopsis

In the *Tagesschau* that preceded this episode, the resignation from the SPD of former finance minister, Karl Schiller, blaming the party's policies for the economic instability and political crisis, continues the political drama involving the dissolution of the West German parliament (*Bundestag*) after SPD chancellor Willy Brandt's vote of no confidence was turned down on September 22. The conservative wing of the CDU/CSU is incensed about the direction of the treaties with the East (*Ostverträge*), specifically their recognition of the existence and legitimacy of the GDR. One of the treaties, the transit treaty (*Verkehrsvertrag* of May 26) regulating traffic between the GDR and the FRG, was ratified two days before and would be fine-tuned for commercial and personal train traffic on the 25th. Due to the new election demanded by the FRG constitution, interviewed representatives from SPD and CDU/CSU traded inflammatory rhetoric on this issue and the political, economic state of the country. Despite the success of the *Ostverträge*, the political situation is highly unstable after the Munich Olympic Village terrorist attack on September 5 and the dissolution of parliament. The continuing Vietnam War dominated international news, as did increased antiterrorism security at airports in the United States and the protest over bilingual Slovenian/German place signs in Kärnten, Austria.

---

[3]Alexander Schuller, "Das stimmt doch gar nicht ... Unverwüstliche Klischees. Wie die anderen auf Hamburg blicken—und wir auf sie," *Hamburger Abendblatt*, March 10/11, 2012: 9.

Thus, the evening news condensed around a breakdown of naturalized borders and trust in leadership. Willy Brandt's ongoing East-West treaty negotiations moved the phantom of the GDR (signaled by *Bild* and other conservative papers by using quotation marks around the name of the other Germany) closer to material historical reality than some dared to acknowledge. The protest against bilingual border signs in Austria indicates a populist resistance to accepting ethnic and cultural heterogeneity within the borders of a German-speaking nation. In the same vein, the German host nation failed the global community in that it did not manage to prevent the anti-Semitic violence committed against Israeli Olympians in Munich. The following *Tatort* episode enters another layer to this array, namely the integrity of the medical profession. In the 1970s, doctors and scientists had just begun to recover from being tainted by severe ethical violations under the Nazi regime. And film and television had played a crucial role in that recovery.

The Doctor Figure in German History and Culture

From the beginning of German silent cinema onward, the figure of the doctor or surgeon has had a dichotomous visual career, either represented as a crazy lunatic à la Caligari or revered à la Albert Schweitzer, traits sometimes attributed to the same person (Ferdinand Sauerbruch as the most famous case in this regard). This trend has only been made more manifest since the discovery of this professional group's disproportional Nazification during the Third Reich and the involvement of its members in some of the most heinous Holocaust-crimes committed in concentration camps and euthanasia clinics (e.g., at Hadamar) established at the first of the *Nürnberger Prozesse* (the so-called *Ärzteprozess* from December 9, 1946, to August 20, 1947). Subsequent attempts by the professional organization of doctors (*Ärztekammer*) to silence its profession's support of Nazi race crimes and crimes against humanity, such as the suppression of Alexander Mitscherlich and Fred Mielke's documentation of the trial from 1949, speak to the continuity of the professional group's internal struggles with political and ethical responsibility.[4]

During the postwar years, films such as *The Murderers Are among Us* (dir. Wolfgang Staudte, 1948) and the film adaptation *Sauerbruch—That Was My Life* (FRG, dir. Rolf Hansen, 1954) reinvested the doctor figure with

---

[4] See Jürgen Peter, *Der Nürnberger Ärzteprozeß im Spiegel seiner Aufarbeitung anhand der drei Dokumentensammlungen von Alexander Mitscherlich und Fred Mielke* (Münster, 1994). See also the podcast of a conference on this topic at the University of Graz, http://gams.uni-graz.at/fedora/get/podcast:pug-veranstaltungen-0911-aerzteprozess/bdef:Podcast/get (accessed September 30, 2010).

"emotionally centered humanity" ("gefühlszentrierte Menschlichkeit"), making the male doctor character the showcase of ethical struggles negotiated between the private and public realms, even redeeming the profession with the task to lead the nation toward democratization.[5]

In mass-produced genre fiction of the time, the doctor-novel (*Arztroman*), based on the "half-god in white" myth, coupled with the nurse/doctor romance trope helped to place the professional group in the center of tenuous postwar gender and class realignments and aided their "normalization."[6] On television, some of the more successful drama series and soaps focused on doctors and hospitals, for example, *Hafenkrankenhaus* (ARD, 1968), *Die Schwarzwaldklinik* (Black Forest Clinic, ZDF, 1985–9), *Der Landarzt* (The Country Doctor, ZDF, 1987–). Until more recently, the genre has favored more rural locations and has therefore contributed to an interweaving of the professional class and the representative doctor figure with issues revolving around the discursive construction and symbolic recuperation of *Heimat*.[7] Character backstories and conflicts in this genre focus on loyalty, trust, authority, and sexual potency of the failed and dethroned father figure as well as the reorientation of the city-educated professional to his roots, roots equated with a regional identity that is configured as essentially German. This is the context that "Worst-Case Scenario" establishes from its title sequence onward and through which a viewer back then likely viewed this *Tatort* episode.

Tatort Synopsis

This episode deals with the criminal meddling with and profiteering from a computer system that determines the ranks of organ transplant recipients. Jill Biegler (Sabine Sinjen), the sister of a patient who died while on the transplant list, takes revenge on the doctor and the system that failed her family. Hamburg's inspector Trimmel has a car accident in Hamburg that leaves him partially incapacitated as he travels to Munich to confront the head of the corruption ring himself. He collapses in the middle of the interrogation and ends up being saved by the criminal surgeon.

The episode deliberately sets up dualities: two sisters, two cities, two attempts on Trimmel's life, two "gods": computer and doctor. The plot

---

[5]*Lexikon des deutschen Films* (Hamburg: Reclam, 1995).
[6]On the different attempts at "normalization," see Heide Fehrenbach, *Cinema in Democratizing Germany: Reconstructing National Identity after Hitler* (Chapel Hill: University of North Carolina Press, 1995).
[7]On the configurations of *Heimat*, see Johannes von Moltke, *No Place like Home: Locations of Heimat in German Cinema* (Berkeley: University of California Press, 1995). This has changed with the influx of US hospital dramas set in major metropolitan areas (e.g., *Chicago Hope, E.R., Gray's Anatomy*) and in the streaming era, where *Charité* is set in a historical Berlin.

points navigate between these dual poles, which contribute not only to the suspense but also to a specific hetero-spatial mapping of desires and anxieties amid ongoing negotiations around gender, class, and national identity formations.[8] The location of Munich takes on symbolic value as the deadly terrorist assault on the Israeli Olympic team took place only three weeks prior to the airing of this episode (September 5, 1972). Munich thus stands for one of Germany's worst-case scenarios, not only because of the attack on Jewish team members, which evokes German crimes of the past, but also because of the utter failure of German police in the rescue attempt.

Yet, none of this topicality made it into the surface layer of the episode. Instead, it was touted for its timely introduction of the criminal organ trade. The ninety-minute episode begins with its title dripping across the screen in Gothic font. It ends with the title in block letters. With the worst-case scenario nominally contained, horror conventions dictate its reach beyond narrative closure outward into interpretative social space. The beginning clearly marks a connection to UK Hammer studio horror productions popular in Germany from the 1950s through the 1970s. It invites viewers to partake in a grisly spectacle that has body parts going to the highest bidder. The esteemed figure of the surgeon, under whose knife the dilapidated Trimmel ends up, is distributing kidneys to wealthy businessmen. He commits these ethical violations to finance his private clinic and to revolt against the nationally sanctioned *Ärztekammer* regulations concerning the determination of end of life and laws governing the harvesting of organs. This episode deals with a capital crime committed against a computer expert on the dole, responsible for matching the available organs with the vetted patient registry. It also throws suspicion on the figure of the doctor, when it outs his stance on euthanasia. The worst-case scenario thus pairs the criminally and ethically tainted surgeon with the anxiety surrounding the dawn of the computer age.

Repeatedly, Trimmel asks the computer technicians and lab workers "Who decides?" and is not satisfied with the answer that each computer-match is discussed and verified by the board, a panel of experts with stock in the business. After checking the data of all previous matches, one name catches his eye, a surgeon, Prof. Becker in Munich (Wolfgang Wahl), who has received more than a reasonable percentage of organs for patients in his clinic. After Trimmel confronts the recalcitrant board members with this data, he asks his question again, only to arrive at the answer that the person interpreting the data wields the power to decide. Murder victim Jakob

---

[8] Bollhöfer, *Geographien des Fernsehens*: "Der *Tatort* scheint zwar insgesamt einem einfachen Dualismus zu gehorchen, indem er von der Auseinandersetzung zwischen den Gegensätzen bestimmt wird, es erweist sich aber nicht immer so einfach, den genauen Grenzverlauf zwischen den beiden normativ besetzten Räumen zu ermitteln" (135).

Tonndorf (Matthias Wegner) presented the computer-based match as a fait accompli to the board, which rubber-stamped every case having fallen prey to the ideology of digitally enhanced objectivity: "the computer decides." The story's thrust insists that a computer is only as objective and ethical as its data analyst, programmer, and supervisory organ and that abuse of power is built into every system, even the digital one.

Until Trimmel suffers a melodramatically timed relapse from his car accident while confronting the surgeon about his criminal activities, the doctor's ethical position is irrevocably compromised. Yet, only Becker can save Trimmel from brain damage and death. The policeman, a representative of the new democratic state's executive wing, is at the whim of the unethical doctor, a holdover from the Nazi past, who ends up saving his life. While Trimmel is unconsciously recuperating, a scene shows Becker and his wife (Kyra Mladeck) in the surgeon's luxurious home-office. He tells her: "Everything is over." She insists: "But he was the only one who knew . . . why didn't you let him die?" He counters: "I am a doctor above all else." After these revelations, the two take their own lives by gunshot. In the next scene, Trimmel tears up upon hearing this news from his hospital bed.

Not only does Becker reclaim his oath to Hippocrates in his final moment, but he also resists his conniving wife's tempting plan to deliberately botch the operation to let the patient die. This narrative twist is noteworthy for its evocation of *Ehrentod* (honorable death) chosen by or forced upon higher ranked political opposition figures as well as Hitler elites during the Third Reich. Thus, the final act of the doctor's life, placing the very life that endangered his future above his own, redeems his honor and integrity as a surgeon while covering up the political implications of his criminal greed and his untenable ethical position on the value of human life. This change in motivation might have allowed contemporary spectators to transfer their feelings for and against Nazis onto reigning capitalists, no matter their actual politics. This transfer aligns itself with the continuity of fascism debate and the notorious continuity of former Nazis in positions of power in the young democracy.[9]

With Trimmel's postoperative tears horror successfully morphs into melodrama. This change takes most of the political thrust out of the computer/doctor dichotomy. The melodramatic redemptive ending disperses blame; it broadly targets capitalism and/or technological progress rather than the criminal collaborative actions of elites upholding and profiting from systemic racism and injustice. As Thomas Elsaesser has shown,

---

[9] By the early 1980s, films and shows intervened in this debate by publicizing the postwar career paths of justices, politicians, and doctors who were demonstrably involved in oppression, persecution, euthanasia, and genocide, for example at the end of *Die weiße Rose* (dir. Michael Verhoeven, 1982).

melodrama excels at wrestling with competing narrative and social crises by "juxtaposing stereotyped situations in strange configurations, provoking clashes and ruptures which not only open up new associations but also redistribute the emotional energies which suspense and tensions have accumulated, in disturbingly different directions."[10]

The font of the end credits appears superimposed on the final scene in standard block letters. These reclaim the episode as a crime drama and release viewers into a structured lawful existence. As credits scroll, Tonndorf's replacement declines to discuss another millionaire's organ request via telephone. But, true to horror protocols, the computer screen's flicker paired with a returning horror score still render this normality fragile. As a repetition of the beginning, the phone rings twice and is answered twice, the plea and—so far—negative answer repeated each time. The pattern of two retains its structural dominance, and its repetition plays an important role in an episode that is dealing with binary computer code.

Critical and Viewer Engagement

"Scandal over *Tatort-Krimi*: Doctors accuse NDR of defamatory statements out of sensationalist greed"—Prof. Klosterhalfen, consulted leader of the kidney-transplant team at the Hamburger University Hospital, beseeched NDR program director Dietrich Schwarzkopf to "toss the discriminating project into the trash." "Out of pure gimmickry, a few TV people wreak havoc with our work and set our public information efforts back years" (*Bild und Funk*, September 23, 1972). Unlike the previous article, it is remarkable how many of the following headlines do not reference the fictional origin of the television story but rather turn it into a national scandal competing with political news. This example displays Thomas Radewagen's triangular rebound effect at work. A network television show like *Tatort* might take its inspirations from current events to represent them in fictional form, but this is not the end of the intermediation. Its narratives flow back into the public sphere accentuating specific aspects that drive a dialogue between social actors and the historical Real that has the potential of impacting political debates and influencing policy with material consequences:

- *Die Welt* (September 26, 1972): "At the Expense of Patients"
- *Tagesspiegel* (September 26, 1972): "Kidney-Scandal"

---

[10]Thomas Elsaesser, "Tales of Sound and Fury: Observations on the Family Melodrama," in *Imitations of Life. A Reader on Film and Television Melodrama*, ed. Marcia Landy (Detroit: Wayne State University Press, 1991), 82.

- *Bild* (September 26, 1972): "Kidney-Transplant only for People with Money?"
- *Hamburger Abendblatt* (October 10, 1972): "The Great Business with Organ-Trading Will Not Happen"
- *TV Hören und Sehen* (October 28, 1972): "Out of Sensationalism TV Shocked Thousands of Kidney Patients"

The headlines suggest that viewers (a.k.a. patients) were morally and politically outraged after this episode. But viewers' own comment letters reveal them generally more grateful to *Tatort* for "courageously handling the hot potatoes of medical ethics, abuse of electronic data, red cells" (*Funkuhr*, October 14, 1972). It was the medical establishment that felt attacked and defamed. In article after article, kidney specialists defended their professional ethics and attacked the scriptwriters and director of misinformation. The surgeon, Prof. Klosterhalfen, who was confidentially asked to review the script of the episode (the NDR would have liked to have filmed it in his clinic in Eppendorf), went so far as to leak the script to the press before its premiere. While the NDR situated the episode closer to "science fiction" than reality, the doctors themselves reacted against the reality effect of the episode:

> Precisely because the film represents the medical facts almost accurately (. . .) the film has to have had a devastating effect on patients. The computer, which holds the data of the potential recipients, really exists. It is located at Scandia-Transplant in Aarhus (Denmark). (. . .) But a director, who could manipulate the data, is unthinkable. (Friedrich Deich, "TV Critique: At the Expense of Patients," *Welt*, September 26, 1972)

It is revealing how the notion of human greed and error, while denied on behalf of three elites—scientists, data-managers, and surgeons—frames the attack against another elite: media representatives. The real battle is waged over who possesses and retains control over public discourse and image. Each side claims to inform and enlighten the public on behalf of the common good. On the one hand, trust in medical progress and accomplishments lays the foundation for saving lives, on the other hand, a heightened awareness of the potential for abuse of power and trust lays the foundation for a democratic citizen's bill of rights regarding data-gathering and mining.

A Crime Out of Time

Videography, score, and mise-en-scène of this episode integrate the computer's binary code semiotically into its aesthetics and narrative. The repeated patterns of two along with the analog/digital divide open up a discursive interstice that reflects on representational systems themselves—telling time, mapping space, gendered embodiment. In the beginning sequence, the church bells are ringing in the background, indicating that it is a Sunday, but *Fräulein* Jill Biegler arrives at her place of work, a modern high-rise office building, wearing a fashionably long white leather coat, just for a minute to check something, she says. We see her car entering the spiral entryway to the underground parking garage, then framed in the doorway of the elevator. We share the watchman's point of view: a close-up of a digital clock—14:26. Then, Jill is shown in relief smoking in front of the eighth-floor office window. We share her view of the distant cranes in the Hamburg harbor. Back to the watchman, who sees Jill's boss, Tonndorf, arrive. The watchman receives and connects a phone call for Tonndorf upstairs. We see Jill's car driving away from the watchman's point of view. The phone rings upstairs. An analog clock is shown—it's 2:37 p.m. Subsequently, we follow Jill's boss, Tonndorf, as he walks through the empty office. At 14:38, another close-up of a digital clock, he is confronted and shot.

This sequence masterfully introduces us to key aesthetic principles of crime fiction at the same time that it sets up the sociopolitical relevance of the episode. The timecode shines a light on the failure to synchronize different coexisting temporalities. In close proximity to the title sequence's pair of scanning and surveyed eyes, the viewer enters the exposition as a watchman, as a mixture of voyeur, witness, and bystander. As is the case with the panel that slides over the pair of eyes in the title sequence, the elevator doors close on victim and perpetrator, leaving the watchman and the viewer in a similar position, the watchman fixed behind his desk and phone station, the viewer's gaze roaming but selectively curtailed, following Jill for a smoke, then Tonndorf through the spooky office only to be placed side by side with the killer. Black screen. For all the privileged position changing, the viewer gets inside the crime scene but not the identity of the murderer. The hook is set. As viewers, we are too close to the crime to change the channel or turn off the television. A classic whodunit is in progress, establishing the viewer as the unseen witness on the scene, allowing her privileged yet limited insight. Connecting the clues is the work of the detective whose historical contextualization of the case plays nursemaid to the reading skills of the audience. Yet in this episode, the structure of connections reflects its visual aesthetics, proving that *Tatort* cherishes and continues the genre-reflective tradition of the *Krimi*.

Digital and analog clocks run side by side, apparently telling the same time, but their pairing diverts attention from telling the time to an epistemological shift itself, to a sociopolitical time-telling rather than a purely temporal one. With the tolling of the church bells, a third time-telling apparatus enters the scene. The three devices connect and contrast traditional and modern times to and with the digital computer age from the very beginning, in a similar way that the secretary's gender and sexuality place her at odds with traditional German society from the get-go. Instead of going to church or preparing Sunday dinner, Ms. Jill drives herself to work on her day off. The old-fashioned use of "Fräulein" immediately marks Ms. Jill as unmarried. It connects her sexual availability to her employment. The long white leather coat and the sporty car seem extravagant for a secretary, adding to the ambiguity of her role. The sequence leads us into thinking that Jill and Tonndorf, her boss, are meeting for a sexual liaison at the office on a Sunday. She waits and smokes, yet, they apparently miss each other in the elevator by a few minutes. Timing is of the essence.

The unanswered phone call, piercing the silent space with its ring, continues the sound motif of the church bells, whose call to morning service similarly invades the public business realm and sounds out the spheres' inherent disconnect. This *Tatort* episode picks up the audio and editing pattern from Fritz Lang's magnificent clock-striking sequence in *M* (1931): shots of empty rooms alternate with clock faces and a mother's increasingly more desperate unanswered call for her daughter Elsie. While the caller does not get a connection in either case, the phone in *Tatort* narratologically connects the beginning of the episode to the end, when Tonndorf's replacement finally picks it up. Like the church bells or the echo-effect of Lang's mother's voice, the ringing phone expresses an unheeded call. The missed connections represented by church bells and telephone stand in for competing and out-of-synch social rhythms, and contrast with the immediate and exact matching of call and response by the central computer in 1972.

The mainframe computer bases its pairings on data collections and programmed task questions, in this case checking for a match in blood type and degree of organ failure. Thus, what church and analog devices cannot manage to connect in any humanistic, social manner, the digital age connects on the basis of numerical data. That this communication is not an improvement, however, is made manifest by the class privilege accorded to the high-stakes briberies from wealthy patients to be moved up on the donor list or to those who commit insurance fraud to retain the wealth within their closest family. Jill's unemployed sister cannot compete with that. Even Jill's attempt to sleep with Tonndorf for a chance to get her sister a kidney fails. In the early 1970s, her sexual availability is taken for granted, does not equal the cash contribution necessary for Tonndorf to facilitate a transfer.

As her bargaining through sex fails, Jill resorts to plotting the perfect crime. If she had been able to act alone, she would have succeeded. Success and eventual failure come in shapes of two. When she engages her and her sister's mutual lover Bertie (Günther Einbrodt) to put on her coat and leave the office garage in her car, she literally and figuratively places her cover on another's shoulders. Portrayed as a nit-witted young long-haired male, who is hopping between the sisters' beds and different left-wing causes, Bertie proves to be the weak link in the cover-up operation. While he physically convincingly doubles as Jill, he does not match her focused intentionality. He talks too much, shows too many emotions, and scares easily: he tries to jump out of a fourth-floor window to evade being questioned. His ambiguous gender presentation, necessary for the alibi, eventually gets Jill into trouble. When asked about her affair with Bertie, Jill shrugs her shoulders nonchalantly: "Should I kick him out?" ("Soll ich ihn rausschmeißen?"). While Jill remains an enigma to the detectives in her transition between witness, victim (of a gas poisoning attempt), and perpetrator, between sexually pliable and intellectually challenging, Bertie is easily readable. Thus, Jill's motives and modus operandi can only be read through her double, through her "female" cover. Because his gender presentation chafes against traditional masculinity, his *Doppelgänger* role is readable to male detectives caught in a heteronormative mode. Bertie's unsuccessful attempts to "take off the cover" and successfully perform according to concepts of traditional masculinity make it possible for Peterson (Ullrich von Bock) to solve Jill's crime. Detective work is thus successful in this episode only by reading reiterations of gender performance (Judith Butler) with and against representation. If we return to the repeated phone calls at the end and Tonndorf's replacement's reiterated negative answers, the reader is structurally invited to repeat Peterson's discovery, forcing the viewer to adapt to the postmodern condition.

A Cop Out of Place

How do Trimmel's travels between the two poles of Hamburg and Munich play into this doubling? Why didn't Friedrich Werremeier have the whole script take place in Hamburg and environs? And why did he write in two attempts on Trimmel's life on top of this spatial instability? When Trimmel's brakes do not engage and he crashes into another car, witnesses spontaneously blame him: "He lost control." Trimmel and his colleagues suspect foul play instead. They see a connection to the pending case, especially after their witness, Jill, is hospitalized after a dubious gas poisoning. Eventually, evidence shows that the mechanic simply neglected to repair the brakes, not because of an attempt to rid the case of the investigating officer. But the accidents leave Jill and Trimmel vulnerable, especially because they both push themselves to the limit. Structurally similar to Bertie's and Jill's gender-based cover-up operation, the car and gas accidents double for a murder attempt, two red herrings, yet it is this narratological device that places Trimmel in the doctor's path, so that the latter is tempted to kill the investigator.

Renowned for his take-charge attitude, the car accident puts a dent in Trimmel's self-control and his public image. Just when he and his fans need him to take control, during the key interrogation scene, his body betrays him. Along with the viewers, he enters a fugue state in between times and places, places him and the audience in suspension. He wants to but cannot deliver. The analogy between Trimmel, who fails not only to accuse Becker of his criminal activities but also to restrain him, and the police in Munich's terrorist crisis is striking. In 1972, a portion of the audience was most likely relieved that the accusations were never made verbal but that viewers could delve as far or as little into questions about "Doctors under the Swastika" and German responsibility for the Munich attack as they dared.[11] In the context of the national news, Trimmel's head trauma can be read as an allegory of the aftermath of the September terrorist attacks in Munich and the subsequent collapse of the German parliament. On television, the lead detective and stand-in *pater familias* of the nation collapses and has his head examined in Munich.

While the NDR *Tatort* producers might very well have sought to highlight the cross-regional, national, and ultimately global aspect of the computer age by relocating the culprit to Munich, that displacement of blame itself has a longer tradition by arguing for or against regional differences during the embrace of fascism, whether based in facts or wishful denial. As has been the case in similar crisis moments, such as Hitler's failed *Beerhall Putsch* (beerhall coup) in 1923 or the ill-fated 1938 Munich conference, "Munich" is synonymous for German constitutional crises. In this *Tatort* episode, the national and individual confrontations with the German past occur in an unconscious state, giving credence to the standardized denial of knowledge—about the Holocaust, about Hitler's intentionality toward a "total war," and so on. While Trimmel is unconscious during the operation, German viewers are coaxed into a melodramatic stupor only to be reawakened to a normalized situation in Hamburg—with his regional team (Trimmel) and his regional bearings (the viewer) reassembled.

The screenplay insists on showing Trimmel en route to Munich, on the plane, ordering a drink, waiting in the doctor's office, his grip on social reality fading as the language and custom differences and upturned hierarchies grow between Hamburg and Bavaria. As Bollhöfer argues, an "inner change set into scene through border crossings" evokes a Romantic style of representation, where the emotional self and topographical conditions are aligned in a precarious mirror-game with one other. "In this case, spatial patterns of movement correlate with symbols for the loss of identity and homeland."[12] Out of his territory, out of his league, Trimmel is stripped of his social and professional power, his forceful patriarchal masculinity.[13] He

---

[11]*Ärzte unterm Hakenkreuz* is also the title of a three-part 2005 TV film by Christopher Paul and Christian Feyerabend.
[12]Björn Bollhöfer, *Geographien des Fernsehens*, 162–3.
[13]On Trimmel and other 1970s *Tatort* inspectors' masculinity as patriarchal masculinity, see Pundt (2000) and Radewagen (1985).

cannot afford to lose control and face in his precinct. He cannot succumb to his injuries from the accident to be hospitalized in Hamburg.

But, once in transit and upon arrival in Munich, the co-identification of space, gender, and power breaks down. His trip down South exposes his control as performance. Trimmel's trespass and resulting predicament are symbolically associated with Bertie's. Trimmel has no jurisdiction in Munich; he has not even received permission to double as a cross-regional agent, yet he refuses to acknowledge it. His attempt at stretching his regional power to a national scale exposes his weaknesses not only as a policeman but also as a man. Trimmel's attempt to reveal the surgeon's criminal greed and unethical stretch of power fail because Trimmel, Bertie, and the doctor have narratologically been positioned as distorted mirror images of one another, weakened by overreaching their areas of competence. Thus, the poles of criminal and cop, North and South, Hamburg and Munich, have collided with one another to give articulation to a tertiary position that threatens to denaturalize the heteronormative axis of power (masculinity and femininity) through the Jill/Bertie narrative strand. The dichotomy has lost its structural soundness and has become precarious because the double is not entirely other and not entirely the same, and because it covers for and reflects on its representation and embodiment of the other.

The structural connections between space, gender, sexuality, and power are crucial for arriving at an understanding of how a naturalized concept of the regional functions in place of nationality in postwar Germany and on network television. While the perpetrator is located in Munich, the computer age brings the crime to Hamburg, thus not only matching organs and recipients but also connecting disparate regions to each other. This is essentially what *Tatort* is doing with its own format during this heyday of the broadcast era, in form of a separate but coequal regional anthology system. The episode's "worst-case scenario" thus also features a media-reflexive element revolving around society's and broadcast media's anxieties around new technologies. If *Tatort*'s regional format and the computer's very building block are alternating between 0s and 1s, each in their respective times and places, this episode produces an uncontainable moment of fusion and hybridity that comments on the system of representation, the system of signification and power itself.

An Untethered Culprit

Hamburg as Trimmel's biophysiological geopolitical center is his True North. The further he moves away from it, the more fragile his hold on his professional, personal, and ethical compass becomes, here equated with a bio-geopolitical principled ethical guidance system. As a red cell sympathizer, the non-Hamburger Bertie lacks such an ethical guidance system. He comes off as the worst-case scenario, rather than the doctor or Jill, who, as femme fatale as she appears, still acts out of a socially respected motivation: love for her family. Bertie does not hail from either region and tramps around Europe. He dabbles in civil disobedience and wants to have it both ways: both of the two sisters, a comfortable materialist existence *and* socialism. Instead of anchoring his representation, his male sexuality becomes as much of a performance as his female impersonation. His sexual and geopolitical identity oscillate as he is yo-yoing between positions. Bertie is depicted as lacking a professional, sexual, regional, and political *Heimat*. Read through the news headlines, Bertie, not quite a Bert, and not a woman either, becomes the poster child for the looming dissolution of the young democracy's fragile status quo.

In a stunning move, rather than the computer-steered medical-industrial complex or the proto-Nazi doctor, it is instead Bertie's untethered-ness that is made to represent the worst of the sociopolitical changes Germany is undergoing in the 1970s. In televisual terms, the ambiguity of Bertie's character makes him a better villain than a supercomputer, which could not be adequately anthropomorphized (as in Stanley Kubrick's *2001: A Space Odyssey* from 1968) on the station's limited episode budget. And the displacement of a stereotypical Nazi villain by a red cell sympathizer makes sense in the context of dominant anticommunism in the West and the fallout from the assassination attempt of a student leader, Rudi Dutschke, in April of that year. According to research of newspaper coverage of the student movement, the *Bild Zeitung* had used rhetoric in line with the scapegoating of Bertie in the Hamburg *Tatort*:

> In the days and weeks prior [to the assassination attempt], the publisher [Springer Verlag] had made little secret of the disdain it held for the 1968 student movement in Germany. Articles urging readers to "stop the terror of the young reds now!" and "eliminate the trouble makers" had appeared in various Springer publications. *Bild*—a paper the leftist students blamed for being partially responsible for the Dutschke attack—led the charge. (*Spiegel International*, November 4, 2008)

Anti-youth conservativeness meets Cold War anticommunist rhetoric and escalates the social unrest leading to the 1970 foundation of the *Rote Armee Fraktion* (RAF) when journalist and sympathizer Ulrike Meinhof springs ring leader Andreas Baader from prison. Until 1998, three generations of RAF members have sought to upend the status quo, resorting to violence, terrorism, and kidnapping.[14]

---

[14]Bundeszentrale für politische Bildung, "Geschichte der RAF," https://www.bpb.de/geschichte/deutsche-geschichte/geschichte-der-raf/ (accessed May 26, 2020).

This episode highlights the anxieties and fascinations surrounding leftist self-representations and embodiments. It uses the popularly drawn connections between left-wing politics and sexual promiscuity to scapegoat and incriminate fluid geopolitical and gender presentations in the 1970s, especially by male-identified bodies. Given the medical context of this episode, and Trimmel's own health and identity crisis, viewers are encouraged to read Bertie in virological terms, as if his promiscuous passing—between cities, regions, genders, sisters—were infectious to the core of democracy and rationality, to the German *patria* itself. As much as this rhetoric echoes Nazi-era racist and anti-Semitic vitriol, its combination of medical, sexual, and geopolitical elements would come back ferociously in the context of the 1980s AIDS epidemic.

Bertie, Jill, and Trimmel are upended by the same kind of transgressions that have become somewhat of a staple in convergence-era shows that utilize the fascination with and narrative/aesthetic potential of gender fluidity in concert with emergent technology in the committing and pursuit of crime (HBO's *The Wire*) along with special-effects television aesthetics (CBS's *CSI*) and complex serial narratives (David Lynch's *Twin Peaks*). In this episode from 1972 trespasses reveal the seams between Germany's region-based federalism and resurgent nationalism, sexism and trans/homophobia, analog and digital media. "Worst case" consequently performs the dilemma of the network crime drama: how *Tatort* has to continuously reach beyond its own technological, fictional, generic, spatial, and temporal boundaries to stay viable for an anxiously changing but broadest possible spectrum of the population while conserving what that audience perceives as a representation of the authentically German *and* regional.

"Voll auf Hass" ("Committed to Hate," dir. Bernd Schadewald; NDR, November 8, 1987)

Tagesschau Synopsis

In German politics, domestic and international events during the fall of 1987 were overshadowed by the *Rainer Barschel Affäre*, the suspicious death on October 11 of the conservative party's prime minister of the state of Schleswig-Holstein. First on the scene was *Stern* reporter Sebastian Knauer, called to the hotel room for an exclusive interview, and his photos of the dead Barschel in a bathtub quickly saturated the national and regional mediascape. Not only was Barschel involved in the Waterkant-Gate corruption scandal involving former Springer journalist Pfeffer and the higher-ups of both Christian and Social Democrats in Schleswig-Holstein, it was also rumored that he was involved with the Stasi (GDR secret service) and a multinational weapons deal gone wrong. The story thus connects the regional (Schleswig-Holstein) and national (inter-German) to the global in criminal terms. Due to the media saturation of the visual evidence shot at the scene, the viewer has already found the corpse before *Tatort* even opens. In the *Tagesschau* preceding the airing of "Voll auf Hass," the ongoing investigations into what would become one of the major political scandals of the FRG were only rivaled by the Remembrance Day bombings carried out by a brigade of the IRA in Enniskillen, Northern Ireland, where twelve people died. It should also be noted that this particular *Tatort* aired on the night before the annual commemoration of *Kristallnacht* (Night of Broken Glass, November 9–10, 1938) lending specific weight to the symbolism of broken glass recurring throughout the episode.

Contemporaneous regional headlines that might have set into motion the specific interracial and neo-Nazi aspects of the storyline: in July 1985, Mehmet Kaymakci (twenty-nine) was killed by three Skinheads in Hamburg. Also, in 1985, the 26-year-old Ramazan Avci died after having been brutally assaulted by young Skinheads in Hamburg. On February 3, 1987, the seventeen-year-old Skinhead Gerd-Roger Bornemann was killed by four of his neo-Nazi companions in Hannover.[15]

Tatort Synopsis

Interracial and intergenerational conflicts take center stage during this Stoever/Brockmöller episode, when the wedding between Turkish-German Erdal Bicici (Tayfun Bademsoy) and his German bride Dagmar Lobeck (Heike Faber) gets crashed by a group of Skinheads, and the bridegroom stabbed and killed by one of them. The crime drama's outcome penalizes the white patriarch Lobeck (Oliver Pleitgen) for his racially motivated masterminding of the attack and seems to be in keeping with the official rhetoric of normalization and democratic stability. But the wedding between a young German woman and her Turkish fiancé produces anxieties over parental authority and the state of Germany as a multicultural society—on all geopolitical levels.

The bourgeois German father bemoans that modern German law does not grant him the absolute power to control his daughter's chosen path—she is of age and already living with her fiancé. However, one year later, the widely watched film *Yasemin* (dir. Hark Bohm, 1988), depicting the paternal power a recently immigrated Turkish patriarch wields over his daughter, stirred up the protective impulses of German viewers. Waters are further

---

[15]Mut gegen rechte Gewalt, *Stern* and Amadeu Antonio Stiftung, http://www.mut-gegen-rechte -gewalt.de/news/meldungen/nichts-erinnert-dieses-verbrechen (accessed July 6, 2012).

muddied as the revised script insists on both of the fathers' acts of vigilante justice, one to keep his daughter from marrying a Turk, the other to take revenge on his son's killers. In a plotline that seeks to recapture postwar efforts to reeducate and denazify, detective Stoever begins mentoring one of the young Skins rather than interrogating him.

The punk music of *Die Toten Hosen* represents the in-your-face antiauthoritarian and antibourgeois politics and sentiments on the left, while the Skinheads ring-leaders' *Führer*-style charisma tips the scale to the extreme right. In the tug of war between too much and too little authority, the democratic structure of the West German state itself is at stake. When should the state intervene or not, when does state power overstep? How can society recover and heal from the domestic terrorism ten years prior (the 1977 RAF violence)? And in its aftermath, what role and powers should the police have without infringing on the civil rights expressed in the constitution? What happens, when former role models disappoint and dangerous new ones appear, when young or old take matters into their own hands, when interracial family building meets Nazi-inspired racial purification?

Critical and Viewer Engagement

Manfred Krug's Stoever became the most popular detective of the *Tatort* franchise after Götz George's reign as Duisburg's Horst Schimanski was over. Krug performed a unification of the previously largely divided audience by heavily drawing viewers from the new Eastern states—reaching market shares between 16 and 35 percent.[16] His claim to fame as GDR's most personable, charming, and talented actor harks back to his roles in DEFA films of the 1960s, and his star-turn in the censored and shelved *Spur der Steine* (Frank Beyer, 1966). After his official East German *Arbeitsverbot* (working ban) and his subsequent 1977 departure to the West, his continued presence on West German screens and stages as well as his social-democratic engagement galvanized an already substantial West and East German fanbase for his arrival on *Tatort*. His previous acting stints included a trucker in *Auf Achse* (*On the Road*, ARD, 1977–86) and the beloved lawyer Liebling in *Liebling Kreuzberg* (*Darling Kreuzberg*, ARD, 1985–98). He would play unemployed East-Berliner Benno Grimm in the *Wende*-themed ARD series *Wir sind auch nur ein Volk* (We are also only a people, ARD, 1994–5, based on a text by Jurek Becker).

"Voll auf Hass" received enough pre- and post-airtime publicity and attention to place it among the most famous episodes of the *Tatort* franchise. As a result of Krug's popularity and the press releases covering the shoot,

---

[16] Holger Wacker and Almuth Oetjen, *Swinging Cops* (Berlin: Henschel, 1999), 86–7.

more than fifteen million viewers watched "Voll auf Hass" on November 8, 1987 (*Neue Presse*, November 10, 1987). It takes on German legacies of racism and the neo-Nazi movement that predates the fall of the wall and the racial riots of the early 1990s. But it also stands out for Schadewald's uncompromising "realist" aesthetic that did not shy away from employing actual Skinheads for the filming of the restaurant's destruction during the wedding sequence, a decision that raised ethical questions for *Tatort* production protocols.

As a rerun in 1993, the episode resulted in viewer telephone protests, public outcries, resulting in a rare cancellation and replacement by another episode after thirty minutes of airtime, right in the middle of its most violent scenes. Regional ARD-affiliated directors decided to stop the broadcast in progress "in order not to intervene in the present situation after the murder of Solingen" (*Süddeutsche Zeitung* June 4, 1993) and not to pour "oil on fire" (SDR press speaker Diethard Härtsch, *Kölnische Rundschau*, June 3, 1993). Neo-Nazis had fire-bombed the home of a Turkish family in the German city of Solingen in May of 1993. Three girls and two women died; fourteen others were injured.[17]

A *Funk-Korrespondenz* critic bemoans that "an unintentional, profiled, original, at least a worthy contribution to the current discussion" was sacrificed not to polarize the population further, but instead ended up revealing the insecurity and "small-mindedness" of SWF and SR directors (*FK* 22, June 4, 1993). It is rather ironic that none of the articles reporting the interrupted rerun from 1993 remember that this very episode became the first ever *Tatort* episode to win the *Fernsehpreis für die Verständigung mit Ausländern* (Television prize for interethnic communication) on December 9, 1988.

Already during its production in 1987, the German weekly *Stern* published a five-page spread with photos from the shoot (June 10, 1987). The full spread glossy photographs of the *Stern* thus connect this episode to the Barschel scandal in more than a formal manner. In the span of only four months, the fictional and the real got equal coverage in the same glossy magazine. In a similarly sensationalist manner, when compared to Knauer's photo spread of the Barschel affair, Schadewald's decision to exploit existing political and racist tensions for a heightened reality mode is questionable. Whether for political power or a powerful aesthetic, both *Stern* spreads reveal the violence done to the body politic.

Advertising the fact that director Bernd Schadewald paid "114 DM per day of the public station's honorarium for Extras" to "real Skin[head]s,"

---

[17]Stephen Kinzner, "Thousands of Germans Rally for the Slain Turks," *New York Times*, June 4, 1993, https://www.nytimes.com/1993/06/04/world/thousands-of-germans-rally-for-the-slain-turks.html (accessed March 2019).

the article shows these "real Skins" with smiling faces as they sit on the set chugging beer and smoking. The essay highlights the fact that instead of the agreed upon broken chairs, the Skins actually caused DM 25,000 in damage to the set. Quoting the episode's dramaturge Matthias Esche: "In front of the camera, the Skins developed a forcefulness that a regular extra on the set never exhibits. When one makes a film with passion, one has to risk something." Schadewald adds, that "Skins were necessary for a certain authenticity" and insists that the ones he hired were "directable, usable." Upon closer inspection of this authenticity-claim, the *Tatort* team supposedly only found a few willing Lübeck and Lüneburg-based Skins at a soccer game. In a further twist, the production team dressed a few Punks as Skins to round out the latter's numbers, while some of the police extras were actual off-duty police officers. The article does mention the evident enmity between the Punks and Skins—two subcultural groups with very different social and political agendas—yet there is no analysis of the implications of the Punks' performance of "the Other" outside of a potential off-screen brawl. This hodgepodge of authentic and performative identities further embolden viewers to ignore the political differences between subgroups and instead label all of them antisocial rather than racist or nonconformist.

NDR producer Dieter Meichsner, fearing the political fallout but foregrounding aesthetic choices, demanded twenty minutes of cuts from the hundred-minute raw cut. According to the director, the delineation of the father's motives suffered as a result. Instead of witnessing the planned peer-pressure that would lead the German father to orchestrate the attack on his future son-in-law, this narrative development was curtailed by the cuts (*Westfälische Rundschau*, November 6, 1987). Schadewald threatened a lawsuit, insisting that the cuts infringed on his creative license, that he was told to "write a different kind of *Tatort*" and was now penalized for doing so (*Westfälische Rundschau* June 13, 1987). Whereas Meichsner argued he needed to save the character from becoming a "Kasperlefigur" (a mickey mouse figure), that character's renowned and here underused actor, Ulrich Pleitgen, countered: "The producers apparently did not want to show that a nice German patriarch can suddenly become a racist" (*Morgenpost*, June 24, 1987).

As the day of the premiere nears, headlines of lead-up articles become more sensationalist, emphasizing "Fear and Terror during the Shoot" (*Fernsehwoche* 45, October 30, 1987), "How real Skinheads devastate an entire TV-Studio" (*TV Hören und Sehen*, 45, October 30, 1987), but they also finally draw connections between political events surrounding the production of the episode: "In Hamburg alone, Skins murdered two young Turks in the span of five months in 1986 [sic!]" (*TV Hören und Sehen*, 45, October 30, 1987). *Neue Presse* reminds readers that "Voll auf Hass" ought to "remind viewers of recent events in Hannover" (November 10, 1987).

After the premiere of the episode, the majority of critics blame the censorship-style cuts for the disjointed narrative but give positive marks to Krug's performance and the didactic qualities of the episode: "An unusually well-targeted detective lesson in social studies of the Eighties" (*Abendzeitung*, November 10, 1987), "Didactic Piece with Thriller Plot" (*Kölnische Rundschau*, November 10, 1987), "Reverberating Flag of Enlightenment" (*FAZ*, November 10, 1987), underscoring the internal contradictions within the *Tatort* series. Several articles lead with "Hatred of Foreigners" (*Niedersächsisches Tagesblatt* and *Tagesspiegel*, November 10, 1987), "Perpetrators were 'ordinary, upstanding Germans'" (*Nordwest Zeitung* and *Wilhelmshavener Zeitung*, November 10, 1987). The *Rheinische Merkur* speculates about living room debates over Stoever's question: "How would you react, if your child wanted to marry a foreigner?" and manages to put a conservative spin on this, when it ambiguously declares "if the not cliché-free episode contributed to a prevention of the shown problematic, then director Bernd Schadewald deserves recognition" (November 13, 1987). The question remains, which problematic the writer refers to the hatred of foreigners or the marriage between Germans and foreigners. *Bayernkurier* goes even further into denial by arguing that the represented attack "is definitely not the pattern, nor the actual example, especially not in this radicalism and brutality" (November 14, 1987).

Some viewer write-ins are critical of the hot-button topic, whereas others are praising it precisely for its "burning contemporariness" (*TV Hören und Sehen*, 50, December 4, 1987). A common rhetoric is of interest: Sabine Bettin from Berlin complains that this episode "was an insult and for me rationally not explainable" (*Berliner Morgenpost*, November 14/15, 1987). The word "insult" appears in several of the write-ins. Most viewers never explicate what they felt insulted by: the German father's collaboration with neo-Nazis? The interracial couple kissing? Krug's references to the German past? All or none of the above?

Breaking Bread and Breaking Glass

In this *Tatort*, glass breaks by accident, under pressure, and by design: the first glass breaks in the restaurant in the very first sequence, the next one during owner Mehmet's confrontation with the local mobster, one of whom threatens: "Glass shards are not for good luck, at least not here in Germany" ("Glasscherben bringen kein Glück, jedenfalls nicht bei uns in Deutschland"). The thug's racist comment is laced with anti-Semitic references to *The Night of Broken Glass*, forging a direct link between the Turkish minority in 1987 and Germany's Jewish community in 1938. The residual memory of the *Tagesschau* commemoration of the forty-ninth anniversary of *Kristallnacht* should coax viewers into a discursive conflation of anti-Islamic and anti-Jewish racism. On the one hand, the connection admonishes viewers to remember and not to repeat fascist Germany's racist crimes with a different minority in a different sociopolitical and economic context. On the other hand, it is doubtful that this moral appeal outlasts the ambiguous drift of the episode's political trajectory.

As Mehmet bleeds from the cut, a melodramatic score accompanies the symbolism of the scene. The father sheds sacrificial blood on his son's wedding day. On this proud day for the future of Mehmet's line, the cut also symbolizes the bleeding of his lineage, since Erdal's death is imminent. I would also argue that the very fact that the patriarch sheds blood before (and here also instead of) the bride feminizes his gender performance. The scene encourages viewers to question the father's support of the couple's premarital cohabitation and the marriage itself as a transgression in gender, cultural, and racial terms. Instead of setting Mehmet up as a role model for German-Turkish/European integration, the first scene questions his ability to be an authority figure and ensure his family's future. Or, put differently, becoming a figurehead for integration automatically disqualifies him from being one on his home front. Whether one is a Turkish, German, or American, a conservative or liberal viewer, this scene brings the role of the father in intimate relation to the effects of modernization, places him at the intersection between gender and race. And as we saw from the viewers' comments earlier, the public compass needle oscillates between sympathy for and against modernization quite rapidly in this case.

Instead of the traditional German *Polterabend* (Mischievous Evening) when guests bring and smash dishes against the stoop of the couple's residence for good luck prior to the wedding ceremony, glass and porcelain are smashed during the attack on the wedding party at the father's Turkish restaurant. Echoes of the Jewish custom of breaking a glass during the wedding ceremony directly intersect with attacks on Jewish businesses on November 9, 1938. Culturally specific elements connoting the beginning of a new family unit are infused with national and racial trauma.

Semiotically, these scenes construct the specificity of the familial, regional event in terms of the national and international debate on the German past. Just when representatives of the two cultures and races were supposed to break bread and join together as a family, neo-Nazis attack. Both the increasing multigenerational integration of immigrant communities in different regions of Germany and the regional success with diversity and inclusion initiatives are erased to show that West Germany has failed to become a modern immigrant nation.

Conflicting with this self-critical appraisal, the heavy symbolism of Mehmet's bleeding directs viewers to accept a discourse that still links belonging and citizenship to bloodline, to the *jus sanguinis*, playing into the white fright pathos of father Lobeck. It doesn't help matters that to German viewers the son's name, Erdal, is less reminiscent of "young person" (in Turkish), but instead of the shoe paste brand ERDAL. If viewers make that association, consciously or subconsciously, their minds don't have very far to go to minstrelsy and 1950s style German racist chocolate or coffee posters of caricatured Turks or 1950s era "brown babies" as guarantors of a "true brown."[18] In a media-specific polysemic manner, the discursive layers fight with one another, pulling the cohesiveness of the text and the stereotypical social-critical message of *Tatort* apart at the seams.

A similar set of contradictions occurs in the choice of local and regional public and private spaces: posh office tower versus rental apartment, restaurant, pub versus kiosk, *Fabrik* (former factory) versus *Fischmarkt*, and again and again, public bathroom scenes. True to the Stoever/Brockmöller era, we get a high-angle view over the *Binnenalster* (Hamburg's interior lake) in the posh German father's office. Several associations compete for attention in this scene: the interiority of the Alster becomes a navel-gazing mirror, in which the usually globally oriented Hanseatic elite (the residents of a city in the Hanseatic league) myopically reflects on its mis/fortunes, but the posh office view also comments on the continuity debate in elite professions after 1945. Paired with the ringing telephone that Lobeck leaves unanswered, this scene symbolizes a refusal to enter into dialogue. As if on cue, Lobeck utters racist slurs and begins to sob.

The scene changes to a close-up of the apartment door sign of bride and groom. If the elevated view in the office signaled a nostalgic postcardicization of Hamburg that eerily accompanies "soon we will be strangers in our own land" ("bald sind wir Fremde im eigenen Land"), the elevated view from the ladder in the apartment the two are renovating evokes the romantic mood of *Singin' in the Rain*. The interspersed scenes of a corrupt yet orderly establishment and the chaos of a beginning renovation make the global intersect with the regional and national. While the well-to-do German father is shown delegating his revengeful racist mission, the young couple takes charge of their own destiny in an approach that Americanizes not just the scene itself but also the European discourse around cross-cultural understanding itself. Their respective intercut mise-en-scènes construct a contrastive tableau of fascist and immediate postwar era. While Lobeck is displayed as a *Schreibtischtäter* (desk perpetrator),[19] the painting newlyweds stand for the rubble-clearing restorative forces.

---

[18] In the German film *Toxi* (dir. Robert Stemmle, 1952), the young white couple using Toxi, the so called "brown baby" (idiom to describe children born as a result of relationships between white German mothers and Black GI fathers), as a photo model for a chocolate brand are portrayed as well-intentioned white saviors.

[19] This term is attributed to Hannah Arendt and refers to Nazi perpetrators like Adolf Eichmann, who orchestrated a bureaucracy of death and murder, including the final solution, without personally killing anyone.

Father-Figure Failures (State, Family, Media, Police)

After the attack on the wedding party and Erdal's murder, the two investigators Stoever and Brockmöller arrive on scene. After interviewing some of the survivors, they meet up in the restaurant's bathroom. Their banter reveals that Skins have been involved in three acts of violence against Turks in the last six months. As Stoever and Brockmöller shake their heads bewildered by race-motivated acts of aggression, they joke that "dafür versteh'n wir beide ja Türkisch" (that's why we understand Turkish). They don't, of course, but here "understanding Turkish" signifies more than the language. It is a shorthand for indicating a humanist appreciation for diversity and a defense of equal civil rights in a multiethnic society. As they wash their hands, Stoever grumbles: "Every single case is reason enough—we already had this—a clean Germany—I assign a political motif to those that want to make me believe that Skinheads are just ruffians and nothing else."[20] This is an important analysis of the German tendency to concentrate on the generational aspect of right-wing violence while ignoring its systemic cause. And with his statement, Stoever indicates a willingness to engage with racism on a systemic level. Brockmöller resignedly calms him down: "We are trying to catch the perpetrator—but that in and of itself won't change anything."[21]

The intentional setting of a public bathroom for two key dialogues about Germany's past and systemic racism calls forth at least two German idioms: *Eine Hand wäscht die andere* (one hand washes the other) and *Sich die Hände in Unschuld waschen* (to wash one's hands of the matter and claim innocence). Similar to the tongue-in-cheek antiauthority punk lyrics and image of the *Toten Hosen* that later perform live in Altona's Fabrik in this episode (they also worked on Schadewald's theater adaptation of Kubrick's *Clockwork Orange*), the act of washing hands here goes both ways. As the gatekeepers of German democracy wash their hands of the right-wing terror, the act of cleansing also points to the "clean Germany" that Stoever sarcastically quips about, and reveals them to be participants, even if well-intentioned ones, of the racially coded privilege that the Skins are trying to reclaim.

After his critical social commentary—a *Tatort* format staple—Stoever identifies one of the apprehended Skins due to the "Spikzettel auf den Pfoten" (cheat sheet on the knuckle, spelling HASS—HATE). With the use of this regional idiom, the aggressor is re-branded as a delinquent

---

[20]Stoever: "Jeder einzelne Fall ist Grund genug—das hatten wir doch schon mal—sauberes Deutschand—ich unterstelle denjenigen ein politisches Motiv, die mir weismachen wollen, Skinheads wären einfach nur Raufbolde und sonst gar nix."
[21]Brockmöller: "Wir versuchen den Täter zu fassen—ändern wird sich dazu nichts."

schoolboy. Contrary to his statement in the bathroom, Stoever (and with him the viewer) can engage the Skin as a misguided young man, instead of as a neo-Nazi and a criminal. He invites the Skin to a beer in a pub at Hamburg's fish market. Stoever educates himself on the youth's attraction to the DAF (Deutsche Arbeiterfront/German Workers' Front, a radical right party, in 2022 this would be the AFD, Alternative für Deutschland). Key but somewhat stereotypical takeaways (backed by psychological and sociological research at the time) point to a chaotic home life, the lack of parental supervision and attention. The Skin tells Stoever that he doesn't know much, that the murder itself "was not planned."

Stoever models how a little attention would go a long way to preserving civil rights. However, one has to wonder why one Otherness is privileged for reintegration efforts over another and why. Is the Skin a better target for reintegration into civil society due to his Germanness? Or a more necessary target due to Germany's past? Stoever's self-righteous general declamation in the first bathroom scene, motivated by a democratic concern on the national level, gives way to the second bathroom scene, in which Stoever's personal interaction with the young Skin has transformed his self-righteousness into a much more general humanistic concern: "When you actually deal with them, then I just feel sorry for the whole lot of them." ("Wenn du dich richtig mit ihnen beschäftigst, dann tut mir die ganze Bande nur leid.") Signifying a shift from condemnation to engagement, this is the classic self-reflexive social critique of the status quo and the "conciliatory move" that Michelle Mattson ascribes to the *Tatort* format in general.[22]

While this is certainly valid here, the politics of the father/son dynamic are especially intriguing, when we consider results from the segmentation analysis: Uwe Barschel's death has become a Jean-Paul Marat-type crime scene, symbolic for the state of German democracy spiraling out of control. A conservative state leader of the postwar generation, the hope of a democratic Germany, drowned or was murdered in a hotel bathtub with drugs in his system, embroiled not only in a regional abuse of power scandal, spying on his SPD opponent Engholm, but also potentially in an international tryst with arms dealers and the East German state police. But *Waterkant Gate* is also about Barschel hiring minions to do his dirty work, just as the bride's father, Lobeck, does in *Tatort*. As a corrupt politician, Barschel is both the wayward son of the republic, who abuses his power to maintain control, and the regional father figure, who gets in bed with the enemy because he fears the loss of his authority—on the personal, local, regional, and national level. When we further think about the name—Lobeck—it appears to be an audial concoction of Lübeck (second largest town in Schleswig-Holstein)

---

[22]Michelle Mattson, "*Tatort*: The Generation of Public Identity in a German Crime Series," *New German Critique* 78 (Fall 1999): 178.

and Lorbeer (laurel leaf/berry). It is thus almost tailor-made to conjure Barschel's death. *Tatort* here intervenes in lieu of the less than democratic and more fiction than real historical world and sends the Barschel-like figure to prison.

However, the script insists on a balanced scale: Mehmet Bicici, Erdal's father, at first speaking German, even within the immediate family, and vehemently defying the protection syndicate is turning into a vigilante after his son's death. He speaks more Turkish, loads his pistol, and goes hunting for the culprits, in short, he is radicalized by his trauma and is shedding his integrationist positionality. In connecting race, language, and violence, however, the whole endeavor delivers the image of a cultural devolution. The scene with Mehmet's bleeding hand can now be added to the enigmas, in that his vigilantism brings him closer to the violent behavior of the mob and the Skins and retroactively forecasts him as having "blood on his hands." The cultural devolution process turns him from a victim into a perpetrator and exploits enduring Islamophobia. Yet, in the polysemic tradition of television, viewers trained on decades of US and European Spaghetti Westerns might also read Mehmet's grief-motivated revenge fantasies sympathetically. His gun-wielding moments might even help him to regain his masculinity in the eye of these viewers.

On the media-reflexive level, we have to think about director Schadewald's own corruption scandal. His "renting" of Skins and Punks to create a heightened reality effect for the shoot takes the format's insistence on "proximity to reality" to extremes. While motivated by his reverence for the gritty urban cinema of Martin Scorsese, Schadewald's offense mimics Lobeck's in the script. Subjecting underrepresented minority actors to their political nemesis in order to milk the resulting confrontational energies is cruel at best, tyrannical at worse. But it also questions the relationship between performance and identity, in this case racial and political identities. The *Stern* feature established that the director groups Skins and Punks (right- and left-wing political subcultures) together. Schadewald's hankering after authenticity sees their "violent public image" but disregards their differing politics and targets. On television, opposite people of color, Skins and Punks are both performing whiteness. When we now consider that Turkish-German actors also play Turkish-German characters in this episode, this double homogenization fuels a racist reductionism that reverberates long after the episode is over. In "Voll auf Hass," race is not a construct.

Tatort presents us with quadruple paternal authority failures that are even if not equal in degree and comment on one another. Reading the pre- and post-production reception together with the intertextual echoes, one could argue that the Erdal and Barschel murders as well as the corruption of parental authority represented by Bicici, Barschel, Lobeck, and Schadewald construct parallel and intersectional scenes that code the nodal point between global, regional, local, familial as the actual crime scene. In *Voll auf Hass*, the discursive shift from national to local and familial is very pronounced in spatial terms, when, at the end, the detectives meet at a local *Alster*-Kiosk—the space indicating a particular local hangout in opposition to the more touristy, regional mass attractions of *Fischmarkt* and *Fabrik*. Here, at this local outdoor food joint, the national perspective on *Ausländerhass* can morph into a "what-if" discussion on a familial, personal level, when Stoever asks: "How would you react, if your child wanted to marry a foreigner?" The realization that in an increasingly globalized culture "Worlds collide" ("Welten prallen aufeinander") leads to the summarizing statements: "I would not send a group of Skinheads to attack my son in law" ("Ich würde meinem Schwiegersohn keine Gruppe Skinheads auf den Hals hetzen") but also to "what a poor sod of a father" ("so'n armes Schwein von Vater"). Yet, like the ghost of the past, structurally brought forth by the geopolitical configuration of the local *Stammtisch* (table reserved for local regulars), the national(ist) discourse reasserts itself with the response: "One shouldn't forget the problems of the Germans" ("Man sollte die Probleme der Deutschen nicht vergessen"). Even if Stoever counters with a flippant "Haven't I heard this before just now?" ("Das habe ich doch eben schon einmal gehört"), the statement leaves Hamburg's cosmopolitan liberal self-image behind to join the broader conservative appeal of "the beleaguered Germany" syndrome. It also transmutes the diverse migrant constituencies and their complex adaptations to the host country into a "German problem."

When Lobeck finally confesses, he lays the blame on peer-pressure. As he is led to the police car, he stylizes himself into another classic German trope, the *Mitläufer* (follower). While Lobeck's apprehension leaves the contemporary civic-minded viewer hopeful at the end of this episode, the tensions between global, national, regional, and local discourses sustain a polysemy that in 2022 could easily tilt toward the right-wing populism of the AFD. Exploiting the precariousness between democratic social critique and populist grievance culture is exactly what *Dogs of Berlin*, an updated version of "Voll auf Hass," projects to a global audience on Netflix, as I argue in more detail in the second part of the book.

"Auf der Sonnenseite" ("On the Sunny Side," dir. Richard Huber; NDR, October 26, 2008)

Tagesschau Synopsis

In October 2008, the ongoing and escalating global recession hits Germany. The automobile industry is in crisis; stimulus packages are being drafted. In September, the *KfW Verwaltungsrat* discovered that a 300 million euro transfer from a German state-owned bank was made to the US bank Lehman Brothers shortly before their bankruptcy. In October, the responsible CEOs are fired, and the government agrees on a 480 million euro stimulus package for banks. The international news segment covers the ongoing Caucasus Conflict that began August 8 between Sakartvelo/Georgia and Russia. In Lithuania's election, the Conservatives decisively beat the reigning Social Democrats. An analysis of the latest polls for the upcoming US election between John McCain (Republican) and Barack Obama (Democrat) on November 4 follows. In national news, the FDP (Economic Liberal Party) affirms that they will be forming a coalition with the moderate right CDU (Christian Conservatives) in Bavaria. This is noteworthy because the right-wing CSU (Christian Social Union) had reigned supreme in that state since the beginning of the FRG. Regional news that gets lifted up to the national level: the opening ceremony for one of the biggest German mosques in Duisburg. And, *Tatort* makes the national news with Mehmet Kurtulus, who becomes NDR's first Turkish-German *Tatort* detective in the following Hamburg episode "Auf der Sonnenseite": a new type of detective and a new concept for the then almost forty-year-old show. As the following synopsis shows, along with minority representation, narrative complexity has arrived in the *Tatort* format.

Tatort Synopsis

Cenk Batu (Mehmet Kurtulus) works undercover at a high-flying German real estate business led by Petermann (Michael Wittenborn) seeking evidence of illicit personal and company activities. When he is finally invited to join the inner circle, the test is staged as a mafia-style execution on the banks of the Elbe, Batu is unable to pull the trigger. The pistol is not loaded, and Batu fails the loyalty test ending the police's long-term investment in the operation. His subsequent debriefing introduces us to his handler Uwe (Peter Jordan), who also feeds Batu's fish, his only companions, during his longer job-related absences. In the laundry room of the complex, we get to meet Anja (Patrycia Ziolkowska), a potential love interest, who is currently annoyed at him for missing a dinner invitation and might not wait around for him forever. Soon after, Batu is tasked to befriend Deniz Nezrem (Burat Yigit), a wounded family member of a Turkish business empire, in the hospital. He does this with aplomb, even saving the young man's life from an assassination attempt. The grateful uncle, Tuncay Nezrem (Aykut Kayacik), offers Batu, whose profile has him play a recent parolee, a job in a tiny Altona Döner booth. A subplot there has Batu interact with the older manager (Demir Gökgöl), who lost his own restaurant and his wife to suicide as a result of falling for a real estate scam called *Sonnenseite* (Sunny Side).

Sonnenseite, a finance scam run through Petermann's office, essentially pitches Turkish vacation and retirement villas to homesick Turkish migrants in Germany. Proving his worth, Batu soon drives Nezrem around, which not only prompts a wardrobe change but also gives him access to the uncle's underground trade practices and meetings. Batu is now juggling three balls: the mystery around Deniz's assassination attempt, the uncle's underground electronic chip trade, and Petermann's real estate scam. All these come to a head, when Uwe finds out that the book Nezrem was holding during one meeting (*Leviathan*) was code for a container ship that a corrupt customs officer was supposed to ignore. Deniz is killed at his girlfriend's apartment and Batu discovers that Deniz and the Döner booth's manager fell victim to the same real estate scam and in Deniz's case also Petermann's virulent racism because the latter happens to be Jenny's (Alice Dwyer) father. Discovering that fact leads Batu to offer his undercover residence in Williamsburg as safe haven to Jenny as he attempts to bring Petermann to justice. Wired for audio transmission, Batu maintains contact with Uwe but goes rogue. He feints wanting to clean out his desk at Petermann's office to gain access and forces his lackey Gregor Winter (Robert Dölle) to delete the old man's debt. When Petermann arrives, Batu manages to get Jenny on the phone to make the father take him to her supposed whereabouts. Instead of meeting his daughter at the specified place in the container terminal, this is the place, where Nezrem was picking up his fake chips. Batu tells Nezrem about Petermann's assassination order on his nephew. The police swoop in and arrest everyone, including Batu to keep his cover. At the end, we see Batu go home only to just miss Anja—once again.

Critical and Viewer Engagement

Spurred on by the *Tagesschau*, the viewer enters this *Tatort* with a specific focus on its new lead detective, Cenk Batu, and his Turkish *Migrationshintergrund* (migration background). The *Tagesschau* coverage further invites viewers to draw a connection between the Duisburg Mosque and the Duisburg *Tatort* of the Horst Schimanski era (1980s). While a historical coincidence, the two highlighted occurrences spawn the realization of a shift in representational power. Mark Terkessidis helps us to contextualize this, when he argues that the first Schimanski "Duisburg: Ruhrort" gave new life to the regional format of *Tatort*, which as he contests was following mostly American crime genre standards through the 1970s.[23] He continues that the ARD begins to classify its *Tatort* episodes as "Heimatfilme" at the same time that "the

---

[23]Mark Terkessidis, "Die Heimatflüsterer," *DU: Tatort: Der Mord zum Sonntag* 779 (August 2007): 26–7. Klaudia von Wick directly relates "Auf der Sonnenseite" to the first Schimanski episode: "There are films that singlehandedly renew an entire genre. In that, 'On the Sunny

self-understood concept of *Heimat* becomes precarious" ("Die Heimat als Selbstverständlichkeit wird prekär") (27). Following the flow between the October 26, 2008, *Tagesschau*, critics and *Tatort* viewers indeed correlated the arrival of Cenk Batu on *Tatort*, the quintessential German crime drama, with the symbolic Islamic marking of *the Tatort* TV region: Duisburg. And Batu does not join any *Tatort* region but the media home of *Tatort* as such— the NDR Hamburg—making this evening's episode symbolic and a cause for a long-overdue celebration by many, a cause for anti-Islam anxieties by others.

The question is, has Batu arrived? 7.07 million viewers (market share of 20.3 percent) "invit[ed] Mehmet Kurtulus into their living rooms."[24] Michael Scholten's phrasing explicitly directs attention to the power of television: in his words, the act of television reception is equated with the gesture of receiving a stranger in one's safe space, on one's property. In delegating that welcoming power to the German viewer, his wording equates the act of actively tuning in to watch a Turkish detective on the national flagship crime drama to Germans welcoming immigrants into their country. Considering the entertainment industry's problematic history with representations of diversity, behind and in front of the camera, this analogy smacks of the plot of *Guess Who's Coming to Dinner?* (U.S.A., dir. Stanley Kramer, 1967). His use of the word "living room" recalls the broadcast era of television, specifically the Vietnam War's televisual "invasion" of ordinary people's living rooms around the world. In 2008, his indirect comparison of the televised Vietnam War and Mehmet Kurtulus's casting as a *Tatort* detective echoes the wartime footage that changed the relationship between viewers, the state, and representation, and the role of television as a medium capable of co-constructing and deconstructing narratives of power and responsibility.

Andrea Kaiser (*epd*, November 1, 2008: 87) goes even further. She deflects the broader sociopolitical symbolism of this television event and decides that the figure of Batu lays ruin to the format of *Tatort* as such. Scorched earth meets tautology: Batu can't arrive on *Tatort*, if *Tatort* is no longer *Tatort*: "Mehmet Kurtulus as undercover agent Cenk Batu is not a *Tatort* detective anymore (. . .) the kernel of the brand [*Markenkern*] is being watered down." This argument is especially odd considering that the entire franchise began with Paul Trimmel (Walter Richter) embarking on a solo undercover operation across the inner-German border in "Taxi nach Leipzig" (NDR, 1970). Later Kaiser adds that the viewer "has every right in the world to expect two 'normal' detectives. And here only gets to see an

---

Side' strongly reminds us of 'Duisburg: Ruhrort' and the young Götz George," *Berliner Zeitung*, October 25, 2008: 33.
[24]Michael Scholten, *Bild am Sonntag*, October 26, 2008: 24.

'abnormal' one" (21). Despite the quotation marks to allow irony to deflect, these contestations are xenophobic to their core: Batu is not and cannot be considered a real detective. His Otherness (in a conflation of narrative format, character, role, and ethnic identity) threatens the very *Tatort* brand. This argument has been brandished by many a television producer asked to cast a member of an underrepresented group in the lead of a flagship show (whether LGBTQ, Black, Latinx, Asian, or Middle-Eastern). But let's be clear—genus and genre are epistemologically related to one another, and Kaiser's argument comes dangerously close to treating the show as a taxonomic guarantor of the genus *Germania*.

Whether Kurtulus or his character Batu or both speak fluent Turkish and carry a German or Turkish passport indeed serves as a hook for many reviewers. Despite the fact that most of them allegedly interviewed the actor, each of them comes to a different answer.[25] Playfully citing the Who's title song for *CSI* (CBS, 2000–2015), Michael Scholten from *Bild am Sonntag* (October 26, 2008: 24) and *Süddeutsche Zeitung* (October 25, 2008: 21) asks, "Who are you, Batu?" This off-the-cuff citation from the popular US crime procedural does more than just reveal the always global *and* local viewer of television crime dramas. It places the new lead investigator of *Tatort* into the position of both unknown victim and perpetrator, whose identities the team of forensic scientists and detectives on *CSI*, and in the case of *Tatort*, German critics and viewers, need to discover. The enigma around Kurtulus's background takes center stage—*Bild* Headline: "First Turk-Detective investigates tomorrow on TV"[26]—and does little to make the actor's own wishes become a reality, namely that "the quality of the performance counts, not the Turkishness [of Cenk Batu]" and that no "*Multikultisauce* will be served."[27] Karen Krüger of the *Frankfurter Allgemeine Zeitung* (FAZ) (October 25, 2008) is in the minority with her assessment that "Cenk Batu is not primarily defined by his Turkish background." Even if critics positively note that certain clichés about Turkish culture and masculinity *cannot* be found in this *Tatort*, they list them just the same. Saturday readers, thus armed with a multitude of listed clichés, watching the episode on Sunday will likely find Batu's representation "lacking." At best, the script and the reviewers confirm that Batu, "the man with the thousand faces,"[28] "has to move between two worlds like a chameleon: on the one side act like a criminal, on the other side make progress

---

[25] Michael Scholten quotes Kurtulus: "Ich habe einen türkischen Pass." The actor is cited as wanting to apply for a German passport. *Bild am Sonntag*, October 26, 2008: 24. Yet Franz Josef Görtz paraphrases the actor as already possessing a German passport: "Natürlich besitze er einen deutschen Pass, sagt er beiläufig, wenn auch nicht ohne Stolz." *Frankfurter Allgemeine Zeitung* (October 26, 2008): 59.
[26] Uli Schüler, *Bild*, October 15, 2008: 5.
[27] Sonja Pohlmann, "Das Chamäleon," *Der Tagesspiegel*, October 26, 2008: 31.
[28] Klaudia von Wick, *Berliner Zeitung*, October 25, 2008: 1.

on his investigations—always in danger that his true identity will be revealed" (*Tagesspiegel*, October 26, 2008: 31).

Franz Josef Görtz of the *FAZ* (October 26, 2008) underscores the pairing of the undercover cop genre with a new *Tatort* aesthetic and is intrigued by Batu's "lithe elegance": "The camera moves, editing and music are up tempo. Not a chamber piece but a report from the street, mistakenly similar to a crude reality." Reinhard Lüke of *Funkkorrespondenz* (Friday, October 31, 2008) spins this argument further by stating that the episode moves "outside of the well-trodden paths of the German TV crime drama." He emphasizes Batu's multiple undercover personalities and that his character profile as "a loner" as well as his unfamiliar contact with the Turkish migrant subculture in Hamburg worked hard to avoid clichés by "appearing like a journey into a world foreign to him" (26). That may be, but what does it signify that, as Karen Krüger of the *FAZ* enthuses, "The camera voyeuristically traces his every step (. . .) At no time do we know more than he does; we pierce the thicket of crime with his eyes." The epistemological gap coupled with the attested voyeurism implies that the point-of-view approach to narration in this *Tatort* Orientalizes the subject, the object, and the format—the detective, the city, and *Tatort*. "Cenk Batu accesses emotional worlds that German detectives have lost somewhere between desk, badge, and coffee machine" (Angela Meyer-Barg, *Hörzu*, October 25, 2008: 10); "And in addition, the Hamburg of this film looks very different and fresh. A whole new *Tatort*" (Klaudia von Wick, *Berliner Zeitung*, October 25, 2008: 33); "Hamburg, a city that likes to call itself 'the door to the world,' and where it's worth to look a little closer in which direction that door opens in reality" (Iris Bents, Interview with producers Heinze and Friedler, *Wir im NDR*, October 1, 2008); "How the actor of Turkish descent, Mehmet Kurtulus, rejuvenates the Ur-German *Tatort*" (Nikolaus von Festenberg, *Der Spiegel*, October 20, 2008: 186). In true Orientalist fashion, the act of rejuvenation is always also an "axe that has been swung at a sanctuary of the Germans, the *Tatort*" (Ibid.), as is the attempt to appropriate, to "eat the Other" (bell hooks), uttered in this case in regional terms: "Unrelenting toughness towards oneself, and a sense of duty that comes before inclination. Is that not also Prussian?" (Ibid.).

Reproducing the Migrant as a Television Trope for the Convergence Era

Sascha Gerhards and Susanne Eichner attribute the international success of the Batu episodes to their transnational *Weltkrimi* appeal:

> *Tatort* episodes from Hamburg present such a global orientation in their style and topics. From 2008 to 2012, chief inspector Cenk Batu

investigated crime cases with international implications. Consequently, his episodes have been sold as a bundle to the United Kingdom's *Channel 4* under the title, *Cenk Batu*. (Episodes 1–6)[29]

While that is surely one reason why the Batu episodes are more readily circulated and appropriated into reception habits of crime drama viewers around the globe, this alone would not explain why the many other episodes in fifty years with a "global orientation in style and topics" did not have the same success. Considering that the story of the first Batu episode essentially updates the 1986 episode "Voll auf Hass" for the new millennium, there have to be other facets besides its "global action appeal."[30]

The sidelined but powerful Hanseatic businessman-father is once again the culprit, not being able to come to terms with the interracial romance between his daughter and the nephew of his Turkish business partner. Instead of Manfred Krug's social democratization experiment on Skinheads paired with Charles Brauer's conservativism, we get Cenk Batu as a cross-cultural undercover agent and his sardonically flippant German handler, Uwe, who doesn't shy away from saying things such as "Ich dachte dass ist so'n türkisches Ding" (I thought that was a Turkish thing) all the while lovingly caring for Cenk's aquarium fish.

Unlike the feminization of the Turkish father in the 1996 episode, Cenk's high-rise suite neighbor, Anja, doesn't seem to doubt Cenk's heterosexuality, even with Uwe walking in and out of his place. Cenk's hetero masculinity seems guaranteed by a combination of Kurtulus's own public image and liaison with television personality Désirée Nosbusch, and the "badass" image of the undercover cop from the long history of crime dramas in film and on television. Yet, the show is not averse to queer-baiting, giving fans plenty of clandestine bathroom and dressing room meetings between Uwe and Cenk, where both of them appear in various stages of undress. In addition, Batu is often shot half-naked in the shower, at the edge of or in the pool. Several of these transitional scenes are so drawn out in duration that their representational aesthetics seem to hark back to R. W. Fassbinder's *Ali—Fear Eats the Soul* (1974), where Emmi (Brigitte Mira) has Ali (El Hedi Ben Salem), her Moroccan-born husband, exhibit his muscles to her German friends as if her living room were a slave market: "Look how strong he is—touch his arm, go ahead." Whereas the 1974 scene draws out the

---

[29]Sascha Gerhards, "*Krimi* Quo Vadis: Literary and Televised Trends in the German Crime Genre," in *Tatort Germany. The Curious Case of German-Language Crime Fiction*, ed. Lynn M. Kutch and Todd Herzog (Rochester and New York: Camden House, 2014), 41–60. And Susanne Eichner, "Crime Scene Germany. Regionalism, Audiences, and the German Public Broadcasting System," in *European Television Crime Drama and Beyond*, ed. Kim Toft Hansen, Steven Peacock and Sue Turnbull (London: Routledge, 2018), 184–5.
[30]Ibid.

systemic connections between sex and race in the colonialist imaginary and critiques the unequal power dynamics of gaze and touch, *Tatort*'s videography re-fetishizes Batu's body as a conduit for the interstitial and distracted televisual look.

John Ellis's argument from 1982, made at the juncture between broadcast and cable eras, has regained some of its validity in our multi-device transmedia age: "[T]he gaze implies a concentration of the spectator's activity into that of looking, the glance implies that no extraordinary effort is being invested in the activity of looking" (137).[31] I would contest that *Tatort*'s self-definition as *Heimatfilm* acknowledges and plays to the viewers that occupy an intermediary position between a concentrated film gaze and Ellis's glance. After all, their large-screen sets, DVRs, and the then new *ARD Mediathek* make it possible for 2008 viewers to pause and rewind the episode, if they find it compelling enough to turn their casual Sunday night glance into a gaze. That spectrum of engagement itself—the mobility between glance and gaze, by text or segment—reproduces the migrant as a media-reflexive trope for convergence-era television. Batu enters the picture as *Tatort* and its network are emerging into a hybrid mediascape, where production, exhibition, and viewer practices are migrating between digital and analog, between devices, between linear and time-shifted reception as well as broadcast and narrowcast environments. Batu's migrations between narrative worlds and environments, between and within sex, class, race, culture, and nationality constructs, represent the convergence of existing and emerging media forms, contents, and practices.[32]

Three specific scenes help concretize my argument. The first one moves us from Batu's thwarting of Deniz's assassination to his next assignment. After an intense interrogation scene, where Batu was threatened with violence by a young cop, a situation he masters with coolness and humor, we see Batu poolside, sitting at the edge with a towel draped over his head. This is too specific a costume choice to be ignored. It captures Batu in a position of exhaustion from fighting the dominant sociopolitical currents and negotiating his multiple identities. The towel over his head visually rebrands him as a Muslim *and* a fighter to the viewer. The image awakens associations to historic and fictional boxing, specifically Muhammed Ali and Rocky, where the former configures Batu in a combination of ethnic and racial Otherness and the latter as a melancholic underdog. In the subsequent head-

---

[31] John Ellis, *Visible Fictions: Cinema, Television, Video* (New York: Routledge, 1982), 137.

[32] As a reminder, *Encyclopedia Britannica* defines convergence as follows: "Media convergence transforms established industries, services, and work practices and enables entirely new forms of content to emerge. It erodes long-established media industry and content 'silos' and increasingly uncouples content from particular devices, which in turn presents major challenges for public policy and regulation. The five major elements of media convergence [are] the technological, the industrial, the social, the textual, and the political."

on long shot, superimposed with the pool image, a barefoot and wet, white towel-clad Batu is seen walking toward the camera in a narrow corridor between dressing rooms in Hamburg's *Schwimmoper* (swim opera), the contender returning from a fight. Water eddies of the superimposed pool scene still surround him and reflect on the walls of this transitory passage. As he walks toward us, he tousles his hair, inviting the viewer to want to do the same. The gleaming white tunnel path draws our eyes to Cenk's upper body. There is literally nothing else to see; everything else lacks pigmentation. The surrounding whiteness of the tiles, ceiling, and dressing room doors accentuate his body's brownness, reproduce it as a consumable visual and haptic spectacle. At the same time, the white tunnel, which encases him completely, makes a point about the straight and narrow path his host-country forces him to navigate. As an undercover agent, who happens to be of Turkish descent, he has to dive into new situations head-on, and the transitional moments between one pool/context and the next do not leave him much time to live into his own personal reality. Batu's wet emergence from the pool down a narrow corridor here metaphorically rebirths him into a new environment and another identity.[33] But on the meta-level, it also constructs that fluid conductivity between segments, genres, narratives, identities, and platforms as *the* televisual spectacle. The emergent medium indeed becomes the new message (Marshall McLuhan).

Diaspora Real(i)ties and Imagined Communities

As demonstrated in this *Tatort*, transitory scenes, often involving water (shower, aquarium, pool) like the previous one, are milked, even fetishized, for their televisual appeal. This practice brings to mind the much discussed— and back then scandalous—network TV moment, when *NYPD Blue*'s (ABC, 1993–2005) first episode featured a naked David Caruso in the shower. But while these types of scenes by themselves might just function as a salacious way of introducing us to a new character, in both cases, 1993 and 2008, they accompany a new aesthetics seeking to adjust the crime drama to a new television landscape. For *NYPD Blue* this meant stylistically differentiating the ABC crime brand and making it compatible with cable and prime subscription channels and their ability to deliver adult-oriented content. *NYPD Blue* thus became known for pushing the envelope on nudity restrictions on the networks along with its dizzying handheld camera style. Yet Steven Bochco saw it as the 1990s version of his acclaimed *Hill Street Blues* (NBC, 1981–7), continuing his visionary stamp on crime dramas, first establishing cross-episode story arcs in the 1980s and then shaking up, quite

---

[33] I thank Ute Bettray for her astute comment about the pool's symbolic function here.

literally, the staid cinematography and editing of police procedurals with *NYPD Blue.*

By 2008, in its thirty-eighth year, *Tatort* is openly in need of a similar genre and brand reformation—of new realty, so to speak—while remaining committed to overall format continuity. Consequently, Christoph Silber and Thorsten Wettcke, the writers, along with Richard Huber's direction and Martin Langer's cinematography, deliberately pair shower with pool, aquarium, and container scenes at Hamburg's industrial harbor.[34] Setting the tone for the episode, viewers enter Batu's apartment through the aquarium. In a close-up shot with a rack focus, we see his tropical fish swim about as we hear Batu from the off: "Hi boys, I'm back." Then we see Batu behind the aquarium, first obstructed, then clearer, but still through the water in the tank. Establishing a pattern that codifies meaning, the use of a rack focus is repeated when Batu takes a shower in his alter-ego's apartment which is situated in the working class and dominantly Turkish corner of Hamburg-Wilhelmsburg.

Like the fish, whose soundscape radically shifts from Chris de Burg's "Lady in Red" on Uwe's watch to Heavy Metal, when Batu is back, Batu is dumped into one container setting, one narrative segment, one legend after another. The show immerses him in liquid environments as much as possible. The formal adherence to utilize water scenes as transitions between contained narrative segments continues until the final resolution at the container terminal, in a location that squeezes everyone between a row of containers and the river. Visually and semiotically, the carefully crafted cinematography marks him as a representative of the region—thriving along/on the water (Waterkant). The ending viscerally stages that *Waterkant* as both crime scene and place of resolution. Yet, I would contend that it also hints at the narrowly defined boundaries of Batu's *Handlungsraum* (action space).

This aspect becomes clearer, when Batu moves from his own sparsely furnished, modern urban Mundsburg apartment to the Wilhelmsburg setting of his undercover alter-ego. While the Mundsburg architecture interconnects different apartments in a suite-style arrangement with doors converging on a communal lobby, Wilhelmsburg gives us the broadcast version of linearly concatenated apartments and rooms along a hallway. Linearity is also emphasized by the external location. The apartment complex is directly situated on the side of the S-Bahn tracks south of center city. In addition, it is styled in 1980s décor harking back to the heyday of

---

[34]This episode was nominated for the *Goldene Kamera*, won the prestigious *Adolf-Grimme-Prize*, and cinematographer Martin Langer received the *Deutsche Fernsehpreis* in 2009. *Deutscher Fernsehpreis*, https://www.deutscher-fernsehpreis.de/verleihung/preistraegerdetails/2009-beste-kamera-martin-langer-fuer-tatort-auf-der-sonnenseite/ (accessed December 3, 2019).

Tatort and the broadcast era. Its décor even features that era's iconic green push-button post office telephone, the dark wood wall paneling, and on the nightstand a *Muezin* alarm clock in the shape of a mosque. That the stereotypical alarm clock is a close relative to the treasure chest bubbler in an aquarium becomes apparent, when bubbles of water droplets run down the glass door of Batu's first shower in the new place. If the show marks Batu as a designated Hamburger through the bountiful use of water imagery and liquid cinematography, the apartment alarm clock as analogous to the aquarium treasure chest bubbler signals that his positioning is controlled by external forces. As Eichner documents, instead of going national, the regional experiment of globalization was shipped abroad and reconfigured in 2013.[35] Batu was replaced by post-1989 German film star Til Schweiger as Nick Tschiller in 2013, who was given a Turkish-German sidekick (Yalcin Gümer, played by Fahri Yardim). Throughout the Tschiller years, the NDR also ran the more traditional German-German pairing of Thorsten Falke (Wotan Wilke Möhring) and Katharina Lorenz (Petra Schmidt-Schaller, until 2016), followed by Julia Grosz (Franziska Weisz).

The mosque clock produces a collision between familiarity and alienation, between stereotypical viewer expectations, historical periods, and complex lived realities. That the 1980s décor additionally makes Batu travel back in time is culturally significant. The set forges a connection between the actor's biography—Kurtulus arrived in Germany when he was a child—and the general history of Turkish-German migration. The scene essentializes Kurtulus and his character, and mines Batu as a representative for this ethnic and cultural group. While upwardly mobile Turkish viewers might reminisce over the long arduous paths their parents and grandparents had to navigate to arrive in and successfully emerge from the Wilhelmsburg high rises, the décor invites viewers to reimagine Batu as a migrant. Considering that cell phones have an important plot function in this episode—Deniz buys a burner for Jenny so her father wouldn't track her, and Batu carefully switches cell phones depending on his intended dialogue partner—the green telephone further gives German viewers permission to feel nostalgic for a post office under state control (against existing decentralized privatization), to remember how the limited choices of models and colors of landline telephones suggested a baseline for a shared national communication that seems lost in the cell phone jungle of 2008.

The mise-en-scène imbues the *Tatort* with the appeal of heritage cinema that Terkessidis mentioned earlier. As we know from Andrew Higson's text on British heritage films, the scrupulous attention to luxurious detail in

---

[35] Susanne Eichner, "Crime Scene Germany: Regionalism, Audiences, and the German Public Broadcasting System," in *European Television Crime Drama and Beyond*, ed. Kim Toft Hansen, Steven Peacock, and Sue Turnbull (London: Routledge, 2018), 184–5.

costumes and sets evoked nostalgia not only for the British past but also for its white homogeneity and status as a colonial power. According to Higson, heritage cinemas like to play progressive representations of gender against regressive representations of race and ethnicity (e.g., *Passage to India*). Here, too, the millennial Jenny Peterman is positioned as the progressive, the one who defies her father's racism and falls in love with a Turkish immigrant. She is also the one who gets to pick up the green phone in the historic setting to symbolically communicate her disdain for her father's, and by extension, German society's systemic racism. Yet the 1980s phone seems to have reoriented her allegiance from girlfriend to daughter, when all she is able to utter is a weepy "Papa?," as if she were a damsel in distress that has been taken hostage rather than secured by Batu. In *A Lover's Discourse*, Roland Barthes contests that the lover is in the position of the one who waits and that this position is coded feminine:[36] Jenny waits for Deniz in a mobile trailer that is going nowhere. And she waits in the undercover apartment weeping for her father and patriarchally contained safety and "normalcy," even though they are responsible for her tragedy and gendered stasis.

Opposite Jenny's immobility, Batu is mobile to the extreme, never in one place for long. The episode highlights this by pitting Döner booth against high-end restaurant, the large and sleek 2008 black-and-white Mundsburg apartment against the 1980s small brown-green rooms in the Wilhelmsburg high-rise, the tiny stationary mobile home, and the upper deck of a moving ferry. The use of water as a visual metaphor provides a fluid conductivity between Batu's transmogrifications. When Batu goes rogue and sets up Jenny in his undercover apartment, he meets Uwe in a parking garage. Uwe is adamant that "Deniz is not our case." Batu disagrees (while having to wire himself produces yet another shirtless moment): "The little one [Jenny] is safe." Uwe: "You and your damn self-righteousness. I am an arsehole when your legends cross each other and what do you do? You put the daughter of your one legend into the apartment of your other one. That is so stupid, I don't even have the words." Instead of following Uwe's plans and staying within the confines of his designated assignment, Batu decides to mix his "legends," to dump some water from one container into the next. Instead of a fish out of water, Batu enacts his own treatment by the script and the press. As a new fish introduced into multiple existing containers, he immerses himself by merging one with the other, going against the purity mandate, his handler, the *Tatort* format, and the press demand of his persona and the actor himself. Batu goes after Petermann *and* Nezrem not for the fake chip deal or for avenging Deniz, really, but for exploiting the diasporic community's dream of returning to their homeland. He seeks justice for diasporic residents, and this justice demands an acceptance of hybridity on

---

[36]Roland Barthes, *A Lover's Discourse: Fragments* (1977) (New York: Hill and Wang, 2010).

the procedural, the professional, as well as the cultural level. As the watery transitory scenes make clear, his precarious positionality between cultures, times, and places, and his professional oscillation between assignments and performances emphasize his diasporic background and raise it to the structural media-reflexive level. The realty scam from the plot level echoes his perpetual migration on the formal and structural level of the early convergence-era *Tatort*.

On the plot level, Batu's mixing of legends reproduces the *Tatort*-inherent preference for meting out justice for big ticket sociopolitical issues rather than dealing with interpersonal strife, and this proves critics wrong who pontificated on the end of the trusted format. On the structural level, the undercover subgenre fuels the hybridity of the televisual Now in 2008: it fuses formulaic broadcast-era segmentation with the new normal—narrative complexity—and it introduces a generically driven niche structure to the format that is both internal to an episode and expands serially across episodes. Essentially, this means that the undercover concept transfers *Tatort*'s regional segmentation onto each episode's narrative structure: each assignment requires a new character performance from Batu; each assignment changes location and characters; and each episode and each assignment within an episode deliver a different social, political, and economic perspective on Hamburg. However, as Uwe states, Batu refuses to abide by Uwe's clean separation of his caseload. His intersectional position in German society and identity-morphing as an undercover cop on *Tatort* make him of necessity and design skilled at interweaving "legends," at code-switching, at mobile reconnections. Essentially, Batu's embodiment of hybridization and decolonization functions as the *Sonnenseite* realty scam for the *Tatort* concept. It pitches the trope of successful migration as a bait and switch for both, the rite of return and diasporic disintegration. The episode stylizes his migrant background into a televisual trope for the convergent mediascape.

4

Tatort Berlin (SFB/RBB)

Berlin in the Crosshairs of Film and Television

In the Weimar years a center for cultural innovation, heavily destroyed as the power center of the Third Reich, divided by Allied occupation, its access routes blocked during the 1948–9 airlift, its Western sectors walled off from 1961 to 1989, renamed as the capital of a united Germany in 1991, the metropolis Berlin and its legacy of modernity figure prominently in national and global memories of the twentieth century. Many of these Berlin-based memories have taken on and have been circulated in visual forms, from the Weimar-era cinema of Fritz Lang, G. W. Pabst, Josef von Sternberg, and F. W. Murnau to the New German Cinema of Wim Wenders, followed by post-wall directors Tom Tykwer, Wolfgang Becker, Florian Henckel von Donnersmarck, as well as their younger peers of the Berlin School (Marco Abel). With the expansion and modernization of Studio Babelsberg after 1989, not only German and US television series (Showtime's *Homeland*, Season 5) but also Hollywood productions (e.g., *Unknown*, dir. Jaume Collet-Serra, 2011) have embraced Berlin as a media center.

The medium of television became inseparably connected to German events when President John F. Kennedy, standing next to the mayor of Berlin, soon-to-be chancellor, Willy Brandt, gave the often abused but nevertheless famous "Ich bin ein Berliner" speech, cementing West German-American friendship. Ronald Reagan's "Tear down this wall, Mr. Gorbachev!" in 1987 received a mixed reaction in both Germanies. The West German state had just gone through several years of democratic upheaval expressed by mass demonstrations against Reagan's so-called Star Wars politics, his missile shield development, and the deployment of Pershing II mid-range rockets in West Germany starting in 1983 (rockets that would land on East German soil). When the wall finally did fall on November 9, 1989, Günter Schabowski's live broadcast blunder on the nightly news, resulting from the *Politbüro*'s frantic crafting of new travel regulations in response to the mass exodus of its citizens from Hungary through Austria, was cited as the most common reason why East Berliners decided to risk a border crossing that evening—"We heard it on the news, couldn't believe it and decided to try it out for ourselves."[1] The botched live television announcement, made in the chaos of the moment, led to the now-famous scenes of East Germans on foot and in *Trabis* passing through official checkpoints. Many of the overwhelmed East German border guards cited the element of surprise as responsible for their largely cooperative reactions that evening. This surprise came in the form of the sheer number of people claiming their rights to cross the border, rights that Schabowski mistakenly announced "effective immediately" on television and which the *Politbüro* could not take back without exerting force.[2]

In hindsight, it is doubtful that events would have unfurled as quickly and peacefully without the intervention of the specificity of the medium: live television. Schabowski's broadcast announcement gained the power of performative speech. The scenes at the border crossings, where West Germans greeted East Germans, among them relatives and friends, with champagne and flowers, people standing and sitting on the wall, were broadcast live on national and international television. The power of these celebratory images along the Berlin Wall should not be underestimated in the pursuant international community's generally favorable reaction to the two Germanys' unification, which, in the international imagination, since that night on television, took the concrete visual shape of the unification of Berlin, of an urban and a once divided national community in celebration.

Within the *Tatort* franchise, one would assume that for all the reasons earlier, Berlin should take a dominant position with regard to funding and development, yet that has not always been the case. Bemoaning a "meager financial budget" of DM 1.5 million per episode, a "Trash-Optik" (trash production values) resulting from its topographical and stylistic emphasis on urban grit was further heightened by the studio's decision to shoot on

---

[1] See Beate Schubert's 1990 documentary *Ein Volk sprengt seine Mauern* (*A People Destroys Its Walls*), produced and broadcast by the NDR and SFB. The Internet Movie Database refers to it as *Ode to Joy and Freedom: The Fall of the Berlin Wall*.
[2] On Sundance and Hulu, *Deutschland '89* (2021) is harnessing the power of live broadcasts by reimagining these scenes with its lead triple agent protagonist as courier of the infamous handwritten addendum. Doing so, the show not only adds a conspiracy twist to the suspenseful developments of that day but also parallels the power of an individual with the power of network television to new audiences accustomed to making and receiving their news on social media.

videotape in the 1990s.³ With its revolving door detectives, none of whom stayed longer than a few episodes, the SFB felt treated like a stepchild rather than the main attraction of the flagship ARD program.⁴ But according to *Berliner Morgenpost*, the *SFB-Rundfunkrat* (advisory board) was itself to blame for much of this bad reputation through the 1970s and 1980s, turning "almost every *Tatort* into a political affair" by interpreting every episode as an attack on Berlin's image and fearing negative socioeconomic as well as political consequences for the city: "Message: Berlin is not worth a trip."⁵ This changed in 1999, when Uta-Maria Heim of *Tagesspiegel* points directly to the regional marketing responsible for Ritter and Hellmann's inaugural and later Ritter and Stark's successful thirty-episode run at the merged SFB/RBB:

> A thriller in Berlin, between remainders of the wall, graffiti, and the TV tower. The red and yellow S-Bahn drives into the station. Sightseeing, romantic, layered with a relaxed musical score. East and West united, blue sky with little clouds, this is how the capital likes to see itself (. . .) like a film trailer courtesy of the tourism industry. (. . .) A new *Tatort*-Duo steps up to the plate, and the city recognizes itself (. . .) With a market share of 20,8%, the duo Ritter-Hellmann played itself into the number one position. (. . .) This is what the Berliners wanted. That's why the "Tatort" produces a communal affect in the Berlin viewers, like a soccer team, even if the plot is fiction.⁶

Stressing the overwhelming and unusually positive response from viewers' letters and emails to the network after the first episode with the new team and revived aesthetics, Heim adds one important ingredient to the current recipe for ratings success: "The Future is here. Ritter and Hellmann are without history. No political/historical baggage, no commitments. Instead, designer jackets. Food cart. Work on a construction site. And a beer for breakfast.

---

³1971/2: Kommissar Kasulke (Paul Esser) criticized the "ridiculous" scripts; 1975–7: Kommissar Schmidt (Martin Hirte); 1978/9: Kommissar Behnke (Hans Peter Korff from Hamburg) was "not enough of a Berliner"; 1981–5: Kommissar Walther (Volker Brandt) took a page from Götz George's playbook but his casual, womanizing ways were found "to hurt the image of Berlin" according to SFB-Intendant Lothar Loewe; 1985–9: Kommissar Bülow (Heinz Drache) "departed angrily after six *Tatort* sleeping pills"; 1991–5: Kommissar Markowitz (Günther Lamprecht) voted the best Berliner detective, but left due to increasingly restrictive financial cuts; 1996–8: Kommissare Reuter and Zorowski (Winfried Glatzeder, Robinson Reichel) suffered under cheap production values and negative media-reception; 1998–: Kommissare Ritter and Stark (Dominic Raacke, Stefan Jürgens/Boris Aljinovic since 2001). "Report Tatort: Zwei sollen aufräumen," *TV-Spielfilm*, July 9, 1999.
⁴*Westdeutsche Allgemeine Zeitung*, June 28, 1999.
⁵Bernd Philipp, "Berliner 'Tatorte': Die Stadt war immer beleidigt," *Berliner Morgenpost*, July 25, 1999.
⁶Eva-Maria Heim, "Und zum Frühstück schnell ein Bier," *Tagesspiegel*, July 30, 1999.

That's how Berlin likes itself." Since 1999 the network has attempted to mark and market Berlin as a region, give it a regional identity aside from its national one. In the Ritter/Stark *Tatort*, this regional flair is based on food choices, beer brands, the different ambiences of its *Kieze* (neighborhoods), scenic views of the Spree, and its high-line public transportation. While this is not to say that the convergence-era brand of Berlin might not intersect well with history on occasion, it can be said that the turn-of-the-century aesthetics encourages viewers to readopt a flaneur-style tourist view rather than the socially critical gaze of the advisory board bemoaned in the 1970s and 1980s.

Before the following analysis of three Berlin-based episodes, one episode from the broadcast era before unification, one from the privatization era shortly after unification, and one episode from the *Berlin Republic* coinciding with emergent media, each segment will prime readers in the politics of the episode's immediate temporal context along with highlighting any resonances of a divided Germany and the German past. The *Tagesschau* synopses will be followed by a reception review of the episode in contemporary public media before turning to the episode itself.

"Keine Tricks, Herr Bülow" ("No Tricks, Mr. Bülow," dir. Jürgen Roland; RBB/SFB, May 28, 1989)

May 1989 *Tagesschau* Synopsis

The May 1 demonstrations in Berlin escalated into the "greatest acts of violence seen in the city since the end of the war" (*Tagesschau*, May 2). Mayor Walter Momper is quoted as describing the motives as "blind hate against state power and the red-green coalition in the city senate." The ramped-up battle between largely anonymous demonstrators and police units is captured in vivid images that make the *Tatort* bank robbery look tame by comparison.

In what was come to be known as the *Raketenstreit* (rocket fight) during the course of May, Chancellor Helmut Kohl and Foreign Minister Hans-Dietrich Genscher continue diplomatic efforts to make Germany's concerns over stationing and modernization of short-range rockets heard by National Atlantic Treaty Organization (NATO) members, especially the United States, without signaling a lack of support for the treaty.

May 2, Hungary, one of East Germany's preferred vacation destinations within the Eastern Bloc, begins to tear down its Western border fencing. Initially, Hungary meant to replace the border with a more modern technical solution, but the television-oriented publicity stunt around the dismantling also signaled a symbolic opening to the West that was loudly heard and taken literally by East German citizens desperate to leave for the West.[7] In addition, on May 7, supposedly 98.85 percent of citizens of the GDR voted for the "National Front" under the leadership of the SED (Socialist Unity Party of GDR) in local elections despite the economic crisis and popular dissatisfaction. Skepticism over the election was mixed with outrage, strengthening the opposition movement and leading to the demonstrations and events culminating in the fall of the wall on November 9, 1989.

The year 1989 also marked the fortieth year since the foundation of both the German Democratic Republic and the Federal Republic of Germany. In January 1989, Helmut Kohl had reminded everyone that it "was no coincidence" that the NATO was the same age as the to-be commemorated FRG (1949–89).[8] Most of the more subdued West German festivities took place in the latter half of May, while East Germany held its customary military-style parade in grand style just a month prior to the fall of the wall, on October 7, 1989. In May, West German newspapers and television specials sarcastically quipped with headlines like "No reason to celebrate" or "Is there a reason to celebrate?" (ZDF special on May 23, 1989). On the one hand, this sarcasm expressed an incredulity that there should be a national celebration despite the ongoing mistrust in the sustainability of German democracy from left and right of center. On the other hand, it acknowledged the unease produced by the official acknowledgment the *Festakt* would confer on the existence of two separate German states. According to *Bayernkurier* (F. M. L. "Stichproben," June 3, 1989), the ARD *Presseclub* (broadcast at noon on May 28) was mostly critical of the state of the nation: "Gender inequality, neo-fascism, animosity towards foreigners, mass unemployment, fate of the underprivileged. Ergo: Hardly a reason to celebrate!" President Richard von Weizsäcker's speech marking the fortieth-year anniversary of the FRG on May 24, 1989, specifically acknowledged the struggle for gender equality in the context of postwar German history.[9]

---

[7] On August 19, 1989, ironically also the anniversary of the border wall itself, at the Pan-European Picknick in Hungary, over 600 East Germans used that "hole" in the Hungarian fence to cross over.

[8] January 18, 1989, Rede des Vorsitzenden der CDU, Helmut Kohl, zur Eröffnung des CDU-Kongresses "40 Jahre Bundesrepublik Deutschland" in Bonn, https://www.kas.de/c/document_library/get_file?uuid=0cc6e897-d4ea-c910-e540-ae7ccee15cd6&groupId=252038 (accessed July 20, 2020).

[9] "Bald nach dem Krieg wurden die Arbeiten und Verantwortungen, die die Frauen während des Kriegsdienstes und der Gefangenschaft der Männer hatten übernehmen müssen, wieder von den heimkehrenden Männern beansprucht. Dennoch gab es keine Umkehr mehr. Der Wunsch nach einem eigenen Beruf wurde für viele Frauen zur Notwendigkeit, für die meisten zur Selbstverständlichkeit. Der Weg zur Ausbildung glich sich allmählich an. Der Zugang zu bislang männertypischen Arbeiten wuchs—wir sehen es hier auf dem Dirigentenpodium. Frauen sind aber nach wie vor zu oft benachteiligt. Sie bekommen es beim Einstieg, beim Aufstieg und beim Wiedereinstieg zu spüren. Dahinter steht die Spannung zwischen Familie und Beruf. Noch

This acknowledgment from the top lifted questions of gender parity further into the limelight and might have encouraged some viewers to redirect their gaze during the Sunday evening *Tatort*.

Tatort Synopsis

This episode is a three-in-one *Tatort* cutting across geopolitical, social, and economic class boundaries: a bank robbery at a downtown thoroughfare, a serial rapist and murderer in a garden colony, a faked kidnapping and blackmail gone wrong in the wealthy suburb of Dahlem. An unarmed Bülow talks down the aggravated gun-toting bank robbers, who turn on each other instead. Eating at a gourmet restaurant to celebrate, Bülow is pulled into the next crime when the chef's wife, Franziska Gellert (Uta Sax), says she is being surveilled. It turns out that chef Walter Gellert (Dieter Kirchlechner) and Franziska's sister Nicole (Eleonore Weisgerber) are having an affair and plan to kidnap Franziska to launder the money, so that they won't have to share it with the restaurant's many debtors. What gives the plotting away? Assistant investigator Karin Jellinek (Christiane Carstens) hears a ringing on the blackmail tapes, the sound of the bell rung by the egg man making his rounds in the well-to-do neighborhood. But despite his foible for Gellert's restaurant, Bülow is not really interested in this case, because a serial rapist and murderer trapping his victims in a local garden colony has been eluding his grip. After the third murder there and the suspicion that the perpetrator is receiving inside information about police activities, he sends newcomer Karin Jellinek through the colony as a decoy. His grumpy secretary (Monika Stenzel) unwittingly serves up the final clue to the killer's identity, when she announces that she will marry Otto Patschke (Andreas Mannkopf) from the garden colony, who happened to serve as an all-too-willing witness to several of the crimes.

Critical and Viewer Engagement

This Berliner *Tatort* is the second to last episode for the "schnieke Hauptkommissar Bülow" (well-dressed detective Bülow) before his retirement from the series. In August of 1989, Heinz Drache's Bülow, "the oyster-slurper in the pinstripe," would be replaced by Günther Lamprecht's Markowitz, "who is more at home with the little men, where he also comes

---

immer müssen sich Familien dem Arbeitsmarkt anpassen statt umgekehrt. Darunter leiden alle. Die Frauen aber tragen den Löwenanteil der Lasten, die sich daraus ergeben," https://www.bundespraesident.de/SharedDocs/Reden/DE/Richard-von-Weizsaecker/Reden/1989/05/19890524_Rede.html (accessed July 20, 2020).

from" (WAZ, May 27, 1989). Bülow's penchant for fashion becomes a favorite tag line for critics: "Heinz Drache is not the only one in the station, but promptly everything gets stuck on his freshly pressed shirts" (Joachim Hausschild, "Gut geschüttelt," *Süddeutsche Zeitung*, May 30, 1989). Luckow counters that Bülow "cultivated his first-class image over his six episodes of *Tatort*" that "every tie matches every jacket." "Celebrating in a gourmet temple," Bülow "believably switches from garden colony to luxury villa, from obsessive petit bourgeois murderers to greedy loud-mouthed blackmailers" (Alexander Luckow, "Herr Bülow überzeugte," *Die Welt*, May 30, 1989). One critic sees a relationship to the US crime hero Kojak (CBS, 1973–8) in Bülow's fashion and foodie sense: "It was, as if author Harald Vock had rifled through the caseload of Manhattan South. Bülow and Kojak are soulmates. Both complain about their civil servant salary, both have an affinity for luxury" (Th. Hellig, "Fast wie Kojack [sic]," *Niedersächsisches Tagesblatt*, May 30, 1989).

"The gentleman in elegant cloth" himself is not happy about his retirement in an interview with *Bild und Funk*: "It is a mystery to me why the SFB upends its most successful program. We had ratings from fifty to sixty percent. Others dream of those numbers." Drache is quoted that he was cast "as the answer to Schimanski." If Götz George's Horst Schimanski is the obstinate unkempt proletariat from Duisburg, Drache's Berliner bourgeois Bülow is the conservative defending the status quo, displaying the power and comfortable life of the privileged. Apparently typecast, Drache has a bone to pick with his network about their social-critical agenda: "As long as this horrible pile of scheming people has the upper hand at the network, I won't set foot in the house again." He insinuates that the new CEO Günther von Lojewski "will not stand a chance against these left-wing people" (Jörn Kluth, "Kommissar Bülow schlägt zurück," *Bild und Funk 21*, June 2, 1989)

Writers are critical of the episode's plot, acting, structure, and direction. Two critics praise the three-crime plot for "believably showing every-day police work," and that it lets Drache's Bülow shine (Alexander Luckow, "Der feine Bülow ganz ohne Tricks," *Hörzu*, June 17–23, 1989). "Even if there was no correlation, and only the inspector and his agile police-officers function as connectors, each episode had its special quality, photographically and character-wise. (. . .) The audience remains involved after the end: Who killed Mrs. Gellert?" (Günther Obitz, "Ein krimineller Knallbonbon," *Weser Kurier*, May 30, 1989).

The majority of critics disagrees with this vote of confidence and bemoans that "the star-director of German crime cinema, Jürgen Roland, has directed better crime series," reminiscing about *Tatort* and Drache highlights from the 1960s like "Dem Täter auf der Spur" and Edgar Wallace thrillers (F.M.L. "Stichproben," *Bayernkurier*, June 3, 1989). Some even go as far as stating that this episode "was deadly boring" and blame Heinz Drache's disengaged "impertinent parallel acting" ("unverschämte Daneben-Spielerei des Herrn

Drache"—teha, "Telekritik," *Wilhelmshavener Zeitung*, May 30, 1989). "Perhaps the actors in the entire team were trying not to leave Heinz Drache as Bülow too far behind." His "performance was once more so colorless, that the inspector's frequently changing wardrobe was able to raise more interest. Also an achievement" (Jbh, *Mannheimer Morgen*, May 30, 1989).

For others, this episode was simply "*Tatort* Average." "The whole thing was a little too much, not only for the inspectors but also for the viewers. Especially since the three crimes had nothing to do with one another." "Roland worked with too many tricks. He tricked himself at the end" (Thomas Schneider, "Ausgetrickst," *Die Rheinpfalz*, May 30, 1989).

> Yes, this script is highly reactionary. But what is even worse, it is conventionally structured and directed in a shuffling and old-fashioned manner by Roland that every *Derrick* has to appear as the height of filmic creativity in comparison. At the end, Heinz Drache walks towards the camera shaking his head. As do we." (Joachim Hausschild, "Gut geschüttelt," *Süddeutsche Zeitung*, May 30, 1989)

> Every case remained a case by itself, and the suspicion that the Sender Freies Berlin cleaned up some of their left overs was as close to the truth as the suspicion that Dieter Kirchlechner played the bad guy once again. (E. Heller, "Berliner Resteverwertung," *Tageszeitung*, May 20, 1989)

That critics and viewers noticed performance, script, and direction is per se not unusual for *Tatort* reception but in combination here nevertheless serves as one of the profounder media-reflexive conversations of any episode coverage from the archives. The episode analysis will thus have to pay attention to how the news' triple themes of street violence in Berlin, gender disparities and violence, and the Hungary-East German border situation intersects with media reflexivity and what this says about Berlin as a region and national symbol, about the format of the crime drama at a crucial juncture between broadcast and privatization.

Broadcasting *Tatort* Average: Episodic Linearity in the Cable/Satellite Era

As many of the critics point out, despite its showcase of talents behind and in front of the camera, this episode is "*Tatort* Average." Yet, at the same time, it is trying to do "a little too much." By 1989, German set owners had begun diversifying their viewer portfolios between the three state-run networks, their regional affiliates, and the cable and satellite newcomers, especially Pro7, Sat1, RTL, each of them offering more targeted niche-oriented programming imported from the United States and the United

Kingdom than their broadcast competitors. The ARD was feeling the pressure and sought to offer a German-produced cinematic alternative in a familiar television format. As a consequence, *Tatort* adapted its *Fernsehfilm* (TV film) concept to the genre-dominated cable era. Although this approach accentuated multiple plotlines and the synchronicity of different crimes, it did so in an episodic, largely linear, televisual format. In order to retain loyal fans of their flagship show and attract new ones, director Roland relied on one of the most conservative middle-class white men in the series' repertoire to anchor an internal niche experiment. In the span of ninety minutes, viewers get an action thriller and a Western (Pro7), a melodramatic whodunit (Sat1), and a horror flick (RTL) without having to switch channels. Yet, instead of interweaving the different subplots and their different genre approaches by dedicating each to a different member of a diverse ensemble cast (such as in *Hill Street Blues*, NBC, 1981–7), Bülow and the *Tatort* concept construct themselves as conduits that seek to channel a divided and dissociative metropolis along with deviating emergent media practices into network patri-linearity.

The first segment begins with police officers on the beat in central West Berlin, driving away from the *Siegessäule*. They banter and stop at a bank, where one of them interrupts a robbery in process and promptly gets shot. For the next ten minutes, we get treated to an action film sequence. Guns are waved around, and there are menacing threats: one of the gangsters enjoys violently pushing uncooperative hostages. All of this is edited in a quick rhythm intercutting between the police team outside and the bank robbers inside. The wounded cop is dragged to the police car under fire. Through the megaphone we hear classic police warnings ("Achtung, Achtung, hier spricht die Polizei!"), one of them an ultimatum, and the tension for all involved rises. The entire segment, especially the free-wheeling use of firearms and the pat genre-typical dialogue between the robbers and hostages, seems ripped from an imported and badly dubbed US action movie of that time on Pro7's late-night lineup.[10]

And then Bülow arrives on the scene in a three-piece suit and tie plus a beige trench coat. He casually leans on the edge of a van as he asks his colleague about the mission status. "Do they know in there that the wounded cop is out of danger? Let me talk to them unarmed." He takes off his trench coat, folds it, and does the same with his jacket. Clad only in his white shirt and a vest that makes him look like a 1980s version of Jimmy Stewart in *The Cheyenne Social Club* (dir. Gene Kelly, 1970), he walks toward the bank. Clearly, the gun violence is meant to signal urban American crime

---

[10]See the 1989 television lineup on *TV Programme von Gestern und Vorgestern*, http://retro-media-tv.de/tvp/show_tage.php?id=1&anf=1989-01-01&ende=1989-12-31 (accessed July 23, 2020).

with a tinge of *High Noon*. A high angle of the scene shows us a divided highway, one direction blocked off, the other one busy with traffic.

The high-angle shot, the Kojak/Jimmy Stewart associations, and the urban gangster genre of this crime Americanize the entire segment. Nevertheless, Bülow's quick and successful diplomatic intervention also insinuates that the bank robbery narrative itself is not homegrown, that the gangsters—like this *Tatort* beginning—are copying their behavior from US media. When Bülow reminds them of German realities on the ground (they haven't killed anyone yet), the more sensible bank robbers immediately turn on their most violent-prone member, after which they rush out of the door with their hands up to surrender. Bülow reverts from urban cowboy to gentleman by reassembling his outfit and apologizing to his colleague for taking over. He suggests a celebratory dinner at his favorite gourmet restaurant to make up for his trespass. Problem solved, end of episode one within the mini-series. After this, we hear nothing about the bank robbery ever again.

The taking off and putting back on of his three-piece suit-ensemble—in that order—suggests that they are removable/combinable pieces and map on to the three-episode linearity of this episode's narration. The assembly permits Bülow and the ARD to adapt to the media situation. The ability to morph into Columbo, Kojak, or Stewart at will suggests that the Berlin detective is superior to them as a conglomerate of their media presences. Indeed, if network viewers were to step out for a few minutes after the first segment, they would think they were in a different episode upon their return—but thanks to Bülow, a *Tatort* nevertheless. Each channel and genre content might have a different look through choices in editing, sound, cinematography, and mise-en-scène, and call up different audience interaction protocols, yet all are containable by the big tent *Tatort* format. Like installments in the long-running crime series itself, the ensemble pieces adjust to the different demands of the changing prime-time television lineup without abandoning their format and specific style entirely. In a mixture of denouncing Americanization but not privatization, the function of Bülow's wardrobe transformation is indebted to the capitalist structure of Taylorism and surplus.

Considering that West Berlin's center city corridor, Kreuzberg along the wall, the villa suburb of Dahlem, or the featured garden colony are distinguishable regions of the city, this Bülow episode demonstrates that the show's cornerstone concept of regionalism has the capacity to layer itself onto the concept of the global, the national, and the new niche-based genre-driven television structure to keep pace with the transformations shaking up the public networks. Bülow's peripherally located yet systemically centralized white male authority is never questioned. Fragmented, niche-based narrative formats in the emergent mediascape match the perception of the frayed sociopolitical landscape in Berlin. Like his pristine suit, Bülow reunites and layers the pieces in the "proper" order, reassembling the "center that cannot hold" (William Butler Yeats), firmly attaching it to his embodiment of middle-class white male authority. Foregrounding Bülow's *reassemblage*, the ARD also hopes to preserve *Tatort* seriality for a new era.

From an action thriller in the midst of urban chaos, Bülow safely commandeers us into the well-worn comfort of a classic salon whodunit. In alternating close-up/medium close-up framing, conniving upper-crust society members indebted to their own upkeep are shown lounging in their gourmet restaurant or opulently designed nineteenth-century villa with rooms the size of an entire garden colony parcel. As a gentleman, Bülow moves in and out of these rooms with ease and ethical but also class-based superiority. He delegates all heavy police work to his associates. While he interviews his "friends" in the salon, his colleagues have to assemble and analyze massive analog data. They have to pursue one of the blackmail suspects into the sanitation tunnels. Bülow neither follows nor waits for them: "By the time they have washed that off, it's time for breakfast." His officers get beaten up and choked in action, while Bülow, the salon detective, simply waits and thinks on the sidelines until the threads come together. In the definitive moment, Bülow suddenly appears in the right place at the right time, insisting on apprehending the suspect himself.

Following the pattern through the three criminal cases, one can glimpse the network's salvaging effort to intervene in the changing media and political landscape of 1989. Jürgen Roland inserts Bülow as a floating switchboard between independent genre narratives that, as one critic reminds us, have "no correlation." "Only the inspector and his agile police-officers function as connectors" between the segments. Bülow functions like Alfred Hitchcock in *Alfred Hitchcock presents*, as a classy yet unassuming host, who channels our forays into depravity but reels us back to safety through his boring old man benevolence.

The three-in-one approach integrates the television medium's episodic linearity characteristic for the television series and the broadcast era into its internal segmentation and format. At the same time, the great resistance to narrative complexity reflects on the cable/satellite era's cross-channel surfing, which fuses action with melodrama and horror not because of their intertextual connectivity or an intentional genre hybridity but because of their scheduled place in the temporal and spatial flow. Surfing began with privatization, the proliferation of simultaneous viewing choices, and the introduction of the remote control along with television sets equipped with cable or satellite connections. This anthology-type *Tatort* follows the horizontal model of cross-channel flow by making it part of its vertical linear flow, pitching thirty minutes each of action, melodrama, and horror at the viewer, facilitated and contained by a *Tatort* detective, to keep them in-house. As the next section will investigate, genre diversification is also mapped onto gender and class distinctions in specific ways that veer from an all-male cast in the shoot-out section, the foregrounding of dueling femme fatales in the melodrama segment, to the sexual predation of women walking home from work at night in the horror chapter.

The Oyster-Slurper in the Garden Colony: The Horror of Gender and Class

In the 1989 *Tatort* episode, a serial rapist and murderer haunts a garden colony. In order to understand why the horror segment within this *Tatort* takes place in a garden colony, one needs to have a sense of what *Schrebergarten*, *Kleingarten*, or *Laubenkolonie* actually signify in the German and Berliner context. Dating back to the first urban garden colony in Leipzig in 1864/5, there are almost a million of these small garden clubs and colonies usually featuring a *Laube* (shack) self-administered by 14,000 *Vereine* (clubs), themselves part of regional garden plot clubs (*Kleingartenverbände*) and the National Organization of German Garden Friends (*Bundesverband deutscher Gartenfreunde e.V.*, BDG) in Germany today. The organization proudly states on its website that Berlin has the most garden plots of any German city.[11] Katrin Schreiter emphasizes the allotment plot as a shared German experience continuing through and beyond 1989: "In the German Democratic Republic (GDR) alone, 1.2 million people—about 10 percent of the adult population were members of the national allotment organization, which was by far the largest non-communist organization in the country."[12]

As part of the physical fitness movement at the turn of the twentieth century, the garden plot concept evolved in response to rapid urbanization, especially multigenerational working-class living conditions in tight, light-, and fresh air-deprived vertical apartment complexes and the Berlin specialty: basement and concatenated rear courtyard dwellings, between one to four labyrinthinely interconnected rear or interior courtyard structures, reachable from the street only by narrow tunnels, corridors, and alleys.[13] Garden plots were supposed to combine exposure to nature and the elements with physical activities, predominantly soccer, and the ability to raise rabbits and chickens, plant and harvest fresh produce, to supplement the vitamin-scarce potato and expensive meat diet in the cities. Pitched as a safer space for small children than the city streets, and a place for seniors to relax and

---

[11]Data gathered from the main website of the BDG, https://www.kleingarten-bund.de/de/bundesverband/zahlen-und-fakten/ (accessed July 21, 2020).
[12]Katrin Schreiter, "The *Schrebergarten* as a Political Space in Postwar German Literature," in *German Division as Shared Experience*, ed. Erica Carter et al. (New York: Berghahn, 2019), 199–218, here 199.
[13]See Gesine Asmus, *Hinterhof, Keller und Mansarde 1901–1920* (Hamburg: Rowohlt, 1982), and Wolfgang Feyerabend's more recent exploration of their multiple use renaissance, *Berliner Hinterhöfe* (Berlin: Thies Schröder, 2015).

remain useful at the same time, same-size parcels were arranged in linear horizontal rows with a conjoint club house plus a playground and/or soccer field.

Walking down one of the central corridors gives members and visitors easy visual access to the different garden plots concatenated like shop displays. The same setup, like a Panopticon, allows the colloquially called *Laubenpieper* (plot gardener, literally translated as garden shack peeper) to peep at their neighbors and whoever walks by day and night. The feeling of being on display and representing the club has the effect of pressuring tenants to conform to set standards and police that conformity. Most individual parcels are fenced with traditional wooden *Jägerzaun* (picket fence), tight hedges, or chicken wire, their gates opening onto one of the straight transecting walkways/narrow streets.

While garden plots were initially meant to function as temporary respites during spare time from work and as retirement activity plots, more and more colonies, mobile homes, and shacks were transformed into semipermanent places of residence, especially after the war, when city infrastructures were destroyed. This move toward residential life also had the effect of turning working-class apartment dwellers escaping to the garden into landholders, prodding them to have more in common with the middle class. Soon, many colonies were split between long-term bourgeois and short-term working-class residents, often signaled by the spatial segregation of parcels with year-round homes, equipped with all the comforts of modern life versus parcels with mobile homes or trailers:

> For the middle classes, allotment gardens became a real and imagined space that catered to bourgeois ideals of order and individuality, which were seen to coexist harmoniously in the gardens to create places of calm and reflection in turbulent times.[14]

Although founder Moritz Schreber's (1808–61) intent for the garden colonies was predominantly guided by medical concerns for the body politic, it was tinged with a "straight back, straight mind" philosophy that combined well with a pathological sense of race and nationalism then as now.[15] The combination of *Vereinsmeierei* (club fanaticism), adherence to and support of law and order, and displayed regional and national pride (whether in the form of soccer club or German flags) supported a growing conservatism in the 1980s.

---

[14] Schreiter, "The *Schrebergarten* as a Political Space in Postwar German Literature," 199–218, here 201.
[15] "Moritz Schreber: Vom Kinderschreck zum Gartenpaten," *MDR*, September 15, 2015, https://www.mdr.de/geschichte/weitere-epochen/neuzeit/artikel124906.html (accessed July 2021).

The sociopolitical and economic changes, along with the topographical allegory the garden colony constructs, are linked to the alterations of the mediascape at the time of this episode. The privatization of radio and television that brought about an explosive growth in niche-based programming was hailed as a liberation from state control by some, a creative and consumer-oriented free market revolution by others. Yet, in actuality, while viewers dispersed across new platforms and services (satellite, cable, pay per view), the results, evidenced by RTL's sexploitation game show *Tutti Frutti* (1990–3), often relished dwelling in and disseminating reactionary class, gender, race, and sexual stereotypes that their competitors, the public broadcast stations ARD and ZDF, had to demonstrably negotiate and carefully calibrate to meet their foundational bylaws.

The first crime scene in this *Tatort* provides insight into *Schrebergarten* culture while simultaneously revealing its own problematic classism. A voice from the off states that the victim's shoes have been found. And that this is not the murder scene. We don't get a view of the evidence or the ground. The camera stays at a high angle. With a tracking shot, it zeroes in on wire-meshed rabbit cages in the foreground, behind which three pedestrians look on. They discuss police evidence and express doubt: "They will never get him" ("Die kriegen den nie"). Otto Patschke: "We should ask ourselves why we are paying taxes? What a bunch of losers."

Patschke, the serial rapist and murderer, utters this critique of the police. His statement coming from behind the wire cages lets us read the garden plot as a colony that is emancipating itself by writing and executing its own laws. As the history of European colonialism has shown, the relationship between the state and its former colonies was fraught with tension over issues of taxation, citizenship, landownership, economic profit, and gender and race. Remembering Jellinek's undercover predecessor, who buddied up to the residents, even state representatives, sent over to keep order, could "go native." Acquired local powers only held in check by remote control left many a colonialist chafing at the imperial bit. In his 1995 landmark study, Robert C. Young argued that "gender, class and race are circulated promiscuously and crossed with each other, transformed into mutually defining metaphors that mutate within intricate webs of surreptitious cultural values that are then internalized by those whom they define."[16]

In the Berliner colony, Otto Patschke has begun to take matters into his own hands to preserve a way of life he sees threatened not only by women's liberation and nonconformity but also by a decline in state power. This neocolonial *Otto Normalbürger* (Joe Sixpack) has a thing for peeking at, raping, and killing women. He hides behind a mask but also craves the

---

[16]Robert C. Young, *Colonial Desires: Hybridity in Theory, Culture and Race* (New York: Routledge, 1995), xii.

limelight, eagerly participating in the interview rounds to identify the culprit. As a long-term resident of the garden colony, he resorts to witnessing and policing in order to redirect the police's attention and fulfill his obligation to the community at the same time. At the station, Otto emulates Peter Lorre from *M* (dir. Fritz Lang, 1931), combining essentialist sexism and victim-blaming with an obsessive compulsion to keep order in the community: "These shameless things, how they dress, those short skirts to arouse men—I have to do what I do."

The camera's look through double wires encases the onlookers in their own community and equates them with the caged animals they sometimes raise. This gaze facilitates a classist perspective on the community, suggesting its members live caged and small lives. But Patschke's compulsory deeds follow this framing. His murder and rape become a crime caused by and about confinement and breaking out (freedom). Aided by the gaze structure of outsider/insider, subject and object of the look, this duality implicates men and women who are confined or crossing boundaries quite differently.

While there are different officers on the team in 1989, who could and do diversify the pool, the script props up Bülow, the white middle-class man, with the privilege and power to access and move between any and all of the individual places, crimes, and genres. He emerges mentally and physically unscathed from any encounter, whether in full suit or just a vest, not so Karin Jellinek, who is introduced to the viewer for the first time sitting with her back to the screen. She wears her hair in a ponytail, making her seem younger than she is. Bülow hands her the caseload, and she asks: "All were rapes?" "All we know." "Always the same location?" "Yes, in the *Schrebergarten*." Without transition, Bülow inquires: "How old are you?" She asks: "Why? 25." After this question, the camera frames her head-on in mid-close-up for the first time, constructing her "being-looked-at-ness" at the very moment he, "the bearer of the look," sizes up her potential to function as a sexual object.[17] Back to Bülow in an over-the-shoulder shot: "And already *Kriminaloberanwärterin* (candidate for the rank of detective)—congrats!" The innuendo is hard to ignore, when countless women reaching higher rungs in their career ladders were accused of using "sexual favors" to get there. His subsequent request makes this worse, since he is requesting that she use her body so that he can clear up the rape and murder case. He informs Jellinek that she would be replacing a "previous undercover colleague, who was very communicative, so everyone, including the dogs, knew she was a cop." Adding insult to injury, Bülow's comment suggests that the previous female colleague was a gossip and couldn't be trusted to do her job.

---

[17] Laura Mulvey, "Visual Pleasure and Narrative Cinema," *Screen* 16, no. 3 (1975): 6–18.

Jellinek expresses concern that she would just be used as a decoy, and she wants to keep doing what she was hired to do: solve murders. What she doesn't say is that acting as a decoy will reduce her contribution to her first murder case to her gender and sexuality, when she is already the only woman on the team. While the undercover activity would put her in more danger than her colleagues, it would also reduce her ability to acquire the career-making skills that her male team members develop on the case. Instead of addressing her concerns, Bülow assures her that "no one will know," that it would be just between her and him. This statement taints the undercover job itself as something to be kept quiet. It concedes that the very act of walking through the garden colony while female is read as a self-prostitution. Repeating the murderer's victim shaming excuse, the criminality of the rape is blamed on the embodied performance of feminine sexuality. Emboldened by what he no doubt considered a trust-building exercise, he gets out two glasses and pours a cognac, moves over to stand behind her chair, and says as he towers over her: "This is a very rich one, especially suited for the ladies. Welcome aboard."

Maybe this scene did not appear as predatory in 1989 as it does in the aftermath of the #MeToo movement. But considering that Alice Schwarzer's feminist magazine *Emma* had been around since 1977 and the need to address gender inequality explicitly made it into the evening news in the form of a speech commemorating the country's achievements of the past forty years, at least some viewers would have sympathized with the tightrope Jellinek was walking her first day on a new job. To quote from President Richard Weizsäcker's May 24 address to the nation:

> Women are unfortunately still too often disadvantaged. They get to feel that disadvantage upon entering and advancing [in a profession], and when they return to the workforce. Underneath that lies the tension between family and career. Even now, families have to adapt to the labor market not the other way around. Everyone suffers from that. But women bear the lion's share of the weight that results from this [tension].[18]

Of course, Jellinek could neither say no to Bülow's request to go undercover nor to the cognac he offered. As is the case with most micro-aggressions that prop up systemic sexism, Bülow does not say anything overtly disparaging, but the combination of his hierarchical superiority, the age difference, his dominating male physique, and the pledge to secrecy as he invades her personal space raises several red flags.

---

[18] Richard von Weizsäcker, "40 Jahre Grundgesetz der Bundesrepublik Deutschland. Rede zum Staatsakt," May 24, 1989, https://www.bundespraesident.de/SharedDocs/Reden/DE/Richard-von-Weizsaecker/Reden/1989/05/19890524_Rede.html (accessed July 20, 2020).

If the scene had been shot differently and not followed a textbook case of the male gaze, and if Bülow's white male authority had not been positioned to ease the *Tatort* format into the next mediascape by, among others, bestowing a B-movie horror veneer onto a rape and murder case, the interview office scene would not take on such importance. But it has to be seen parallel to the scenes featuring a grinning mask-wearing rapist, who is, after all, also sneaking up on women from behind. Like Jellinek in the office, the women the perpetrator pursues are already on high alert. They already know that they are not safe, no matter where they are. All of them have a specific reason to be where they are and a clear destination in mind. But they know that their path forward and toward that destination is precarious.

The first victim, Ulla, for example, returned to Berlin to be by her mother's side. Ulla needs to use the corridor through the garden colony to get to her house on the other side, as she tells her worried friend before she drives off: "But I run like lightning." No skill, natural or trained, can save the women from the systemic predation by men, here executed by the apparatus itself that assumes that predatory look. As Ulla brusquely walks through the brightly lit central corridor of the garden colony, the camera zeroes in on her legs from behind. In a cinematography borrowed from Fritz Lang's tunnel sequence in *Metropolis* (1927) and the opening sequence of *M* (1931) with a dose of F. W. Murnau's *Nosferatu* (1922), the long shot becomes a close-up of the leather-gloved shadow outline of a man, then a shadow with one hand extended like a claw. A close point-of-view shot frames the woman from behind. She turns around and screams. The reverse shot captures a man with a clownish brown mask on his face. He grabs her and pulls her down.

A key mise-en-scène ingredient that connects the diverse socioeconomic locations and micro-societies functions as a one-way mirror in this episode: German *Gardinen* (translucent window treatments). Originally a luxury interior design staple of the upper class, cheaper versions soon became ubiquitous in working- and middle-class households. Unlike shades that obscure views in both directions, *Gardinen* offer a modicum of privacy while allowing residents relatively unobstructed views of the outside. Bülow has them on his office windows. Gellert's villa features them. And all we see from the prime suspect, Patschke, when Jellinek rings the bell of his up-converted garden shack are the slight ruffles of the *Gardinen*. Even the small camper functioning as Bülow's command central in the *Schrebergarten* has a set of *Gardinen* through which Bülow takes stock of Jellinek's operation. The *Gardinen* level the class differentiation in this episode, not in the sense of erasing them but in Helmut Schelsky's sense of portraying Berlin and Germany as a "nivellierte Mittelstandsgesellschaft" (leveled middle-class society). Yet their function as a partially opaque and translucent surveillance tool speaks to the power of looking: that is, a dominant horror genre element and one which is elevated here by a specific cultural context.

For Ulla and Karin, there are no places to hide in the brightly lit alleyway between fenced-off rows of garden parcels. Like border-jumpers that are spot lit by surveillance tower guards and hunted down by dogs and rifles, female bodies become an allegorical casualty of the German-German border along with embodying the specter of channel surfing. While their right to transfer is denied, their images are trafficked between ARD, ZDF, RTL, Pro7, and SAT1. Yet entrenched network television audiences on both sides of the Iron Curtain and the political aisles are reunited in watching *Tatort* on Sundays. Scopophilia and fetishism also come together to produce a classic horror scenario that reflects on the looking relations of network television at this media moment. The women are channeled by and channeling the veiled and multidirectional bourgeois male gaze through a linear episodic corridor that has served as a thoroughfare for niche-interests since the late 1950s. Bülow and his alter-ego voyeur, Patschke, watch from the sidelines, expecting and producing the violence that they supposedly aim to police in the streets of Berlin. Key for the crime drama at this junction is that the murderer's obsession and victim-blaming are neither opposed by Bülow in the television text nor by the network's format mode or the director's aesthetic choices. Just the opposite, in fact. This episode demonstrates that the network's anxieties surrounding audience drift manifests in a multi-genre attempt to redirect parceled attention to a central passage of televisual flow, where divergent desires and fears unite in the monstrous embodiment of female spectacle and proletarianism, repeatedly enacted and vanquished.

The penultimate Bülow episode could have been a lesson for the SFB to rethink its overreliance on solo male detectives. Yet it took until 1996 to install the first team (Roiter and Zorowski) and until 2015 for the first woman, Meret Becker, to be cast in the Rubin and Karow team in Berlin. Since then, pairing two investigators with different gender/race/class intersectionalities has become *Tatort*'s default attempt to represent diversity, synch with contemporary lived experiences, and treat gender and race-based violence with more sensitivity. Episodes from the convergence era cast doubt on whether that approach alone suffices.

"Berlin, beste Lage" ("Berlin, Top Location," dir. Matti Geschonneck; RBB, January 10, 1993)

Tagesschau Synopsis

The Social Democrats (SPD) voted to allow German troops to enter regional conflicts in the capacity of United Nations units, in this case the ethnic conflict in the former Yugoslavia. This decision has to be seen in the context of the ethical and political effect of founding FRG chancellor Konrad

Adenauer's shift from vehemently supporting disarmament in the course of the Morgenthau Plan to endorsing rearmament in 1955 with the help of the US Marshall Plan. After 1945, many Social and Christian Democrats never wanted to be responsible for the actions of German troops (and Germany) in wars in greater Europe again. In 1993, then chancellor Helmut Kohl's siding with Catholic Croatia against Serbia was interpreted as a personal bias of his Christian Democrat Party and as setting a precedent for German military involvement elsewhere.

Former GDR state secretary Erich Honecker's trial accusing him of giving "shoot to kill" orders at the wall occupied much public attention. The trial had the potential to out the crimes against humanity committed by the regime to keep its citizens from exerting their right to free movement. Yet before a true public reckoning could begin, the trial ended with dismissal for health reasons on January 12. As the government, opposition parties, and states agreed on the financing of the reconstruction effort in former East Germany,[19] Kohl insisted that the "Solidarity Tax" would create "Blühende Landschaften" (blooming landscapes).[20]

Because of racially motivated riots against migrant families in their residences in Hoyerswerda, Mölln, and Solingen (1991–3), hundreds of thousands demonstrated against domestic racism in Berlin and elsewhere, seeking to make visible to the anxious world that the German past is not repeating itself.

The internal flow of news segments opens up the ongoing tension between Germany's responsibility for initiating two world wars and once again becoming a global player extending its military and economic power into greater Europe and beyond. The combination of ethnic cleansing in the war in Yugoslavia and the hate crimes committed against migrants in Germany highlight the prominence of race and racism as a constitutive element of German national identity. Kohl's plan for the five new states' (agri)cultural revitalization backgrounds the reckoning with East Germany's civil rights oppression and industrial abuse while echoing the US postwar plans for West Germany. For West German viewers, the reported ferry disaster with fifty-five people onboard perishing in the crossing between Poland and the island of Rügen might also make visible the new proximity of a united Germany to Poland and other Eastern Bloc countries.

---

[19] ARD Tagesschau Jahresrückblick 1993, http://www.tagesschau.de/jahresrueckblick/meldung118396.html (accessed July 11, 2011).
[20] Helmut Kohl, German chancellor in a televised address, July 1, 1990: "Durch eine gemeinsame Anstrengung wird es uns gelingen, Mecklenburg-Vorpommern und Sachsen-Anhalt, Brandenburg, Sachsen und Thüringen schon bald wieder in *blühende Landschaften* zu verwandeln, in denen es sich zu leben und zu arbeiten lohnt."

Tatort Synopsis

West Berlin Kommissar Markowitz (Günther Lamprecht) investigates the murder of a carpenter from the *Scheunenviertel*, the centrally located former Jewish district in what was East Berlin. The crime involves property speculations in the aftermath of 1989. Since the victim happens to look like Markowitz, the *Doppelgänger* scenario mirrors the configuration of the two Germanies. Because of this twinning, the West Berliner detective's investigation in the East leads to literal and figurative misappropriations. The *Tatort* episode following the news thus connects questions of genetics, ethnicity, and the perpetrator/victim dichotomy to the redistribution of property in the post-*Wende* real estate boom and the mass-scale reconfiguration of urban and regional mapping. The episode builds a relay between the still outstanding reparations owed to German Jews and the West German financial support for a radical reconstruction effort of the five new German states that just got passed by parliament.

Viewer and Critical Engagement

Günther Lamprecht became famous as the actor portraying Franz Biberkopf in Fassbinder's 1980 television mini-series adaptation of Alfred Döblin's *Berlin Alexanderplatz* and for being wounded during the amok-run of a teenage shooter in 1999 (*Bild*, November 2, 1999). He played Markowitz in eight episodes of the Berliner *Tatort*. His highest-ranked episode was watched by fifteen million viewers nationwide (*Berliner Morgenpost*, 25 July, 1999). Critics either characterize the actor as a *film noir* stylist (*die tageszeitung*, January 12, 1993), a thinking detective: "a quiet, contemplative Berliner" (*Tagesspiegel*, January 10, 1993) or a non-gun-wielding "decent human being" (*Die Welt*, January 11, 1993). That Markowitz is not as fully fleshed out as a character is attributed to the SFB's lack of funds, that is, not being able to pay for an apartment studio-set to give him a private life (*Tagesspiegel*, January 10, 1993).

Berlin-Beste Lage received many and widely diverging critiques in national, regional, and local papers. It was called "an oasis in everyday crime television" that takes advantage of the fact that "film means a chance to tell a story through images and to paint atmosphere" (*Funk und Fernsehen 5*, February 6–12, 1993). On the other end, Knut Hickethier pans Geschonneck's long takes, which he considers "superfluous," and Ulrich Gumpert's 1960s style Jazz score, which he considers "too idyllic." Further, Hickethier argues that writer Rainer Berg brings in "the unfortunate German past" for lack of ideas on how to deal with the East meets West phase in German politics (*epd 2*, January 13, 1993). By contrast, Erich Emigholz sees the story as delving into "complicated circumstances" comparing the real estate bonanza of

1938 with that of 1989 (*Weser Kurier*, January 12, 1993). This implied conflation of fascism and socialism leaves Manfred Riepe of *die tageszeitung* with a "stomach upset" (January 12, 1993). Thomas Linden of *Kölnische Rundschau* disagrees and calls the "macabre" *Doppelgänger* episode an "intelligent lesson in dealing with the past" (January 12, 1993). The East German *Leipziger Volkszeitung* and *Magdeburger Volksstimme* claim the episode as "Tatort Ostberlin," praising the "always surprising perspectives of *Hinterhofarchitektur*" (rear courtyard architecture) underscoring the fact that the episode's touted "best location" is actually "in the Berliner East in Oranienburger Strasse" (January 12 and 11, 1993). By arguing that "there is no route that leads to the West (...) the *Hinterhof*, as full of flair as it may be, becomes a dead end," Stefan Stosch takes note of the director's conscious mapmaking: "The Eastern part of Berlin, one learns, lies much closer to Poland than to the Western part of Berlin" (*Hannoversche Allgemeine Zeitung*, January 12, 1993).

Doppelgänger Geography and Aesthetics

This episode begins like a film, dominated by establishing long and traveling shots of a rural area, open fields, and winding tree-lined streets. An older truck makes its way slowly through the fields to encounter a farmstead fortified by a surrounding wall. When the truck passes through the gate, we witness playing children and an assembled group of adults who greet the two arriving workers warmly and familiarly in Polish (not subtitled). Everybody helps to unload the truck's goods, which consist of used furniture items, from appliances to carpets. From the very first frame, it is obvious that we are not in Berlin anymore. But at the same time, the sequence is shot like a homecoming. The viewer expects a murder or a corpse to turn up, but is motivated to dread its inevitable discovery within this lovingly depicted family circle. When legs protrude from a pulled carpet, a non-Polish-speaking viewer only understands the excitedly pronounced word "police," upon which the camera cuts to the arrival of a moped-driving policeman arriving at the farm in a replica of the representation of the truck's arrival in the previous sequence. With these parallel arrival scenes, time and space coordinates have been set backward into a homestead-time out of synch with united Berlin in 1992, but the spatial configuration symbolically connects the gold-rush mentality in post-*Wende* Berlin to the frontier atmosphere of the mythical Wild East, that is, Poland.

> Over the course of the century preceding the National Socialist rise to power, a complex discourse developed representing past and present German engagement in Poland and further stretches of the East in colonial terms. Depictions of German colonial endeavor and its purported impact circulated in novels and atlases, political speeches and press publications,

feature films and history textbooks, printed scholarship and classroom lessons. These visual and narrative representations arose out of specific political contexts but ultimately came to define the nation's collective sense of its colonial identity.[21]

The setting of the fort-like farm serves as an allegory of former West Berlin's fortified insularity between 1961 and 1989. Additionally, the wide-open landscape that needs to be traversed in order to arrive at the farm is iconographically reminiscent of a classic US Western. If we remember that both East German and West German television and cinema have not only had a long and fond relationship with classic US Westerns but also with Italian Spaghetti Westerns and *Indianerfilme* (both GDR and FRG varieties), then the combination of wide-angle, long-shot, and long-take codes the Polish terrain as a wild (old and new) frontier adjacent to and constitutive of the freshly united states of Germany.

Given the established colonial discourse Kristin Kopp contests earlier, it is likely that viewers would have speculated on the guilt of the truck drivers just because they speak Polish and have "taken stuff from a Berlin household." Anxious anti-Polish sentiments, especially regarding car thefts, were rampant in the early 1990s. But this prejudicial perspective does not gain track due to the configuration of the truck's journey as a symbolic homecoming, as a journey into the past of Berlin as a village (depicted like this in novels by Theodor Fontane, for example) into what looks like former German Silesia or East Prussia. The episode utilizes these anxieties and colonial desires to set the hook and to compel the viewer's associations backward in time (1881–1933) and space (Germany in its borders before the Second World War) while moving the narrative forward into unified Berlin and its reopened Eastern corridor in 1993.

Director Matti Geschonneck refrains from showing us the contrastive arrival of a Berliner CSI team and detective Markowitz in their flashy Western cars. Instead, he and script writer Rainer Berg let the viewer, and the Berlin police, follow the trail of the unknown victim's photograph, taken at the scene across the border in Poland and sent via fax to Berlin headquarters. Thus, the film camera—and we as spectators—arrive in Berlin along with the teleported image. A secretary receives the fax in the communication office of police headquarters without the viewer being able to see the photograph. She erupts disbelievingly and anxiously: "Oh no, that's not possible" to speedily make her way along empty seedy-looking corridors, down a Paternoster, through more corridors to finally arrive in a deserted office. Through her point of view the camera glances into several empty rooms until she pushes

---

[21]See Kristin Kopp, *Germany's Wild East: Constructing Poland as Colonial Space* (Ann Arbor: University of Michigan Press, 2012), 202.

open a closed door. Her expectation of finding but her failure to locate someone (what we later discern must have been Markowitz) in these deserted rooms directly ties this beginning to the sculpture "der verlassene Raum" (the deserted room) that Markowitz later visits on his rounds through the formerly Jewish *Scheunenviertel*. From behind another closed door within the empty office, Markowitz suddenly appears as if he has cheated death. He takes one look at the photograph and follows the secretary outside. As we discover at this moment, comparing photograph to diegetic reality, the victim could be Markowitz. The *Doppelgänger* motif, structurally introduced by the two takes of near-identical homecomings (via truck and moped) and repeated by the secretary's path through headquarters, now takes on physical form.

The long horizontal path the secretary travels through the innards of the police headquarters matches the winding horizontal path of the truck through the Polish landscape. The photographic match of physiognomies between Markowitz and the victim (a carpenter from the formerly Jewish *Scheunenviertel*) finds its structural equivalent in the aesthetic matches of the two establishing shots, one in the Polish province and the other in Germany's metropolis. The film has us "arriving" three times and equates the two very different spaces with each other through its elaborate documentation of the journeys (by truck, moped, and secretary). John Berger's emphasis on the "always already dead" relation of image to index informs the film. But the consistent structural and physical matching defers death and becomes very close to a denial: "oh no, that's not possible."

The implementation of the *Paternoster*, famously and comically employed by Doris Dörrie in *Men* (1988) to stand in for the roll of credits at the end of a film (featuring the responsible parties for specific production duties in their individual boxes), points the viewer in several directions: the *Paternoster* is a British invention from the late nineteenth century and was adopted by Germany in the 1870s. While the UK abandoned most of theirs, as of 2015 Germany still had 250 in use.[22] A *Paternoster* is an open-face double elevator on an automatic continuous loop, in which one party goes up while another goes down. Its name refers to the Catholic rosary. Its eleventh bead is reserved for the Lord's Prayer—the ten preceding for Ave Marias. Since the old-fashioned elevator was originally used as the entrance into mines, entering it was often accompanied by a prayer for safe return. Its revolving mechanics also mirror the use of a rosary in praying. In addition, the insertion of a *Paternoster* in the photo's traveling scene also establishes a

---

[22]Kate Connolly explains how the Paternoster is tied to German history and why it suits German customs in "Lovin' Their Elevators: Why Germans Are Loopy about Their Revolving Lifts," *The Guardian*, August 14, 2015, https://www.theguardian.com/world/2015/aug/14/elevator-germans-loopy-revolving-lifts-paternosters (accessed November 19, 2020).

link to the history and mechanics of motion pictures. When Oskar Messter invented the Maltese Cross/Geneva Drive *c.* 1896, the small part moved the film strip forward at precise temporal and spatial intervals.

The *Paternoster* visualizes how structural, aesthetic, industrial, and narrative layers correspond with and represent each other in the first two sequences of this *Tatort* episode.[23] Thus, the *Doppelgänger* motif takes on self-referential implications for the history of film as a medium itself, a theme that needs to be intersected with the trajectory of the narrative, which leads Markowitz to ensure reparations are paid to the children of evicted Jewish owners. The question remains whether the viewer is supposed to notice the apparatus—as in the case of the *Paternoster*—or be sutured into the narrative by means of the perfectly spooled and projected movements (which the invention of the Maltese Cross helped smooth significantly). However, Geschonneck's three arrivals make the beginning narrative "stutter" with similar, yet not identical, repetitions despite or because of their aesthetic and mechanic finesse.

Let's keep in mind that the border crossing into Poland is spatially and emotionally represented as a repeated homecoming despite the discovery of the corpse. The journey through the austere, deserted, seedy Berlin police station not only postpones the moment of the photograph's arrival in the hands of Markowitz and for us, but it also alienates us from Berlin. The third arrival in the echoing deserted and outdated halls of a Berlin institution contrasts with the sounds and sights of a family welcoming their loved ones in Poland. Traversing the corridors also temporally and spatially stretches the match of signifier and signified to increase the tension inherent in the perfect physiognomic match and transfers this tension unto the space, which is emptied of people, defamiliarized to the point of uncanniness. When muffled sounds of a celebration come out of a hidden interior office, the secretary's interruption—"I am sorry, you have to see this"—is no match for the open arrival to hugs and kisses in the Polish homestead. The image transported under cover—similar to the rolled-up corpse in the carpet—is a near-perfect match to Markowitz.

If the discovery of the match between Markowitz and the photographed victim is the uncanny shocker usually reserved for the murder scene at the beginning or sometimes provided in a flashback, one can further extrapolate that the faxed image of the victim functions as more of a corpse than the actual one in the pathologist's lab. The transport of the image makes the sender-message-recipient process visible on camera but refutes the unique identity of each station in the communication process. It scrambles their codes and unsettles the departure-arrival function within the system of

---

[23]This aspect is beautifully conceptualized by Steph Ketelhut in the experimental short film "Pater.Noster," http://vimeo.com/8569529 (Dortmund 2001) (accessed October 27, 2010).

narration. The message resets the enunciated positions in the process. Instead of a whodunit in the traditional criminal style, it implicates (mechanical) reproduction itself in the case.

The shock effect Markowitz's *Doppelgänger* status provides threads itself through the entire narrative, for example, gaining him unusual insight into each suspect's emotional relation to the victim. Lacanian mis/recognition, the moment where, for a toddler, the stabilizing ego-function of the mirror also becomes a deeply unsettling one—"that is/is not (yet) me"—runs through the film as a leading structural theme. Markowitz himself is spooked enough to ask a geneticist to check his own DNA against the victim's. There is no currently attestable relationship but a relationship link could have existed hundreds of years ago surmises the specialist. What does the viewer take away from this? On the one hand, that this uncanny resemblance is a genetic accident, on the other hand, that this means any of us could have a *Doppelgänger*. For the specific German-Jewish-Polish case presented in this episode, the reference is precariously ambiguous. While the attested distant relationship lends itself to a social practice of collective guilt and reparations, it also comes precariously close to repeating the Nazi-era gesture of genetic tests done to specify Aryan or Jewish heritage. This is especially crucial since the victim was not Jewish but died alerting the Nazi owner's son to the unresolved property rights of the housing block in the recentered topography of united Berlin. But coupled with Markowitz's Polish-sounding name, the very insertion of the DNA test discursively refers the viewer to Jewish Holocaust victims despite the fact that neither Markowitz nor the victim of the crime is Jewish. As a result of the physical similarities, Markowitz steps into the role of the collective conscience that Mr. Printz, the Nazi owner's inheriting son, wanted to silence in order to become rich. At the same time, the serial concatenation of arrival scenes points toward *both* a continuous deferral of involvement in and acceptance of the committed crime *and* the ability to retain the affective relationship without the historical specificity, a structural coup d'état for television, the medium, where seriality is king. This would, of course, also necessitate a rereading of the repeated arrivals as epistemological attempts to get close to, yet always misrecognize the basis of ethnic and racial difference and/as Polish, Jewish, German, Other.

Markowitz's reproduction as discursively Other-ed implicates, as I have explained earlier, the very act of reproduction. But what is (not) being reproduced and why? Markowitz, with his Polish last name, is reproduced as kin to the slain carpenter who died because of his ethical conscience and the official German stance of "never forget." If the carpenter's goal was to hinder the reproduction of Nazi-era crimes against the children of Holocaust victims, then Markowitz steps into his shoes to prevent history from repeating itself. As a civil servant, he stands in for the public consciousness, as many other *Tatort* detectives have done before and will after him. If that were all, the *Doppelgänger* motif would be superfluous, even a bit extravagant for the narrative. Like Hamlet, who is spooked and traumatized by the ghost of his father that appears to him in the dark of night, Markowitz's walking about during day and night produces constant uncanny misrecognitions in others, at the bar, in the *Scheunenviertel*, on the street. Looking at him as the return of the repressed confronts the individuals with their disbelief. His *Doppelgänger* status performs what the Americans attempted at Buchenwald: they marched residents of the town of Weimar—young and old—up the hill to confront what they mostly denied existed, the concentration camp and its barely alive, liberated inmates. In the episode, Markowitz comes across residents of the victim's block or confronts suspects in his *Doppelgänger* role. As he does so, his appearance elicits responses from denial and justification to infatuation and guilt. Their misrecognition of him performs their roles in the murder and cover-up— and the crime itself takes on much larger, much more general sociopolitical contours.

A dramatic shift within the discursive construction of Markowitz as Jewish-Polish defined Other occurs: a West German detective with a Polish name, a member of the Berlin police, signifies "victimhood" to the newly "liberated" East Berlin residents, many of whom saw themselves as double victims of global capitalism and state-sponsored communism. Long-held myths of the working class ruling over East Germany's official policy of antifascism collide with the post-wall economic opportunism exhibited by the royally named Printz and others. The episode can thus also be read as a West German attempt at correcting the East German victim myth, as an intervention into the East's double standards (profiting from Jewish-owned center city properties despite official reparation policies) at the same time that it implicates its own capitalist frontier greed in the crime—the realtor collaborating with Printz is a West German. And the episode conspicuously does not express alienation and Othering in the form of the inner-German East-West conflict itself, nor in the Southern European migrant situation contextualizing the show's first airing in 1993, but represents it in the historically traumatic pairing of Jew and German. While this move may have the result of insisting on a continued united responsibility of all Germans for the Holocaust and its aftermath, at the same time it also codes the inner-German conflict as a Self-Other, a racially configured conflict.

Topography of Terror as Film Noir

As a representative of a West Berliner, Markowitz's forays into the other Berlin remind spectators that West Berlin itself was an island cut off from West Germany by the surrounding East German state of Brandenburg and the infamous Berlin Wall from 1961 to 1989. It was displaced from its own center—Berlin Mitte, where the *Scheunenviertel* harboring the crime scene lies. Instead, at its core lay the "empty center" of former Potsdamer Platz (Hito Steyerl's 1998 film of the same name makes this viscerally apparent), itself the disputed space where property interests, former ownership rights, and politics (Hitler's Bunker) collided with each other. For many without direct familial reasons for visiting the East, elevated subway journeys and outlook towers were the only methods for sneaking peeks at the other side.

It is worth remembering that in 1993, the images that have since become reclaimed common Berlin iconography with the help of *Run Lola Run* (dir. Tom Tykver, 1999), *Goodbye Lenin* (dir. Wolfgang Becker, 2003), and television series (e.g., the 2002–5 ARD series *Berlin Berlin* or *Verliebt in Berlin*, Sat1, 2005–6) did not and could not yet visually represent a united Berlin. Visually, the West had relied so long on studio shots of supposed East German locations in connection with the cultural memories of historic Berlin, pre-1933 and after the bombing raids in 1945, that any actual filming on location would remain without much regional or cultural signification to a majority of West German viewers that early after unification. Solving the *Scheunenviertel* crime as a German crime against Jewish owners thus eschews representing the specific topography of a divided Berlin struggling to reunite in favor of reconnecting Western viewers' imaginary of Berlin Mitte to wartime footage or the late Weimar years.[24]

In his interior and exterior shots, Geschonneck relies on high-contrast low-key lighting and the sparse street-film aesthetics of Weimar cinema.[25] Markowitz's wardrobe, his trademark fedora and duster, his stubble, and Third Man-like emerging and disappearing from and into shadows contribute to the temporal shift. To add to this, Helga Seelitz (Renate Küster) as the widow functions in duplicitous femme fatale mode, flirting with her husband's murderer for her economic survival. While the cinematic aesthetics of the episode thus reconnect the Western viewer of *Tatort* to visions of "a better Germany," as Kracauer called the Weimar era, Markowitz's travels through the *Scheunenviertel* only become significant and readable through his retracing of the topography of terror. The director treats the viewer to selective identifying shots of Berlin Mitte, including the hovering golden dome of the New Synagogue in *Oranienburger Straße* (that has attained a purely representational and symbolic meaning, since it no longer serves the Jewish community as a meeting place for worship). Further, Markowitz stops to glance at Karl Biedermann's installation "Der verlassene Raum" commissioned in 1988 to demark the fiftieth anniversary

---

[24]This is the choice that Wim Wenders made in his 1988 *Himmel über Berlin*, which features a long flashback sequence of late Weimar and wartime footage.
[25]On this, see Sunka Simon, "Weimar Project(ion)s in Post-Unification Cinema," in *Berlin: The Symphony Continues*, ed. Anne Costabile-Heming et al. (Berlin: Walter de Gruyter, 2004), 301–20.

of the Night of Broken Glass (November 9, 1938). Markowitz will repeat this attentive look at a roadside memorial to the Holocaust on his way into the *Scheunenviertel* upon his exit from it at the end of the film. At that moment, he stands respectfully reading in front of the black and gold memorial plaque dedicated to the oldest Jewish gravesite in Berlin and its destruction by the Gestapo in 1943.[26]

The bookend scenes at the memorial to orphaned Jewish children, framing Markowitz's investigatory route in this episode, connect themselves to his interaction with some Berliner youths curious about meeting a detective. When the free-ranging kids ask him whether he carries and uses a gun, Markowitz replies, "Nee, ick mach det allet mit de Hände" (in Berliner dialect: no, I do all of that with my hands). While the youths have been influenced by American crime series and movies to expect a Western detective to carry and wield a weapon, Markowitz's reply intimates that physical strength and mental capacity suffice for his job and his authority.[27] Markowitz's response also recalls a well-known German hero's privileging of the fist over the gun, namely Karl May's alter-ego Old Shatterhand, thereby countering the American gunslinger expectation with a decidedly German translation of the same.[28] This dialogue scene between two generations further pays homage to the legacy of a rubble film like *Somewhere in Berlin* (dir. Gerhard Lamprecht, 1946, no relation). As a figurative *Heimkehrer* (returnee) standing in for most of the West German audience, Markowitz engages symbolically orphaned children, whose role models, as is intimated here, are not their compatriot fathers and brothers but American cops and gangsters on television. In *Somewhere in Berlin*, the returning POW father comes across a youth gang involved in war games amid the rubble and admonishes them that the war is over. He later smashes his son's prized possession, a toy tank. The film ends with adults and children removing rubble and rebuilding their district in solidarity. By stylizing Markowitz as a combination of *film noir flaneur* and *Heimkehrer*, Geschonneck builds parallels between Weimar, the rubble film,

---

[26]There are two sites close to one another that memorialize the specific moments of deportation, one "Der verlassene Raum," the departed/left-behind room, http://www.fotopolitics.org/fotopolitics_thumbnails.php5?galleryid=7&topicid=4 (accessed May 8, 2013) and Will Lammert's statue from 1957, http://de.wikipedia.org/w/index.php?title=Datei:Skulptur_Juedische_Opfer_des_Faschismus_(Foto_2008).jpg&filetimestamp=20090407094349 (accessed May 8, 2013).

[27]By contrast, his younger *Tatort* colleague Till Ritter (Dominic Raacke), whose physical frame dwarves Markowitz's, brandishes a gun whenever he can.

[28]German author Karl May (1842–1912) penned over thirty bestselling Western and colonial-era novels that are still popular today. While he declared them travel adventures, with a few exceptions, he never visited the locations of his tales. His most famous Western trilogy is *Winnetou I-III*, whose bromancing partners are a German immigrant and an Apache chief, https://www.karl-may-museum.de/en/collections/karl-may/biography-works/ (accessed March 15, 2020).

and his 1993 *Tatort* that configure Markowitz's meandering investigations in East Berlin as a homecoming, as if he—a West German—along with the Jews, had been evicted. The double life of Markowitz thus includes a reference to his East German alter-ego, whose demise is enabling his symbolic return to the center of Germany's former power.

This message intersects with the musealization of Berlin *Mitte*. In tracing his alter-ego's footsteps, the topography of terror positions Markowitz as an engaged participant in active memory culture. In the larger context of post-1989 unified Germany, these related scenes have Markowitz function as a decidedly democratic subject and a German father figure who counters the violence and capitalist fervor of mainstream US crime narratives. His reflective silence at the memorials proves that he has learned the lessons of the Second World War and the Holocaust. Further, his no-gun rule appeases European and international fears of a militarized unified Germany. This episode thus configures the German placeholder of state powers to be a trustworthy ally with the necessary moral fiber to reunite the two Germanies with an eye toward European integration—even if, or especially if, the West re(dis)covers the former East.

However, the first memorial's disarranged domestic scene also points to the current unstable national climate and reverberates in the racially motivated attacks on the Hoyerswerder (Saxony) migrants, who had their new homes destroyed by citizens of the town turned into an angry German mob.[29] The slogan coined by the neo-Nazi inspired yet collectively fueled pogrom during 1991—*ausländerfrei* (free of foreigners)—finds its equivalent in the featured absence of Jews portrayed by the first memorial and by Printz's sought-after eviction of his tenants to remarket the properties. Due to the discursive references built into the performative and narrative doubling, repeated misrecognitions and misappropriations become a motif that problematizes the projection of unification as a seamless "organic" merger or as former West German chancellor and mayor of Berlin, Willy Brandt, commented on the fall of the wall: "Es wächst zusammen, was zusammen gehört" (What belongs together, grows together) (November 9, 1989).

"Eine ehrliche Haut" ("An Honest Skin/Man," dir. Ralph Bohn; RBB, January 4, 2004)

Instead of a *Tagesschau* summary to establish the circulation between television segments during the Sunday evening lineup, I will focus in more

---

[29]See the documentation assembled from various news outlets by the Initiative Pogrom 91, http://pogrom91.tumblr.com/dokumentation (accessed May 8, 2013).

detail on the televisual flow between the ARD crime drama at 8:15 p.m. and the successful ARD political talk show *Sabine Christiansen* following *Tatort* at 9:45 p.m. between 1998 and 2007.

Tatort Synopsis

Young idealistic politician Körner (Heikko Deutschmann) drives home from a talk show and runs over Sammy, a drug dealer. He is brought down by his old-guard party leader, Heinrich Paulsen (Dietrich Mattausch), who aligns himself with a career-hungry journalist to produce a smear campaign. Distracted by his girlfriend, Judith Klee (Stefanie Stappenbeck), at the moment of the accident, Körner uses the excuse that "the young man ran in front of the car out of nowhere," not realizing that the man was already dead before he hit him. Investigator Till Ritter (Dominic Raacke) thinks he is guilty; Felix Stark (Boris Aljinovic) believes there is more to the case. Meanwhile, the media(ted) Berlin Republic, represented by a highly publicized *Sabine Christiansen* (ARD, 1998–2007) talk show segment in a television-on-television scene, is as much the focus of the episode as the crime itself.

One of the key suspects and boyfriend of the actual culprit is called Nato (Toni Snétberger). His name signifies the prefix nat- (as in native or born) to make a claim for Nato's ethnic background *and* his right to be considered German but is obviously also an association to the NATO. In March 2004, two months after this episode, Bulgaria, Estonia, Latvia, Lithuania, Romania, Slovakia, and Slovenia formally became members of NATO. As their membership applications were pending, pros and cons were frequently debated in the news cycle in 2003 and early 2004. While Nato's ethnic background is not revealed in the episode (he always speaks German), the name's history suggests a Southern European origin (Spanish or Portuguese). At first it appears that Nato would have the most to gain from Sammy's demise, but it turns out that Connie, in a melodramatic turn, had been so traumatized by her older brother's death from a drug overdose that she slapped and accidentally pushed Sammy off the staircase when she found out he was dealing.

Nato's aggressive stance toward the police and politics—he imprisons Ritter and Körner in the basement with an open canister of gas—is motivated, as Stark concedes, by "trying to protect his girlfriend all along." Loyalty comes in different shapes, and one could surmise that *Tatort* is sending a post-9/11 message about the need for an expanded trust base, including integrating former *Ostblock* members, for NATO's more aggressive push in the Middle East. The can of gas, on the other hand, sends a more troubling message about genocide—alluding to the Holocaust and the recent ethnic cleansing during the Yugoslav conflict, respectively, and perhaps also signals to Germans to assume a watchful role in assuring that the United States does not overstep as they did in the recent Abu Ghraib torture and prison abuse scandal (2003).

By 2004, the 24/7 news cycle on television has become part of the investigation pipeline—as have rumors, conspiracies, and defamations. When we consider that Peter Meckel, the careerist reporter in this episode, works for a cable news service rather than a newspaper or a network, "Eine ehrliche Haut" updates Heinrich Böll's and Volker Schlöndorff's/Margarete von Trotta's *Lost Honor of Katharina Blum* (1974 and 1975) for the new millennium. The sensationalist journalism of the national *Bild Zeitung* from the 1970s has morphed into alternative media outlets with tabloid standards in 2004. The smear campaign is fueled by increasing competition between news agencies amid a proliferation of German, European, and international channels and viewing choices within the niche-based cable and satellite era as social media and web-based content are gaining steadily. Pitting Sabine Christiansen's champagne talk show against the beerhall journalism of Peter Meckel not only offers a glimpse at the media spectrum but also implicates the increasingly opinion and celebrity-oriented political coverage of the talk format as such in the Berliner Republic's state of hypermediation. And of course, this being *Tatort*, broadcast on the original German network ARD, this entire episode is a thinly veiled critique of privately owned cable and web services that fall outside of the control of public policy and—as is hinted at here—any obligation to a nationally agreed-upon code of journalistic conduct and ethics.

Critical and Viewer Engagement

The majority of critical coverage reads the *Tatort* episode as a self-reflexive tour de force of Berlin's obsession with itself at the media(ted) intersection between local, regional, national, and global. The FAZ calls the episode a "*Berliner Republik* Krimi" (January 5, 2004) devoted to political intrigue and journalistic careerism. As a reminder, Bonn had been the nation's capital due to the special status of Berlin under Allied occupation until the fall of the wall in 1989. After the official unification in 1990, the Berlin Republic emerged from the shadows of history and the realm of symbolism to reclaim legal and executive powers under the refurbished transparent Reichstag dome in 1999. By 2004, Berlin had thus emerged from a decade of local and national recalibration that included anxious global attention. "*Tatort* has been accused of avoiding the *Berliner Republik*, this mixture of Christiansen, political vanity, boomtown, media city, drugs for celebrities" (*Der Tagesspiegel*, January 4, 2004).

With Sabine Christiansen's cameo, playing herself in the episode's opening talk show segment, several critics are intrigued that the televisual flow has been inverted. That Sunday, the highly ranked national political talk show,[30] which was on hiatus during Christiansen's vacation, took place in and as *Tatort* and not after the crime drama. "*Tatort* plus Talk in one" (Ibid.). *Bild* (January 3, 2004) even titles the article "*Tatort* on Sabine Christiansen": "I was intrigued by the surprise for Sunday evening viewers who could see 'Sabine Christiansen' at 8:15pm." Malte Betz and Hans Wilhelm von Saure add that "Now she talks on *Tatort*" (*Bild am Sonntag*, December 21, 2003). They stress Christiansen's rise to fame "from stewardess to Germany's most successful talk show host and now film star." *Süddeutsche Zeitung* argues that the ARD is "baiting the viewer with audience flow" (December 22, 2003).

Der Tagesspiegel goes on to argue that Christiansen's guest stint creates "[a] nice alienation effect, to experience the weekly talk-punching as a fictional crime show." The same article also suggests reading the episode like a roman à clef: "A bit of Spreegate! Dieter Wedel! Rise and Fall!" "Similarities with real people are not completely accidental: Westerwelle, Friedman, Christiansen, who is supposed to be who?" This assessment continues in Thorsten Wahl's "Dead guys don't jump" (*Berliner Zeitung*, January 3, 2004), who relates the episode's plot revolving around politicians' corruption and personal life scandals to the Ronald Schill affair in Hamburg. The right-wing leader of the so-called Party for a Rule of Law Offensive or Schill Party was accused of cocaine use in 2003. He was removed from the Hamburg senate after threatening Mayor Ole von Beust (Christian Democrat) with outing him as homosexual (August 19, 2003). Viewers of the show also read the episode in the context of prominent Free Democrat politician Jürgen Möllemann's suspicious June 5, 2003, sky diving death: "This *Tatort* came shortly after the affair and suicide of Möllemann. Government propaganda is totally transparent."[31] Twenty-two minutes before his death, his parliamentary immunity was dissolved, a decision that would have allowed an investigation into his alleged illegal arms deals and tax fraud.[32]

Post-1989 Reorientation

The title sequence of the episode pauses on individual shots of the lead investigators in their respective cars before ending on a grainy extreme

---

[30] According to *Der Tagesspiegel*, Christiansen received "9 million Euro for production of her weekly political talk show" during the height of her fame (January 4, 2004). See also Tanja Thomas, *Deutschstunden: Zur Konstruktion nationaler Identität im Fernsehtalk* (Frankfurt: Campus, 2003), 377.
[31] YouTube viewer comment at https://www.youtube.com/watch?v=Afs67OkOKxI (June 29, 2020).
[32] BBC News from June 6, 2003, http://news.bbc.co.uk/2/hi/europe/2970066.stm (accessed June 29, 2020).

close-up of Christiansen's eyes, here taking over for the famous *Tatort* title sequence's eyes. Ritter's frame pauses in front of the *Volksbühne*, Stark's in front of *Kino International*. Both of these legendary cultural establishments are located at crucial locations in the former East Berlin, the former on Rosa Luxemburg Platz, the latter on Karl-Marx Allee. On its homepage, the *Volksbühne* proudly announces that true to its motto "Die Kunst dem Volke" (art for the people) its construction was financed solely by donations from members of the *Verein Freie Volksbühne* (Association for a Free People's Theatre). Throughout its history, the Volksbühne has been shaped by directors, authors, and artists who constantly challenged the boundaries of classical spoken theater—names like Max Reinhardt, Erwin Piscator, Benno Besson, Heiner Müller, Frank Castorf, Christoph Schlingensief are intrinsic to the theater.[33] *Kino International* was built to premiere DEFA studio films from 1963 through 1989 and has functioned as one of the main locations of the Berlinale since 1989.

On the one side, there is the revolutionary theater built by and for the proletariat in 1914 "challenging boundaries" of representation throughout its history. Under Frank Castorf's extended leadership (1992–2017), it became a world-renowned stage for its avant-garde experimental productions. On the other side is a cinema built along the boulevard used for frequent military parades that occasionally showed socially critical films until the censorship purge of 1965, the year of the shelved *Keller—* or *Kaninchenfilme* (basement or rabbit films), named after Kurt Maetzig's banned film *Das Kaninchen bin ich* (The rabbit/guinea pig is me).[34] Until 1990, the cinema functioned mostly as an exhibition outlet for state-approved content and image control.

Why choose these two backgrounds for an episode focused on the hypermediation of the Berlin Republic? The frozen shots in front of the two establishments prime domestic viewers to reflect on the interrelationship between arts and politics, representation and power. The two scenes stand as frozen counterpoints along a continuum of revolutionary, independent, subsidized, and state-controlled media forms. With tongue in cheek, the two cultural tastemakers situate *Tatort* in their midst and simultaneously reflect *Tatort*'s long history of seesawing between contained social-critical message plots and oppositional cinematic strategies, between staid and revolutionary aesthetics. Yet the two pauses in a mind-numbingly fast-cut prelude also mark *Tatort* as a reliable *Ruhepol* (rest stop) amid the rapidly changing cityscape, cultural mediascape, and sociopolitical climate.

---

[33]Volksbühne Berlin, https://www.volksbuehne.berlin/en/haus/529/about (accessed July 6, 2020).
[34]Sebastian Heiduschke, "Film Censorship, the East German *Nouvelle Vague*, and the 'Rabbit Films': *Das Kaninchen bin ich* (*The Rabbit Is Me*, Kurt Maetzig, 1965)," in *East German Cinema* (New York: Palgrave, 2013), 77–83.

Ritter and Stark both emerge from the East to head West. This is a significant optics when compared to the large-scale migration to culturally and materially privileged sites in West Berlin on October 9, 1989. "We just want to see it for ourselves." That statement was common from interviewed East Berliners flocking across the suddenly open border. Their spectatorial migration was recorded and disseminated widely on television, radio, and film. The subsequent migration in the other direction—not just to see but to stay—did not garner such attention, but that does not mean that it didn't happen. In 2004, the two frozen tableaus also acknowledge the Berlin Republic's Eastern real estate boom and subsequent replacement of West Berlin's central corridor from Ku'damm and Kaufhaus des Westens in favor of Weimar era and East Berlin's city center, with its mix of dilapidated chic and frontier spirit.[35] Everyone who thought of themselves as young, hip, and urban flocked to cheaper or newly restored housing stock in the former East. In the process, previous student hangouts in Charlottenburg or even Kreuzberg seemed boringly petit bourgeois by comparison. When Ritter is seen driving to a West Berlin crime scene in Moabit from Rosa Luxemburg Platz while Stark, whose actor is German-Croat, joins him there from Karl Marx Allee, their transit stops register the new reality and serve up the historical memory of fifteen years ago with irony, especially when they pull up their cars to the scene of the crime at the exact same time. Much has changed in unified Berlin, but punctuality of German civil servants is still a virtue.

Symphony in Blue and Tan—Talk on *Tatort*

The blue and tan leitmotif dominates the episode's mise-en-scène and connects the talk show to *Tatort* in critical media-reflexive ways. Understanding the surface layer of costume choices will help to draw connections on the structural level later. Blue and tan tones signal clean and conservative. For a host, who not only broke with the gendered history of the genre in a male-dominated network but also succeeded in the ranking wars between networks, cable, and internet offerings, the combination allows Christiansen to radiate nonthreatening femininity and competence.[36] As her guest in the *Tatort* segment, Körner's colors match hers. In the majority of scenes, he

---

[35]Bundeszentrale für politische Bildung: "Abschied von West-Berlin," March 4, 2010, https://www.bpb.de/apuz/32893/abschied-von-west-berlin (accessed July 6, 2020).
[36]To this day, daytime talk show hosts tend to be women or male and female co-anchors, while solo political evening talk shows are predominantly hosted by white men. Sabine Christiansen's success in a male-dominated genre is extraordinary, especially when considering how her show culturally intersected with and branded the newly reminted capital, Berlin, and how it accompanied and negotiated the cable/satellite to digital decade between 1998 and 2007.

is seen wearing a long tan wool coat. While his dominantly blue shirts and ties underneath slightly change, this wardrobe staple never does. He even wears the coat in indoor scenes. Since the German title of the episode literally translates to "An Honest Skin," the color of this full body wrap is significant. Körner's caramel coat and Christiansen's suit as well as their hair colors are not brown or black but match the race-based skin-tone imaginary of Germanness—blonde and tan. That Körner's coat is not white announces that there is no such thing as innocence in politics. In an indoor scene with his girlfriend Judith, where his media-fueled paranoia is threatening to get the better of him, the coat functions as a crutch to hang on to his integrity, when she spits out: "Now you are close to what you feared you might become." Körner is manufactured to be Sabine Christiansen's tan and blonde equal, a unicorn among the corrupt politicians, just as she is the trusted navigator in a sea of superimposed, replaceable shady blue figures. He might be a compromise-ready pragmatist, but he has not shed his ethics and idealism completely. That stance would be in keeping with the era of great coalitions between left (SPD) and center right (CDU) under Schröder and in the upcoming Merkel years. Costume choices guide viewers to an answer about the "honest man" enigma long before the crime is solved.

Connie Siegel, the victim's blond sister, is another character whose wardrobe is intentionally color-coded. We don't get to see much of her until the middle of the episode. She sits on bar stools on the sidelines, but as her character becomes more central to the storyline, and Stark and Ritter take an interest in her, so do we. A dedicated crime drama viewer knows by her peripheral existence in the detectives' blind spot that she must have played a role in the murder. Absent from where she is supposed to be, when someone is actively looking for her, she pops up when least expected. At several points in the episode, her sudden and unmotivated presence or absence seemingly delays the plot progress. When she discovers Nato's drugs, she throws the baggies out of the window and jumps out after them. Stark catches up to her as she tosses the drugs into the *Landwehrkanal*. When confronted, she claims Nato is innocent: "He might deal drugs but he didn't have anything to do with Sammy."

During these outdoor scenes, Connie always wears a mid-length leatherette coat with tan and blue patchwork squares. The colors are faded, but the checkerboard pattern is distinctive and intimately relates to Sabine Christiansen's and Körner's signature color-palette. Connie's coat advertises that its wearer has an ambiguous ethical compass that has her waver between a perpetual blue state of mourning over her older and younger brothers' deaths, her own guilt, and her loyalty to a boyfriend with the telling name Nato. In televisual terms, her dis/appearances tear at the narrative continuity. Whenever she interrupts linear progression, she forces Stark and Ritter on detours that stitch segments together that seem to be superfluous or not to belong together. Her femme fatale motives are as checkered as her coat, and its pastiche pattern maps onto the aesthetics of the opening montage of the talk show and this episode, compelling viewers and detectives to connect the multiply mediated layers of this crime. Connie's case makes clear that the blue and tan notes are not limited to ethnicity, costume, or styling but extend to narration. They color the hyper-medial exchange between fictional crime show and political talk show. How does this *Tatort* utilize the genre-specific aesthetic aspects of the talk show to develop its representation of and critical commentary on the Berlin Republic? And what effect does the media reflexivity and genre hybridity have on the format of the crime drama itself?

Network talk shows in the United States and Germany are embedded into the daily or weekly TV lineup and viewers' routines. The format is designed to pluck people, issues, and curiosities from the flow of time and space, and add them to the segmented flow of the broadcast to bring viewers who are immersed in their own flow of work/life schedules to integrate them into theirs. Moving between expository, self-reflexive, and participatory reality modes, the talk genre takes advantage of the myth of live television, even when it is prerecorded in front of a live studio audience. This allows viewers to feel directly addressed by the host, who often breaks the fourth wall and to identify with historical actors that appear in their stead. As Jane Feuer argues in "The Concept of Live Television" (1983), ideological and technological concepts and forms of liveness are "exploited in order to overcome the contradiction between flow and fragmentation in television practice."[37] Inserted into the televisual flow of parallel and consecutive programming, life or prerecorded guest interviews are contained in often rigidly formatted segments strung together by aesthetically repetitive expository and transitional shots utilizing brand-identifying sound and image cues.

This episode features two-in-one title sequences and reverses the flow of *Sabine Christiansen*'s and *Tatort*'s traditional windowing. Both sequences stay within a blue and tan color scheme that is combined with fast-paced graphic and rhythmic editing. The original *Christiansen* opening sequence features a faded blue side-scrolling filmstrip background in which one blue-shaded politician and celebrity is replaced with the next. The right to left scrolling headshots of her famous guests is repeatedly punctuated by Christiansen's face and upper body in tan colors, topped by her trademark blond bob. When her image is reinserted after three to four guests, her posture is slightly turned sideways to signal her attentiveness to both her individual guest-segments *and* the continuation of the flow. The opening sequence ends with a glowing beige Reichstag with a blueish cupola.

---

[37]Jane Feuer, "The Concept of Live Television: Ontology as Ideology," in *Regarding Television: Critical Approaches*, ed. E. Ann Kaplan (Los Angeles: The American Film Institute, 1983), 14.

The color scheme suggest that all politicians are the same, whether German (Angela Merkel) or American (Bill Clinton), man or woman, Black or white, straight (Joschka Fischer) or gay (Klaus Wowereit), liberal (Claudia Roth) or conservative (Ursula von der Leyen). Only the host, Sabine Christiansen, stands out, seemingly infused with an inner light that she graciously imparts on some of her guests, as its cone briefly extends to their silhouettes only to be displaced by the next guest. Her talk show, branded with her own name, was broadcast from the blue-tone Globe Studio close to the *Gedächtniskirche* ruin. The show made a bigger than usual impact during a crucial phase in the new capital and the country, especially when considering that Angela Merkel (CDU) would assume the chancellorship in 2005, the first woman to take that office since the inception of the Federal Republic in 1949 and the first East German since unification in 1989. Indeed, at the end of the opening sequence, when Christiansen's tan image dissolves into an equally tan light-infused montage of the Quadriga atop the Brandenburg Gate followed by the Reichstag, it becomes clear that Christiansen's image is meant to rank next to these multiply mediated yet steadfast monuments of Berlin's past and present.

The *Christiansen* introductory sequence reshot for this *Tatort* proceeds along a mixture of Walter Ruttmann's city symphony, *Christiansen*, and *NYPD Blue* (ABC, 1993–2005) aesthetics: short takes, handheld camera, low/high-angle contrasts, quick zooms, and grainy combinations of everyday locations (high-rise complex, Istanbul Grill, S-Bahn, cars at intersections) with intentionally unphotogenic shots of iconic buildings (Reichstag and Brandenburg Gate appear as silhouettes on the edges of the screen), mixed together with production studio images (sound mix, multi-camera selection screens, news, and sports segments). A jazzy score with a strong brass section accompanies *Christiansen*'s original opening segment and this *Tatort*'s rapid rhythmic editing.

This *Tatort* of the new millennium mimics its own production by starting in the network studio and ending on television. In a Moebius twist, the episode's bookend beginning and ending scenes are both part of the opening sequence. The first is a studio camera's image recording live television, the final one is the fictional show's wrap-up dialogue filmed in the Istanbul Grill, both shots are part of the title montage. The episode opens with a television-on-television shot of a small studio camera screen that captures a young tan-hued Körner on what is later revealed to be the *Christiansen* set in the Globe Studio on Breitscheidplatz. In a sentence fragment, he states that "die Vereinzelungen nehmen zu" (atomization is increasing). This is as much an argument about social alienation in the hyper-real internet era as it is a description of the aesthetic choices portraying a geographically reunited yet increasingly sociopolitically and economically fragmented cityscape. Körner, the lead character, is here literally and figuratively constructed by a multiply mediated process—by a television studio camera on a television talk show in a crime drama on television. As much as politicians are constructed as media-personalities in this process, Nick Couldry argues that "media rituals, such as the talk-show form, are formal means of making media power seem natural."[38] What he means by this is that the camera constructs a "ritual boundary" between ordinary life and media as a "rite of institution (Bourdieu 1991)."[39] The talk show guest confirms this boundary when seeking it as a means to gain symbolic capital. The network hosting a fictional character on its evening talk show and inserting the talk show into its crime drama bear a similar result. At this point in the early convergence era, the network's pastiche of the two genres makes that ritual boundary visible in the very attempt to harness its media power. And it allows the network to recast the crime drama as ordinary life in the process.

Inserting Körner's and the Istanbul Grill's images in the opening flow amid other vetted indexical images attaches their indexicality to the fictional scenes later in the episode. The process repeats the inversion of the flow from the broader evening lineup—*Talk* usually follows *Tatort*—in its inner episode segmentation—a scene from *Tatort* appears in the *Christiansen* segment, which introduces us to *Tatort*. This inverted flow inserts *Tatort* into Berlin's urban life and infrastructure, reconnects it to its regional and temporal context, and adapts the crime drama for a hypermediated decade with the help of the genre characteristics of the talk show.

Watching Television in the Istanbul Grill

The Istanbul Grill's bright yellow neon sign stands out in the tan and blue opening montage. The choice to highlight a restaurant with that name intentionally refers to Berlin as the city with the most Turkish residents outside of Istanbul. To *Tatort* fans, the Grill is recognizable as the local dive Stark and Ritter frequent when they have a hankering for a Döner Kebab. The Grill's featured dated television set also suggests its clientele's hankering for the media staple *Tatort*, emphasizing the ARD's semi-successful campaign to reach a shifting demographics. The detectives are regulars at this joint, alone or together, and usually self-confidently occupy the middle table. Ritter must be at least six and a half feet tall; Stark is a foot shorter. Their blocking in the middle, with other customers usually occupying the periphery, has to be seen as an attempt to reassure viewers that Germans feel at home and are welcome in diverse multicultural settings. Indulging in television's proclivity for polysemy, the social blocking also purposely inverts the right-

---

[38]Nick Couldry, *Media Rituals: A Critical Approach* (New York: Routledge, 2003), 120.
[39]Ibid.

wing rhetoric of a "Muslim invasion" because it is Ritter who invades every room through his sheer size.

That the Istanbul Grill is used as a location four times in this episode alone also seeks to normalize the existence of Turkish culture within the German capital and within its flagship crime drama, albeit in the stereotypical shorthand of reducing a culture to its cuisine. Revising detective Bülow's center-right bourgeois proclivity for fancy restaurants, Ritter and Stark have a foible for working-class staples. And thus, the Istanbul Grill serves as a symbolic meeting ground of the workforce across ethnicities and professional niches, where German state authority and people of color co-define the public sphere, eating together, making and watching television together. As a public network, the ARD takes its role in maintaining and managing the changes of and in the German public sphere very seriously. Following Habermas and Bollhöfer, the Istanbul Grill scenes make explicit that *Tatort* is intent on representing and performing the "mediated positioning of cultural practices."[40]

And even if the quick opening montage shot of the Grill just serves to trigger an unconscious familiarity in casual viewers, when its neon sign reappears in the episode, the insertion of the Grill into the rapid flow of seemingly random cityscape images and everyday situations into this *Tatort*'s version of Christiansen's opening montage is self-referential. Using a crane, the quick shots look down on the Grill from above and quickly zoom in on its window façade. In every scene of the episode, the camera approaches the Istanbul Grill in exactly the same way. Despite the likely economically driven decision to milk the expensive shot for all it is worth, the pattern of this cinematographic and editing approach also creates additional meaning.

The second scene featuring the Grill cuts to inside, where we watch Ritter gobbling down a quick bite. The daily news running on a small television set on a corner shelf features an image of the suspected victim Stark identified from the surveillance camera near the crime scene. But viewers and Ritter can only see the image because the set is on mute. As a child of the 1960s, Ritter was socialized with manual set-controls. In his urge to turn the volume up, his body acts before he can think. Only when he cannot find knobs on the TV set does he remember to look for a remote. By the time he locates it, the newscast has solved the dilemma for him with the use of close-caption: Sammy Siegler. This short and simple scene exposes not only how television as apparatus has constructed viewers' body memories and *habitus* but also how the successive manual knob-remote control-mouse click-touchpad navigation changes have resulted in an increasingly fast adaptation rhythm for viewers. Ritter's hunt for the controlling device and the need for a chair to reach the set (remembering that he is very tall) make him appear old, out

---

[40] This is the title of Björn Bollhöfer's important book. Ibid.

of sync with technology and the intensifying news cycle. Who or what is in control, this is the question the scene raises, as Ritter mounts the chair like a trained seal.

Furthermore, this self-reflexive scene goes against all rules for maximum televisuality: a tiny set, no diegetic dialogue, and no sound from the diegetic television image. But because television identifies the victim for Ritter and the viewer, the television apparatus and the viewer also become parallel and competing investigative bodies. Cable and internet news identify the victim for us, not the police. Ritter is learning critical case information from television as he is eating. We watch the detectives watching. And Ritter models for us how television can turn a casual into a dedicated viewer. During this scene, synchronous viewers will have to lean in to read the tiny image, exasperated at Ritter. 2004 middle-class German viewers who are getting accustomed to ever larger television screens with the ability to play back in HDTV (2003) might feel superior to Ritter but they have to crane their necks just the same.[41] Ironically, his bumbling delay produces a mise en abyme that is mimicking and intensifying our very viewing experience. While lack of image or sound quality and lag is becoming increasingly unacceptable in an age of instantaneous access to high-definition information, it is both effectively used and affective here. The scene performs how television utilizes redundancy and any means at its disposal (text, image, and audio) to reach the audience. What used to lack a clear and vivid televisual aesthetics is regaining it in an era of high definition, even if only by contrast. Ritter's fumbling to turn on the sound transports viewers into a time-shifted mediascape. As we watch *Tatort* asynchronously on DVD or a year later on YouTube (2005), we can pause and rewind the scene to lip read if need be. This scene is training us to adapt our viewing practices from deducing or merely guessing who the murderer is (a crime drama fan practice since the genre's inception) to become interactive, collaborative, and competitive partners in the investigative decoding process of televised images from and reinscribed into the emergent digital mediascape.

A different use of intentionally low production value that gains televisual appeal as a result is the scene in which Stark catches up with his colleague withdrawing money at an ATM around the corner from the crime scene. After having surveilled the crime scene without a corpse in sight, we get a point-of-view shot at the two men from the grainy black-and-white surveillance camera just as Stark states the obvious, "there must be a surveillance camera in there." And indeed, at the police station, he reviews the video footage from the ATM camera and finds a man that fits the witnesses' descriptions

---

[41] "Europe's First HDTV Channel Completes Trial Broadcast," *TV Technology*, September 22, 2003, https://www.tvtechnology.com/news/europes-first-hdtv-channel-completes-trial-broadcast (accessed July 14, 2020).

withdrawing money around the time of the crime. The body is located alive on video before the coroner has a chance to autopsy it. This reverses the temporal flow and the drama's usual internal segmentation pattern. As viewers and investigators rely on mediated images to identify and find the body, the wired city becomes the powered apparatus that controls the look and constitutes the subject of the look.

In the third scene at the Grill, Stark and Ritter discuss politicians, catching a glimpse of Paulsen on the television news. Ritter exclaims: "Paulsen is a pig! How does someone manage to stay in power that long?" Stark cannot stop thinking about Connie and her questionable choice of Nato as boyfriend. Ritter adds, as they leave the Grill: "Good Times: no wives, lots of overtime, and a bad paycheck." Immediately after he ends, the medium close-up switches to the disembodied high-angle camera which pulls back and zooms in on the Berliner *Fernsehturm* (TV tower). This time the shot is revealed to be part of the title sequence of a morning talk show with the feature "Ist Körner eine ehrliche Haut?" (Is Körner an honest skin/man?). In quick succession, snippets of street interviews with pedestrians show a range of different opinions. The television-in-television sequence ends with a man stating: "Because he became a politician, he can't be honest." A voice-over transitions with "Now, we head over to the *Bundestag*, where there are more of those."[42]

The Grill scene, where Ritter and Stark offer their civilian opinions about their prime suspect, is edited together with a street-interview scene of civilians giving their opinions, itself embedded in a morning talk show segment. I read this interlaced segmentation as the show advocating for its media-savvy precognition. The scripted scene already possesses the slice of life aesthetics that the street-interview scene offers. And the pull-away shot to the TV tower seems to suggest that *Tatort*'s detectives are already part of the street wisdom the morning talk show thrives on. The redundancy of these concatenated scenes from the two different television genres is another example of inverted flow to accentuate how the crime drama simulcasts its representation of regional and historical reality. At the end of the episode, we again see Ritter and Stark's silhouettes behind the Grill's window before we join them around the table for the classic *Tatort* wrap-up. The insertion of the Istanbul Grill into the talk show's opening sequence accomplishes a decontextualization that facilitates a reinsertion of the scripted *Tatort* narrative into the historical Real. The same camera move locates the two detectives in the Grill at the end and releases them into the urban flow as it releases the viewers into theirs. Media power naturalized.

---

[42]The title and transition line reveal that race-based thought patterns are deeply ingrained in the German language.

5

Tatort Dresden and Leipzig (NDR/MDR)

Bruno Ehrlicher (Peter Sodann) and Kain (Bernd Michael Lade) were the first post-1989 investigative team in Dresden (in the state of Sachsen). From 1992 until 2007 they contributed forty-four episodes to the franchise and left a lasting legacy in documenting a tumultuous period of *Zeitgeschichte* through on-location videography capturing the rapid de- and reconstruction of Dresden immediately after unification.[1] For fifteen years, writers and actors explored the sociopolitical and economic fissures that opened in the aftermath of the fall of the wall. With regularity, these *Tatort* episodes approached immediate and long-term effects of life under and after the collapse of the GDR regime with a modicum of realism. Network television delivered during a decade of cinematic delay due to major restructuring of DEFA film production and political reckoning within the creative pool. A rerelease of banned DEFA films in late 1989 (e.g., *Spur der Steine* from 1966) and the *Wende*-comedy hit *Go Trabi Go* (dir. Peter Timm, 1991) were followed *a decade later* by *Sonnenallee* (dir. Leander Haußmann, 1999), the critically acclaimed *Good Bye, Lenin!* (dir. Wolfgang Becker, 2003) and *The Lives of Others* (dir. Florian Henckel von Donnersmarck, 2007). Unlike these delayed filmic representations, the three to four yearly episodes of the Dresden *Tatort* ensured both a stable focus on the region and a diachronic representation of process and change. The popularity of the more recent television projects *Weissensee* (ARD, 2010–) and the

---

[1] The forty-four episodes place Ehrlicher and Kain in first position followed by the popular Stoever and Brockmöller team from Hamburg with forty-one episodes. For comparison, Schimanski and Thanner contributed only twenty-nine episodes from Duisburg. "Die ehemaligen Kommissare," *daserste.de*, https://www.daserste.de/unterhaltung/krimi/tatort/kommissare/kommissare-ausser-dienst-100.html (accessed August 20, 2020).

coproduced international hit *Deutschland '83* and its sequels *Deutschland '86* and *'89* (RTL/Sundance TV, 2015–21) speak to the thirst for filling that audiovisual gap in the form of the extended story arcs of soap opera and melodrama.

A new team, Karin Gorniak (Karin Hanczewski) and Peter Michael Schnabel (Martin Brambach), began regional coverage of Dresden in 2016. They were joined by Henni Sieland (Alwara Höfels) until 2018, followed by Leonie Winkler (Cornelia Gröschel) in 2019. When *Tatort* productions resume after the Covid-19 pandemic, Dresden is slated to be represented by a team of three women, a first in *Tatort* history (the third played by Jella Haase).[2] Between 2000 and 2016, the MDR shifted its focus to Leipzig and began establishing new regional coverage in the picturesque towns of Erfurt and Weimar (both in the state of Thüringen). At the time of writing, only the Dresden and Weimar teams were operational. Some cultural and network-based reasons for these regional shifts will become clearer in the following city section and in the individual episode analyses.

Dresden is the capital of Saxony. Its center hugs the river Elbe on the easternmost border of Germany with Poland and the Czech Republic. In the United States, the city is known predominantly for the February 1945 firebombing by American and British air forces. The scale of the bombing was controversial, especially when it became apparent that women and children suffered disproportionally. Images of the skeletal remains of the city core and Kurt Vonnegut's representation of "the necropolis of Dresden" in his novel *Slaughterhouse-Five* (1969) outlasted many a resident's or tourist's attempt to tell a different story about the city and the region.[3] Subsequently, the city's unwavering and costly intent to rebuild the *Frauenkirche* ruin and renovate most historic center city buildings made an impact abroad. Due to the symbolic importance of postwar and post-1989 reconstruction, national and international acknowledgment was pivotal for the city's sense of healing and self-understanding. For this reason, many Dresden citizens still smart from the UNESCO's removal of the city as a world-heritage site due to the construction of the modern *Waldschlösschenbrücke* across the Elbe.

After 1989 Dresden became Germany's Silicon Valley with several global tech companies making it their chip-production and semiconductor site. Tourists, however, are steered toward the *Semperoper*, the art museums in and outside of the *Zwinger* palace, including the *Grüne Gewölbe*, the largest

---

[2] "Neuer Sachsen-*Tatort*: Drei Engel für Dresden," *daserste.de*, https://www.daserste.de/unterhaltung/krimi/tatort/specials/neuer-sachsen-tatort-drei-engel-fuer-dresden-100.html (accessed August 20, 2020).

[3] This is how James Parker refers to Vonnegut's Dresden in his article "The Meaning of *Slaughterhouse-Five*: 50 Years Later," *The Atlantic*, March 31, 2019, https://www.theatlantic.com/entertainment/archive/2019/03/why-slaughterhouse-five-resonates-50-years-later/586180/ (accessed September 20, 2020).

exhibit of ostentatious historic household objects of the aristocracy and the wealthy in Europe. The guides on the frequently docking river cruise ships generally avoid pointing out the high-rise concrete slab apartment complexes built for industrial workers on the city's outskirts (e.g., in Gorbitz) during the GDR, although some of them have now been placed under protection themselves.

Whether it is the city's near-total destruction and subsequent collective pride in the rebuilding efforts, its proximity to Eastern Europe with the result of being a first encounter and landing spot for Eastern and Southern European migrants, a rapid de- and re-industrialization process that left many residents without the skills or too old to acquire them unemployed, or a combination of all of the above, Dresden is also the birth place and hotbed of the Pegida (Patriotic Europeans against the Islamization of the West) movement. The party was founded by Lutz Bachmann in Dresden in 2014. As an intentional historical commentary on the Monday demonstrations that contributed to the eventual fall of the wall, he orchestrated weekly Monday demonstrations to protest Germany's immigration policies, many of the slogans directly directed against Muslim migrants. At the height of its populist message in 2015, up to 25,000 Pegida supporters marched through Dresden any given Monday. In 2016 Bachmann founded the *Freiheitlich Direktdemokratische Volkspartei* (Liberal Direct Democratic People's Party or FDDV). Together with the *Alternative für Deutschland* (AFD), they make up a significant portion of the political spectrum on the German right and have been successful in entering legitimate political representation in several states and the federal government.[4]

Radebeul, a suburb of Dresden, is the birthplace of global bestseller author Karl May (1842–1912), whose house, the Villa Shatterhand, named after his Christian German protagonist, functions as the Karl May Museum. His fictional exploration tales of the US frontier, the Middle East, and Latin America have sold over 200 million copies worldwide. The museum houses May's own collection as well as more recently curated anthropological artifacts of Native American tribes. For locals and out-of-towners, but especially school classes before and after the fall of the wall, the museum and its event center were and remain a regular destination.[5] The influence of Karl May's vast generation-spanning readership in East and West Germany in combination with Harald Reinl's 1960s film adaptations of his *Winnetou* novels, the East German *Indianerfilme* based on James Fenimore Cooper's

---

[4]In 2020, the AFD held 91 seats of 709 in the *Bundestag* parliament. For comparison, the Green Party, which has been a registered part of German politics since 1980, held only 67, https://www.bundestag.de/en/parliament/groups#url=L2VuL3BhcmxpYW1lbnQvZ3JvdXBzL2d yb3Vwcy1kaXN0cmlidXRpb24tMTk3NjQ0&mod=mod487054 (accessed August 11, 2020).
[5]Karl May Museum website, https://www.karl-may-museum.de/en/collections/karl-may/biography-works/ (accessed August 10, 2020).

(1789–1851) novels, and the Italo-Westerns of the 1970s should not be underestimated for research into German media-reception patterns along with national and regional identity formation.

Leipzig, the most populous city in the state of Saxony, is situated halfway between Dresden and the former border of West Germany. *Messestadt* Leipzig (trade fair city), whose importance as a center for European trade goes back to the Holy Roman Empire, and is also known for its deep connection to learning, music, the arts, and print publishing. During the GDR, Leipzig functioned as the headquarters of the Stasi (*Staatsicherheitsdienst*). The *Runde Ecke* (Round Corner) in center city is now a museum depicting the regime's surveillance apparatus, the scope of its unofficial informant network, and the history of incarceration and torture of the country's citizens. The museum memorializes the victims of Stasi repression and violence. Between the 1960s and 1989, the suburbs of Leipzig saw the development of heavy industry that not only caused severe pollution but also contributed to urban flight after unification, since a majority of the industrial sectors were neither sustainable nor competitive with West German technology.

In the summer of 1989, the city became the center of the opposition movement, beginning with peace, environment, and human rights groups gathering for service in the *Nikolaikirche*. On Monday, September 4, about a thousand attendees spilled into the streets calling for freedom of movement and human rights: "Stasi raus!" (Out with the Stasi) and "Wir sind das Volk!" (We are the people). These calls resulted in rapidly growing weekly demonstrations on Mondays that took root in other cities and put enough pressure on the regime to lead to the resignation of SED (Socialist Unity Party) general secretary Erich Honecker on October 18. Since 2000, as its current nickname *Hypzig* attests, an extensive urban renewal project has reversed the drain and has resulted in Leipzig becoming Germany's fastest growing as well as one of its youngest, most livable cities.

"Taxi nach Leipzig" ("Taxi to Leipzig," dir. Peter-Schulze Rohr; NDR, November 29, 1970)

Tagesschau Year-End Synopsis

The year 1970 was the year of West German chancellor Willy Brandt's *Ostpolitik*. In short, through several diplomatic missions and signed treaties, the chancellor assured Eastern Bloc neighbors that West Germany accepted the new postwar borders of the Oder-Neisse line, an admission of the new geopolitical map that strove to normalize relationships strained by the lingering Cold War but also recognized the existence of the GDR as a coequal neighboring country. Brandt's *Ostpolitik* included two state visits with his East German counterpart Willy Stoph, one in Erfurt in March and one in Kassel in May. While the West German conservative parties voiced their vehement opposition, accusing Brandt of selling out Germany's right to self-determination, East German citizens' enthusiasm for his diplomatic efforts could barely be contained by the *Volkspolizei* when he stuck his head out of the Erfurt hotel window in greeting. The domestic right-wing backlash against the intimated "abandonment of reunification" led to street battles around the state visits, wherever conservative demonstrators met anti-Vietnam, anti-establishment student demonstrations in West Germany.

On August 12, Chancellor Willy Brandt and Foreign Minister Walter Scheel signed the Treaty of Moscow. On December 7, a week after the first *Tatort*, Chancellor Willy Brandt signed the Warsaw Treaty, acknowledging and accepting the new Polish borders. In Warsaw, the German chancellor unexpectedly kneeled at the memorial for the victims of the Warsaw Ghetto Uprising signaling West Germany's acceptance of responsibility for the atrocities of the Third Reich and the Holocaust.

Willy Brandt, who fled to Sweden and Norway to escape the Nazis, was governing mayor of West Berlin from 1957 to 1966 and stood by John F. Kennedy's side during the historic 1963 "Ich bin ein Berliner" speech. Throughout the year of 1970, in televised segments featuring Brandt attending events, at conference tables in Bonn, Moscow, and Warsaw, *Tagesschau* viewers heard his trademark rolling "r's" intonated in his gravelly accented smoker's voice. He appeared at turns serious and laid-back, a lit cigarette in his hand in many shots. But most of all, he exuded competence, confidence, and a deep commitment to direct diplomacy. In retrospect, the casting of Walter Richter as *Tatort*'s first detective appears modeled after Willy Brandt, in posture, speech, and behavior. Following in Willy Brandt's footsteps, inspector Paul Trimmel inaugurated the longest-running West German crime drama by going on a diplomatic mission to the East, demonstrating that mutual respect and collaboration were not the same as abandonment of reunification or self-determination.

Critical and Viewer Engagement

Being the first to launch half a century of subsequent *Tatort* episodes, *Taxi nach Leipzig* has received a good amount of critical and viewer attention, especially around the crime drama's anniversaries. While these later write-ups are instructive for the sociopolitical associations drawn between the 1970 episode and their own contexts, the first reactions from 1970 give a sense of the domestic network's competition with US and UK imports but also ZDF's lineup of prime-time entertainment. It is fair to say that *Tatort*, as the first coordinated regionally produced and nationally exhibited series, initiated a change in the crime drama format that, in turn, led the way to current domestic and trans-regional, transnational production and reception practices. This section will highlight critical engagement around the series premiere in 1970 and its twenty-year anniversary in 1990, a year after the fall of the wall. Because the series' first episode deals with a case that crosses the inner-German border, reactions to the rebroadcast will be especially illuminating for the continuity of *Tatort*'s regional concept.

Before the premiere in 1970, Gert Kistenmacher addresses medium specificity and network strategies to increase ratings for domestic fare on Sundays—"Sunday was dead, long live Sunday"—stressing the new regional concept of the show: "Every TV station has its own detective" (*Süddeutsche Zeitung*, October 16, 1970). To ensure the execution of Gunther Witte's explicit demand for *Tatort* scripts to reach for the greatest possible proximity to domestic historical reality, the ARD hired the long-term legal journalist Friedhelm Werremeier for the first of many *Tatort* scripts.[6] And due to the limited casting pool in the 1970s, the ARD set up a clearing house to "avoid having the detective of one region play the murderer in another" (*WAZ*, December 4, 1970). The multi-prong strategy paid off. Almost 23.4 million viewers watched the ARD premiere and more than 60 percent of viewers tuned into subsequent *Tatorts* on Sunday evenings.[7]

While *Neue Revue* reasons that viewers "are delighted with German crime-reality" "after the surplus of foreign crime shows" on television, Ingo Mummert of *Konkret* disagrees and believes that a "depressing reality creates the willingness to submit to the illusion of a logical and manageable world." Mummert draws on *Taxi nach Leipzig* to stress that the viewer "knows" that the "friendship between a Hamburger detective and a high functionary of the Stasi [state security service] in the GDR, who lends him an illegal hand—after 25 years of separation—is (. . .) unrealistic." He sees the "key to success of the *Tatort* series" in the show's ability to make not Los Angeles but "the German city of the present a medium of that desired illusion" (February 25, 1971). The *Frankfurter Rundschau*, however, finds "the basic idea to include the GDR" in the episode plot "praiseworthy" while somewhat forced and stereotypically executed (December 1, 1970).

Günther Kriewitz of the *Stuttgarter Zeitung* sees its "hope for closeness to everyday life" dashed, even though the "federalist tendencies [of the series concept] had the potential to deliver an image of police work with a higher degree of realism." He bemoans the "illegal Wild West manners" of Trimmel's rogue investigation within GDR borders, a character profile "modeled after

---

[6] "Überwiegend Trimmels: Interview mit dem Fernsehautor Friedhelm Werremeier," *Funkkorrespondenz* 42 (October 22, 1999).

[7] Ingo Mummert, "Der deutsche Sonntagskrimi: Warum die neue Fernsehserie 'Tatort' so erfolgreich ist," *Konkret*, February 25, 1971. Among the non-news programs, *Tatort* landed in second place nationally behind the second installment of a ZDF crime mini-series: "Die Erfolgs-Sendungen vom 28. Nov. bis 4. Dez," *Funkuhr* telemeter, December 19, 1970.

an American P.I." (December 1, 1970). Compared to the reigning German inspector of ZDF's *Der Kommissar*, played by Erik Ode, Richter's Trimmel comes across as a buddy cop with "farmer-smarts and a soothing fatherly thick-headedness" (*Lübecker Nachrichten*, December 1, 1970). One author thus views the ARD's *Tatort* concept as a domestic adaptation of the US crime drama format, leaning on established character types and narration elements known to German viewers from *Alfred Hitchcock Presents* (1955–65), *Perry Mason* (1957–66), and *Columbo* (1968–2003). The other sees it as an attempt to compete with the ZDF and their flagship crime drama by introducing regional episodes, each with different backstories and character profiles, and different approaches to their jobs. In 1970, at the cusp of Brandt's East-facing *Entspannungspolitik* (détente), the ARD presents Trimmel, their first detective, as a man of the people eager for dialogue, even if it means sidestepping official protocol.

On November 29, 1990, marking the twentieth anniversary of the series, *Taxi nach Leipzig* was rebroadcast three days before the first "German-German election." Its writer, Friedhelm Werremeier, is adamant: "The Berlin Wall might be gone, but there are still walls in the heads of people. The film might be called historic now but it is definitely not outdated."[8] The year 1990 was not just a crucial turning point in the country's history, after 236 episodes *Tatort* had arrived at an average of 30 percent of viewers per episode, half of its original network ratings. One of the most pressing issues in 1990 was the onboarding of East German viewers, those that preferred homegrown fare such as *Polizeiruf 110*. The ARD thus fired on both cylinders: in the course of two months around the election, it rebroadcast its 1970 German-German episode and a crossover episode between *Tatort* and *Polizeiruf 110*. *Unter Brüdern* (October 28, 1990) ran on ARD and DFF channels. The episode featuring a montage of the shows' title sequences and the Duisburg *Tatort* and *Polizeiruf* teams was watched by almost 44 percent of viewers.[9] Nevertheless, for a show that garnered an "unbeatable 76% with the 1974-episode *Nachtfrost*" (NDR) and successfully sold the 1976-episode *Reifezeugnis* (with Nastassja Kinski) as a stand-alone film internationally, the reduced viewership is largely seen as a direct consequence of competition from cable and satellite. Yet critics also note that private sector programming was bound to change reception habits and viewer expectations: "'Too little action and too many long-winded dialogues,' say younger viewers. The older ones criticize 'too much psycho-stuff'" (*Stader Tageblatt*, November 29, 1990). Still, viewers and critics agree that *Tatort*'s "marketing concept, a crime drama lucky bag,

---

[8]Ingeborg Müntze, "Taxi für Trimmel," *Hamburger Abendblatt*, November 29, 1990.
[9]Peter Hoff, *Polizeiruf 110. Filme, Fakten, Fälle* (Berlin: Das Neue Berlin, 2001), 150.

out of which fall the most distinctive characters and stories," will survive.[10] After all, if some viewers were tired of Schimanski, they could wait until the following Sunday, and if they didn't care for a "Killer-*Tatort*," next Sunday might bring a "Literature-*Tatort*" or a "Mob-*Tatort*" expanding the format bible with a multi-genre approach in step with the cable era (*Fernseh-Dienst*, November 11, 1990).

Tatort Synopsis

The very first *Tatort* episode comes from the NDR out of Hamburg but takes place along the transit corridor between West and East and in an imaginary Leipzig. It features the plot of a child swap between the FRG and GDR. Erich Landsberger (Paul Albert Krumm) from Hamburg exchanges his son who succumbed to leukemia for the healthy result of his affair with Eva Bilsing (Renate Schroeter) from Leipzig. There, Eva and her military officer husband-to-be Peter Klaus (Hans-Peter Hallwachs) trade the boy to Landsberger, her former West German lover, so that they can begin their marriage unhampered by baggage from the past. The GDR first asks for West German police help to solve the case but soon withdraws it. But when Trimmel hears that the dead child found along a stretch of the transit highway in East Germany was wearing a West German shoe brand, he becomes suspicious. He takes matters into his own hands and begins an undercover cross-border investigation with the help of a GDR friend and former colleague. He feints a breakdown along the transit highway and calls a taxi to Leipzig from an East German gas station. Mirroring Chancellor Brandt's initiated *Ostpolitik* (1969–74) between the two countries, this episode manages to entice the two involved civil servants (GDR officer and FRG policeman) to cooperate on the basis of their common humanity, their privileging of ethical concerns over political, ideological ones.

ImagiNation: One Nation under Network Television

Taxi nach Leipzig—the very title pronounces an impossible feat in 1970 but cleverly toys with viewers' longing for unification. It is still an odd choice for the pilot of a series whose concept insists on regional realism, since this episode could not be shot on location and features the Hamburger Trimmel (Hans-Werner Richter) in an unauthorized undercover operation. In 1998, Helmut Böttiger underscores the importance of the episode's imagined

---

[10]Frank Thomsen, "20 Jahre lang Tatort-Spannung," *Bremer Nachrichten Weser Kurier*, November 29, 1990.

encounter with the East and what had become an alien nation to most West German viewers: "*Taxi nach Leipzig* had something of a concrete utopia in 1970; it was reminiscent of *Raumpatrouille* and *Star Trek*. (. . .) The East, that was Science Fiction back then. The territory of the GDR was almost as removed as space station Alpha 1 or the intergalactic cruiser Hydra." One needs to remember that this episode as well as the rest of West German television could transmit "few optical and acoustic signals to the viewers that signaled: Aha—GDR!" (*Frankfurter Rundschau*, September 12, 1998).

Böttiger writes from the vantage point of the late 1990s. And he clearly exaggerates for effect, considering that the wall had been up for nine years in 1970 and there still was plenty of back-and-forth movement throughout the 1950s. Yet he is right in assessing the situation for the West German generation coming of age in the 1970s. Some still had family on the other side, but not many went through the bureaucratic ordeal to travel there. For a visit beyond a day pass to East Berlin, West Germans had to register months in advance with state and local authorities. In addition, the GDR required a forced exchange of D-Mark for Mark at a 1:1 rate on a daily basis. Once the visit was approved, movements within the GDR were severely restricted, and surveillance of oneself and of those visited was all but guaranteed. Experiences were bound to remain localized and impressionistic at best.

Except for official news coverage, television did not help to fill that void. Outside of the daily dose of *Unser Sandmännchen* (GDR, 1959–), children and teenagers were rarely exposed to films or television shows that could have provided an extended look, even if fictionalized, of everyday life in the GDR. Younger West German viewers were thus more clueless about East Germany than most East German viewers about the West, even from the so-called "valley of the clueless." In the GDR, the station handle ARD was satirized as *Außer Rügen und Dresden* (Outside of the island of Rügen and Dresden) as up to 87 percent of viewers in the East could receive ARD's signal on VHF in the 1970s.[11] By comparison, "fewer than one-sixth of West Germans [were] able to receive GDR TV."[12]

Keeping in mind that the wall went up in 1961, viewers from either side would have approached the premiere *Tatort* episode after nine years of closed borders with curiosity and critical anticipation. Knowing that direct access to authentic locations was impossible, how would the writers, actors, and videographers depict the East? What would be recognizably West

---

[11] Screening Socialism Project, Loughborough University, UK, https://www.lboro.ac.uk/subjects/communication-media/research/research-projects/screening-socialism/television-histories/tvinthegdr/ (accessed August 7, 2020).
[12] Jan Palmowski, "Narrating the Everyday: Television, Memory and the Subjunctive in the GDR 1969–1989," in *German Division as Shared Experience*, ed. Eric Carter et al. (New York: Berghahn, 2019), 31–55, here 31.

German disguised as approximations of East German locations, designs, and apparel? How would they portray mannerisms, speech, and behavior patterns? Eastern viewers would get a mostly benevolent if conjectured glimpse of how the West saw them. Western viewers would have to deal with a televised fiction of their imagination, hoping for a glimpse of authenticity underneath the self-posturing exhibited by both sides in the evening news programs, a peek at ordinary life behind the Iron Curtain. This *Tatort* episode is one of the few attempts to dramatize "life over there."

Taxi nach Leipzig opens with a low-angle shot of the shiny black boots of a uniformed GDR border patrol agent. While the waxed boots draw an immediate comparison to the Nazi-era evoking the long-held fallacy of equating the two totalitarian systems, they also establish a contrast with the rest of the dilapidated border station, its white paint peeling off. Only a bright red "Frieden und Sozialismus" (peace and socialism) sign draws our eyes. In a manner that merges boredom, arrogance, cool detachment, and chicanery, the agent's requests to open trunk, suitcase, and hood of the car would have been familiar to West German viewers having endured these on the heavily traveled transit highway into and out of Berlin. Because the child stretched out on the backseat "is sleeping and not feeling well," the owner of the Mercedes does not have to show and lift up the rear seat.[13] As the Mercedes drives in the direction of Leipzig, the episode title appears in the form of what will later be known as the *Star Wars* crawl, here matched to the perspective drawing of the *Autobahn* sign.[14] The three-dimensional graphics suggest that *Tatort* seeks to lay the path into a new era of television, a decidedly modern one, forging connections not only between places but also between past, present, and future.

The following scene is as phone conversation between Trimmel from Hamburg and an old friend and former colleague in East Berlin. Both men recline in their living rooms adorned with neutrally patterned wallpaper, the Hamburg version more ornate, the East Berlin version more geometric. Both men drink a similar beer straight from the bottle while they talk. They joke that as professionals they "sometimes even speak the truth." Trimmel messes up official titles, is corrected by his East German friend, whose *Berliner* accent and barking at his constantly yapping dog go a long way to make him familiar to the viewer. This sentiment is enhanced when his wife comes in and uses that day's issue of *Neues Deutschland* (the official party newspaper) to place under her husband's feet on the couch and informs him she is off to a *Schulungsabend* (evening training session), a copy of a Friedrich Engels book under her arm. In one sweep, Werremeier is able

---

[13]Without a permit, it was illegal to stray from the *Transitstrecke*.
[14]Helmut Böttiger, "Die heile Welt der Sozialliberalen," *Frankfurter Rundschau*, September 12, 1998. Seen from 2020, the title aesthetics underscore Böttiger's "the East as science fiction" argument from above.

to communicate the coexistence of and daily navigation between official and unofficial positions, between performances of conformity (attending a *Schulungsabend* discussing Engels) and acts of nonconformity (treating the central party's paper as dirt catcher).

Even though the props bear different names, gender roles and the men's *Feierabend* (Miller-Time) rituals are portrayed as strikingly similar in their stereotypically petit bourgeois ways. While the two men are quick to break household and national rules, the wife is just as quick to enforce middle-class standards of cleanliness and order, all the while exhibiting loyalty to the communist party and career. The point of this scene is that (a) the middle-class lifestyle and its idiosyncrasies have survived the onslaught of official antibourgeois communism in the GDR and the student movement in the FRG, transcending class and region to symbolize an essential Germanness and that (b) the German-German dialogue could just as well have taken place between two colleagues and their eavesdropping wives from West Berlin or Frankfurt. Keeping Böttiger's alienation statement in mind, Werremeier and Schulze-Rohr deliver a shorthand for establishing an implicit kinship based on everyday routines and middle-class foibles, and the three actors convey the back-and-forth phone dialogue in an effortless, naturalized manner.

Consequently, *Tatort*'s first episode styles itself as a crossover episode between the two Germanies as two German-language regions. The mirrored rituals of everyday life in their regionally defined variation do as much to normalize the existence of the two Germanies with their own specificities as they maintain that continued familiarity and kinship outweigh political differences. Even a former secret service agent from the SSD is shown to be a *Mensch*. Both engage in intentional double entendres that make clear that they expect their call to be monitored and recorded. The script handles the intentional double-speak with humor, so that viewers from both sides can read between the lines and enjoy the irony dripping from statements by the former secret service agent such as: "You causing me difficulties? We don't have any difficulties here." The suspicious clicking in the phone line cutting off the connection to Hamburg proves them right to be as guarded as possible under the circumstances. The surveillance apparatus spies on its own, yet does not deter the two from pulling off a job together ("ein Ding drehen").

The diegetic five-party telephone conversation—the two men, the wife, who listens in from the same room, and the potential state security agents monitoring calls between East and West—highlights the process of a multiply mediated communication. The complex triangulation also reveals the active role television is playing in the German-German dialogue, how *Tatort*'s dedication to contemporary historical realism utilizes the official rhetoric to feed another version of *Ostpolitik*, based on an unspoken yet resonating code of understanding—from friend to friend, from region to region—back into the line. This scene entices viewers to share a laugh based on their superiority in intercepting the coded messages.

Yet at the same time, the outing of power hierarchies involved in communications and their technological transmissions also implicate the medium of television in the act of surveillance and countersurveillance. Viewers here and there have to become active listeners and viewers to milk every word, syntax, emphasis, every gesture and facial expression for clues to distill the implicit meaning resonating between explicit statements. The scene is a reminder why the crime drama was the perfect genre choice for West and East Germany at this historical juncture, when a simple telephone conversation could be a committed crime. The genre prods viewers to take initiative and analyze clues, invites them to become part of the investigation *and* part of the opposition. While schooling viewers on both sides how to decode implicit meanings (the Stasi-light approach), the scene also exemplifies how to obscure critical statements and crucial information without sacrificing understanding for the right ears and eyes. And, most importantly, it underscores that the foundation of a successfully communicated veiled message is mutual trust, respect, and above and beyond all, being united against authoritarian structures on both sides. Comparing Trimmel's subsequent icy dialogue with the wealthy father in Frankfurt to the warm telephone call between the two former colleagues establishes that *Tatort* producers and writers believe that this foundation is based on shared life experiences and the dominance of middle-class values and not on whether one lives in the West or East.

Of course, Trimmel himself drives to Frankfurt to check on the former Hamburg resident Erich Landsberger, the father of the dead child. The car radio, announcing station handle and time, functions as a sound bridge to inform us where Trimmel is seen reversing his car to park in what appears to be a luxury residential area. After he is invited inside the stately villa, he and the viewer are treated to two jump scares. One takes the form of a bulldog on the floor revealed to be a porcelain statue, the other occurs after a slow 360-degree pan around the office, which is richly adorned with antique clocks and various wooden artifacts. The deep gong of the grandfather-clock announces the full hour just as the camera speeds up to return to Trimmel and the closely hovering vampiric landlord behind him. Recovering from the initial shock, Trimmel takes his place in one of the leather seats while Landsberger ghosts around him displaying his nerves and sense of dislocation even though he is the one questioning Trimmel's legitimacy to be in Frankfurt. Landsberger reveals only that the dead boy's biological mother passed away from leukemia. Just then an apparently healthy blond boy jumps into the room calling Landsberger "Babba" (Papa) with the soft-consonant inflection typical of *Sächsisch*. Believing this to be too much of a coincidence, Trimmel vows to travel to Leipzig to solve the mystery.

When Trimmel reverses his car to park in Frankfurt, he arrives in a different region, social class, and era. The sudden appearance of the hovering host completes the feeling that Trimmel, the fish out of

Waterkant, is trespassing on turf ruled by the landed gentry and that this upper-class lifestyle in Frankfurt is more unfamiliar than everyday life in the other Germany. While both jump scares have a comedic effect, they also serve as a social commentary on how the wealthy pharmaceutical entrepreneur is exploiting the health and lifeblood of the working and middle classes. The upper-class milieu and antique castle-like décor imbue the scene with a lifeless museal quality, in which Trimmel acts like the actual bull(dog) in the proverbial china shop. He calls Landsberger a "Kotzbrocken" (piece of vomit) for lying and refusing to help him solve the case. *Tatort* viewers are introduced to the first of Trimmel's many takedowns of the high and mighty. After surviving "count Dracula" and his evasive maneuvering, Trimmel's trip to Leipzig seems even more like a homecoming by comparison. He gets his hands dirty to remove the belt from his car's engine, takes public transportation, and amiably chats with everyone he meets.

Two more scenes bear crucial information: the rehearsal scene for the trip and the arrival in Leipzig. In a traditional German *Kneipe* (bar), drowning six rounds of beer and *Korn*, Trimmel seeks advise from a friend who frequently has to travel to trade conventions in Leipzig. The friend advises him to change his wardrobe to an older two-piece with an open collared shirt, to exchange some money and take plenty of D-Mark coins with him. In the end, it is both his *Westgeld* and his straightforward unassuming manner that endears him to the locals. Even though Trimmel complies and changes his attire, he is immediately spotted anyway, underscoring that costuming alone does not suffice to pass, that vocabulary, intonation, mannerisms, and posture, especially in everyday interactions with a highly ritualized component, contribute to regional and national identity structures, and that these as well as knowledge archives change from region to region. The episode tries to undercut the assumption of national homogeneity in a comic fashion, when the first gas station attendant tells Trimmel in what sounds like the local dialect "I am not from here," when Trimmel asks him where he could find an engine belt. When Trimmel wants to know, where he is from, the man proudly announces the name of a village most Western viewers would not have recognized. Besides emphasizing regional over national identity structures once again, this scene also makes it easier for *Tatort* to pass off its costume drama as historical reality. The scene and the episode at large foreground the default performativity of national identity vis-à-vis the assumed naturalness of performing regional belonging, even if or precisely because the latter cannot be read by some or a majority of outsiders.

In the bar, the friend also tells Trimmel that East Germans no longer have to identify themselves when they use hard currency to purchase international high-end products at the infamous *Intershops* located throughout the East. What might seem simply an aside today was actually a useful bit of information for viewers from the West.[15] Originally, the state-run *Intershops* were supposed to attract visiting Western customers, but they also showcased what kind of products were available in the West that were not available for purchase in regular GDR shops. West television, its content, and its commercial breaks functioned alongside *Intershop* displays to advertise the ongoing discrepancy between the two Germanies' economies. Decades of watching products advertised without the ability to purchase most of them also built up an eager customer base for Western household staples after 1989, initially all but eradicating the demand for East German products, which also included the majority of East German television programs.[16] With this crossover episode, the ARD calculated that *Tatort* would invite both sets of viewers to buy into its regional concept, to get an inside view of the different German regions they could not visit. And the network encouraged viewers to welcome the series into their lives as a regularly available high-end product. Unlike the sudden appearance and disappearance of citrus fruit in a local GDR store, *Tatort* would arrive reliably every Sunday.

Another sound bridge connects Trimmel's first border crossing: a sickly sweet children's choir intoning a favorite FDJ (Free German Youth organization) folk song is blasted through the loudspeakers at the checkpoint, moving from diegetic to extradiegetic score as scenes alternate between the two lovers breakfasting in bed in Leipzig and Trimmel driving. As a monocultural sound source, the song permeates all three scenes indicating the pervasive way in which private and public spheres, but also education, the arts, and politics, are entangled in state ideology. Once Trimmel manages to stray from the official path, the song ends, letting us know that we are about to get a peek underneath the party cover. From here on out, even though the viewer gets treated to camouflaged West German buildings and costumed actors doing their best to speak *Sächsisch*, viewers eagerly pick up any fictionalized hints of everyday life socialist-style.

Before Andrew Higson coined the term "heritage film" for 1980s and 1990s British films depicting the empire's bygone colonial past in enticingly vibrant colors, textures, scores, and immersive exterior and interior landscapes, *Tatort* sends us on a similarly engrossing journey in a wooden streetcar complete with functioning pull-string and bell. We join Trimmel on the tram and people-watch as they go on with their daily business. Whereas Higson states that heritage films "seemed to articulate a nostalgic and conservative celebration of the values and lifestyles of the privileged classes, and (...) in doing so [reinvented] an England that no longer existed (...) as

---

[15] By 1974, East Germans were officially allowed to hold foreign currency to purchase hard-to-get products at *Intershops*.
[16] *Good Bye, Lenin!* (dir. Wolfgang Becker, 2003) derives most of its humor from *Ostalgie* by reconstructing a GDR mise-en-scène for the party-loyal mother, who spent November through spring 1989/90 in a coma.

something fondly remembered and desirable," Phil Powrie argues that the "alternative heritage film" focuses on "difficult moments in the national past which indicate contemporary fears."[17] What makes Powrie's study interesting for the case of the divided Germany and *Tatort*'s regional concept is that he emphasizes the geographical and class-based fragmentation between the different regions in Thatcher's England and therefore suggests that a heritage film "in the imagination at least, resolves separateness, difference, fragmentation" and restores the image of the nation (Ibid., 325).

The first *Tatort* episode delivers a combination of these different nostalgic projects to its divided screens. For West Germans, it functions as an alternate history, a time-travel device back to a German counterpart from the 1950s. The camera does not give us industrial wastelands or vast agricultural communes but instead foregrounds parklike streets, suburban gardens, scenes of manual labor, friendly and prompt service, quaint and historic methods of transportation, and an idyllic, comfortably gender-typed domestic sphere. West German viewers would probably have argued that most of these societal aspects were embattled in the West in 1970. In addition to the student and burgeoning women's movements, the rapid technological modernization was threatening to do away with treasured aspects of urban life, most poignant in the context of this episode: the streetcar. The tracks and the trolleys themselves provide a visual affirmation of German endurance going back to the 1880s. As remnants of an intact prewar German cityscape and infrastructure they function as reassuring continuity devices. In the West, Hannover was one of the few cities that kept theirs in the course of the nationwide orientation toward cars and buses, while Hamburg abandoned most of their lines in the 1970s.[18] This *Tatort* produces a look across the wall that is more enchanted and melodramatic than hostile, more nostalgic for a bygone era than expressively yearning for a united future. The crime drama represents the results of the difficult German past and present but does not recuperate the loss incurred by the division as much as fills that loss with an enticing visual and audial landscape of the imagination.

To East German viewers, being represented in a West German television show in a somewhat fair, if still problematic fashion, this episode must have appeared as a unicorn. The very fact that their main representatives on screen are beautiful young people, allowed to have a love life, feed each other in bed, listen to pop music, and wear fashionable haircuts and clothes in a

---

[17]Andrew Higson, *English Heritage, English Cinema: Costume Drama since 1980* (Oxford: Oxford University Press, 2003), 12. Phil Powrie, "On the Threshold between Past and Present: Alternative Heritage," in *British Cinema, Past and Present*, ed. Justine Ashby and Andrew Higson (London: Routledge, 2000), 316.
[18]Per Hinrichs, "Der lange Streit um Hamburgs Straßenbahn," *Die Welt*, February 4, 2012, https://www.welt.de/regionales/hamburg/article13849372/Der-lange-Streit-um-Hamburgs-Strassenbahn.html (accessed August 13, 2020).

modern middle-class environment provided a counterpoint to the *worker-farmer* self-image privileged in domestic East German television projects and export-oriented features. On top of this, GDR viewers could feel superior when critiquing the details the show got wrong, including regional specificities. Both sides were invited to window-shop their way through a fictionalized East Germany, and East German viewers additionally got the pleasure and pain of nit-picking at the appropriated and rear-projected cultural spectacle of their own lives.

The Body Politic

Neither here nor there, the episode takes place in a different time and a proverbial no one's land. On the one hand, Werremeier's script "feverishly attempts to avoid prejudices and not promote the cold war mentality," on the other hand Trimmel's Freudian "*Über*-Father of all of Germany" outplaying the "minions of a totalitarian system" underscores "West knows best."[19] The first we see of Trimmel is his white suspenders holding up a portly physique and the half-smoked remnants of a cigar. His tie matches the suspenders, suggesting that he might like his food and drink but that he cares about his job and his appearance. He is reading the telegram about the suspected child murder out loud. When the camera reaches his face, he spits out a few tobacco crumbs. From the very beginning, Trimmel's body is our anchor: Trimmel practicing his aim, driving, being driven in a taxi, in armchairs and on sofas, the camera encircling him in medium and extreme close-ups, lingering on his stately paternal body smoking and drinking in recline, confidently taking a seat even where he is not welcome (as in Landsberger's house). Especially on the way to Leipzig, the shaky handheld camera from the passenger seat seeks stability by framing Trimmel's profile in extreme close-up. This scene lends a documentary feel and suspense to the drive East. It is as if Trimmel's body has become the viewers' replacement location, anchoring and reuniting their dual screen and dual country experience.

The body politic comes into play right away. First, his assistant and then the boss himself are keen to disregard the GDR's telegrammed ask for help. While it is true that German-German affairs were generally not part of the job description of the murder commission, the disregard is telling. It is only after his assistant tells him that the East German office has withdrawn its request because "the child was one of their own" that Trimmel springs into action. He senses a cover-up. His investigative instincts are thus awakened not by the case itself but by the withdrawn request and the national paternity acknowledgment of the dead child. The case he is interested in investigating

---

[19] Böttiger, "Die heile Welt der Sozialliberalen."

is about national and regional belonging, legacy, and progeny. When he finds out that the child's West German shoes were a present from its biological father with an address in Hamburg, Trimmel aims his gun at the camera and pulls the trigger, a camera angle choice indicating that he will not do any favors, that he takes aim at German viewer's perception and their biases, at state-sponsored ideology here and there as much as at any wrongdoing, no matter on which side of the Iron Curtain the crime originated.

In the context of national politics, Trimmel adds some of the force to Willy Brandt's *Ostpolitik* diplomacy that conservatives from the opposition were missing. The CDU/CSU accused Brandt of forfeiting Germany's right to self-determination by conceding too much (e.g., the post-1945 borders). While Trimmel, like Brandt, goes East and builds his investigation on dialogue and cooperation rather than rhetoric and force alone, Trimmel is clearly not just motivated by the prospect of unification, but he also models that a successful *Entspannung* (détente) only comes after a cleansing post-conflict conversation. The *Tatort* version is not as simple as reunification on the basis of a former union. Trimmel needs to make sure the dead child is identified, and the surviving child is with the right parent.

Even though Trimmel himself fails to reunite the parents—as does Brandt—their respective fictional and real-world activities succeeded in reframing the political rhetoric in familial terms. The idea of a united postwar Germany in its prewar or Third Reich borders is dead and has to be abandoned to the reality that Germany's instigation of war and genocide resulted in the adjusted central and Eastern European map and a divided Germany. Following Bertolt Brecht's play *The Caucasian Chalk Circle* (1948), in which the mother that lets go of the child is pronounced the real mother, the episode suggests that letting go is best for all parties. After all, the child's mother gets a fresh start, a chance for a new union, the father gets a do-over with a healthy child. And that child gets to live a more economically advantaged life in the West. But Trimmel's undercover investigation also makes clear that treaties and policies involving the divided Germany should and could be entrusted to Germans accepting these conditions. From its first episode, *Tatort* reflects, evokes, and constructs anxieties over paternity and maternity, over national belonging and its connection to and severance from biological, national, and regional ties. At the same time, it seeks to contain these instabilities by directing our identification toward a paternal substitute who surreptitiously and successfully works both within and outside of the constraints of global, national, and regional authority (not the only time, as "Rechnen Sie mit dem Schlimmsten"/"Worst-Case Scenario" proves).

Peter Klaus, the GDR officer and husband-to-be, tracks Trimmel down and apprehends him using his official connections. Instead of bringing him in, Klaus absconds with Trimmel and stops on an open field to find out why he came to see his fiancé. Trimmel provokes the young man intentionally to get under his skin and abandon his officer decorum: "Is she good in bed?" After

Klaus has punched him in response: "Human reactions are pretty similar in East and West." They scuffle, Klaus wants to draw his gun but Trimmel counters: "Leave it be, my son. Everyone can shoot when they don't know how to go on. Can we talk?" Both men stray from their official paths, even though they are both state employees sworn to uphold state power. Trimmel plays the wise father to the hotheaded son, seeing himself in the young man.

The fight scene and dialogue encourage viewers to read national politics as a costumed performance that once exposed reveals the familiar—and presumably real German subject—underneath. Trimmel's body looms large accentuated by the camera's frequent close-ups. His corporeality, broad face and smiles, and his sexist affront accentuate his physical presence. The young man, who starts out in full uniform, remains cold and official at first, but once the hat comes off, his body betrays his intentions and opens him up for connections on an interpersonal level, even if the first one is his fist and Trimmel's face. Afterward, in a public restroom, they wash the fight marks off their faces, symbolically wiping the masks off. Only then they introduce themselves by their first names, announcing a fresh start.

The two end up in Eva Bilsing's living room, where the silver-gray wallpaper matches Trimmel's own from Hamburg, last seen during the telephone call with his old friend. As the wallpaper suggests, he is just as much at home in Leipzig as he is in his own four walls in Hamburg. During Eva's difficult confession of swapping out one child for the other, Klaus and Trimmel share a Bulgarian cognac that Klaus drinks straight from the bottle. His Trimmel-gesture and the matching wallpaper in the West and East living rooms let us view Leipzig as a mirror image of Hamburg.

That element is strengthened, when the next scene in Frankfurt features another fist fight, this time between Landsberger and Trimmel, adding a more recalcitrant Frankfurt, West Germany's economic center, to the fold. The mirror scenes include the drawing of a gun, the drinking of cognac from a bottle, and the words "Leave it be, son!" Had viewers just watched this scene or were they imagining it? The viewing experience is very similar to the premise of the 2018 Starz series *Counterpart*, where two *Doppelgänger* live in slightly altered yet still similar-looking apartments on both sides of alternate versions of Berlin. If the fight scenes in this *Tatort* are engineered to get the body into play to facilitate the return to the Real in form of a pre-symbolic communal connection, to use Jacques Lacan's terminology, then the wallpaper posits that the German-German living room has no walls, that it is one continuous mise-en-scène—united and not fragmented—in the Imaginary.

Seriality and Geopolitics

Toward the end, all four protagonists gather at a *Transit* rest stop. Eva and Landsberger talk, while Trimmel and Klaus walk in circles in view of the café window. Eva admits that she will not marry Landsberger and seek their son's extradition, upon which he gives her a 6,500 DM bracelet. Landsberger is keen on determining a value for the child swap, showing that he has not yet understood the lesson Trimmel was trying to teach him. The show revels in his cruel materialist and sexist gesture, and lets Eva just stare at him with disgust. Landsberger would rather resurrect the symbolic order to rescue his slipping patriarchal control than live with the precarity of his guilt and his wounded ego, so he rebrands the child swap as a commodity transaction—a "sale." (Fittingly, his Mercedes cross is visible when Landsberger later wonders out loud whether Eva would even risk wearing the bracelet.)

The regained power of the symbolic carries over to the final scene at the rest stop, when the three say their good-byes in front of a "Verkehr-Verhalten-Verantwortung" (Traffic-Behavior-Responsibility) sign that bookends the "Frieden und Sozialismus" banner from the beginning. As Landsberger insists on Trimmel's promise to keep the child swap a secret and respect their "Individualsphären" (individual spheres), a very Western concept, the sign behind the protagonists publicly announces the group's different irresponsible and illegitimate actions and behavior—and by intimation here also Eva's and Landsberger's extramarital interzonal affair (*Geschlechtsverkehr* is the formal term for intercourse). The blocking is precise and leaves Trimmel out of the group. The sign dispenses its symbolic moral judgment on the three culprits in the shape of an official GDR dictum. The GDR's ideological apparatus gets to speak the truth on West German television.

The camera pulls back into a long shot as both parties depart, a contemporary pop tune begins to swell, but this is not yet the end. What follows is a series of strange epilogues performed with an almost Brechtian approach to dramaturgy and acting. Trimmel insists Landsberg drive to the crime scene, and once there that Landsberger reenact the burial scene with the help of a gnarly tree branch. Unwilling at first, Landsberger plays along only for Trimmel to interrupt his performance three times, until the camera moves to a close-up on Erich's hands, which mimic how he smothered the still breathing child with a pillow. But this grisly reveal is still not the end of the episode. In the next shot, Trimmel is behind the wheel and Erich is finally talking, yet Trimmel interrupts his narrative repeatedly to get him to verbally admit that his son was still alive. At one point, Landsberger pummels Trimmel like an enraged toddler and endangers both of them. Finally, as tears are streaming down Erich's face, a catharsis has been reached and an era of new understanding is dawning. In the next shot, Landsberger is behind the wheel, a sign that Trimmel now entrusts him with leadership. Night falls, the two approach the border, and viewers get treated to a close-up of the GDR agent's golden wedding band just as Trimmel finds a photo of Erich with his son, and as Landsberger finishes saying "You have to believe me, I wouldn't have done this, if I didn't want them to live with me and believed she wanted to marry me." The image of the ring as a transition shot as the two get ready to cross back into West Germany figuratively weds the two countries to one another. The wedding ring confirms that East and West share the same moral code and that marriage and family life are common goals. But like the rest stop sign, the wedding band creates another foray into the Imaginary. While the narrative of Erich and Eva ends in separation, the ring lets viewers see the border not just as that which divides but also as something that (re)connects.

At the same time, since the two men's cathartic journey together raises the professional relationship between cop and suspect to a level of intimacy that charges the homoerotic energy of these final scenes, the wedding ring at the border seeks to put a stop to wayward imaginations, channeling multidirectional desires, whether political, national, or sexual, into a clear heterosexual linearity. That these desires resist suppression is emphasized by a trip through the unconscious in the form of a joke. The next shot is of the car's engine block, where the border agent curiously inspects an oblong box: "What is that?" he asks. Erich presses a button and the car's radio antenna extends automatically. While the antenna provides comic relief after the climactic display of masculine vulnerability we just witnessed, it also reconfirms the techno-phallic superiority of the West. The two drive off toward the West German control station. The third end—with the car suspended in limbo between East and West control booths—is the final end.

It is tempting to read these serial endings and the freeze-frame on the border as a continuation of the three interruptions at the burial site and the three-worded signage at the rest stop. The reiterative cycles of threes borrow from Greek tragedy. Like a combination of psychiatrist and Brechtian dramaturg, Trimmel kindles and oversees the younger East and West German men's maturation processes by getting them to drop their territorial posturing, to let go of Eva and the East (Erich Landsberger) and jealousy of Landsberger and the West (Peter Klaus). In the process, as one dichotomy is breached, others are being denied or renegotiated, suspending the two men in a rupture between Symbolic and Imaginary realms and between past and present—at the caesura.

Walter Benjamin's rethinking of history and the flow of time become pertinent for this episode, because (a) the inability to portray the present of the GDR resulted in its substitution through its representation of material German history (the boots, the tram) that clashes with the concept of modern love and romance, and (b) the catharsis-oriented structure places this episode's serial endings in close proximity to the three-act Greek tragedy that Benjamin theorized. The freeze-frame mid-border thus points to the mechanics of representation itself, suspending time in a spatial rift, while creating a televisual Now through serial repetitions and interruptions that open up the past to the present and vice versa.

Only where the linear course of time is burst open and interrupted can history and the present appear as reciprocal processes. In this sense, one's own time should be thought as a moment that is not causally determined by the past, "but in which time [. . .] has come to a standstill" (Benjamin [1940] 2003, 396). Accordingly, the horizons of the past and present cannot be reconciled. The present, which according to Benjamin is won from this historical work, is not a self-contained presence; rather, the creation of a historical constellation brings about a split in the present—it creates a "now-time" (*Jetztzeit*), which opens itself to an other.[20]

This episode introduces seriality as a caesura machine that transforms Trimmel's psychological interventions and *Tatort*'s cinematographic aesthetics into the collective "historical work" that creates this "now-time." In that moment, the division between past and present, the two Germanies, is *aufgehoben*—preserved *and* undone.

While Werremeier's approach is symptomatic for the German time period of the late 1960s and early 1970s, which brought a lasting change to the concept of criminality, away from a biological and toward a more complex psychological understanding of motivations and affect, it would also continue to be the privileged method in the network crime drama *Tatort*.[21] On the one hand, this speaks to the real-life court-room drama that inspired law journalist Werremeier; on the other hand, the heightened attention devoted to character psychology has a long history in German visual culture, going back to the silent era. Films like *Der Student von Prag* (Stellan Rye, 1913), *Der letzte Mann* (F. W. Murnau, 1924), and *M* (Fritz Lang, 1931) were dedicated to the anxieties around gender and technology, specifically exploring the fragmentation of German masculinity during rapid modernization processes. The psychological approach to narrative and character development set German films of that era apart from their US counterparts.[22]

The first *Tatort* holds on to this tradition, adds a televisual spin to it, and reacts to a contemporary social climate that is in the midst of rethinking the connections between nature and nurture. Trimmel's rogue police activity, its aim therapeutic, conciliatory, and pragmatically result-oriented—like Brandt's—reinvests the global and national narratives

---

[20]Matthias Dreyer, "Caesura of History: Performing Greek Tragedy after Brecht," *Performance Philosophy* 2, no. 2 (2017), https://www.performancephilosophy.org/journal/article/view/107/143 (accessed August 15, 2021).
[21]Hilden Clages/Zeitner, *Einführung in die Kriminologie* (Verlag deutscher Polizeiliteratur, 2016), https://www.vdpolizei.de/shop/out/pdf/leseprobe/100985(1).pdf (accessed August 17, 2020).
[22]See the first two chapters in Sabine Hake, *German National Cinema*, 2nd ed. (New York: Routledge, 2007).

coming out of the Cold War with the power of critical self-renewal. Similar to Trimmel forcing Landsberger to the burial site, the crime drama takes viewers into familiar and unfamiliar places that are both feared and desired. The deferral and multiplication of the episode's ending through the three consecutive epilogues socialize viewers in the serial mode. The series extends the televisual suspension of departure and arrival within its serial elements to the suspension between and within German regions, including East and West Germany. After the *Tatort* project's imaginary foray across the German-German border, viewers can return to their historical worlds having been saturated with the reinvigorated power of *imagiNation*. Seeing Germany through *Tatort* thus reveals a televisually mediated geopolitics that reconstructs its national self-understanding through serial cross-regional facilitation. Within the regional series concept always lies the possibility of new additions, as the next episode from 1994 proves.

"Jetzt und Alles" ("Now and Everything," dir. Bernd Böhlich; MDR, July 31, 1994)

Tagesschau Synopsis[23]

The United Nations Security Council passes a resolution to intervene in Haiti's military dictatorship. Egyptian president Hosni Mubarek and Israel's premiere Yitzhak Rabin meet in Taba to discuss a peace accord between Hafiz al-Assad in Syria and Israel. A special report emphasizes how the United Nations is delivering aid to 1.2 million Rwanda refugees after the humanitarian catastrophe at Goma refugee camp, where thousands died of dehydration, starvation, and disease.

Bankruptcy of Russian bank MMM: neither the company nor the government will reimburse approximately ten million small-scale investors whose dream of "fast money" has become a nightmare. Some put their whole savings on the line after promises of profits of up to 8,000 percent. There is no discussion or willingness to curtail or outlaw speculatory and predatory bank practices, not even to forbid MMM to continue advertising for its supposed profit margins on TV, while the CEO reportedly keeps speculating and putting new shares into circulation.

It is the fiftieth anniversary of the Polish Warsaw Uprising. The German army suppressed the uprising and punitively destroyed what was left of

---

[23]This *Tagesschau* is available in the ARD archive, https://www.tagesschau.de/multimedia/video/video-10558.html (accessed July 27, 2020).

Warsaw. In a historic first, German president Roman Herzog is to join Lech Walesa for the commemoration in Poland.

The *Oberschlesier Landsmannschaft*, an organization of c. 1.7 million German-identifying expellees from the formerly Prussian province Silesia between 1945 and 1947, holds a three-day celebration in Essen. Speeches emphasize "working in partnership with Poland" but stress support of an autonomous *Oberschlesien*: "*Oberschlesien* must live." To run these two segments back-to-back casts a light on the reason for the expulsion in 1945 as much as it makes the cry for an autonomous German Silesia within the ratified Polish borders highly problematic.

Rita Süssmuth's speech about the negative consequences of poverty for social peace and justice notes that seven million people live below the poverty threshold in Germany. She highlights the unemployed, single mothers, and families with more than three children as especially affected.

The rest of the *Tagesschau* dwells on sports—among them a rather lengthy clip from the Hockenheim Ring German Grand Prix car race, which was won by an Austrian driver in a Ferrari—and the heat wave in Europe. Kurt Töpfer (CDU) warns about this as a precursor to climate change and challenges Germany to drastically reduce emissions.

Several of the reports match up with plot points from the Dresden *Tatort* that follows. The news flow places European aid for the Rwandan refugee crisis in relationship with the refusal of the Russian government to help those who lost all their savings, which in turn links with the data on German poverty. Since divorce rates skyrocketed after 1989 at the same time that most childcare facilities in the East closed, many children were left in the care of single parents, most of them mothers, while the economy was in upheaval. More than 2.5 million East Germans lost their jobs between 1989 and 1991, mainly as a result of the rapid deindustrialization. Women in the East, who reportedly had achieved an employment rate of 89 percent during the GDR years, were harder hit than men. Even by 2008, their unemployment rate still ranked around 9 percent higher than those of men.[24] The Dresden episode endorses Süssmuth's concern over the intersections between gender, class, poverty, and crime.

The insistence on Silesian autonomy might evoke sympathies with those viewers that believed in a third-way approach to German unification, namely for the five Eastern states to retain some autonomy rather than be folded into the existing political and economic structures of the FRG. While the climate change narrative finds an echo in the dominating postapocalyptic ash-gray tones in the episode, the contradiction between climate catastrophe

---

[24]Melanie Booth, "Die Entwicklung der Arbeitslosigkeit in Deutschland," *Bundeszentrale für politische Bildung*, March 30, 2010, https://www.bpb.de/geschichte/deutsche-einheit/lange-wege-der-deutschen-einheit/47242/arbeitslosigkeit (accessed July 28, 2020).

and the spectacle of auto racing carries over into the chase scenes in the episode.

Post-1989 Media Integration

Viewer comments will be integrated into the episode analysis. Here, I will focus on in-house publications reflecting on the unification of the network with the MDR (Mitteldeutscher Rundfunk) and the role of the Leipzig and Dresden *Tatort* in that process after 1989, a period that coincided with the increased competition between the existing public broadcasting structure and the emerging private media market.

The selected episode of the Ehrlicher/Kain team was the sixth since the official July 1, 1991, merge of Sachsen, Sachsen-Anhalt, and Thüringen into the triple-state public broadcasting station MDR. For its foundational bylaws, the new unit used the model of the NDR. In November, the umbrella network ARD decided to admit the MDR into its fold. Two programs exhibiting the MDR's approach to retain regional specificities while embracing new cross-country connections are the continuation of *Sandmännchen*, the GDR's legendary early evening children's program, and the regional contribution to the *Tatort* series "with a detective from Leipzig."[25] Allowing the MDR to expand and join the *Tatort* family serves as the most public signal of accepting the new regions into the German federation of states. That Leipzig serves as the headquarters of the MDR and also of the hometown of the first GDR inspector for the new *Tatort* offers the middle German region a much more visible profile, both a chance to retain a geopolitical identity and the ability to broadcast a successful path to integration. Similar to the new MDR structure, Ehrlicher and Kain investigate cases in all three states. By comparison, Brandenburg and Mecklenburg-Vorpommern have a delayed start into the new broadcasting order and would be fused with the SFB/RBB to a much higher extent.

Even more crucial is the self-congratulatory awareness that the regionally organized ARD, according to Dietrich Schwarzkopf,

> will be the only program that will offer the public broadcasters of the new states the chance and responsibility to portray the states and their people, their landscapes and institutions, with their concerns and their hopes, with their problems and their successes, in a self-determined form, to the viewers of all of Germany.[26]

---

[25]Thomas Nissen, "Drei Länder—ein Sender," *ARD Jahrbuch* (1991): 138–43.
[26]Dietrich Schwarzkopf, "Integration und Integrität," *ARD Jahrbuch* (1991): 118–25, here 118.

This claim to full representation needs to be seen in the context of Eastern viewers flocking to private media to a higher extent than their Western peers, a result of distrusting state media, and the eagerness to choose and experience new commodities.

By 1994, Jürgen Kellermeier argued that the competition between public broadcasters and commercial services should have revealed a lack of demand for the *Fernsehfilm* (film made for television). Instead, he contends that because of the "creative power of television," "the future of the *Fernsehfilm* has just begun." Again, *Tatort* serves as the key example of the legally enshrined responsibility of the three networks to heed their "cultural responsibility" and produce and disseminate a "program for the whole population, that can withstand the competition with the private sector" (*Bundesverfassungsgericht* decision from February 1994). Because the ARD has the repertoire and proven ability to produce "films that entertain, and films that artistically and dramatically represent the questions and problems of the day," the author sees a reason for optimism in a proclamation that leans heavily on Gunther Witte's foundational format bible for *Tatort*.[27]

Tatort Synopsis

The episode's storyline involves human trafficking (*Mädchenhandel*) and the so-called crash kids of the communist system failure, who spent their time competing in drag races and crashing stolen cars. Young adults with local high school diplomas had low upward mobility prospects amid the rapid changes after unification. After the recent fall of the Iron Curtain and Soviet rule over the CSSR (1948–90), young Czech women are hoping to find gainful employment in the West. They entrust shady West German middleman Ollenberg (Winfried Glatzeder) with their undocumented transfer to Germany. As a halfway stop and layover, while Ollenberg prepares the arrangements for their ultimate destination in Western bordellos, his accomplice's Dresdner *Spielothek* (arcade) serves as a hideout. Its manager, the disgruntled socialist party-loyal Wille (Henry Hübchen) used to be a social science teacher in the GDR and had to seek new employment after 1989. He is beholden to Ollenberg, who invested in his establishment. His wife, Jutta Wille (Renate Krössner), has an affair with Ollenberg and is eager to become financially independent to be able to leave her husband. One of the trafficked women sequestered in the basement is Katja (Lenka Jelinkova). Her father, fearing the worst, followed her to Dresden to get her back only to be murdered by Wille. Waiting for Ollenberg to arrive, Wille places the body in the trunk of his Mercedes. Soon after, the car is

---

[27]Jürgen Kellermeier, "Zwischen Tatort und zweiter Heimat," *ARD Jahrbuch* (1994): 37–42.

stolen by local teenagers for a joyride. When Lucky (Niels Bruno Schmidt), Falco (Oliver Bröcker), and Marko (S. Recznicek) steal the Mercedes for a road race, they discover the corpse in the trunk and attempt to hide the evidence by setting the car on fire. Unable to leave it at that, Falco hatches a blackmail scheme putting pressure on the Willes to help himself and his friends "get out of Dodge." The police soon link the car to the Willes and thus the two storylines of the crash kids and the Willes are connected. The episode alternates between the two plots, depicting the derelict transitional existences of both generations with visual acuity.

Inter-Medial Integration

One of the ways to interpret the three boys' fates is that the episode mourns the missed opportunity of a "third way" in 1989, a way forward that honored the East's differences instead of plowing them under existing Western economic and political structures.[28] Instead of getting the support to discover their own path forward, their emancipation endeavor traces a media- and genre-based trajectory from East to West. Their attempted East-West resettlement is paralleled in the genre-switch from *Indianer-* and *Trümmerfilm* toward video game, Hollywood action and heist films, ending with a High-Noon shoot-out. Integration is displaced from the narrative to the inter-medial level. Lucky dies in a Western-style duel, Falco gets killed during his blackmail attempt, and Marco is hauled off to the reservation. In the end, this episode re-essentializes the East German teenagers as a "lost tribe," because it resorts to comparing their desperate acculturation struggle to the colonization of indigenous peoples as represented in the *Indianerfilme*. Neither assimilation nor defiance works for them.

The culturally specific intertextual, film historic echoes evoked by the cinematography and mise-en-scène together with the issue-centric contemporariness seem to follow Dietrich Schwarzkopf's recommendations *against* "the artificial construction of harmony" and "a nostalgic orientation along the status quo." Yet, the three boys' fates could well resonate with his condescending definition of the "emergency community of offended, outmaneuvered or helpless 'Ossis.'"[29] With its inter-medial narration structure, "Jetzt und Alles" manages to take into account that East German overall media usage was "more extensive," generally around 10 percent higher than in West Germany before and shortly after unification.[30] The episode also leverages the seven points of the ARD network's official

---

[28]This is not to be confused with the right-wing "Third Way" party that formed in 2013.
[29]Schwarzkopf, "Integration und Integrität," 118–25, here 122–4.
[30]Ernst Dohlus, "Augen und Ohren nach Westen gerichtet?," *ARD Jahrbuch* (1991): 80–95, here 88.

integration goals for implementation in its content, most of which circle around increasing understanding for each side's cultural, linguistic, regional, and historical specificities. One point specifically addresses the importance of representing and appealing to younger viewers, a coveted age bracket and one increasingly likely to desert the networks for cable and satellite faire catering to their interests.

ARD and MDR approached these concerns and opportunities head-on with an updated episode entrance. "Jetzt und Alles" features not only an unusually long cold open but also a music montage that functions as a delayed title sequence—a first in the *Tatort* franchise. A German rock ballad score that has a *Stairway to Heaven* motif morphs into a Western score complete with howling steel guitar strings as a montage introduces us to the major characters. While the graveyard scene from the cold open lays an intertextual and inter-medial path to iconic cemetery scenes in Italo-Westerns—*The Good, the Bad, and the Ugly* (dir. Sergio Leone, 1966) and *My Name Is Nobody* (dir. Tonino Valerii, 1973)—the music montage updates the media references and resonance to the 1990s. Together, the two sequences unfold a road map between regional, national, and global media cultures and their reception.

The establishing shot as music montage mixes black-and-white news footage of car crashes with color shots of the three boys, Ehrlicher and Kain investigating the local crash, Ollenberg and Katja on the road, Ollenberg and Frau Wille in bed, Herr Wille at his bar. The title sequence capitalizes on the popularity of music videos and MTV, and its videography copies aspects of contemporary US teenage drama imports (e.g., *Beverly Hills 90210*, Fox, 1990–2000). Both styles aim to appeal to a younger demographic, enticing its distracted viewers to remain in front of the screen with inter-medial audio-cues and a teaser-reel. At the same time, following its mandate to educate the citizenry at large, the ARD manages to sneak in a public service announcement about the dangers of road racing, a message that would appeal to older viewers concerned about the "crash kids" of the 1990s. The result is an attempt to overcome its narrative of cross-generational German-German disintegration on the inter-medial level. The spectacular, melodramatic way this attempt is shown to fail on the plot level creates a televisual feast for engaged viewership that has turned this episode into cult television.

The year 1989 marks a deeply ambiguous, in turns traumatic and hopeful watershed moment for the social, political, and economic lives of teenagers and adults. The easternmost German city of Dresden functions as the frontier, where reorganized local, regional, and global concepts and connections are embodied and performed. Changing concepts of femininity and masculinity clash with economic despair and symbols of wealth. What dominant media outlets and Kohl's fantasy of "blooming landscapes" largely ignored in stories about the *Wende*, this episode makes self-reflexively clear:

how access to local, national, and global media, and the constellation of old and new reception habits, contributes to the fashioning of a post-*Wende* identity—of self, region, and nation.

Throughout the episode, Dresden's outer limits appear as a postindustrial wasteland of perpetual grayness. Nothing blooms in this concrete mud desert. The scenery is almost completely devoid of color. A thin rivulet of dirty water runs through a ruinous landscape flanked by concrete apartment silos and barren agricultural fields. For Katja, the trafficked protagonist, this is indeed a rain to trough situation, especially when she finds out that her handler Ollenberg plans to prostitute her instead of getting her into a job training program in the West as promised. Lucky, Marko, and Falco have their own dreams of escaping their inhospitable surroundings and their families' meager existences in outmoded communist-era *concrete slab* high rises. Yet these dreams take on an exceedingly morbid undertone.

In a shallow with some trees, overseen by a barren hill, underneath which the Second World War rubble mingles with GDR reconstruction debris, a cemetery is visible, where a young man, one of Lucky's classmates is laid to rest officiated by a priest. The first view of the three teenagers is a low angle from the cemetery. They appear as backlit silhouettes against the gray sky on the ridge of the hill. Instead of joining the mourners, they applaud the dead classmate for "making it." "That will be me at some point." Lucky emphatically retorts: "Fuck it, main thing is that it's quick and doesn't hurt." As it becomes clear, the death was a result of street racing, and while Lucky is eager to resume the race—"New game, new luck"—the others are less enthused: "Now, when all the cops have descended on this place? Are you nuts?" For Lucky, the cops just add excitement to their otherwise bland existence. They walk off, agreeing on a stretch of road and time for their next road race.

For the construction of regionally and nationally specific meaning, it is significant that the low-angle shot of the three silhouettes on the ridge of the stony hill approaches post-*Wende* Dresden with the iconography of the Western. The reverse shot looking up at Lucky, Falco, and Marko on the ridge turns the three disaffected teenagers into Native American warriors spying on the unwitting settlers and planning their raid.[31] Like the ambiguous figure of the "Indian Scout" in many Westerns, Lucky flaunts a blue bandanna with white stars that gathers up his long black hair throughout the entire episode. He follows in the footstep of the so-called Chief Indian of the DEFA, Gojko

---

[31]That viewers caught the association is demonstrated by a comment on tatort-fundus—"a rather melancholic Eastern with beautiful locations" (eher ein melancholischer Eastern mit schönen Locations). https://www.tatort-fundus.de/web/rangliste/folgen-wertungen/rangliste-auswertung/einzelwertungen-einer-folge-tatort.html?Nr=9&folge=294.0 (accessed July 30, 2020).

Mitic's *Chingachgook, die große Schlange* (1967),³² when he embarks on a rescue mission to save Katja, the kidnapped yet reluctant damsel in distress, and return her to her people. The climax occurs on a hilly meadow, the only undamaged piece of nature in the entire episode. Instead of a trusted steed, Lucky commandeers a stolen car, but the boys still strategize around a campfire, albeit in a dilapidated former greenhouse-tent, where they, like the weeds around them, cling to life.

The genre-specific cinematography is partially a citation of US Westerns. German viewers East and West would have recognized the signs, having been inundated with US movie imports since the dawn of television. Yet, as a scene playing on Germany's new frontier, it capitalizes on the unifying success of Italo-, East, and West German *Indianerfilme* at the divided nation's box offices between the 1960s and 1980s. While the West German films were based on Karl May's *Winnetou* novels, the East German films (sometimes called *Easterns*) loosely adapted the *Leatherstocking* novels by James Fenimore Cooper while retaining an ethnographic approach to tribal rituals and life. Thus, in Dresden, the traces of the Western and Eastern come together uniting German media consumers on the basis of their preoccupation with, some say obsession with, ethnographic and fictional Native American cultures.³³ Evan Torner discusses the appeal and identity-formation potential of the DEFA *Indianerfilme*:

[The] Indianerfilm's apparently ineluctable appeal stems (. . .) from the genre's unwitting success at creating what Michael Saler might call an "immersive secondary world" of heroic Indian adventures within the post-industrial socialist GDR, a fantasy world that successfully captured popular attention and crossed national borders by addressing universal values held by many Eastern Bloc populations. These films appear authentic in their gestures toward transnational and transhistorical solidarity by being 1) openly artificial (overcoming 20th Century socialism's lack of transparency) and 2) jointly Eastern European as well as German (overcoming national difference). These films are certainly artifacts of resistance, in the sense that they have their own hidden lives and agendas (. . .). They are ambiguous, commodified, ever-circulating celluloid

---

³²"Mit elf Millionen Zuschauern in der DDR und fast 30 Millionen in der Sowjetunion und vielen anderen Ländern in Europa, wurde es einer der größten Kinoerfolge der Babelsberger Filmstudios. Gojko Mitic wurde mit jedem der insgesamt zwölf zwischen 1966 und 1983 von ihm gespielten Indianerfilme der absolute Star der Defa und Liebling der Zuschauer." Eberhard Görner, "Der Ober-Indianer der DEFA Gojko Mitic feiert 80. Geburtstag," *Moz*, June 30, 2020, https://www.moz.de/kultur/artikelansicht/dg/0/1/1808495/ (accessed July 29, 2020).

³³See *Germans and Indians: Fantasies, Encounters, Projections*, ed. Colin G. Calloway, Gerd Gemünden, and Suzanne Zantop (Lincoln: University of Nebraska Press, 2002) or H. Glenn Penny, *Kindred by Choice: German and American Indians since 1800* (Chapel Hill: University of North Carolina Press, 2015).

fantasies that are screened as both illustrations of a dead country's media history and as a form of rebellion against some pernicious threat (be it capitalism or Soviet occupation) through the haunting, active bodies and talents of fake indigenous people depicted onscreen.[34]

As Torner points out, the *Indianerfilme* enabled a displaced tribal identification path for East German citizens that allowed them to imagine themselves as an oppressed and defiant people. While the state rhetoric of the "fascist capitalist aggressor" on the other side of the Iron Curtain encouraged East German citizens to identify as a defiant tribe, the Easterns also facilitated an imagined identity that coagulated around a collective resistance against an oppressive communist system: the GDR and the USSR. "Wir sind das Volk" (We are the people) was the official banner call of the Monday demonstration in the summer and fall of 1989. The imagined and felt tribal identity of being united in resistance against the state denied the existence and humanitarian consequences of the sometimes willing, more often coercive, collaboration with the Stasi in the form of the "unofficial colleague" program that had neighbors and friends spy on one other. Despite this reality, the call to a tribal unity found great resonance on both sides of the border, and as Torner contends, helped to "overcome national differences." The difference between a unification based on essentialist and one based on policy categories is apparent in the two terms ascribed to the 1989 event. The more dominant term "reunification" (*Wiedervereinigung*) implies an organic sense of tribal belonging, "joining together what belongs together" (Willy Brandt's words in 1989). In contrast, the competing word "unification" (*Vereinigung*) tends to acknowledge the two states' separate sociopolitical and cultural developments over their forty-year separation from one another.

One of the divisive issues in the 1980s was the party leadership's steadfast refusal to recognize the GDR's own socioeconomic, sexual, and ethnic diversity along with a brazen exploitation of the environment leading to water, soil, and air pollution within and across the inner-German border. The denial became especially precarious during the AIDS crisis in the 1980s. Both homosexuality and drugs were described as "capitalist plagues" and would not exist in the "perfect lifestyle" of the communist East, if they had not been imported from the West.[35] This "import theory" found its representational equivalency in *Indianerfilme*, which portrayed how alcohol and smallpox threatened the survival of native tribes. It is thus

---

[34]Evan Torner, "The DEFA Indianerfilm as Artifact of Resistance," *Frames Cinema Journal* 4 (2013), https://framescinemajournal.com/article/the-defa-indianerfilm-as-artifact-of-resistance/ (accessed July 28, 2020).

[35]"HIV in der DDR: Die Mauer als Kondom," *MDR Zeitreise*, December 16, 2019, https://www.mdr.de/zeitreise/aids-ddr-104.html (accessed July 31, 2020).

not a coincidence that this *Tatort* casts a West German, Marlboro-smoking Ollenberg, in the role as an unethical capitalist super villain, who traffics young women and extorts Wille, while sleeping with his wife. In a dark twist, the "import theory" is made manifest by the GDR's garbage deal with West Germany, which included toxic waste that would be shipped to GDR landfills over decades.[36] Natural resources, on the other hand, were readily exported to the West.

Similar to the train tracks laid to conquer the US frontier and transport its resources back to the cities, this episode connects the issue of human trafficking with the gas-pipeline that siphons off local energy to the West for *Devisen* (foreign currency).[37] The winding self-contained pipeline that expedites the flow of energy across the former border projects a global mobility that does not apply to the residents in its vicinity. Just the opposite, the energy trafficking has left local residents in a social and environmental desert. The ash-gray landscape inundated by rubble that the pipeline dissects makes apparent the explosive combination of a cycle of violence amid structural paralysis. For example, Gaby's father beats her up in front of Kain and Ehrlicher, before they have had a chance to explain to him that they just need her as a witness. And Marko's television-hypnotized mother resorts to committing him for juvenile delinquency.

While viewers get a depressing close-up of the socioeconomic and cultural clash between West and East in the five years after unification, the echoes of the *Indianerfilm* feed into the long-standing East German media practice of resorting to allegorical representations that turn victims of colonization and genocide into defiant protagonists. Judging from anonymous viewer comments, this tactic was partially successful. While many viewers praised the sense of realism for this post-*Wende* Dresden profile, others criticized the corrupt West German profiteer Ollenberg as the cause of all evil. The cross-generational cooperation between Ehrlicher and Kain, especially the latter's energetic attempt to understand Lucky and rescue him from himself, rang sympathetic to viewers from both sides.[38]

---

[36] Claudia van Laak, "Dreckmüll gegen Devisen," *Deutschlandfunk*, April 15, 2019, https://www.deutschlandfunk.de/westmuellexport-in-die-ddr-dreck-gegen-devisen.724.de.html?dram:article_id=446426 (accessed January 11, 2021).
[37] Transcontinental pipeline projects have also been the focus of indigenous peoples' protests in Canada and the United States: for example, the Clayoquot Protests in British Columbia in 1993, the Iowa protests in 2014, and the Dakota Access Pipeline protests in 2016.
[38] Viewer opinions on tatort-fundus: "realistic portrayal of social despair" (realistische Darstellung sozialer Abgründe), "record of the times and social study" (Zeitzeugnis und Sozialstudie)," and "The enjoyable interaction of Kain and Ehrlicher saves a lot, but this episode still falls rather flat" (Die angenehme Art von Kain und Ehrlicher rettet einiges, aber trotzdem ist diese Folge eher mau), https://www.tatort-fundus.de/web/rangliste/folgen-wertungen/rangliste-auswertung/einzelwertungen-einer-folge-tatort.html?Nr=9&folge=294.0 (accessed July 30, 2020).

Mobility at a Standstill

The *Indianerfilm*'s genre characteristics combine action, documentary, and melodrama. Close-up dialogue blocking interchanges with fast-paced wide-range mobile camera use. This is what the road races, car crashes, and chase scenes accomplish in this episode. But there is another angle to be taken into consideration. For that, we need to go back to the cemetery and the sterile *Plattenbauten*, back to the three backlit silhouetted figures on the mount of the Second World War and GDR reconstruction rubble.

An iconic scene in Wolfgang Böttcher's *Born in '45* (1966), East Germany's New Wave pendant to Godard's *Breathless* (1960), features three friends on top of the barren rubble mountain overlooking Berlin's center—both East and West—discussing their personal and their countries' past and future. Usually subsumed by the minutiae and drama of their everyday lives, on top of the mountain they realize that it is up to their generation to overcome the fascist past and the Cold War's present animosities. Jaimey Fisher has termed this the "panoramic gaze" and "panoramic memory."[39] Bearing in mind that the wide-angle landscape panorama is a cinematographic characteristic for both the Western and the rubble-film genre, *Tatort* merges these two landscapes, gazes, and culturally specific memory tracks. For the return shot from the low angle of the cemetery, Eric Rentschler also reminds us that the

> [s]hots of devastated German cities provide stirring vistas in postwar rubble films (*Trümmerfilme*). As low-angle compositions frame monuments of destruction against the vastness of cloudy skies, the shattered expanses of a depopulated metropolis assume the countenance of natural landscapes.[40]

Dresden's burnt-out skyline in 1945 is mapped onto Monument Valley vistas. The three boys, representing the future of their country, are framed as hollowed-out ruins of their fathers' and forefathers' wars, and as a premonition of the fate of their own rebellion. The rubble aesthetics explicitly codes 1989 in war terms. One of their soldiers has already fallen. And just as every *Indianerfilm* ends on the sobering realization of an already written history, that the war is lost, even if a battle was won, he won't be the last. But as the continuing appeal of the *Indianerfilm* attests, the pre-scripted ending did and does not mean that the ruinous attempts dissuade viewers

---

[39] Jaimey Fisher, "Wandering in/to the Rubble-Film: Filmic Flânerie and the Exploded Panorama after 1945," *The German Quarterly* 78, no. 4 (Fall, 2005): 461–80.
[40] Eric Rentschler, "The Place of Rubble in the *Trümmerfilm*," in *Ruins of Modernity*, ed. Julia Hell and Andreas Schönle (Durham: Duke University Press, 2010), 418–38, here 418.

from tuning in. Even today, television reruns of both East and West German *Indianerfilme* still garner respectable ratings.

In "Jetzt und Alles," the three teenagers view death and the ruins of their upturned lives—the "exploded panorama" (Fisher) of the present—from the rubble of the previous generation's war. But the panoramic gaze is that of a new media generation as the next scene in Wille's videogame arcade makes apparent. We enter the scene through a point-of-view shot from the videogame monitor, at which two teenagers point their joystick guns. They are shooting directly into the camera and at the viewer. The raid has begun. The scene assaults our casual interaction with the television set. This is an assault at looking at "the East" as a form of entertainment similar to the Western tourists gawking from the tour buses and watchtowers installed along the wall. While this scene coaxes Western viewers into some self-reflection, the youth's hair-trigger gaze is immersive and mobile rather than reflective. Their sideways scroll leads to a serial self-refraction among the multiple targets and the next levels in the video game. In retrospect, the shoulder shrugging in response to the death of one of their own merges with the gamer mantra of "One down, two lives left." While *Tatort* dresses the youths' resistance in the combined iconography of the national and regional rubble- and *Indianerfilm*, their rebellion takes the form of interacting with and immersing themselves in globally circulating media forms and fantasies.

As the boys' names suggest, their reception habits vacillate between US film, television, and videogame content. National DEFA *Indianerfilm* elements join the fantastic journeys in local author Karl Mays's Wild West novels and their West German adaptations in the form of steady reruns on television. Like Karl May, who mostly traveled in his imagination, until 1989 East Germans were restricted to Eastern European countries and could only fantasize about exotic travel destinations. The youths' attempt at friendship and love hovers between FDJ camaraderie, campfire romanticism, and appropriating German, American, and global screen cultures. Lucky is eager to practice his English on Katja, his Russian from the GDR school days (with Wille as his teacher) all but forgotten. At the kitchen table, Marko's mother is smoking and makes an attempt to have a conversation with him as he stares at the television set. When we hear police sirens, it remains unclear whether these are part of her program or diegetic to the scene in *Tatort*. And when the boys run to meet up with one another after the money heist, their jog is matched to the rhythm of rap music that starts extradiegetic and becomes diegetic only when we see a group of young men dancing to a boom box in a pedestrian tunnel. With the fall of the wall, the borders between media projection, reception, and historical reality have become porous. From Gaby's (Sandra Lindner), Falco's girlfriend, perspective, the attempt to combine the disparate socialization and identification maps fails for adults and the boys, who are constantly projecting their desires onto mediated screens that leave them too self-involved and in denial about "real existing conditions" on the ground.

The road race scenes connect the ethnic drag of *Indianer* hobbyism to masculinity models from *The French Connection* (dir. William Friedkin, 1971) and *The Getaway* (dir. Sam Peckinpah, 1972). Due to the low production budget, the *Tatort* race scenes are slower and tamer by comparison. The night-time race happens on a stretch of urban highway surrounded by sound barrier walls still under construction. The highway fragment has the racers do a U-turn at the end and drive back the way they came from for the second lap. When Lucky triumphantly passes Falco and looks behind him in the second lap, he crashes into the backhoe parked at the turning point. Thus, Lucky figuratively crashes in(to) *Die Wende* (the turn), a term used to describe the post-1989 political moment.

This scene encapsulates mobility at a standstill. The freedom of movement the teenagers hanker after is still severely impacted in all directions. Even though the border wall has been torn down, new barriers emerge daily. There is no visibility, no horizon to reach for, and there is no destination. The incomplete walled-in track forces them to go back to where they started. The unfinished highway is a race track full of construction rubble and machinery. In a video game, these obstacles would add to the thrill, here they become deadly. The highway fragment highlights that Saxony's infrastructure is still being assembled, and that older roads, including the concrete slab utility lanes between the fields, would not accommodate these speeds. Even though the teenagers attempt to emulate the *Mutproben* (tests of courage) characteristic of *Indianerfilme* and teenage media fare, and even though they manage to become mobile, the conditions on the ground negate their momentum. The rapid socioeconomic and geopolitical changes, including large-scale shifts of the local and regional infrastructure grids, mess with the young protagonists' orientation. Their race symbolically ends when a parked backhoe figuratively scoops up the Mercedes as if it were another piece of debris to be removed. Lucky and his friends run up against the reconfigured geopolitical map. The new networks that are being laid have not yet been integrated into everyday memory paths to facilitate a connection. Right now, in this state, they obstruct rather than assist mobility. And as the kids drive into the construction vehicle, they are contributing to the rubble mountain of their future, instead of dealing and working through the ones of their past.

Even though Marko begs him to stop, Lucky follows his bad-guy script and burns the car with the corpse in the trunk: "The cops won't ever believe we had nothing to do with this." Once the deed is done, all three meet up at the rubble mountain: "I'm out of here." But Falco reminds him: "We can't get out without money." The plan to extort money from Wille takes shape. When Marko finally gets his cut from Falco, his mother locks him in his room, having notified social services. He will move on but only to a youth detention center. Falco ends up getting shot by Ollenberg and joins his buddy in the cemetery, where the episode started.

The sense of perpetual persecution by the *Volkspolizei* and Stasi still hanging over his generation, Lucky is convinced he is next. He steals a white BMW and pursues Ollenberg's golden Mercedes heading West with Katja in the backseat. The James Bond-style battle of the brands has begun. When the Mercedes with Ollenberg gets totaled in the inevitable crash, it proves that its gilded veneer cannot deliver on its promises. The white BMW, while dented, is still functional, and Lucky and Katja speed off. The bad condition of the back-country roads in the GDR makes the camera on the dash bounce, lending the clichéd scene a documentary but also haptic videogame controller feel. The heavier rock score from the road race switches to a country ballad: "I want to meet you in big sky country," as Lucky and Katja smile at each other, cruising westward through the rolling hills like Bonnie and Clyde. Along the way and fitting into the new self-conception as Clyde, Lucky holds up a deserted rural gas station with his toy gun and laughs. The country ballad repeats "big sky country" as the camera pans to reveal open skies and fields in a long shot of the disappearing BMW.

In the last sequence, Lucky and Katja are cut off by the police and flee on foot across a barren field. Kain pursues them, quickly out of breath. Lucky waves his gun around; Katja screams at Kain "Don't shoot." Just as Lucky enters the confines of a tractor-lane on the field instead of forging his own path, the country ballad portents how this duel will end: "Death and life are so close to one another. Red is my blood, and it seeps into the field. This day was beautiful, too beautiful for this world."[41] As Lucky turns around, he grabs his pistol with both hands and aims. Kain reacts to this stance as he was trained to do and shoots to kill. Katja cries, "It's not loaded, it's just a toy." If Lucky's holdup of the gas station was his dress rehearsal, Kain is trained to read Lucky's performance on the field as a threat. In the very moment that Lucky is taken seriously as an adult, he dies.

The East German teenager follows a script that is conjured by the preceding car chase, the iconographic Western setting, an ill-fated gangster-style romance, and a gun prop, combining globally circulated film, videogame, and television genres into a deadly semiotic cocktail. The attempt to move from one genre to and through the next to find a form of expression that can sustain his drive, his coming of age through the *Wende* (the 1989 turn), ends in parallel to Lucky's drag race. Here, it is Kain, the West German investigator, who dead-ends the turn, reading his and Lucky's performances within the borders of policing and the conventions of the crime drama. After the shot, as Kain walks away in despair over taking Lucky's life, *Tatort*'s

---

[41] "Der Tod und das Leben sind einander so nah. Rot ist mein Blut, und es sickert ins Feld. Dieser Tag war der schönste, zu schön für die Welt" (lyrics by Ben Becker).

own genre-dependent and geopolitical blind spots are reflexively examined by this cult episode.

While seeking to appeal to a different demographic by revising the aesthetic format of *Tatort* through an inter-medial design, a music-montage title sequence, and an extended cold open, while depicting and reflecting on the sociopolitical and economic moment achieving the sought-after "proximity to reality," while promoting complex psychological profiles of detectives and suspects, *Tatort* is still bound by the crime drama format. At the end of this episode, perhaps, one can see, for the briefest moment, an inkling of regret and anxiety about contributing to a discourse of criminalization that enforces a weekly body count rather than providing substantial support for critical emancipatory developments in the East and the West.

"Todesstrafe" ("Death Penalty," dir. Patrick Winczewski; MDR, May 25, 2008)

Tagesschau Synopsis

The recent Burma hurricane disaster begins the evening news program. Jens Hofer, the anchor, emphasizes the fact that international humanitarian aid is now being accepted by the military government.

The next segment switches to domestic politics without any transition—the party convention of *Die Linke* (Party of the Socialist Left that emerged out of the former GDR)—and just as swiftly continues with an official review of the states' social service structure in Germany, especially federal subsidies for lower income residents to offset rent and utilities costs. These subsidies are allegedly given too freely in most states, except Bavaria. The following segment takes viewers to the former GDR, to Leipzig, where the SPD commemorates the foundation of the *Allgemeinen Deutschen Arbeitervereins* in 1863, out of which the party later emerged. Editing these four topics together brands the social support network in Germany with a socialist label and compares aid to flood victims with government subsidies. It also aligns the Left with the much more moderate SPD, even though the latter officially refused to enter a red-red coalition and continued to work with the Greens or the FDP, even the CDU. And it maps socialism onto the East with its focus on Leipzig.

In the fifth segment, we are off to Schleswig-Holstein in the Northwest, where the CDU emerged victorious in the state's elections, improving on their historically low results from the previous election. Striking a balance to the segments covering the left end of the political spectrum, viewers are subsequently treated to a report on the 97th German *Catholic Day* in the West German city of Osnabrück, attended by approximately 25,000 believers. As if he had watched the earlier segments, the headlining bishop is quoted as reprimanding an "over-reliance on and elevated levels of requests" from the states and the federal government.

The final segment of the news goes to Lebanon, where after a long and arduous process of negotiating with the Hezbollah, Syrian and anti-Syrian factions, army chief Suleiman has become the new president. The *Tagesschau* ends with coverage of the annual national science youth fair, *Jugend Forscht*, and the Eurovision song contest winners and losers (Russia won, Germany lost).

To understand the programmatic multifaceted embeddedness of *Tatort* into the network's televisual flow, it is worth noting that the ARD *Tagesthemen* following this evening's *Tatort* episode from Leipzig devotes its opening segment to missing and abused children in Germany. While activities surrounding the official international day of the missing child and the media frenzy around the 2007 disappearance of Madeleine McCann from a Portugal hotel room brought this topic into renewed focus, it is clearly intentional on part of ARD's producers to provide the greatest possible integration between the network's factual and fictional content. Confronting the mass hysteria over child abuse with some actual statistics, the report underscores that most missing children in Germany turn up after only a short absence. Yet the anchor also reveals that 1,600 children to date have never been found. The subsequent exposé on a missing Trier university student not only touches on the ongoing psychological trauma suffered by parents and siblings but also stresses the support networks in place for them.

As the evening schedule crisscrosses between different forms and practices of representation, between international and domestic news coverage, a regional crime drama, and a case study, the focus topic is approached from different angles in each segment. On the one hand, this cements Gunther Witte's foundational *Tatort* doctrine and extends its mantra to the network lineup. The lineup serves *Tatort* as much as *Tatort* anchors the lineup. On the other hand, the continual inter- and intra-program focus on an issue resonant on global, national, and regional levels furthers general accessibility, especially in the time-shift era. If multi-platform viewers missed one segment but found the focus topic relevant to their interests or concerns, they can watch the other in real time or find more on the topic online afterward, where the ARD *Mediathek* will return several results under the same search terms.

Tatort Synopsis

In their first case, and *Tatort*'s 700th episode, the formerly married Eva Saalfeld (Simone Thomalla) and Andreas Keppler (Martin Wutke) have to investigate the stabbing death of Hans Freytag (Tom Quaas), the proprietor of the "factory," a local youth center. The words "death penalty" and "pedophile" are found sprayed on the walls of the center and on the boat Freytag was restoring there. Prior to his death, he had been accused of abusing the young daughter he shares with his wife Sibylle (Julia Richter). When that accusation becomes public, some locals suspect Freytag of having something to do with the mutilation and murder of two children the year before. Investigations zero in on two suspects: one of the teenagers, Max Lornsen (Joseph Bundschuh), and the leader of a local organization calling for the death penalty for pedophiles, Kurt Steinbrecher (Matthias Brenner). Saalfeld and Keppler are dropped into a district of Leipzig where broken families are the new normal, and disenfranchised locals' dog whistles have led to mobbing and vigilante justice.

Critical and Viewer Engagement

Doing triple duty as the 700th episode, the introduction of a new team in a new city, critics and viewers paid attention and had ample reason to tune in. Leipzig presented a chance at a homecoming and a new direction after thirty-eight years of the series. Sylvia Staude refers to the videography as "a jump into a new visual frontier" and highlights the director's visual concept of Leipzig as a "Las Vegas" look-alike (*Frankfurter Rundschau*, May 24, 2008). Jochen Hieber remarks how "the camera scans the terrain and delivers elegiac scenes from the restored city center as well as from a Leipzig periphery that still reminds one of GDR times" (*FAZ*, May 25, 2008).[42]

The script of this *Tatort* episode resurrects national trauma around state executions during the Third Reich and the GDR. But it also brings to the surface regional trauma around instances of abuse and murder of children in Leipzig and environment: the three Erwin Hagedorn murders between 1969 and 1971, the case of Mitja in 2007. In addition, the script uncannily foreshadows the mass hysteria around Michelle's murder in August 2008 and Corinna's in 2009.[43]

---

[42] Jochen Hieber, "Das leise Lächeln am Ohr der Kommissarin," *FAZ*, May 25, 2008, https://www.faz.net/aktuell/feuilleton/medien/tatort-mit-neuem-team-das-leise-laecheln-am-ohr-der-kommissarin-1546497.html (accessed August 21, 2020).
[43] These two child murder cases from Leipzig made national news between 2007 and 2010. See Gisela Friedrichsen, "Mordprozeß im Fall Michele [sic]," *Spiegel Panorama*, August 17, 2009, https://www.spiegel.de/panorama/justiz/mordprozess-im-fall-michelle-geschaendet-getoetet-entwuerdigt-a-643338.html and Lars Radau, "Trauer und hilflose Wut," *Stern*, August 22, 2008, https://www.stern.de/politik/deutschland/kindermord-in-leipzig-trauer-und-hilflose-wut-3754492.html and Christiane Kohl, "Ermordet in der Gartenlaube," *Süddeutsche Zeitung*, February 26, 2007, and May 17, 2010, https://www.sueddeutsche.de/panorama/fall-mitja-ermordet-in-der-gartenlaube-1.674793 (accessed August 21, 2020).

The Hagedorn case helps to clarify why the call for the death penalty makes an entrance and how it resonates with a certain contingent of the population's dissatisfaction with the new legal parameters in the united Germany. At the same time the scandalous focus on child abuse and murder obscures politically motivated abuse during the Third Reich, whose pattern of repression against the political opposition continued in the GDR. There were twenty acts punishable with the death penalty in the GDR, one of them attempted *Republikflucht* (fleeing the republic). In 1949, West Germany decided not to reinstate the death penalty (West Berlin had a special status and repealed the death penalty in 1951). Between 1949 and 1981, the GDR sentenced over 600 citizens to death of which over 200 were executed in secret, first by guillotine and later by a shot in the neck. The cause of death was always labeled as a medical one. The majority of executions took place under cover of darkness at the Central Execution Center of the GDR in Leipzig. Corpses were anonymously laid to rest at the city's South cemetery.[44] Until 1968, the GDR adopted paragraph 175a of the Third Reich that criminalized the so-called unnatural desire between men, specifically acts with those under twenty-one.[45] The blending of homosexuality and pedophilia also signifies a displacement of the historical reckoning with large-scale systemic executions of politically undesirable citizens onto undesirable social, racial, and sexual minorities. That a subsector of Leipzig and former GDR residents call for the death penalty for pedophiles in the 2008 *Tatort* script and the Michelle case thus establishes the existence of continuities not only between pre- and post-1989 but also between pre- and post-1945.

Even though Michelle's murder took place two months after the episode aired, I include it here because her case exemplifies how complex and multidirectional televisual flow can become. The coverage in *Stern* magazine reads like the official *Tatort* episode description on the ARD website:

> The murder of eight-year-old Michelle brings emotions to a boil in the Leipzig district of Anger-Crottendorf. While schools and authorities urge calmness and the police feverishly look for traces, some residents demand draconian punishments for the perpetrator.[46]

The article goes on to describe how public mourning mixes with mass hysteria, how residents "quickly drop names of this and that neighbor, who came to

---

[44]Hans Michael Kloth, "Der Henker kam von hinten," *Der Spiegel*, July 13, 2007, https://www.spiegel.de/panorama/zeitgeschichte/todesstrafe-in-der-ddr-der-henker-kam-von-hinten-a-494202.html (accessed August 21, 2020).
[45]For more information, see Josie McLellan, *Love in the Time of Communism: Intimacy and Sexuality in the GDR* (Cambridge: Cambridge University Press, 2011).
[46]Radau, "Trauer und hilflose Wut."

attention because of 'something with kids' or because they have a criminal record." Similar to the divided community in the *Tatort* episode, exemplified by the contrast of opinion between Herr and Frau Kühne (the bakery owners), during the Michelle case, one interviewed resident wants "the electric chair" for the culprit, and the other wants to wait and "see what actually comes out of the investigation." While these diverging reactions to a child murder case are common, the connection to the neo-Nazi scene connects the August case to "Todesstrafe" in the way both address the German past and the resurgence of German fascism in the 1990s. When Frau Kühne confronts Kurt Steinbrecher, the head of a local right-wing organization, at the scene of the crime in the *Tatort* episode, he loses his grip on some flyers. The flyers demand the death penalty for pedophiles and homosexuals. After Michelle's murder, the local organization Initiative of Upstanding Citizens, among them reportedly many neo-Nazis, held a *Mahnwache* (vigil) in front of her school. A school official ordered the removal of two flyers demanding the "death penalty for child abusers" that were posted on the gate. In addition, according to the two articles about Michelle's murder, a Nazi rune was found at the crime scene, and right-wing extremists were mobilizing through an internet list serve.

The supporters of the "cultivation hypothesis" seek to prove a direct connection between the portrayal and consumption of violent acts on television to committing these acts. That is not my goal here. Instead, the similarities between "Todesstrafe" and public reactions to the August murder case detail how mediated depictions of public reactions to violence can turn into social scripts for public mourning: when and how to mourn, how to mark the occasion as an individual and as a community, what to leave at the site when demonstrating one's respects, how to make protests against locally committed violence legible to a national and global audience, how to use the rarity of the media spotlight to air local and regional grievances and make them heard on a national and global level. The cross-pollination is crucial. Television crews descend on crime scenes that have become sites of public mourning precisely because they often feature visual displays, thereby further strengthening the social scripts resulting in the displays. While the feedback loop of hypermediated events retroactively attributes a prescient sense of social realism and contemporariness to the May *Tatort* episode, the flow also ensures that future scripts with public displays of mourning and mass hysteria will follow "Todesstrafe's" lead. Scholars who have studied the differences between culturally specific rituals of mourning through the ages have wrestled with the way the internet and social media have affected these rituals on a global scale since the 1990s.[47] In the oft-desperate attempt

---

[47]Martin Gibbs, James Meese, Michael Arnold, Bjorn Nansen and Marcus Carter, "#Funeral and Instagram: Death, Social Media, and Platform Vernacular," *Information, Communication & Society* 18, no. 3 (2015): 255–68.

to find a meaningful way to memorialize the dead, to participate in publicly legible mourning rituals, and to process incomprehensible acts of violence, the source for the inspiration of one's reaction and the specific form it takes is often elided. But that erasure does not mean that a discursive and media-specific intersection did not and does not exist.

The Post-Network Crime Drama between Soap Opera and New German Cinema

The episode explores different positionalities within the globally connected cityscape—Keppler arriving in Leipzig from the West, Saalfeld coming back home to a new post, and Freytag, the local, losing his life in the process of improving the lives of local youths. The intentionally intertwined backstory of the new investigators, including the loss of their child and Keppler's struggle with alcoholism, plays a significant role in the course of their twenty-one episodes together. The soap opera aspect that allows viewers access to Saalfeld's and Keppler's private lives—the stolen glances and smiles, their fights, the chess games with his landlord, her nephew's visits—capitalizes on genre-hybridity and narrative complexity, both characteristics of the emerging multi-platform mediascape in 2008.[48] The backstory constructs both a residual love interest and an intractable conflict between the partners that teases with but prohibits the happy-ever-after of Bruce Willis's and Crystal Shepherd's *Moonlighting* (ABC, 1985–9), which famously led to the demise of that show.

The cold open is structured as a cross-cut montage between Freytag on his way to the bakery and his youth center, and the spray can in action. The white mist of the spray can is used for the dissolves between shots indicating that he is the intended target. The hidden graffiti sprayer and knife wielder set up a classic whodunit. Is it one and the same, or are they two different people? The mystery is complicated by the fact that the whole district seems

---

[48] Tilmann Gangloff of the *Kölner Stadtanzeiger*, May 23, 2008, points specifically to Keppler's "autistic traits," when he compares him to the introverted title character in *Monk* (USA, 2002–9) and notes the "new challenges" of this type of "romantic potential." In a 2008 interview celebrating the 700th episode of the series, *Tatort* director Sven Döbler explains what makes this duo unique in the series: "Eva Saalfeld und Andreas Keppler sind eine Frau und ein Mann, die gleichberechtigt ermitteln, beide sind in den besten Jahren, in der Mitte des Lebens, und sie waren mal miteinander verheiratet. Also haben sie beruflich eine Menge Erfahrungen gesammelt (und tun es auch weiterhin), und sie kennen sich persönlich sehr genau. Das erzeugt, bei aller Unterschiedlichkeit ihrer Ermittlungsweisen und den Krisen, die sich daraus ergeben, immer wieder die Möglichkeit einer große Nähe und Wärme zwischen den Kommissaren, die ich als sehr wohltuend empfinde." Francois Werner, "Wie machen wir dem Zuschauer Lust darauf, das nächste Mal wieder einzuschalten?" https://www.tatort-fundus.de/web/folgen/chrono/2000-bis-2009/2008/700-todesstrafe/interview-mit-sven-doebler.html (accessed August 21, 2020).

to have taken a position on Hans Freytag's personal and public life. We find out immediately that even Herr Kühne, the proprietor of his favorite bakery, has joined in mobbing Freytag: "You don't get anything from here anymore." When the first sequence ends with Freytag staring at his killer, the camera pulls back into a long shot of Saalfeld beginning her new job with warm welcomes and handshakes. The following sequence alternates its shots between Saalfeld's, Keppler's, and Frau Kühne's (the baker's wife) arrivals. Keppler hauls his own suitcase through the train station while Saalfeld receives cards and trinkets. Going against her husband's explicit order, Frau Kühne delivers rolls to the factory only to find her murdered customer. These interlaced arrivals effectively contrast the two investigators' and Freytag's experiences of Leipzig and open up the contested spaces between and within the local, regional, national, and global.

Andreas Keppler, aptly named after Johannes Kepler (1571–1630), the German mathematician who laid out the law of planetary motion, is introduced to viewers as a one-suitcase kind of guy. He moves a lot and does not have many possessions; and he is not picky where he lays his head. He generally goes his own way, and prefers to do things himself. If at all, he follows Trimmel's path. The network clearly wants to forge that connection in homage to television history. In front of the central train station, he studies a map and gets on the next streetcar to the crime scene. Like in 1970, viewers hitch a ride with him, getting (re)introduced to the city and region on *Tatort* for the second time. This time around, bright restaurant and shop awnings beckon from the sidelines, the city humming with pedestrians, bikers, and cars, the staged setting exchanged for on-location realism. "Taxi to Leipzig" and its unification mission are made real thirty-eight years later.

When he arrives at the converted brick-factory backlot on foot, Keppler has to wait in front of the police line like the other spectators. Unlike Saalfeld, he observes how looking and public mourning become spectacle. He sees the youth center's teenagers, one of them grim and aggressive, the others setting up a memorial display for Freytag. Keppler's nonlocal "embedded" position thus gives him a level of access the investigators cannot recapture within the interview setting. By portraying Keppler as an "Ortsloser" (without a place of origin), Klaus Raab argues that producers are avoiding the pitfall of "overly exaggerating the regional so that individual mannerisms of characters are elevated to mentalities of an entire region" (*taz*, May 25, 2008). But when he does not shake the offered hand of the crime scene technician Wolfgang Menzel (Maxim Mehmet), he comes across as a stereotypical *Wessie*—impolite and snobbish. His West German identity thus becomes a marker formerly reserved for regional characteristics. If Keppler's homelessness avoids regional stereotyping, it also resurrects a specific "homeless" masculinity from New German Cinema, the eccentric world wanderers in search of themselves and Germany.

When Keppler retires at his *Pension*, he lies on the bed in his suite. The camera frames him in front of the mid-window gauze curtains with the hotel's neon lights bathing the room in pastel colors. As Silvia Staude remarks, this aesthetic turns Leipzig into Las Vegas. For example, R. W. Fassbinder used highly stylized lighting to color-code his characters in *Lola* (1981). In Wim Wenders's *Alice in the Cities* (1974), Philip Winter (Rüdiger Vogler) lies on his Vegas hotel bed watching television, while the neon lights turn him into our flickering screen. Even if these film historic citations are unintentional, the similarity in character type, blocking, and lighting constructs a connection between the way the auteurs of New German Cinema and television writers employ iconic US locales and media culture for both their sociopolitical and reflexive effects. While Wenders's male protagonists were living through a post-1968 disenchantment with their home country and suffering from postmodern ennui, they were taken in by US popular culture. New Hollywood and US popular music became a community-surrogate for the displaced generation. The Baudrillardian simulacrum of Las Vegas with its strip combines with the nomadism of New German Cinema's soul-searching protagonists and the televisual flow of broadcast television.

In the 2008 *Tatort*, New German Cinema aesthetics combine with melodrama and soap opera conventions. The characters' backstory and lingering tensions are applied as an allegory for the German-German relationship. While he shares his restlessness with Philip Winter, Keppler's uprootedness seems to be the combined result of his devotion to his job, his antisocial tendencies, and the end of his post-1989 romance with Saalfeld (East). From dialogue fragments, we know that the two broke it off in 1996, when major differences (re)asserted themselves. The ebb and flow of the team's relationship directly graphs onto the honeymoon and disenchantment phases of German unification. The scene in his hotel room exemplifies that Leipzig might as well be Vegas for Keppler, that his desire for a reconnection matches his anxieties for the same, reaching a state of paralysis that leaves him fully clothed with his eyes open on his dingy hotel bed, the neon lights becoming the only animated element of the scene. Instead of watching television, he is breaking the fourth wall, looking at us watching him on television, watching the lights of the new Leipzig flow over his still body, which turn his animated silhouette into our projection screen. While the camera solidified Trimmel to make him an anchor in the push and pull of the Cold War in 1970, it makes Keppler's body fluctuate despite its stillness.

The flickering neon transforms him into a chameleon, who adapts to his surroundings and "plugs and plays." He barely sets a foot in the lobby of his hotel, and he is already playing chess on the proprietor's board, calculating the moves that lead black to the win. This character profile is in keeping with the hybrid genre approach of the new series entry as well as reflective of the post-network era. One of his first complaints is that his computer is not installed, when he arrives at headquarters. As the two investigators walk down the central hallway, he ducks into offices to compare technology setups, disappearing off-screen only to reappear in front of the camera, while Saalfeld is still looking for him further down the corridor. Keppler's zigzagging (dis)appearances add time-shifting to his *Ortslosigkeit*. The at turns comical and aggravating scene demonstrates his tendency to act without communicating his intentions or plans, but it also maps his behavior onto the time-shifted viewing habits of the DVR and streaming era.

While Saalfeld progresses along the linearly configured publicly accessible network corridor and expects him (and network viewers) to follow her, Keppler navigates hyper-textually, stepping sideways and utilizing interconnected rhizomic pathways, before joining her at the point in time and space where she was originally headed, before she backtracked to find him. The time- and space shifts do not make him lose sight of the destination or the schedule, just the opposite. Embodying post-network reception practices during his onboarding as a new investigator in Lepizig, Keppler expresses the network's hopes of attracting nonlinear multi-platform viewers while retaining *Tatort* regulars. The scene is also useful in refreshing staid narration patterns and in keeping both Saalfeld and viewers on their toes.

Later, Saalfeld and Keppler briefly share the same seat in front of Saalfeld's PC to research a website that was advertised on one of the labels found at the crime scene. For a precious synchronous moment, the scene models how *Tatort* unites time-shifting, web-savvy, and old-school investigators and viewers. When the two discover that "pfarma" is a chat room, where people "flirt with one another," Keppler immediately gives himself a fake persona to interact with the chat online, prompting Saalfeld to get off the chair to fondly remember and quote a sentence from one of his love letters to her. The brief moment of living in the same time and space has passed, when Keppler says: "I never wrote that." His answer is telling. It could imply that he courted Saalfeld like Christian woos Roxane in *Cyrano de Bergerac* (Edmond Rostand, 1897), treating literature like a template for a "cut and paste" or that he took on a persona to fit Saalfeld's expectations. In either case, this sets up the complexity of their backstory and underscores her preference for linear modalities vis-à-vis his "textual poaching" (Henry Jenkins).

While it is encouraging to have a female lead in the Leipzig *Tatort*, Saalfeld's two soap opera storylines cast her as a love object caught between two leading men and as a maternal figure. When the handsome pathologist checks in on her and invites her out for dinner, she declines: "It was a big day." The next day, Saalfeld forgets to pick up her nephew Lukas from daycare. When she remembers, she loads Keppler, who protests against this "waste of time," into the car. They pick up the jovial Lukas a half hour too late. "You are getting better. Last time it was an hour, aunt Eva."

In trend with portrayals of career-mothers in romantic comedies (e.g., *One Fine Day*, dir. Michael Hoffmann, 1996), the progressive packaging is undermined by a conservative reprimand. Even though Lukas makes light of Saalfeld's lack of dedication, and Saalfeld is not his mother, Saalfeld gets stuck with the quickly dispensed *Rabenmutter* (neglectful, uncaring mother) label, especially in an episode that revolves around the dangers that could befall unattended children. In a 2007 interview, Leonie Herwartz-Emden contends that the continuing polarization of motherhood in Germany goes back to the Third Reich:

> The woman was incorporated into the ideology of National Socialism. She had to wage the war on the home front. A child rearing book from that time, financed by Joseph Goebbels, had a high rate of circulation. It was reprinted with only slight modifications in cover and text until well into the 1970s. With it, the heroicized portrayal of the mother continued uninterrupted. We are still dealing with that national socialist inheritance today.[49]

The scene in this episode is designed to represent Saalfeld as a typical overcommitted modern woman, devoted to her job at the expense of her family. This matters because their backstory points to a trauma involving the loss of a child. The belated pick-up scene prods viewers to wonder what happened and who was to blame. Since we have not seen Keppler relapse and fail as a father, we only see Saalfeld fail the punctual mother test. By contrast, Inge, her mother, depicts the ideal of dedicated German maternity, selflessly caring for her grandchild, ready with coffee and cake when they arrive. Her domesticity and natural authority play favorably off of Saalfeld's perpetual hurrying. Saalfeld delivers Lukas to her mother with a quick hug. Inge stares at Keppler until he gets out of the car. An awkward moment later, he nods his head "Inge," whereupon she asks: "Is that all after twelve years?" "You look good." "So do you." Even scenes designed to support Eva's storyline end up revolving around her "lack" as a mother and daughter—and around Keppler.

Following soap opera conventions, a woman's face with large eyes is preferably captured in suspended close-ups, inserted as a mirror for unspoken and unspeakable emotions. Employed in this fashion, Simone Thomalla's classically beautiful face is at turns quizzically tuned into or reacting to people, scenes, words, or actions. Her face expresses the nurturing maternity she was found lacking in the scene earlier. Her steadfast conductive

---

[49]Pia Volk, "Das deutsche Mutterdilemma: Rabenmutter oder Hausmütterchen," *Deutsche Welle*, April 13, 2007, https://www.dw.com/de/das-deutsche-mutterdilemma-rabenmutter-oder-hausmütterchen/a-2440659 (accessed September 4, 2020).

televisuality merges her maternal and her detective selves. Whenever the camera frames her face, she appears to know exactly what someone is going through, smiles when that is required, or beckons encouragingly to tell her more. Like a convector, she circulates warm air to make others feel comfortable. Her face ensures continuity between segments. Unlike her soap opera peers in television, for example Linda Gray as Sue-Ellen Ewing in *Dallas* (1978–91), whose quavering lips and high-rise eyebrows conveyed the results of suffering sustained systemic abuse at the hands of the patriarchy, Thomalla's close-ups function as resets and resting points within a narrative dominated by Keppler's unpredictable time- and space-shifting movements and occasional angry outbursts. Like Hannah Schygulla in *Die Ehe der Maria Braun* (Fassbinder, 1978), Saalfeld's face most often exudes a mature confidence gained by having dealt with and moved past trauma, a face that reflects what it looks like if one managed to refocus on the positive rather than the negative—of people and memories, of regional and national history. She is indeed the face of a city that wants to live into its presence rather than its past. In doing so, the MDR provided viewers with a team that managed to restore Leipzig in a *Hypzig* format.

Sounding Out (Re)Unification

When the team decides to pay Steinbrecher's organization a visit, the sound of a choir singing "Am Brunnen vor dem Tore" ("At the Well before the City Gate," Text: Wilhelm Müller, 1823; Musik: Franz Schubert) greets viewers in the street, before we can identify where it comes from. Since neither of the two characters react to the sound, it is ambiguous whether the source is ambient, off-screen diegetic, or extradiegetic. The effect is disconcerting in the context of the episode's focus on nationalism. After a cut, we find out that a choir's rehearsal seeped out of a dark-paneled bar cellar into the public sphere, mingling with everyday noises of traffic and conversations. Considering that Leipzig is famous for its *Auerbachskeller*, a wine cellar dating back to the sixteenth century, the below ground setting seems too specific to ignore. While this is not the actual *Auerbachskeller*, where German author Johann Wolfgang Goethe, who was a frequent patron during his studies in Leipzig, reportedly found his inspiration for his adaptation of the *Faust* legend, it obviously triggers that reference to anyone even remotely familiar with German literature and Leipzig's main attractions.

The nineteenth-century *Volkslied* evokes the dualities of *Heimat* (home and homeland) and *Fremde* (foreign and foreign land), spring and winter, as a man turns toward the city gates away from the linden tree facing the cold, blowing winter wind head-on, without the safety of cover. In subsequent stanzas, the linden tree and the village become a longed-for memory from abroad. Depending on the context, the winter wind blowing the subject's hat off has been interpreted to signify the period of political restauration, war, the human drive to explore, and more generally life's struggles. The blooming linden tree at the spring or well in the village has been seen as the symbolic center of the community, where love and death intersect.

This in and of itself sounds innocuous, and most readily available information on the song does not explore the adaptation of this and other *Volkslieder* by the Nazis following the movements' fervent return to a Germanified nationalist song canon. In that context, the linden tree became a symbol of a racially defined Germanic family tree. During Hitler's reign, the strong headwind was reconceptualized as the force to be conquered, which included Jews, who throughout German history were often denounced as well poisoners by fervent anti-Semites. The first stanza visualized soldiers heading into battle, at home and abroad, to battle forces endangering the source (in Nazi rhetoric, Germany's "blood and soil"). Later stanzas expressed the longing to return to a vision of home that remained unchanged and pure.

This *Tatort* makes the connection between Nazi ideology, the neo-Nazi scene, and this folk song explicit. In the German language, the word for pedophile is *Kinderschänder* (child abuser), the same word stem used for anti-Semitic propaganda accusing Jews frequenting the company of so-called Aryan women as *Rassenschänder* (race abuser) during the Third Reich. The word *Kinderschänder* was written on Freytag's door before his murder. Keppler helps us connect the dots, when Steinbrecher emphatically denies having "consorted with the likes of a pedophile": "Mit wem pflegen Sie denn zu verkehren, mein lieber Herr Gesangsverein?" (Literally: Then, with whom do you consort, my dear Mr. Singing Club?) And a bit later: "I am going back in there—Steinbrecher *fallera*." Keppler barks out the add-on chorus fragment—"fallera"—a typical rhyming device in German folk songs (e.g., "Im Frühtau zu Berge, wir zieh'n fallera"), indicating his disgust with the resurrection of German nationalism and Steinbrecher's right-wing witch hunt.

The fact that the folk song carries from below ground onto the street suggests that nationalist discourse, forced underground by East Germany's official antifascist stance and suppressed during West Germany's official wrestling with collective and cultural memory, is emerging into the open, that it is saturating the public sphere of a unified Germany under the thin veneer of its back catalogue. The well-known nostalgic chorus hovers in the air, functioning like Laura U. Mark's "radioactive memory," a memory that is called forth from a shared cultural archive whether one wants it to or not.[50] Sung by a community of ordinary-looking middle-aged women and men, the song is bound to resonate with viewers in some way or another, sneaking

---

[50]Laura U. Marks and Dana Poland, *The Skin of the Film* (Durham: Duke University, 2000).

up on them before its identity and problematic history are consciously identified. When Saalfeld and Keppler enter the restaurant, the chorus finishes the final stanza of the song, while the camera pans over the singers in medium close-up and through the busy restaurant. As the two detectives stand by, a waitress asks them if they want anything to drink, normalizing the spectacle as regular entertainment. True to television's medium-specific penchant for polysemy, this shot turns the team into our stand-in diegetic audience, and it allows viewers intent on ignoring or agreeing with the Nazi echoes of the song to delight in hearing one of their old favorites while providing an eerie warning for progressive viewers at the same time.

In a later scene, when Saalfeld meets with Klaus Arend (Roman Knizka), he suggests the same traditional cellar bar. She announces her astonishment: "I would not have thought that you come here." The very fact that the writers Mario Giordano and Andreas Schlüter chose to revisit the locale of the choir scene is significant. Saalfeld and Arend sit in the same corner that was formerly occupied by the choir, now a quaint and appealing corner niche, each a drink in front of them. The room appears cozy, evenly and warmly lit lit in mellow brown tones, unlike the low-key lighting during the daytime choir scene. The camera captures the two in close-ups. It is as if the writers want to advertise the local flair of a classic Leipzig establishment, extending an invitation to viewers to bask in the glow of a shared social evening among old friends.

Yet, as it turns out, Arend is also the lawyer involved in the pedophilia suit against Freytag. And as Freytag's ex-wife's lover, he helped pay one of her outstanding loans. Behind them, in deep focus at the bar, we recognize Kurt Steinbrecher and both of Max Lornsen's parents. Her lawyer friend as well as Lutz Lornsen trained under Steinbrecher in the *Bundeswehr* "right after the Wende." This scene connects the comradery of military service with the regional and suggests a continuity of power hierarchies in the local community.

In the context of Steinbrecher's organization advocating for the death penalty for pedophiles, a victim has turned into a perpetrator, when Lutz Lornsen is revealed as the murderer. A former soldier and victim of sexual abuse himself, he is convinced that his son, Max, is being abused by Freytag. In a move rather typical for soap operas and crime time on television, popular science tag lines—in this case "sexual abuse victims are predisposed to become perpetrators themselves"—are converted into plot lines so that the political can be expressed through the personal. Saalfeld, who cites this very line to Elle and Lutz Lornsen, does not mention the fact that the likelihood of childhood abuse victims avenging themselves on a suspected or proven adult perpetrator is lower than the likelihood of reproducing the abuse.[51]

---

[51]Bundesministerium für Arbeit, Familie und Jugend: "Prädisponierte Täter waren selbst Opfer von psychischem/physischem und/oder sexuellem Missbrauch und richten ihre unverarbeiteten

The scene also implicates the structure of child and youth activities in the GDR, from daycare and school to hobby, athletic, and political youth organizations. Younger and older adults in charge in these organizations likely became role models, confidantes, and friends but were also more likely to be drafted as unofficial informants for the Stasi due to their strategic positions in interacting with kids and parents. Consequently, the sense of betrayal and abuse must have been considerable when names and surveillance protocols could be accessed by individuals after 1989. For this reason, Lornsen's unprocessed childhood trauma is still readable as the lasting fallout of the GDR state's systemic abuse his generation has carried into unification. His wife's partially apologetic yet also aggressive bystander rhetoric additionally evokes the haunting paralysis of those citizens pressed into functioning as unofficial informants and the knowledge that they would endanger their friends and neighbors and uphold the system of surveillance and repression in East Germany's regime.

Family Therapy

Whether intended as an outright homage to the very first *Tatort* and Trimmel's armchair psychology or whether simply a sign of the continuous preference for pop-psychology in this crime series or a mixture of both, this episode ends with a psychological intervention at the scene of the crime. Utilizing the tactics of a dramatic *Familienaufstellung* a la Virginia Satir (authoritatively adapted in Germany by Bert Hellinger),[52] Saalfeld and Keppler unite to position Lutz and Elke opposite each other and the boat at the scene of the crime. Saalfeld assumes the therapist's position up high, whereas Keppler confronts Lutz from the side with a GDR file of the abuse report. Assuming the role of Steinbrecher, another authority figure who abused his sway over Lornsen, Keppler hands him the spray can to "finish the job." When Keppler places the file picture of the uncle—shown with his arms around Lornsen's younger self—on the rim of the boat in the middle of the circle, Lornsen's legs begin shaking in response. The placement of the image propels him to assume the positionality of a son—his son—in the circle. The intervention is deemed a success when he breaks down and admits his guilt.

The placement of the image on the upturned, unfinished boat that his son was repairing with Freytag is ripe with symbolism. In comparison to

---

Erlebnisse als sexuelle Gewalt gegen Kinder," https://www.gewaltinfo.at/fachwissen/formen/sexualisiert/taeter.php (accessed September 9, 2020).
[52]Colin Goldner, "Familienaufstellung nach Hellinger: Wenn Ahnen krank machen," *Süddeutsche Zeitung*, May 8, 2010, https://www.sueddeutsche.de/wissen/teil-8-familienaufstellung-nach-hellinger-wenn-ahnen-krank-machen-1.863677 (accessed September 9, 2020).

the 1994 Dresden *Tatort*, where the youths were spinning their wheels but not getting anywhere, here it is a representative of the older generation, who interferes in a multigenerational restauration project because he is stuck in his personal and his generation's national trauma. Like the defunct brick factory which houses it, the boat is and will remain stranded. With a dig at the undelivered promise of prosperity following unification in the East, what stood for dreams of social mobility and freedom has been reduced to the empty hull of a stifled, land-locked potential.

The ending makes apparent the discontent of a large minority within the new states, who have turned to a broad spectrum of right-wing alliances in a combination of xenophobia, anxiety over rapid social changes, and disillusion with economic progress and democracy. *Tatort* writers approach this phenomenon through the format-typical psychological lens, emphasizing the personal pain underneath the political and criminal actions to appeal to similarly disenchanted viewers. Producers bank on diverse psychological profiles in combination with backstory secrets and hyper-medial imagery to provide enough eye-catching visuals and serial accents for nonlinear and cross-platform engagement. Because this pits its regional approach against the expected social-critical assessment of lived realities, *Tatort* aims to have it both ways: acknowledge the dissatisfaction in the East *and* show Leipzig as a burgeoning youthful center of innovation and commerce. The camera shows us one thing, the crime plot and soap opera storyline tell us another. Gender norms that are broken within the diegesis are resuscitated on the media-reflexive level. The open female face in close-up situates viewers "at home with television"; the male body becomes a projection field for and embodiment of nonlinear mobility. This episode exhibits the synchronous existence of parallel worlds that try to but never quite come together, not even in Saalfelds's and Keppler's collaboration. And with this, network protocols have found a representational model that at least acknowledges the post-1989 disconnect along with post-network media practices.

Conclusion

The nine analyzed episodes between 1970 and 2008 illuminate the format adaptability of the ARD network's regionally structured franchise concept for its flagship crime drama *Tatort*. Over a 38-year span, changing concepts of gender, class, and race infuse the narratives thematically and consistently tackle issues that interconnect regional with national and global discourses. When the German past is referenced, it is often directly connected to the criminal plot of the episode. Several episodes wrestle directly with the legacies of the Third Reich, the Holocaust, the divided Germany, and the Cold War and relate that past to the emergence of Islamophobia and racism from the 1980s to today. Thus, the German history of twentieth-century genocide committed in the name of nationalism continues to frame present-day conflict negotiations, even in the convergence era. *Tatort* therefore assumes the role of a crucial conductor and shaper of, as well as contributor to, ongoing memory work in the German public sphere. Even with its penchant for social critique, the program's longevity and iconic standing have endowed it with the power to broadcast a sense of stability, normalcy, and belonging that have made the show itself a signifier of the national.

While the success of *Tatort* has placed enormous expectations on its format's viability for economic return, its built-in regional rotation has not only proven to support creative experimentation (within limits) since the program's inception but also socialized viewers to accept and expect variation as an integral part of the program's feature. While the regional structure essentially provided a niche-oriented experience prior to privatization, in the convergence era it offers the reliable continuity of a homing beacon for proliferated viewing practices across devices and platforms. Rather than an either/or, viewers tune in to their trusted networks to recharge their connectedness to a communal sense of self and in between watching globally circulating content from Netflix or Sky.

Over the years, the network crime drama format has repeatedly adapted to change, sometimes with innovative grace and at other times under pressure. *Tatort*'s focus on homicides shifted to include a wide-ranging array of crimes and frequently investigated murders as symptoms of broader socioeconomic and political crimes and issues. While some city productions stressed the murder of the week series aspect, others built in multi-episode story arcs or deeper character backstories that created serial elements driven by and feeding into a growing transmedia pollination through fan culture, *Tatort* tourism, and social media. In some cases, the franchise revolved around the charisma and failures of a single detective (e.g., Horst Schimanski vs. Klaus Bülow in the 1980s), in others the actor's portfolio and large transmedia fanbase allowed for genre-expansions, for example, Manfred Krug as the singing detective in Hamburg, while genre hybridity emerged through on-screen chemistry in the Münster team with Thiel (Axel Prahl) and Boerne (Jan Josef Liefers) as the comedic duo. As the series faced competition from other networks and platforms, it could rely on ample experience with balancing its offerings and adapting its narrative strategies to broaden its appeal across demographics and viewing habits. In 1990, this meant integrating GDR's most popular crime drama *Polizeiruf 110* into its lineup. Imbuing some of its regional contributions with serial elements aided in retention efforts of engaged viewers while still providing an on-ramp for casual and new viewers in other regional offerings that featured a case of the week.

Since the crime drama franchise had to integrate different production values as the result of diverging regional budgets, low-concept episodes mingled with high-concept episodes throughout the decades. In the network era, critical and viewer reception in print form reflect a lively engagement week to week but especially around the introduction of new teams, a new region, or a new visual style. *Tatort* continues to become news as television *and* as a window onto the state of the nation, continuing the fiction/nonfiction intersection of its lineup with the *Tagesschau*. During its long run, producers had to learn that big budgets dedicated to action sequences did not equal an increased market share in every case and that sometimes they even hurt the brand requiring a re-set of the creative team in charge (e.g., Hamburg *Tatort*'s movie spin-off failure *Tschiller-Off Duty*). Even so, as routine television production *and* talent factory for actors and directors, the crime drama often functioned as a laboratory for the genre by expanding the crime format into subgenres (e.g., undercover cop) or genre hybridity through soap, horror, or melodrama elements. Cinema/television crossover directors accentuated inter-medial relationships with the integration of media-reflexive cinematic and televisual codes, and they explored broadly circulating intertextual resonances through appropriating German and global visual culture history. The public network's ongoing self-assessments and adjustments due to rapid changes in technology and industry along with the regional variations have left traces within the program's format structure and aesthetics, which reflect on contemporary medium specificity in a dialogic polysemic fashion. How this compares to German crime dramas on Netflix is the focus of the second part of the book.

Regions and/as Mediascapes

The global convergence between and across media, and between production and reception, has affected concepts of the regional and national, and how viewers and creators interact with regionally and nationally modulated genres and media forms. Since the 2010s, the network's online *Mediathek* has offered snippets of its vast *Tatort* archive to the global German-speaking public. This feature has also expanded advertising and branding opportunities for the network. Interested viewers are guided through the archive of articles, images, and videos by actor or character name or in form of city or historical search categories, aided by maps and chronological lists. In addition, viewers are posting about *Tatort* in the blogosphere, adding detailed episode information or commentary on existing fan sites, producing and circulating *Tatort* videos on YouTube. Actors are using their *Tatort* casting as narrative fodder for other crime dramas. All of these activities have contributed to the world-building energies of the *Tatort* franchise and have, in turn, been thematized or self-reflexively integrated into episodes. At the same time, *Tatort*'s attachment to sociopolitical and regional expressions of German culture seems to still be prohibiting it from crossing over onto streaming platforms. However, the lessons it has provided in surviving through the different television eras have been pivotal for domestically produced crime dramas for streaming platforms.

One of these lessons is that the regional aspect can be productively, reflectively, and critically interwoven with changes in the mediascape. *Tatort* tourism and social media interactions with the locations of the series successfully co-construct a region and/as mediascape. A region conceives of it as such if it has a *Tatort* team that represents it, which adds it to the national look-book of the franchise and subsequently attracts not only domestic and international tourists but also investors. Every week, viewers expand their horizons by gaining access to regionally accented social milieus from urban apartments and office complexes to suburban houses and allotment plots, even rural lifestyles at times. In turn, the investigating detective would function like a mix of tourist guide, social worker, and real estate agent. On the flip side, the 2008 Hamburg episode evidenced not only the race-based anxieties around "inviting" the first Turkish-German detective into "viewers' living rooms" but also the way in which *Tatort* had inserted itself into the dominant culture's concept of *Heimat*. This episode drew attention to the way imagined communities for diasporic minorities and the German majority fail to manifest in "real" estate. Instead, the episode offers up its migrant undercover cop as a trope for navigating a multifaceted and diverse city-state (Hamburg) and the convergent mediascape.

By contrast, the Berlin *Tatort* between 1989 and 2004 struggled with conceiving of and branding itself in regional terms because of its hypermediated position that projected its intersectionality between national and global discourses of and to Germany. As production, casting, thematic concepts, and formal styles were quick to be politicized, the quest for adequate self-critical representation continued, and the format never quite settled into a routine. Despite taking place in Berlin, the three episodes showcased the *Tatort* format's flexibility in that each took a distinctive approach to capitalizing and reflecting on their sociopolitical moments while immersed in a dialogue with their respective contemporary mediascapes. Episodes matched different crimes in different socioeconomic sectors to different generic structures, approached post-unification Berlin through a mix of Weimar cinematic and film noir aesthetics, or integrated not just the style but the reality modes of Berlin's favorite talk show into the concept of an episode.

In kinship with Berlin's *Tatort* that wrestled with the city's past and present role in the nation and the world, the Leipzig/Dresden episodes grappled with imagination. In a rare foray into televised West German conceptions of East Germany, the inaugural *Tatort* episode dared to imagine and represent life behind the Iron Curtain, conscious that it would be watched on both sides and thus could and did insert itself in ongoing official negotiations between the two Germanies. Fast forward to two years after economic unification (October 3, 1990), the focus on three Dresden teenagers again foregrounded imagination—what could, should, might be, but was falling short of hopes. With inter-medial integration advancing ahead of and often functioning in opposition to sociopolitical and economic integration after 1989, this episode mobilized the intertextual and intermedial synergies between rubble film, *Indianerfilm*, New Wave and MTV aesthetics to lift up obstacles to the integration between East and West—lingering traumas from the past along with inhumane profiteering in the present—at every turn. And finally, the convergence-era Leipzig episode investigated the potential of time-shifted engagement with(in) a network format, at the same time that its storyline stressed the intersections between sustained dissatisfaction, moral panics, and tribally inflected imaginations of community and nation.

Investigating how nationally coded and regionally accented political and personal histories shape the present emerged as one of the crime drama's dominant thematic emphases. Formally, *Tatort*'s resourceful variations in narration, cinematography, and editing display a constant tweaking of the genre format that reacts and contributes to transformations at the home network and within German and global mediascapes. Combined, *Tatort*'s internal format adaptations demonstrate how strongly the German genre's cultural and discursive practices are interwoven with its acute awareness of television's powerful role in society, of medium specificity and media hierarchies.

PART TWO

Netflix

1

Introduction

This introduction to German crime dramas on Netflix has three purposes: the first is to find out how the crime drama emerged as the leading umbrella-genre; the second is to assess more broadly how the digital revolution and streaming services have changed the mediascape in Germany and for German television products abroad; the third is to probe the current situation for continuities to and departures from the network era that reach beyond the confines of Netflix and the crime drama per se but constitute crucial structural and formal intersections propelling a show like *Babylon Berlin* to global popularity. The remaining chapters in this part focus on three of Netflix's first-generation German-language crime dramas and discuss how each develops specific formal and generic strategies to navigate the local-global challenges of the new mediascape while adjusting to post-network storytelling modes. The textual analyses of the three Netflix crime dramas *Dark* (2017–20), *Perfume* (2018), and *Dogs of Berlin* (2018) continue the explorations of spatial and geopolitical situatedness from Part I and ask how these dramas are screening regionally or nationally accented cultural specificities, for which reasons, and to which effects.

Converging on Crime

While Germany has been a successful media exporter to the Global South and laterally to other European countries,[1] it could not crack the glass ceiling of the North American market in the broadcast or cable eras. From

---

[1] Kaarle Nordenstreng and Tapio Varis, *Television Traffic—A One-Way Street? A Survey and Analysis of the International Flow of Television Programme Material* (Paris: UNESCO Reports and Papers on Mass Communication, 1974), 30.

zero German television shows on US network or cable television prior to 2014, the last years have seen a meteoric rise in production, content diversity, and global audience awareness, even cult fandom, of German projects while another international cinema success like *Run Lola Run*, *Goodbye Lenin*, or *The Lives of Others* remains unlikely in the current mediascape. The prevalence of crime dramas and crime drama hybrids from Germany merges with the way "Netflix is feeding America's love for serial killers."[2] This genre choice, more than any others, has allowed the platform to cater to American tastes as it widened the shares of domestic audiences watching foreign and domestic productions on its service. Because German crime dramas on Netflix reverse-engineered fifty years of the US-Germany "one-way flow," how their format stayed the same or changed from their network predecessors and how each embraced or reflected on the medium specificities of the streaming era deliver crucial information at this juncture.

In close readings of the intersections between network flow, television text, aesthetics, and geopolitical realignments, Part I revealed how the crime genre facilitated not only format adaptations and genre reconfigurations but also adjustments to viewing habits and media practices that primed it to become a convergent agent. Based on Jean K. Chalaby's research on transnational television in the European markets, Ramon Lobato discusses Netflix's strategy of "long distance localization."[3] Netflix has had to learn that "it must localize if it wishes to compete on a global scale."[4] As the investigation of *Tatort* showed, German television crime drama exhibited its steadfast ability to productively interconnect local, regional, national, and global discourses within its format while reflecting on and adapting to rapid mediascape changes. And even if the results of its geopolitical and aesthetic engagements were not primarily aimed at or always accessible to the global market, the crime genre also provided a meeting ground between the local and the global because of its deep international and intertextual resonance archive (e.g., *Sherlock Holmes* novels, films, series).

It is this resonance that Netflix explored, when it launched its first European-Netflix coproduction, *Lilyhammer* (2012–), using the transnational popularity of HBO's *The Sopranos* and the comedic chops of its actor Steven van Zandt as an audience magnet to follow his criminal antics across both continents (North America to Norway) and platforms (from HBO to Netflix). *Lilyhammer*'s premise trained viewers in seeing

---

[2] Amanda Riss, "Netflix Is Feeding America's Love for Serial Killers," *Pavlovic Today*, June 16, 2019, https://www.thepavlovictoday.com/en/netflix-feeds-americas-love-affair-with-serial-killers/ (accessed June 26, 2019).
[3] Jean K. Chalaby, *Transnational Television Worldwide. Towards a New Media Order* (London: Tauris, 2005).
[4] Ramon Lobato, *Netflix Nations. The Geography of Digital Distribution* (New York: NYUP, 2019), 133.

television from and on both continents, switching the glance from outsider to insider, from global to local and vice versa, in the format of a classic television trope: the fish-out-of-water scenario. This theme of two worlds, dual screens, an increasing plurality of perspectives and glances, threads itself through the narratives and structures of a significant number of television projects developed or licensed for the convergence era. This doubling in narration, plot, mise-en-scène, and character development is a prominent feature of *Dark*'s time-traveling paradoxes and *Counterpart*'s (Starz, 2017–18) alternate Berlin realities, as well as of the East-West spy thriller *Deutschland '83-'89* (RTL/AMC/Sundance).

At its most revealing, the self-referentiality to the mediascape appears in the branding of the crime drama itself. The thumbnail of *Criminal Germany/UK/Spain* (2018–) features a two-way mirror encased in neon red, taking on the look of the Netflix logo itself. The pan-European concept of *Criminal* demonstrates how Netflix conceives of itself: as a conduit of and to the transnational. As a two-way mirror, Netflix invites viewers to take part as investigator, witness, or prosecutor gazing at unfolding criminal cases from an adjacent room. The criminal case is recast as the part of the global mediascape that is nationally accented (in language and kind) but the cinematographic approach and the genre format are reissued as global and branded in Netflix colors. Furthermore, the German chapter of *Criminal* was directed by Oliver Hirschbiegel. Considering that Hirschbiegel's Hitler bunker film, *Downfall*, was one of the more celebrated film/television coproductions between Constantin Film and the NDR/WDR in 2004, with him as director, Netflix embraced not only Germany's fruitful coproduction practice between television and cinema but also the high-quality limited series and *Fernsehfilm* tradition. Not only does *Criminal* retain the one-room setting of *The Downfall*'s bunker across the inner-European borders, it also draws on the tradition of German cinema (*M, The Last Laugh*) and Hirschbiegel's partiality to portray psychological deterioration under pressure. The chamber format and shared mise-en-scène of the limited series *Criminal* thus most clearly demonstrate in aesthetics, narration, and production (all using the same studio space and setting) how the concept of the (trans)national has merged with media capitalism, especially franchise seriality, brand recognition, and diversification. In a way, *Criminal* mobilizes the national for global consumption as *Tatort* mobilized the regional for national consumption.

As these post-network crime drama examples illustrate, that the genre relies on contrastive or alternating storylines (police, detective, defense and prosecution, victim, witness, perpetrator) has turned it into a blueprint for (trans)national television engagement under the auspices of US-dominated globalization. The examples also show that crime dramas can accommodate episodic storytelling (*Tatort, Law and Order*), become a limited series (*Criminal*), or expand into multiple seasons (*Dark, How to*

Sell Drugs Online (Fast)). Even at its simplest, the format combines a goal-oriented narrative trajectory with serial elements and interactive viewer components. As Part I showed, throughout the network and cable eras, the crime genre successfully navigated stasis through self-reflection, spin-offs, and hybridization, introducing gender, class, race, cultural, temporal, and regional inflections (e.g., *CSI SVU*, *Homicide: Life on the Streets*, Nordic noir, period crime, urban crime) along with subgenre specializations like true crime (*Aktenzeichen XY Ungelöst*, *Making a Murderer*) or serial killer horror crime (*The Following*). Thus, the crime drama amply demonstrated that it can thrive along a spectrum of genre conventions, work with series and seriality components, as well as survive varying emphases on brain or brawn and different reality modes, and that its built-in decoding process made it transmedia-ready.

Unlike situation comedies which heavily rely on linguistic, physical, and cultural specificity besides a shared archive of foibles and recognized behaviors for their humor, crime dramas offered Netflix a shortcut to what Jean Chalaby termed the "localization knowledge curve."[5] As a standard on network and cable television and an export success, Netflix could count on a broad viewer base for the crime drama. Searchable by genre category, and by already established inter-medial and international crime connections between literature, film, and television in the United States, Germany, and Europe, the crime drama helped to attract Netflix viewers to adjacent content. Crime dramas therefore increased the crossover appeal of original or acquired programming to global and domestic audiences and ensured that the platform's original language productions were worth the investment.

Netflix and the German Mediascape

This section will cover both the obstacles and entrance points during the convergence between German and US mediascapes. Specifically, it will discuss the television knowledge differential between US and German viewers, the connection between Germany's leadership in smart television ownership and user preferences in the first Netflix decade, and end with an assessment of the changing attitudes to the text-image relationship in the evolution of original language series.

Outside of the group of New German Cinema films enjoying high critical acclaim in the United States in the 1970s and early 1980s and arguably exporting a national German media brand, only singular German box-office hits and occasional foreign language Oscar contenders made a splash stateside. Until the second decade of the new millennium, US broadcast

---

[5]Chalaby, 193.

television audiences have not had much exposure to serialized fiction focusing on Germany and no television projects made in Germany. With *Dark*, *Perfume*, *Dogs of Berlin*, *Babylon Berlin*, *Charité*, and *How to Sell Drugs Online (Fast)*,[6] a potential audience consisting of c. 200 million Netflix subscribers in over 190 countries are given complex narratives that open new windows into and out of globally related national and regional histories.[7]

In 2014, Netflix introduced itself to the German media market. In 2015, RTL and AMC's Sundance TV coproduced the first two installments of the series *Deutschland '83* and *'86* (showrunners Anna and Jörg Winger, directed by Eduard Berger and Samira Radsi). Distributed by Fremantle Media, it became the first ever German-language television series to air on both German and US television. While the ratings were not stellar in Germany, the series became a success across the ocean, enough to be renewed and reimported with rising viewership for a second season. This reverse flow soon became a pattern for other original language productions. "Suddenly the whole world seems to want German TV," writes Adam Lusher of *The Independent* and quotes a British source at Fremantle Media International:

> It is so different from almost anything else Germany has produced. There are bits of humour in it. It's quite unusual to see this kind of humour in a German drama, and that's one of the reasons why everyone is so excited about it.[8]

His quote illustrates a prevailing opinion about German film and television that glosses over the fact that prior to 2015, the majority of German television projects remained inaccessible, linguistically, technologically, and infrastructurally, to the majority of US viewers. Thus, broad-strokes representations of Germans as Nazis or villains in popular US films (e.g., *Die Hard*), combined with spotty appreciation for the output of the self-reflexive and system-critical New German Cinema auteurs, filled the lack of access to domestically created and produced long-form serial narratives

---

[6] The production rate and genre diversity are increasing. In 2021, *Tribes of Europa* sought to cash in on the popularity of *The 100* (CW, 2014–21). In October 2020, Netflix released the historic epic *Die Barbaren* (*Barbarians*), a Swiss-German coproduction between Gaumont and Netflix that unofficially adapted the successful *Vikings* (History Channel, 2013–20) for Netflix.
[7] Netflix announced that its subscriber base soared over 200 million in late 2020. Its competitors Disney Plus, Hulu, and HBO Max were each well below 100 million. Joan E. Solsman, *CNet*, January 20, 2021, https://www.cnet.com/news/netflix-fourth-quarter-subscribers-soar-past-200-million-members-stock/ (accessed January 25, 2021).
[8] Adam Lusher, "Deutschland 83. Scandinavian TV Takes a Back Seat as New Show Ushers in Golden Age for German TV Dramas," *The Independent*, May 15, 2015, https://www.independent.co.uk/arts-entertainment/tv/news/deutschland-83-scandinavian-tv-takes-backseat-new-show-ushers-golden-age-german-tv-dramas-10254241.html (accessed November 18, 2020).

for broadcast television. While German dramas—single episodes or entire series—were exported near and far with varying case-by-case success, until 2015 especially the US market had been the equivalent to Fort Knox for German television.[9]

For the launch of its original German-language series, Netflix thus had to employ a triple strategy. First, the streamer partnered with producers and showrunners steeped in the traditions and formats of domestic crime series, including *Tatort* directors like Christian Alvart (*Dogs of Berlin*) to entice domestic viewers to follow them across the digital divide to watch a German show on an "American" service. Second, Netflix sought out vetted creators that had already delivered cultural crossover hits, like Tom Tykwer (*Run Lola Run*, *Babylon Berlin*), and third, they engaged showrunners who had projects in the works that could provide multiple points of access during genre-based searches and thus generate adjacencies within the existing US-centric global Netflix library. The latter was the case for *Dark*, which became the first multi-season German series to be globally accessible on Netflix.[10] Due to its success, *Dark*'s showrunners, Baran bo Odar and Jantje Friese, garnered a contract for a subsequent series. In the competitive race for transnationally appealing content, Netflix purchased, licensed, and coproduced several original German-language projects that contribute to a growing cross-cultural and transnational television archive.[11]

Globally dispersed pockets of communities made up of socioeconomically, racially, and sexually diverse members hailing from one or a set of different countries have clamored for easy and expeditious access to representative content in their own languages for a while. Thus, foreign language productions are filling the needs of a sizeable group left underserved for decades. For most Netflix subscribers in middle-class households, Ramon Lobato is right, when he argues for a both/and approach to local and global content instead of an either/or. German crime drama fans watch *Tatort* on ARD or its online portal and move to a streamer for *Breaking Bad*. As we saw in the close analysis of the proximity between local, regional, national, and global input and output in the *Tatort* chapters, "[a]udiences do not choose between the local and the global but combine both in their everyday lives; they move between these scales of identification, at different times

---

[9]According to Timo Nöthling, Germany's image as global export champion is diametrically opposed to its image in television exports. Only individual, mostly light entertainment, crime series (*Kommissar Rex*, *Tatortreiniger*) attracted interest from abroad until 2015. *Quotenmeter.de*, May 19, 2018, http://www.quotenmeter.de/n/101107/noch-keine-export-weltmeister-so-schlugen-sich-deutsche-tv-serien-zuletzt-im-ausland (accessed November 23, 2020).

[10]*Dark's* second season dropped on June 21, 2019. The third and final season aired in the summer of 2020.

[11]Amazon, Pantaleon, and Warner Brothers coproduced cyber-thriller *You Are Wanted* (Matthias Schweighöfer and Bernhard Jasper, 2017).

and for different purposes."[12] Christian Stiegler points to the "Deutsch" search engine integrated into Netflix Germany's launch site as one of the strategies employed to facilitate that cross-platform viewership.[13] On a daily basis, millions of multilingual viewers in Northern Europe migrate between different languages and media platforms: they scroll through their social media feeds on public transportation, sit down and watch the news on network television, enjoy family movie night courtesy of cable, satellite, or DVD, *and* access curated storyworlds from a streaming service in the original and/or subtitled version of their choice.

Yet, succeeding with a global and domestic reception surge of German shows on Netflix required not just convincing domestic viewers to subscribe but also moving past initial skepticism and long-standing associations of German crime series as a high-quality staple of domestic network television and of US dramas with quality serial narratives. The first Netflix German crime drama *Dark* could be called a born-digital series, because it did not, like *Babylon Berlin*, resurface on network television close to or interwoven with its premiere season on Netflix. And its hybrid genre features also assured that it would not be limited to these preconceptions, neither in its format nor in its algorithmic distribution in existing search categories on the platform.

Although the Netflix transition between the United States and Europe signals the arrival of one type of borderless mobility, it also evidences residual television practices that prohibit seamless integration. Further, subscription-based television marks economic privilege at the same time that it emphasizes the success of the long-term socialization of viewers around the globe to accept US storytelling formats and character types. In the second decade of the new millennium, streaming catalogued and customized content also revealed itself to be both a contributor to and a symptom of the tribal, niche-based isolationism that has accompanied a resurgent populism in Europe and the United States. This digitally enabled mobility coincided yet also competed with greater active steps to incentivize investments and subsidize financing for pan-European and national film and television projects. The EU facilitated open borders for traveling and working, and enhanced opportunities for physical, social, and economic mobility. Yet Britain's Brexit, Hungary's and Poland's right-wing turns, a global pandemic, and the Russian invasion of Ukraine (February 2022) have threatened that very openness. The latter directly affected the local-global media integration on Netflix, when in late February 2022, Netflix officially announced that it would not bend to the Russian demand to host its official television channels.

---

[12]Lobato, *Netflix Nations*, 160.
[13]Christian Stiegler, "Invading Europe: Netflix's Expansion to the European Market and the Example of Germany," in *The Netflix Effect*, ed. Kevin MacDonald and Daniel Smith-Rowsey (London: Bloomsbury, 2016), 243.

Along with these geopolitical developments, the might of globally connected US streaming services threatened to upset the carefully calibrated entertainment ecosystem of European countries. While the freshly minted networks in the 1960s and 1970s, and later cable and satellite stations had filled their rosters with cheap imported US content in the 1980s, from the 1990s onward, European television productions had become increasingly successful due to improvements in the industry's homegrown infrastructure and an interest in domestic projects representing national as well as regional locations, stories, and characters. In 2014, US catalogue behemoths Amazon and Netflix stomped through that proverbial porcelain shop. The streamers enticed baby boomers who grew up on dubbed US series back into the fold and attracted those who still found domestic alternatives lacking. Netflix facilitated access to coveted US series in the original format without synchronization and eliminated the lag between episodes and seasons.

In this context, it is understandable that in October 2018, the European Parliament voted for a 30 percent quota of European content for video-on-demand services that were also

> asked to contribute to the development of European audiovisual productions, either by investing directly in content or by contributing to national funds. The level of contribution in each country should be proportional to their on-demand revenues in that country (member states where they are established or member states where they target the audience wholly or mostly).[14]

This policy at least partially explains Netflix's intensified push for coproduced content and for retaining rights to original language productions, of which *Dark* is one. And it shows the delicate balance of acquisition and coproduction protocols. Catherine Treyz adds a few other reasons that have turned Germany into the "shining light" of home entertainment consumption in Europe: "Germans [are] embracing TV streaming services in record numbers." She continues, "*Futuresource* estimates a quarter of Germans utilize one or more subscription video services. Germany's subscription video-on-demand market is projected to double in the years between 2017 in 2019, and exceed €1 billion in 2020."[15] Two related reasons are the dynamism of television access (integrated

---

[14]European Parliament News Press Release, "New Rules for Audiovisual Media Services Approved by Parliament," October 2, 2018, http://www.europarl.europa.eu/news/en/press-room/20180925IPR14307/new-rules-for-audiovisual-media-services-approved-by-parliament (accessed June 20, 2019).

[15]Catherine Treyz, *The Local.de*, January 9, 2019, https://www.thelocal.de/20190109/netflix-and-amazon-primes-popularity-continues-to-grow-german-home-entertainment-market-passed-9-billion-euros (accessed June 10, 2019).

offers and uses of video on demand, subscription, satellite, cable, etc.) and that "Germany has one of the highest levels of smart TV ownership in Europe." The threshold to adding another layer of streamed content is thus relatively low for a country with a large middle class and when the Netflix app is preloaded on a viewer's smart television set. Yet, lest we forget *that* Germans watch on streaming platforms does not mean they actually watch *Dark, Perfume,* or *Dogs of Berlin* at all or on Netflix. A majority of Germans only watched *Babylon Berlin* when it became available on the network ARD/Das Erste.

The results of a comparative study of what German demographics refers to as "online moving image content" (Online-Bewegtbild-Inhalt), between 2011 and 2018 shows that while in 2011 about half of the German population accessed television among other media digitally, by 2018 this percentage grew to 75 percent.[16] According to the 2019 study "ARD/ZDF-Onlinestudie," which was conducted on the basis of data garnered from 2,000 interview subjects in April–May of that year, 76 percent of the German population still watched linear television and 79 percent listened to broadcast radio.[17] While older Germans spent up to seven hours a day on various audio and visual media forms, the age bracket between fourteen and twenty-nine was watching less television and was slowly inverting the pyramid in favor of nonlinear programming (33 percent on linear vs. 67 percent on nonlinear offers).[18] 2020 data on audience shares reflects this. Whereas ZDF and ARD reached the highest overall viewer shares within the divided mediascape (13.6 percent and 10.7 percent respectively), the percentage of viewers between fourteen and forty-nine years of age distributed themselves to a higher extent over the six included private cable and satellite services.[19] But according to the 2019 study, even this age group acknowledged that ARD and ZDF featured qualitatively higher programming. And as my in-depth study of *Tatort* and the ARD's championing of the genre showed, the crime drama in its specific format as a high-quality *Heimatfilm* project combined with a deep-rooted ritualistic reception structure was a major contributor

---

[16] A. Poleshova, "Anteil der Personen, die zumindest selten Online-Bewegtbild-Inhalte abrufen in Deutschland in den Jahren 2011 bis 2018," *Statista.de*, November 21, 2019, https://de.statista.com/statistik/daten/studie/163165/umfrage/abruf-von-videodateien-im-internet-seit-dem-jahr-2006/ (accessed October 7, 2020).
[17] Natalie Beisch et alii., "ARD/ZDF-Onlinestudie 2019: Mediale Internetnutzung und Video-on-Demand gewinnen weiter an Bedeutung," *Mediaperspektiven* 9 (2019), https://www.ard-zdf-onlinestudie.de/files/2019/0919_Beisch_Koch_Schaefer.pdf (accessed November 21, 2019).
[18] "ARD/ZDF Massenkommunikation-Trends," *ZDF.de*, September 5, 2019, https://www.zdf.de/nachrichten/heute/ardzdf-massenkommunikation-trends-2019-100.html (accessed October 7, 2020).
[19] Bernhard Weidenbach, "Zuschauermarktanteile der TV-Sender im September 2020," *Statista.de*, October 1, 2020, https://de.statista.com/statistik/daten/studie/75044/umfrage/zuschauermarktanteile-der-tv-sender-monatszahlen/ (accessed October 7, 2020).

if not guarantor for this cross-generationally perceived quality difference between cable/satellite, streaming, and the public broadcast networks.

Convergence-era technologies and media practices have also altered seemingly entrenched attitudes toward the image-text relationship in historically subtitle-weary Germany and the United States. Subtitles and closed captions are no longer the obstacle to English-only viewers or German audiences accustomed to dubbing as they once were. The centrality of daily life revolving around mobile small screens makes subtitles and closed captioning almost a necessity both within and outside of a show's diegesis. From the late 1990s onward, television shows consistently featured characters talking on their mobile phones and reading SMS messages, making the over-the-shoulder shot of small screens a regular storytelling and editing device. Despite some experiments with multiple language- and dubbed versions, YouTube's (2005–) championing of closed caption and translations for those viewers needing accommodations has pushed the envelope further in the direction of general acceptance of the image-text relationship.

Netflix took up the challenge to modernize the mundane shots of text/image on tiny screens with its first original production. *House of Cards* (2013–18) made extensive use of text message bubbles and breaking of the fourth wall to invite viewers to access a privileged means of communication. Instead of cliché-driven close-up shots of mobile devices that still required viewers to lean into their television screens, the videography posts them on the current mise-en-scène, thereby turning the Netflix screen itself into a mobile device that directly corresponds with its diegetic and extradiegetic "inner circle" confidantes. Possibly, this strategy did its part in training hesitant viewers to accept text-based information as part of the television experience. In 2019, the German crime-dramedy based on a true story, *How to Sell Drugs Online (Fast)*, cleverly expanded and energized the text-image relationship with innovative editing more suited to Generation Z viewers. Further, the trend to integrate global travel into a series' narrative ecosystem (*Homeland*, *Game of Thrones*) and the expectation to inclusively represent diversity on screens have resulted in more original language dialogues appearing in subtitles rather than being delivered in English and actors with native fluencies being cast in international coproductions.

In the form of a big picture case study, the following sections read the post-network German crime drama *Babylon Berlin* as a continuation of rather than a rupture with German media history. Continuities from the German network era conjoined emerging preferences at Netflix to engineer a launching pad for the multi-season series *Babylon Berlin*, which has become the star of the first-generation German crime dramas. Consideration will be given to the coproduction history between German cinema and television, the limited series and *Fernsehfilm* (television film) tradition, the preference for literary adaptations and period dramas, the role of unofficial US format adaptations for linguistic and cultural authenticity, and finally, confluences in transnational television production and casting practices.

From *Berlin Alexanderplatz* (1980) to *Babylon Berlin* (Netflix/Sky/ARD, 2017–)

When network television began to be integrated into the 1950s German mediascape, it not only threatened German cinema economically, it also interacted with its aesthetics and laid down ritualized pathways of reception and identity construction (global, national, regional, and local) that competed with cinema's star-, genre-, and event-driven structure of engagement. There is a creative, if anxiety-producing, intersection between cinema and television that is often neglected. From the 1960s through mid-1980s, German cinema was, as it is now, made *on television*. The limited series *Berlin Alexanderplatz* gave Fassbinder the space and time to make his vision come to life and share it not just with the bourgeois film buffs and critics buying tickets to a German movie back then but with a cross-constituency of millions over a span of three months. It was must-see television. This history is a key reason why each ninety-minute episode of *Tatort* is classified as a *Fernsehfilm*.

In 1978, R. W. Fassbinder, the venerated New German Cinema auteur, called attention to the porous nexus between both media forms:

> I do know of course that critical films in the Federal Republic—with whatever limitations; that varies from network to network—were possible only on television, or at least in collaboration with television... and that on the other hand, more directors are in danger of succumbing to an aesthetic specific to television.[20]

He points to the ability to innovate on television, to experiment with long-form narration and character development, but he is also worried about a crossover effect. His limited series adaptation of Alfred Döblin's novel about released and relapsed murderer Franz Biberkopf, *Berlin Alexanderplatz*, would air on the West German broadcast network (WDR) from October to December 1980. Its production model could be called a precursor to the current era of transnational coproduction. The more than thirteen-hour-long series was coproduced by German and Italian public and private broadcast

---

[20] R. W. Fassbinder, "The Third Generation (1978)," in *German Essays on Film*, ed. Richard W. McCormick and Alison Gunether-Pal, trans. Krishna Winston (New York: Continuum, 2004), 230.

entities (WDR, Bavaria Film GMBH, Italian Network RAI). Looking at his 1978–81 *BRD Trilogy*, it is clear that televisual aesthetics, especially the generic conventions of the close-up small screen melodrama, contributed significantly to his signature "cinematic" style.

The Film Funding Act of 1967 inscribed moral and political guidelines into its statutes leading to, what Martin Leiperdinger calls, "an absolute dearth of critical filmmaking."[21] In addition, wrangling over age appropriateness for broadcasted films brought the conservative film censorship board (FSK, Freiwillige Selbstkontrolle der Filmwirtschaft) more power in decision-making, leading to a period of paternalism, declining audience numbers and revenue for films shown on television.[22] Counter-measures building a pipeline between cinema and television took root from 1963 onward, but became more successful a decade later with the Television Framework Agreement and the promotion of innovation labs like *Das kleine Fernsehspiel* on ZDF. The *Talentschmiede* (talent factory), as it is often called, not only promoted work by burgeoning male auteurs but has been influential in supporting women and minority filmmakers until today.[23] Continuing this tradition, the regionally organized ARD more recently developed an "amphibian production and financing model, in which a film destined for the cinema is developed alongside an original television version (. . .) with high financial participation by the television networks."[24] This hybrid model has been lucrative not only in financial but also in critical terms. Coproduced films from *Das Boot* to *Lives of Others* have garnered acclaim domestically and abroad. Broadening the spectrum from issue-films (e.g., *Contergan*) to event films (e.g., *Baader Meinhof Complex*) to deliver a diverse coverage within the *Grundversorgungsauftrag* (basic supply requirement) of the public networks, the ARD believes that "quality and quota (. . .) do not have to be in contradiction to one another."[25]

Since the 1980s, privatization with cable, satellite, and subscription services brought another layer of competition to cinema and the networks that has only been amplified by the continuous proliferation of streaming platforms within the last decade. In this context, Randall Halle makes clear how the 1993 FFA transformations "opened the film market to new cooperative joint ventures, reduced state control, and instigated a

---

[21]Martin Leiperdinger, "State Legislation, Censorship, and Funding," in *The German Cinema Book*, ed. Tim Bergfelder et alii (London: BFI/Bloomsbury, 2020), 323.
[22]Ibid., 324–5.
[23]Claudia Sandberg, "*Das kleine Fernsehspiel*: Model of a TV Avant Garde," in *The German Cinema Book*, ed. Tim Bergfelder et alii (London: BFI/Bloomsbury, 2020), 331–3.
[24]Verena Kulenkampff, *ARD Jahrbuch 2008*, 118.
[25]Ibid., 120.

liberalization of the film market."²⁶ On the one hand, he argues this also meant that what was considered "German" was broadened significantly and could include transnational projects. On the other hand, new regional film boards could connect more easily with their regionally structured counterparts in broadcast media, especially because the film boards were "organized as public-private joint ventures . . . to profit their respective regions" (Ibid.).

More recent German funding, production, and distribution strategies share some characteristics with the older cross-fertilization model from the 1970s. The 20 percent domestic production rule, for example, ensures that tax-based funding at least partially goes to German production companies while making Germany attractive to global media companies. Capitalizing on the success of the first two seasons and investing in the future of this model, the German Motion Picture Fund (GMPF) subsidized the production of *Dark*'s third season with 3.6 million euro. The subsidy nevertheless initiated a lively debate in the German press, because the produced content was often exclusively available on the streaming platforms, which are not accessible to all taxpayers:

> The money flows from the German Motion Picture Fund (GMPF) directly to domestic production companies, which produce series like "Dark" under contract for Netflix and Co. The fund was established to strengthen Germany as a competitive film location within the international market. The productions qualify for annual subsidies up to 15 million Euros by proving a 20% minimum participation of German financing on the series. The third season of the mystery series alone received a subsidy of 3.6 million Euros.²⁷

Netflix and Amazon therefore circulated a German imaginary that bypassed a large sector of the domestic audience, reversing on a smaller scale the bifurcated television screens of the network and cable era. That creation of parallel nation- and world-building and reflection will be an important aspect in the close textual analysis of each show. To some degree, the proliferation of curated domestically produced content on streaming platforms also repeats the case of 1970s New German Cinema. Most of the movements' films were watched and critically acclaimed abroad but failed at domestic box offices. It will therefore be important to keep in mind how distribution and accessibility patterns intersect with (self)representations and (un)conscious cultural biases.

---

²⁶Randall Halle, "German Film: Transnational," in *The German Cinema Book*, ed. Tim Bergfelder et alii (London: BFI/Bloomsbury, 2020), 519.
²⁷*Future Zone*, October 18, 2019.

One final aspect that needs to be discussed in this context is the "reverse" flow of domestic German coproductions with Netflix. For *Babylon Berlin*, the premiere dates looked like this:

- Season 1 and 2, October 2017, on Sky One (Sky Deutschland, on-demand/subscription channel since 2016)
- Season 1 and 2, January 2018, on Netflix
- Season 1 and 2, September 2018, on ARD/Das Erste
- Season 3, January 2020, on Sky One
- Season 3, March 2020, on Netflix
- Season 3, October 2020, on ARD/Das Erste

These dates exhibit three things: for one, they constitute a delayed German arrival of domestically produced content rerouted through a US streamer; second, the reverse flow from post-network to network means that on average five million German viewers in 2017–18 watched episodes of *Babylon Berlin* once the show returned to German network television;[28] and finally, German-language originals produced with or for Netflix have not altered but joined the directional media flow from the United States to Germany. This rerouted flow also sheds some light on what has become a transnational proving ground, in which the pilot season of a domestic show is coproduced or purchased by a streaming service to receive the attention of the global media industry. The potential for broader exposure to industry, media, and viewers is expanded through social media publicity in English. Upon returning to the home market, the show is then predisposed to achieve higher market shares than competing network-born projects. In return, the creative team is likely to receive higher funding for the production of subsequent seasons, continuing the cycle.[29]

What counts as "German" and "domestic" within the parameters of the current funding law and the post-network to network flow for first-generation German-language originals is thus bypassing a not insignificant sector of the German audience. The "domestic" label is applied to private

---

[28] While one cannot be certain how many of these viewers were first time versus repeat viewers, the assumption is that the majority of network viewers were not repeat viewers of the series from Netflix. Domestic audience and market share for *Babylon Berlin*'s first two seasons: "4.92 million viewers saw the 16 episodes with a market share of 15.9 percent. The market share of the 14- to 49-year-old audience was 12.0 percent. (. . .) 14.53 million viewers saw at least one episode of the successful series on DasErste [ARD]." *DasErste.de* (accessed July 12, 2021).

[29] "Die Film- und Medienstiftung NRW fördert die dritte Staffel von 'Babylon Berlin' mit 1,25 Millionen Euro. Erst vor wenigen Tagen wurde bekannt, dass die Produktionsfirma X Filme Creative Pool vom Medienboard Berlin-Brandenburg 1,7 Millionen Euro erhält." *DWDL.de*, May 4, 2018, https://www.dwdl.de/nachrichten/66674/medienboard_berlinbrandenburg_frdert_babylon_berlin/ (accessed July 14, 2021).

entities and corporations that maintain a location in Germany, whatever their configurations might be. Given the globalization of the media industry as such amid an always rapidly changing owner- and partnership infrastructure, this revision of the local and regional needs to be monitored as streaming becomes the norm.

Despite these changes, some German/y-specific media conventions have been retained. Among these are the preference for literary adaptations and *Fernsehfilme*. Within the transmedia coproduction model between television and cinema established back in the 1970s, adaptations have always held a central position. And they continue to do so.

Fernsehfilm, Limited Series, and Period Drama

Like Fassbinder's *Berlin Alexanderplatz* from Alfred Döblin's novel, the heritage crime drama *Babylon Berlin* (2017–), is based on a literary adaptation from the period *Krimis* by Volker Kutscher. Yet, it is domestically and transnationally coproduced by a public network (ARD) and a domestic subscription-based satellite platform (Sky Deutschland). It is distributed by an international company (Beta) and licensed by a global streamer (Netflix). The show thus exemplifies the convergence momentum, including a porous interchange between German literary, televisual, and cinematic traditions that merge with current funding and production practices. In a continuation of broadcast television habitus, innovation meets the status quo. Tom Tykwer, one of the directors of the show, addresses this very issue but fails to acknowledge the continuities from the subsidy era for *Fernsehfilme* that Fassbinder characterized earlier:

> "The biggest challenge, really, was convincing people here in Germany that German audiences were already watching shows like this, that they were ready for it," says Tykwer. "We have a very successful TV culture here focused on crime series—a hundred different variations, all very successful—so it looked like there was no need to change. But we noticed that people we knew were watching fewer and fewer German series because they wanted the long-arc storytelling, the immersive, novel-like stories, and German television wasn't making those shows. . . . We had to all shed our skins, leave the old ways behind, to make this work."[30]

---

[30] Scott Roxborough, "How the *Babylon Berlin* Team Broke the Rules to Make the World's Biggest Foreign Language Series," *Hollywood Reporter*, December 26, 2018, https://www.hollywoodreporter.com/news/how-babylon-berlin-team-broke-all-rules-make-worlds-biggest-foreign-language-series-1171013 (accessed October 15, 2020).

By treating Netflix-type storytelling as a new realm and the future of television, the self-stylization of Tykwer as a frontiersman in some way Americanizes not just *Babylon Berlin* but the entire coproduction process with Netflix. In the same breath that Tykwer voices his goal to produce the German equivalent of American "novel-like stories," he calls for the necessity to abandon "the old [German] ways." In one fell swoop he fails to acknowledge crucial precursors like Fassbinder *and* actual audience data that would attest to the both/and that Lobato and others have evidenced (watching German and non-German content on the same or different platforms).[31] Further, if domestic crime series are as successful as he says, then why are supposedly fewer and fewer people watching German series? Obviously, the need to break with the past, with the national/regional label, and with German network storytelling practices, is stronger than reality. Even though denied, continuities remain and deserve to be acknowledged as significant contributors to convergence-era successes. One of these is the myth of the nonexistence of serial storytelling on German television.

Since the 1990s, as Jason Mittell has shown, serial narrative complexity has become American television's privileged media-specific storytelling mode.[32] Socialized through and familiar with US American television since the dawn of domestic television, German viewers in the 2000s eagerly awaited delayed season releases of *The Sopranos* (HBO), *Mad Men*, and *Breaking Bad* (AMC). But in contrast to Tykwer's assessment, German viewers' taste for domestic television projects with similar storytelling modes had been fed by domestic serial dramas as well, judging by the early critical and audience successes of limited fictional series and multi-season docudrama series. However, instead of being defined as or reviewed as serial dramas, they were produced, advertised, and consumed as limited series or television films (*Fernsehfilme*) that were especially popular in the shape of period dramas.

The success of Fassbinder's literary adaptation in the form of a limited series, *Berlin Alexanderplatz*, helped greenlight Edgar Reitz's extensive serial saga *Heimat: Eine deutsche Chronik* (1984), which he stylized as a German response to the US limited series *Holocaust* from 1978. With the latest instalments from 2013, Reitz's entire five-part television film series is almost sixty hours long with a cast size comparable to *Game of Thrones*. During the cable/satellite era, the ZDF managed to recoup viewer losses through their televised fiction-documentary hybrids exploring every sensationalist nook and cranny of the Hitler era. Directed by Philip

---

[31]As an example, the three-part limited series *Der Laden* (*The Shop*, 1998) came together as a coproduction between Bayrischer Rundfunk and European public service channel ARTE.
[32]Jason Mittell, "Narrative Complexity in Contemporary American Television," *The Velvet Light Trap*, 58 (2006): 29–40.

Kadelbach, serial heritage projects like *Generation War* (ZDF, 2013) trail the interconnected experiences of five everyday Germans in the Third Reich, garnering astonishing ratings at times.[33] The ARD followed suit with its heritage melodrama *Weissensee* (ARD, 2015) covering the rise and fall of a family in the German Democratic Republic (GDR) with an average 4.6 to 4.9 million viewers per episode.

This is the context in which the late Weimar-era *Babylon Berlin*, the 1950s era *Ku'damm* as well as the *Deutschland '83–'89* series have to be seen. It becomes clearer in trade journal statements that lauded *Ku'damm* as "Germany's answer to *Mad Men*" (*The Hollywood Reporter*). Like *Babylon Berlin*, both series cash in on the retro-mania of a content- and eyeball-hungry diversifying mediascape but also follow in the footsteps of *Fernsehfilm* biopics, period and docudramas from the German 1990s to today. The women-centric *Ku'damm* not only allowed German and US viewers to fill the nostalgia gap after *Mad Men* ended but also provided them with the enticing opportunity to see more of the 1950s and 1960s from Peggy's and Joan's perspectives, rather than from Don Draper's. And both *Ku'damm* and *Deutschland* opened a window onto the network-era Germany of the 1950s to 1980s that US viewers never got to see on television in the first place. But these television successes also continued and reintegrated a cinematic trend from the 1990s, when German period dramas like *Comedian Harmonists* (Josef Vilsmaier, 1997) and *Aimee und Jaguar* (Max Färberböck, 1999) became box-office gold. Like *Babylon Berlin*, these films combined the sounds and mise-en-scène of Weimar era and Third Reich popular culture (e.g., the rise and fall of a famous barbershop quartet) with a biographical truth claim wrapped in soap opera-style melodrama and progressive-looking romance (e.g., a Jewish bohémienne and a Nazi officer's wife step out and explore the LGBTQ underground).

Babylon Berlin heeded these lessons and steered clear of untranslatable German comedy conventions while delivering the grimness associated with German history projects. But it also immersed audiences in a sensorily rich period mise-en-scène and soundscape that let viewers marvel at the ill-fated vibrancy and debauchery of pre-Hitler Berlin. In the basement of a dance club, Charlotte (Liv Lisa Fries) is occasionally seen offering BDSM services to higher ups from the executive and legislative branches of government. And when following Gereon Rath (Volker Bruch) on an investigation into one of Berlin's infamous rear courtyard communities, we can almost smell and taste the rancidness of the meat and human flesh on display. As a literary adaptation and period crime drama, *Babylon Berlin* allowed both casual domestic and global viewers to indulge in pre-fascist Weimar

---

[33]For more information, see Wulf Kansteiner, *In Pursuit of German Memory. History, Television, and Politics after Auschwitz* (Athens: University of Ohio Press, 2006).

"lifestyle modernism" (Hake and Elsaesser), the film buff to access a Tom Tykwer project that comes across as an updated version of Fassbinder's *Berlin Alexanderplatz*, and the European history aficionado to read the sociopolitical clues to the inevitable rise of Hitler as well as echoing the contemporary rise of populism for more invested political viewers.

It is thus important to clarify that Netflix did not depart from but instead capitalized on the German *Fernsehfilm* tradition, when it licensed the mini-series *NSU: German History X* in 2016. Since then, Netflix has innovated on the limited series concept, most notably with the anthology format and interactive television experiment of *Black Mirror: Bandersnatch*. On the German side of Netflix, the recent Emmy success of the limited series *Unorthodox* (Maria Schrader, 2020) and the (trans)national concept of *Criminal* (2019) attest to the versatility and adaptability of the *Fernsehfilm*/limited series combination to global television.

Unofficial US Format Adaptations and Cultural Authenticity

Besides the productive tradition of limited series and *Fernsehfilm* in the shape of literary adaptations, period, or docudramas, German networks also unofficially adapted US television formats for their domestic audiences. Post-network original language series have to be contextualized within these cultural appropriation endeavors. The efforts to localize US formats without retaining the US branding (as in *Germany's Next Top Model*) provide an archive of understudied experimentation for any showrunner and CEO wrestling with Chalaby's "localization knowledge curve." One example: the ARD turned the popular, transmedia innovator *Dawson's Creek* (WB, 1998–2003) into *Sternenfänger* (*Star Catchers*, ARD, 2002), relocating the show from North Carolina to Lake Constance while retaining most of the character portfolios and major narrative enigmas (e.g., love triangle, new girl, urban-rural relocation). Since it aired alongside the original *Dawson's Creek* run on the competitor channel (ZDF), it served as a direct domestic competition and point of reference: "We can make shows like this with people and places that look like us with content that speaks about us." The shows' comparable and competitive popularity among younger German viewers ushered in a growth of domestic productions that turned to serial narratives. Because *Sternernfänger* was produced prior to streaming for ARD's early evening slate of regional programming, it never made it back across the ocean. But shows like *Sternenfänger* revealed the medium's potential for culturally attuned German-language dramas with serial narration.

Viewers had to watch *Dawson's Creek* dubbed. But they could watch *Sternenfänger* in the original German. Fan studies have shown that the sustained daily or weekly engagement with television furthers a different fan engagement than cinema. A show in the target language assists the experience of "unmediated" access beyond the star's circulated image and in Germany's case beyond the audibly familiar ensemble of standard voice actors. While Germany's reliance on dubbing initially reduced the obstacles to accessing foreign content and formats in its history of imported film and television projects, dubbing also represented a dominant act of cultural appropriation, of speaking over and in place of the Other. And, given the overreliance on simplified and cheap dubbing of foreign language television, original language scripts could set themselves apart with intentionality, especially as they developed more complex character portfolios, serial enigmas, and exploited the increasing fluidity between period drama, melodrama, mystery, fantasy, musical, horror, and comedy. Insisting on *Babylon Berlin* as an original language drama thus capitalizes on this momentum while complicating what is defined as German in other ways. In the *Hollywood Reporter*, Stefan Arndt recalls the critical decision in pre-production:

> "It was just too big, too expensive," he recalls. "We were almost ready to start shooting and I thought, 'If we do it in German, it won't sell.' I panicked." (. . .) "Tom [Tykwer] just pushed his chair back from the table, stood up and said: 'OK then, I'm out. I won't do it unless we do it in German,'" says Arndt. "Of course, he was right." (. . .) "You have to remember, this was before Netflix even arrived in Germany. That was still way off on the horizon," he recalls. "And the rules of German TV were very strict—it was still one story arc per episode—and you focus on your one hero. . . . But our story had 157 characters, all very specific, all very individual, and all with their own interacting stories."[34]

Tom Tykwer's refusal to concede German history and content—and the term of the national—to the monetary, linguistic, and geopolitical dominance of America and English is only possible in a global mediascape, in which television shows have merged more fluidly with analog and digital popular culture as well as global media content. The ability to do the show in German without losing Netflix's buy-in is due to Tykwer's verified ability to connect with American cinema-going audiences despite or because of language and culture barriers (e.g., *Run Lola Run*), to retro-mania in television in general (reboots, period dramas), but also to Netflix's willingness to experiment with the limited series and *Fernsehfilm* concept for German-language content (*German History X: NSU, Criminal Germany, Unorthodox*). During the 2010s, another factor emerged on the casting and production side that

---

[34]*The Hollywood Reporter*, December 26, 2018.

needs to be lifted up in the context of confluences between US, global, and national television practices.

Transnational Casting and Production Practices

In 2010, Sibel Kekilli followed her lauded launch in Fatih Akin's *Head-On* (2004) with a fourteen-episode contract as Sarah Brandt on the Kieler *Tatort* (2010–17) to be cast as Tyrion Lannister's lover Shae on the global HBO hit series *Game of Thrones* (2011–14). Shooting indoor scenes in Belfast or on location in Croatia and Spain rather than in LA made it possible for her to fulfill both contracts. Unlike actors before her, like Nastassja Kinski, who often felt pressure to move to the United States when Hollywood called, at the prospect of abandoning their German careers, the new production models in transnational European cinema and television allow an actor like Kekilli today to remain active on both continents.

The attractiveness of European locations coupled with financial incentives through regional, national, and transnational funding opportunities have also prompted US-based shows, like *Game of Thrones*, to shoot in Europe and do postproduction in LA. This has also resulted in a greater exchange of German and US-based actors into and out of US and European projects, as demonstrated by Claire Danes and Damien Lewis in Showtime's fifth season of *Homeland*, which was the first US show to film an entire season at Studio Babelsberg in Berlin, followed by J. K. Simmons's show *Counterpart*. Furthermore, as these multilingual shows demonstrate, casting agencies seek out domestic talent to work alongside their own stars, for example, Sebastian Koch (*Homeland*) and Liv Lisa Fries (*Counterpart* and *Babylon Berlin*), providing actors with global exposure and networking opportunities, while broadening their own talent pools significantly.

Unlike the fluid actor exchange, however, domestic German television projects for Netflix seem to be continuing a cinematic tradition in directing. Television productions usually employ a slew of single or multi-episode directors that work with a steady location team. Shows like *Tatort*, *SOKO*, but also *Game of Thrones* or *The Wire* generally have four to six directors in any given season, which (a) allows producers flexibility, (b) enshrines the power of the format bible overseen by writers and showrunners over the auteur vision of a single director, and (c) gives multiple directors an in-road to boost their experience with different formats and genres, garner critical attention, and foster their transmedia networks. Agnieszka Holland (HBO's *The Wire*, *Tremé*) and Anca Miruna Lazarescu (Netflix's *We Are the Wave*, HBO Europe's *Hackerville*) are examples of European directors, evidencing the opportunity for international, female, and minority talent to find a creative path to hone their skills, gain recognition, and translate that back into clout for their next film or television venture.

Deutschland '83 was created by the US/German couple Anna and Jörg Winger (who also co-created *Hackerville*) and directed in rotation by Edward Berger, a Tisch School graduate with both German and US-based film and television credentials (*Jack, Tatort*), and experienced German television director Samira Radsi (*SOKO, Verbotene Liebe*). Yet looking at *Dark* and *Babylon Berlin*, both shows have retained their directors for multiple seasons, fusing the roles of writer, producer, and director. While *Dark* has a famous duo at its helm (Baran Bo Odar and Jantje Friese), three white men, Tom Tykwer, Hendrik Handloegten, and Achim von Borries, steer the course of the Netflix showboat *Babylon Berlin*, two of them filmmaker transplants, the other a television writer and director. *Ku'damm* (ZDF/Sundance) gives writing credits to Annette Hess but sole directing credits to Sven Bohse. And the trend continues in *Dogs of Berlin* (Netflix, 2018–), where Christian Alvart is the mastermind.

The pattern wouldn't be quite as clear cut, if Netflix had not canceled its Turkish-German hip-hop show *Skylines* after only one season, despite its popularity in Germany and on Netflix. *Skylines* was the only German Netflix show directed and produced by a diverse team of women (Soleen Yusef and Maren Ade). If we take Tykwer and Alvart's rather than Radsi's and Yusef's cases as symptomatic for this period of transition, one could argue that the role of the German cinema auteur has fused with a slightly more collaborative but vision-centric and still male-dominated approach in German television projects for streaming platforms. *Babylon Berlin* has continued this German film tradition as it has also continued the tradition of literary adaptations and combined it with the stalwart genre of the crime drama, three trusted standards for cinema and television development since the auteur-heavy days of New German Cinema (e.g., Fassbinder's *Berlin Alexanderplatz*, Schlöndorff's *Der junge Törless*). *Babylon Berlin* could essentially be called the new *Fernsehfilm* on transnational television. While retaining many of the outlined aesthetic, narrative, and production patterns of their peer, *Dark, Perfume, and Dogs of Berlin* follow different convergence paths, each informative about post-network genre format, storytelling, and directing strategies.

2

Crime Time

Dark (Netflix, 2017–20)

Each of the first-generation German-language Netflix shows is succeeding *Tatort* in stretching and redrawing the generic boundaries of the crime drama. Like *Babylon Berlin*, *Dark* revolves around a series of murders, environmental crimes, and abductions. But in *Dark*, uncovering the motivations and causalities takes characters and viewers to different periods in German history and into the future. Similar to *Babylon Berlin*, *Dark* invites viewers to indulge in period mise-en-scènes. In *Dark*, time travel takes viewers back to Germany in the 1920s, 1950s, and 1980s, continuing the pleasure of the former's Weimar look-book through the postwar era. But its narrated time also transports the 2017 audience forward to 2019 and a postapocalyptic 2050s, and in the third season to parallel worlds.[1] *Dark*'s narrative trajectory is motivated by the contrast between good and evil, as is *Babylon Berlin*'s portrayal of rising fascists and opposing forces. In the latter, the rise of capitalism and fascism combines with representations of historical atrocities committed in the name of fervent anticommunism and anti-Semitism mixed with personal desire, spite, and greed. *Dark*'s character designations experience radical revolutions as good intentions in one timeline engineer bad outcomes in another and vice versa. Each script features strong women and vulnerable men with diverse sexual orientations, carrying on a trend inherited from post-feminism along with the penchant of heritage dramas for modern gender portrayals amid the display of

---

[1] *Dark* showrunners Baran bo Odar and Jantje Friese are planning to continue that look at the past with their *1899* project, April 25, 2019, https://media.netflix.com/en/press-releases/dark-showrunners-jantje-friese-and-baran-bo-odar-unveil-1899-as-next-project-for-netflix (accessed June 2020).

aggressive containment energies. And both shows deal with foundational questions about humanity.

As a result, whereas *Babylon Berlin* is recognized as a period crime drama (not least because it is an adaptation of Volker Kutscher's Weimar-era *Krimis*), *Dark* has been categorized divergently as science-fiction noir, as fantasy-horror mystery, as time-travel crime drama. Each show, in different ways, violates generic boundaries, at the same time that the crime narratives, their acts and images of violence, revisit and redefine German conflictions about a national identity defined by *jus sanguinis*, on the one, and *Erinnerungskultur* (culture of remembrance), on the other side. While viewers can scan *Babylon Berlin*'s narrative for clues to the impending Third Reich, we get to see Germans dealing with its aftermath in *Dark*.

As survivors of the Nazi genocide are dying out, right-wing populism is on the rise in different guises around the world. It is at this juncture that German television projects are reaching a more diverse audience than ever before. Though the crime drama still plays a leading role in representing and responding to German history, cultural specificity, and memory, it is central to investigate how convergence-era television is reconfiguring this dialogue on and through global screens and what traces that leaves on the genre itself. With its time-shifted system of narration that mirrors the medium specificity of convergent television practices, *Dark* explores how anxieties about the human potential to commit atrocities are repressed or rerouted, temporally, physically, and spatially. The drama employs serial narrative complexity with the purpose to connect contemporary environmental, economic, and social crises to long-spanning historical as well as deeply individual causes and effects. Along the way, active viewers are encouraged to assemble and interact with knowledge that implicates every character in their own chain of causalities as they are torn between believing in choice and agency and succumbing to predestination.

This chapter traces the German crime drama's efforts to transform itself into transmedia television. To do justice to the interlacing of narration, aesthetics, and medium reflexivity that are responsible for this development, the different sections of this chapter are concerned with the way *Dark* mines the convergences between genres, between globally resonating and culturally specific discourses, between popular, material, and "high art" cultures. The chapter shows how *Dark* builds a recombinant modular television architecture that entices avid viewers to explode the borders of its textuality and contribute to its enigmas' de- and re-mystifications. In a similar way, watching, interpreting, and writing about cross-cultural transmedia television require tracing some of the convergences at these intersections beyond the dominant points of access and inquire into the genre's and the medium's ability to deal with origin stories as well as their subversions, among them memory culture and national identity construction.

Dark Synopsis

Dark is set in the fictional small postindustrial town Winden two years in the future from 2017 (2019). It is a brooding philosophical crime drama hybrid with a cross-generational appeal. The premise of the show is built around a set of child abductions and murders, an impending energy- and climate catastrophe, and the fatal attraction between two young lovers. Its plot pits two sides against one another: one side actively seeks to avoid a nuclear Holocaust, whereas the other deems it unavoidable and a necessary reset for humankind. Agents of both sides travel through time to reach their goals or alter the course of events.

The serial narrative revolves around the intertwined close-knit community of the fictional town Winden (meaning: warping, winding, writhing, twisting) that is portrayed through the lens of four families across the generations: the Kahnwalds, the Nielsens, the Dopplers, and the Tiedemanns. A series of children alternately gone missing or found murdered have plagued the town at certain temporal junctures and forged complicated social—romantic, economic, and antagonistic—relationships complete with anxiously guarded secrets between the families. At the center of the mystery is a tunnel under the now-defunct nuclear reactor that warps time in 33-year increments: 2052–2019–1986–1953–1920, and so on. Intentional time travelers or unwitting trespassers travel from 2019 Germany to 1986 or 1953 and even into an apocalyptic future in the second season.

As a preteen, Mikkel Nielsen (Daan Lennard Liebrentz), son of stubborn police investigator Ulrich Nielsen (Oliver Masucci) and high school principal Katharina Albers (Jördis Tribel), disappears from 2019 and ends up in 1986, where he is adopted by nurse Ines Kahnwald (Angela Winkler). His two siblings, Magnus (Moritz Jahn) and Martha (Lisa Vicari), remain in 2019 in the first season. Mikkel stays in the 1986 timeline and eventually marries Hannah Krüger (Angela Winkler). They have a son, Jonas Kahnwald (Louis Hofmann), begotten out of linear time, who unsuspectingly falls in love with his aunt, Martha, in 2019. Nearing the anniversary of his disappearance in 2019, adult Mikkel/Michael (Sebastian Rudolph) commits suicide and bequeaths Jonas a letter and map to the caves under the reactor. This begins lead character Jonas's process of discovering time travel and puts him on a mission to blow up the time tunnel to restore linear history, but without sacrificing Martha and his love for Martha. We find out that Michael killed himself so that his younger self, Mikkel, can disappear in 2019 and travel to 1986, so that he can meet Jonas's mother, Hannah, and so that Jonas can be born to put into motion and/or thwart the world-ending or power-balance restoring plans of Noah (Mark Waschke), Adam (Jonas's future self), and Eva (Martha's future self).

This synopsis cannot cover all the intricacies of the twists and turns that accumulated in three seasons. For each of the time periods, the show engaged different actors portraying the lead characters at distinctive ages (the actors in parentheses are from the 2019 timeline, unless otherwise specified). While the casting and the script gave clues to specific identities throughout, some of the connections provided viewers with unforeseen plot twists, for example, that a daughter gave birth to her own mother: Charlotte Doppler (Karoline Eichhorn), Ulrich Nielsen's colleague on the police force, is the adopted daughter of time-machine maker and time-travel author W. G. Tannhaus (Axel Werner) but the biological daughter of Elisabeth Doppler (Sandra Borgmann) and Noah from another timeline. Charlotte gives birth to that same Elisabeth in the 2019 timeline.

Transmedia Families

The narrative complexity of *Dark* carries forward into its reworking of kinship networks, how they are represented and mobilized, within the diegesis, between diegetic and extradiegetic worlds, across platforms and media. *Dark* deals with its German families' past as one of its narrative drives, but it also employs its multilayered family tree as a self-reflection of the convergence mediascape. The family structure in *Dark* explores Jacques Derrida's "law of genre" as a self-transgressive system that continuously exceeds and redraws its boundaries.[2]

The show's anthology of time-travel segments turns *Dark* into a nonlinear television primer, each becoming a teaser trailer for post-network German period dramas from *Babylon Berlin* and *Charité* (1920s/1930s), *Ku'Damm* (1950s), to *Deutschland '83* and *Perfume* (1980s). In the process of exploring nodal intersections between families, characters, and their timelines within the diegesis, *Dark* is also advertising them as genre and media-family connections to engaged viewers. Each segment is long enough to contribute to the growing enigma or its solution but short enough to leave viewers wanting for more. Thinking about each timeline as a spin-off from the 2019 story-world, each setting with different genre accents (horror, crime, melodrama) also mimics the franchise-making of broader media worlds. Character and family timelines thus interconnect genres with the discourse of the national to produce a post-network German media family.

When the question "What makes a murderer?" is the leading enigma for the ninth episode of season one taking place in 1953, the episode also serves as an embedded advertisement for another original Netflix production

---

[2]Jacques Derrida, "The Law of Genre," trans. Avital Ronell, *Critical Inquiry* 7, no. 1 (Fall 1980): 55–81.

Making a Murderer (dir. Laura Ricciardi and Moira Demos, 2015–18). Its placement as an episode header advertises the crime drama connections existing on Netflix and encourages viewers to add that show to their queue mid-stream, if the algorithm didn't do so already. The show's self-awareness therefore extends to its position among a family of crime dramas on its host platform. Its writers reveal themselves as media consumers, even platform junkies. In tongue-in-cheek fashion, *Dark* acknowledges its production and distribution parent as the global part of its domestic DNA, at the same time that the German show is merging with that global television flow. As a German-language genre-hybrid, *Dark* surreptitiously installs one of its genre parentages as a nonfiction crime show and a global Netflix ratings success. *Dark* thus reconstructs the television family tree by asserting that its long-standing incorporation of global content and innovative appropriation of multiple genre elements have earned it its rightful place in the Netflix family.

The family-tree string walls making a repeat appearance on the textual level in the first and second seasons connect that medium reflexivity to narration and reception. The string walls show how characters are linked directly or indirectly, biologically, by adoption, by marriage. Within the serial cross-season context, every entry on the string wall plays a part, if not in one episode or season, then in a later segment. Some that appear to be connected in only one way become implicated in several relationships and actions deeper in the nestled Winden timelines. An unconnected face reads like a potential for narrative exploration, a chapter down the road, emulating a writer's room scenario that is eagerly grasped by avid "textual poachers," Henry Jenkins's word for viewers or users that become media-makers through engaging in participatory cultures around their fan-experiences of television.[3] Functionalizing the interactivity of time-shifting and cross-platform viewing throughout the seasons, viewers add their own vectors to screenshots of the string walls to connect those characters surreptitiously liaised. On social media, fans share and publicly debate speculations about relationships and lineages. As they do so, their pages include hyperlinks that lead to other fan sites and to official channels, containing both visual and textual elements, thereby recreating the model of the photo string wall and extending television flow.

This multi-nodal representation and transmedia practice goes against the representation history of the family on television with its focus on members of one or two families (in dramas and comedies). *Dark* is reshaping generic codes in this area, broadening the format of crime-family peers on HBO (*The Sopranos*, 1999–2007) and Netflix (*Bloodline*, 2015–16, *Ozark*, 2017–22).

---

[3]Henry Jenkins, *Textual Poachers: Participatory Culture on Television* (New York: Routledge, 1992).

Instead of focusing on one family or a feud between two families, *Dark*'s plot is driven by the ongoing relationships between members of four Winden families: the Kahnewalds, Nielsens, Dopplers, and Tiedemanns. In addition, *Dark* is reworking the family relationships from docu-melodramas such as the US series *Holocaust* (1978/9) and its more recent successors *Weissensee* (ARD, 2010–19) and *Hotel Adlon* (ZDF, 2013), and the period drama *Ku'Damm*. *Dark*, instead, takes its cues from long-running soap operas and teen dramas like *Riverdale* (CW, 2017–22), where everyone is involved, in past, present, or future, with one another, biologically, romantically, economically, socially, professionally, or criminally. In the footsteps of *Dr. Who* (BBC, 2005–), *Dark* adds the fantasy element of time travel. Characters travel back or forward in time to prevent or commit crimes crossing not only ethical but also familial boundaries. They become historical witnesses as well as culpable participants. They see their grandparents as ineffective or criminal adults, their parents as brooding, violent, or abused kids and teenagers. When they act or intervene in actions, fall in or out of love, have affairs, they remake their family tree: after Elisabeth sleeps with Noah, she gives birth to her own mother, Charlotte; Jonas commits incest with Mikkel's (his father's) sister, Martha Nielsen, his aunt.[4]

But instead of connecting characters directly to these themes individually, as the series *Holocaust* and *Weissensee* did, *Dark* offers a labyrinthine network of personal, political, and economic motivations. Unlike the categorical impersonation of political violence in the melodramatic format of *Holocaust* (one individual = one category of victim or perpetrator), *Dark*'s representation of collaboration, guilt, or resistance is not embodied by one source. In multiple origin stories that twist around one another, each character's action or inaction results in an array of effects down the road. Unlike the formulaic linkage between characters and categories of victim or perpetrator, *Dark* provides characters that are stuck on, progressing or regressing along the knowledge continuum of duplicated and corrupted cause and-effect chains. Viewers, similarly, can only make sense of certain scenes-and storylines, once they have watched the final season, which entices them to go back in time and watch the show again from the beginning. Violent psychological and physical acts in 1953 are interlaced with those in 1986 and 2019, prompting the viewer to analyze how they relate to one another. A lie with catastrophic results is driven by greed in 1953 (Bernd Doppler) but by passion in 1986 (Hannah). Not showing up to protect a friend as promised ends badly in 1986 (Ulrich) and in 2019 (Jonas). Viewers are made to care

---

[4] In season one, we cannot be sure that Michael Kahnwald/Mikkel is Jonas's biological father, since Hannah Kahnwald's and Ulrich Nielsen's affair goes back a long way. If Ulrich is Jonas's biological father, then that would make Martha his half-sister.

about sociopolitical circumstances, about intersectionalities, and how these contribute to motivations for committing, preventing, or solving crimes.

Tragically, going back to change the past proves illuminating but futile for most characters within the narrative. The dense net of personal and societal *Fehlleistungen* (performed failures) extends from 2019 back to the 1980s and the 1950s. For that period, *Dark* heavily borrows from Fassbinder's mise-en-scène in *The Marriage of Maria Braun*, 1978. Fassbinder intended for his *BRD Trilogy* to expose bourgeois complicity with fascist continuities after 1945. Viewers similarly leave *Dark*'s 1953 scenes, tinged in perpetual brown-green tones, with the uneasy sense that "this is where things went wrong." Not only does economic greed sow the seeds for the environmental disaster that spawns *Dark*'s 2019/20 apocalypse, but bourgeois values and the institution of the family are shown to be inherently unstable and prone to reproduce interpersonal and systemic violence rather than buttress the tenets of democracy.

When Ulrich looks for his son, Mikkel, in the tunnels under the reactor, he travels to 1953 by accident. On the road into town, he meets his grandmother, Agnes Nielsen (Antje Traue), and his father, Tronte (Joshua Marlon), as a young boy. Embodying the connection between personal and systemic oppression, Agnes hints that they are on the run from Tronte's father and have crossed over from East Germany. Instead of rescuing his son, Mikkel, Ulrich thus comes face to face with his father's rescue. Agnes and Tronte room with the Tiedemanns, where she begins an affair with Doris Tiedemann (Luisa Heyer), Egon's (Sebastian Hulk) unhappy wife.

Dark continues Fassbinder's nod to the 1950s penchant to represent the structural fragility of the post-1945 society through unruly female sexualities. Women's anxiety-producing endurance under pressure is extended to sexual appetites in the films of that era: *Die Sünderin*, dir. Willy Forst, 1951, or Rolf Thiele's *Das Mädchen Rosemarie*, 1958.[5] *Dark* attaches this allegorical packaging to Mikkel's displacement from 2019 to 1986, literalizing Heide Fehrenbach's argument of postwar demasculinization, when the adult Michael returns as the preteen Mikkel. More importantly, his father Ulrich's and his own storylines respectively mirror and reverse the experience of prisoners of war, whose return to partners and children was delayed and their integration complicated by changes in familial situations. While Mikkel acquiesces to the new reality, is subsequently adopted by Ines Kahnwald, and forms a new family unit, Ulrich's desire to be recognized as his 2019 adult self results in his commitment to a mental ward.

While *Dark* follows the gender-genre connections that 1950s era German films forged to explore and contain social tensions and persisting

---

[5]See Heide Fehrenbach, *Cinema in Democratizing Germany: Reconstructing National Identity after Hitler* (Chapel Hill: University of North Carolina Press, 1995).

realignments of gender, race, and class in the family structure of the postwar era, it explicitly uses Ulrich's journey to the past—to 1953—to critically assess the dominance of the family, along with its pictorial equivalent, the family tree, as a representation of reality. Sexual violence but also homosexual and asexual relationships are invisible on the tree graphic, even though they are crucial for the time travel and crime drama aspects of the show: Greta Doppler is raped during the occupation and raises Helge with his nonbiological father Bernd Doppler in 1953; Doris Tiedemann and Agnes Nielsen have a steamy romance in 1953; Bartosz betrays Jonas with Martha in 2019; Peter and Charlotte Doppler live in an asexual marriage; Peter has an affair and later continuing relationship with the trans-prostitute Bernadette Wöller; Charlotte cheats on Peter with Ulrich in the alternate reality of season three.

Ulrich, in particular, rather than the single-minded Hannah, who is fixated on Ulrich since her teenage years, is the poster child for the productive connections between nonmonogamous relationships and fiction. "Indeed (...) it is the unstable triangularity of adultery, rather than the static symmetry of marriage, that is the generative form of Western literature," constituted Tony Tanner.[6] Following Tanner's instrumental assessment of the function of adultery for the genre of the novel, adulterous activities across the sexual spectrum and their restructuring of family ties prove seminal for the narrative structure, hybrid genre format, and media reflexivity of post-network crime dramas as well. In *Dark*, transgressive sexualities install obstructions that lead to redirections, entice involved parties to obsessively read each other for clues which lead to misreadings and forked paths, which create more obstructions in need of containment or closure, and so forth. As a result, *Dark*'s time-travel structure instills a general skepsis into origin stories that destabilize not only bourgeois but also national, heterosexual, and race-based family concepts, a destabilization that extends to assumed lineages photographically documented on the string wall—and even further to the genre's and television's representational relationship with the historical world.

The bourgeois concept of the family as a forked but linear biological series is further torn asunder by hints and evidence of sexual and domestic abuse. In Season 1, Episode 9, the extradiegetic viewer, not Ulrich, is made aware that the child Helge, whom he suspects as the future murderer, might have been abused. We observe how his mother Greta Doppler first coldly admonishes, then makes Helge strip naked in the entryway of the house. During her admonishments, she remains halfway up the stairs, her position combining institutionalized authority with spectatorship. While historically savvy viewers can speculate that Helge might be the unwanted result of an

---

[6]Tony Tanner, *Adultery in the Novel* (Baltimore: Johns Hopkins University Press, 1979), 12.

occupation-era rape, a fact that would explain her coldness toward him, the scene remains disturbing, whether as an original form of abuse or as a consequence and repetition of her own victimization.

In the 1986 timeline, a teenage Katharina gets beaten by her abusive mother Helene Albers (Katharina Spiering), who returns home with blood on her hands. It is only until much later in the next season that viewers find out where the blood came from. Before Helene returned to the house, she had killed and drowned the time-traveling adult Katharina from 2019. Katharina had tried to get Helene's key to free the adult Ulrich from the mental hospital, where Helene works as his nurse in that time period. At that juncture, another enigma is solved: the spooky tale the 2019 teenagers, among them the victim Katharina herself, share about a woman having drowned in the lake, where they like to party.

With its foregrounding of adultery, sexual, and domestic abuse, *Dark* reformulates representational approaches to the idea of blood lines and the assumed analogous relationship between family and nation. It makes viewers aware of the multi-laminated a/synchronous in/visibility of private and public relationships. Intimate and family relationships are established as criminal (abuse) or criminalized (homosexuality), visible (adultery) or invisible (asexuality) in different time periods, not just within the diegesis but also for viewers, who discover some of these connections temporally delayed. The serial's complex interpersonal structure is nonlinear and transgressive.

In Winden, multiple temporal versions of characters exist at the same time, with different gender identities and dis/abilities. And since the string wall modal is expandable and malleable, fans can insert vectors between LGBTQIA characters or ship their favorite characters against the biological determinant of the family tree. But in this nodal network, where mothers kill their progeny, and daughters give birth to their mothers, perpetrators also turn into victims and vice versa. Noah and Claudia, Jonas and Martha, Adam and Eva connect to and transform into their dialectic opposites many times. Serial violence here is not the repeated acts of violence by a single killer, nor is violence enshrined in a continuous national family tree leading from Nazis to neo-Nazis. Instead, the media reflexivity of the Netflix series itself unearths the serialized formations that violence has taken and continues to take from the postwar period to today—on television. National, regional, personal, and fictional origin stories thus merge, reverse, and rewrite one another, deconstructing the biological parameter of family and lineage. Considering the importance of the race-based jus sanguinis for German national identity formation during and after the Third Reich, *Dark*'s revision of kinship structures and their representations on and through television, which includes a media-reflexive acknowledgment of the show's own production and distribution network, thus continues the crime drama's contributions to German memory culture.

Time-Shifting as a Post-Network Formal and Narrative Device

The ability to shift time, in historical and technological meanings of this phrase, unites delivery form, genre format, narrative structure, aesthetic choices, viewing experience, and audience expectation in *Dark*. Paradoxically, serial continuity is enhanced through binging, just as the post-network era is reportedly all about time-shifted "nonlinear viewing."[7] Here, Amanda Lotz specifies the drama as the genre form, for which "viewers particularly desire a different experience (. . .) than traditional television experience has allowed" (2014, 13). Thus, linearity is very much desired yet neither in fixed weekly increments nor at the mercy of broadcast offerings and tastes. Instead, post-network era viewers can view "prized content" (2014, 12) in a continuous loop or out of synch, whenever they so desire, from a growing set of narrowcast libraries (e.g., Netflix, Hulu, Amazon). While growing the potential audience for an original language production, streaming loses the big tent synchronicity inherent to broadcast and cable "event TV." Unlike the ritualized viewing of *Tatort* that continues to this day among a large network demographic, the "now trending" portions of the Netflix audience are watching different scenes in their different time zones and in different places on different screens.

Elizabeth Evans has summarized the importance of time for the medium television as follows:

> Time is built into the way television is structured and scheduled in more fundamental ways than is the case with these other media (see Doane 1990). Thinking about television in relation to time brings together storytelling and industry strategies. The nature of most television narratives as episodic and serial speaks to the importance of time passing—of spreading narratives out over long periods of time—to the way that television tells stories. (. . .) More than in other forms of narrative, time plays a crucial role in structuring both television's storytelling practices and its audiences' experiences of them.[8]

A time-shifted narration connects with the ability for viewers to scroll back and forth, review episodes for greater clarity, and gather information about or engage simultaneously with fan sites on a second screen. This has affected the way stories are conceived, aesthetically formulated, shot, and narrated. And it has encouraged expansive transmedia storytelling through

---

[7] Amanda D. Lotz, *The Television will be Revolutionized* (New York: NYU Press, 2014), 15.
[8] Elizabeth Evans, "Layering Engagement: The Temporal Dynamics of Transmedia Television," *Storyworlds: A Journal of Narrative Studies* 7, no. 2 (Winter 2015): 111–28, here 114.

engagement portals across devices. Aesthetic choices and exhibition formats are thus deeply interconnected and pushing each other to the limits.

Dark features a rapid editing pace between different times, characters, and storylines that requires perseverance and attention. There is only so much a graphic match between an "old" and "young" face between timelines and scenes can achieve, when dealing with such a large interconnected cast and complex storytelling. Frequent quick cutaways to unfamiliar characters and timelines leave strictly linear viewers relatively clueless until later seasons. Even with editors exploiting the gamut of editing conventions, keeping track of time-traveling *Doppelgänger* and parallel worlds relies on transmedia viewer engagement.

This type of multimedia, cross-platform engagement is modeled by *Dark*'s narration in the form of the time-travel cave under the nuclear reactor. The cave system composes different temporal versions of characters and storylines creating micro-seasons within and across the segmented structure of a television drama. Thinking about the cave's labyrinthine structure as a transmedia story-engine helps us understand the different media-archaeological layers of this enigmatic story space.

In the first two seasons it remains unclear how and why the different underground doors function or refuse to function, when and for whom. The thirty-three-year interval as well as the thunderstorms and occasionally flickering lights prompt reflections on an active and a passive state of the cave's time-travel aspect, but akin to the spectrum of viewer engagement, the cave's internal machinations peak with their audiovisual manifestations. These take the form of ominous sounds and wind emanating from the cave, along with successfully time-traveling characters entering into and emerging from it (e.g., Mikkel, Jonas, Ulrich, Katharina). Viewers hitch a ride with characters that sleuth out the traces left by the adult Jonas, combine the philosophies of clock maker Tannhaus with Helge's rantings and Noah's appearances, or are shocked by the return of missing and mutilated children. When the minor 2019 characters, Erik and Yasin, are found with mutilated ears and eyes, their deaths serve to sustain crime genre elements as Mikkel's disappearance retreats as the major topic from the 2019 storyline and is replaced by our curiosity about his life in 1986. The cave makes material the generic energies that both sustain each genre and contribute to generic drift between crime and horror, crime and melodrama, and so on. As many of the lead characters double and triple up, each version adds a specific genre spin to their featured segment: Jonas Kahnewald is at turns the star of a teenage romance (2019 version) and the underdog in an apocalyptic science-fiction plot (2052 version).

Thus, the cave as story-engine is producing and spinning off characters and narratives in serial fashion, demonstrating the very concepts of generic hybridization, televisual innovation, and convergence. And, in a multi-platform era invested in transmedia convergence, the cave is also functioning similar to a computer algorithm that produces forking paths and altered character developments for interactive game worlds. It is as if *Dark* lets viewers observe a single-player game in multi-player format, so that one sees a cross-section of different versions of characters at different stages of narrative gameplay interacting with one another in the same story-world. Thus, the story-engine feeds the different generic demands—the gruesome deaths of minor characters and the timeless romance between Martha and Jonas—and integrates spatially dispersed and temporally shifted post-network viewing and gaming practices into its very narration system. *Dark*'s writers and showrunners manage this without recourse to the platform's interactive television experiment (*Black Mirror: Bandersnatch*).

As Will Brooker and John Caldwell suggest, viewers and content are interconnected through transmedia and ancillary activities. While Brooker advocates for extending the concept of flow to "overflow" in his reading of *Dawson's Creek*'s pivotal online summer diaries, Caldwell deems it important to consider viewer migrations across programs, channels, and platforms. Following the work of Henry Jenkins, both argue that even though viewers might be asynchronously displaced, they are actively engaged in locating themselves and each other vis-à-vis the complex narratives they enjoy as well as extending these storyworlds beyond official channels and boundaries.[9] This structure of emergent convergences mirrors the very narration format of the crime series *Dark*. Along with expanded cross platform storytelling material that is bending the time of *Dark*'s narrative content, spatially and temporally dispersed viewers are mining each other's investigative clue-finding to either reestablish linear chronology or add their own twists to the narrative. How *Dark* constructs transmedia engagement is best exemplified by a closer look at the narrative functions of the string wall and the built-in detective modes.

The string wall is a crime drama staple in that it visualizes otherwise tedious and not very televisual police work or the displayed obsessions of a stalker-killer. The string wall reveals investigative process and progress (or the lack thereof) as well as gives police and viewers access to perpetrator obsessions (of the voyeuristic kind) and mind sets. The graphic critically visualizes existing parallels between state power and criminal elements along with a model of engaged knowledge production that maps onto viewers' collaborative online gathering of clues to ever more complex relationships, characters, and plot developments.

---

[9]Will Brooker, "Living on *Dawson's Creek*: Teen Viewers, Cultural Convergence, and Television Overflow," in *The Television Studies Reader*, ed. Robert C. Allen and Annette Hill (London: Routledge, 2014), 569–80, here 569. John Caldwell, "Second-Shift Media Aesthetics: Programming, Interactivity, and User Flows," in *New Media: Theories and Practices of Digitextuality*, ed. Anna Everett and John T. Caldwell (London: Routledge, 2003), 127–44, here 136. See also Henry Jenkins, *Textual Poachers* (2012), *Participatory Culture in a Networked Era* (2015) and *Spreadable Media* (Reprinted 2018).

An actual string wall features prominently in the first season of *Dark*, parts of it "coming to life" in dispersed indexical evidence in different eras. When Mikkel's and Ulrich's photos show up in the glass cabinet of the school in 1986 or the 1953 newspaper, respectively (in their 2019 bodies), they become diegetic proof of life for family members looking for them in subsequent times but also Easter eggs for non-diegetic viewers in our own time zones. Online fan sites accomplish the detective work by constructing maps to help decode complex narratives and relationships, whether factual or fictional (Figure 1).

While watching *Dark*, viewers can pause the show for a closer look at string walls in the bunker at the Doppler hunting cabin and in the Stranger's (a.k.a. 2052 Jonas's) hotel room. While the purpose of the cabin and its bunker forges a connection between the string wall and hunting, investigator work at its most target-oriented, the hotel room, where the adult Jonas resides when returning to 2019, produces for us a revised Raymond Williams experience. In the latter, the subject (Jonas and the viewer) is temporally and spatially dislocated and seeks to orient itself within the flow and transmedia overflow. In the former, the subject/object dialectic is taken for granted, despite the shifts in time. Taken together, both locations of the complex maps demonstrate television's polysemic textual codes that produce diverging reading and interpretation modes.

Setting up this dialogue between the two poles on the hermeneutic continuum and between diverging investigative drives in crime dramas, *Dark* reproduces fan practices within its narration and connects network to post-network storytelling and viewing practices. Comparing the two string walls is painstaking work that is rewarded by placing time-bending fans in

FIGURE 1 *String wall in* Dark *from a fan site investigating family connections. Still from* Dark *as featured on: https://25yearslatersite.com/2019/06/27/in-dark-season-2-everything-is-connected-and-everyone-is-related/ (accessed May 15, 2022).*

a community-acquired elevated knowledge position to their fellow diegetic time travelers. On their different screens, active viewers can post a screen-grab or scroll through fan sites with helpful time-coded family trees, further informing their viewing experience and interpretation of unfolding events in each timeline.[10]

Time- and place-shifting Netflix viewers alternate between their roles as content-managers and creators, critics, fans, or casual viewers in a similar fashion to the three investigative models that are embodied by Mikkel, his father, detective Ulrich Nielsen, and Jonas in *Dark*. Like Mikkel, who continues his life from 1986 onward after accidentally traveling to the past from 2019, casual viewers lean into the serialized narrative rather than fight against it. But like Ulrich, more engaged viewers may begin looking for cues, observing people and scenes, but then also react viscerally to what they originally "just wanted to watch"; they get immersed in their reactions to a script they want to but can't quite control (like Ulrich in 1953). Socialized to seek even more investment, fans are invited to partner with the different versions of Jonas and fellow fans in the decoding process and time management on a meta-level. Netflix viewers' multiply mediated viewing experiences and oscillation between different viewing modes, including second screens, continuous binging as well as delayed viewing, mirror Mikkel's acquiescence to the flow of narrative time and Ulrich's parallel, alternatively on-hold and accelerated lives with his family and lover, Hannah, in 1986 and 2019. But streaming the show also "cuts them loose" like Jonas, who seeks to outsmart the system of narration itself by inserting and removing himself in and from it more strategically. For example, at the exact moment that the 2019 Jonas is bent on rescuing Mikkel/Michael from 1986, his older self appears next to him to talk him out of it (Season 1, Episode 7).

The ability to remember which storylines are open, continuing, and as yet unresolved, which characters are attached to them, and which subplots are either completed or in a holding pattern and in which time achieves the best results for an enjoyable comprehension of the complex storytelling mode. The Jonas traveling between 2019 and 1986 or 2052 does not change very much. It is up to viewers to interpret each opening shot's audiovisual codes and any physical and material cues to discern which version of Jonas they are beholding in any given scene, all the while being mindful of the twists and turns that the fantasy and time-travel genre elements are bringing to the crime narrative. Even careful attention to embodied causalities, such as that Jonas from 2019 does not bear a scar around his neck until after his visit to 2052, or continuities, namely that Elisabeth is hard of hearing in

---

[10] Thinc's *Dark* Family Tree, https://taylorholmes.com/2017/12/22/netflix-series-dark-family-tree-poster/ (accessed June 9, 2019).

2019 and 2052, refuses to help much in transitioning one's comprehension between the third season's alternate worlds, referred to as Eva's and Adam's worlds, where causalities and embodiments have disappeared or been switched between characters (e.g., Elisabeth does not have a disability in the alternate world).

To counterbalance the narrative complexities associated with the storylines of several lead characters, the writers embed Ulrich's storyline as a crime series within a serial narrative format. Ulrich not only embodies a network-era detective, but his storyline is also reflective of the linear mode of series-style storytelling, segmentation, and reception. One could call his forked path narrative a 1.0 version that conduits network-rehearsed newcomers into digital hypertextual storytelling. Ulrich's storyline exhibits a series of repetitions that turn them into signposts in the swirl of serial narration. Time travel does not make Ulrich a world wanderer like Jonas. Instead, he is stuck in a loop that repeats in every timeline, even in the alternate world, whether he is married to Katharina or Hannah, so much so that he muses at one point: "I am betraying the woman [Charlotte] I betrayed my wife [Hanna] for with my wife [Katharina]."

Ulrich cannot comprehend how time travel affects the very structure of cause and effect. As a 2019 policeman and affected father of a missing child, he is stuck in cause-and-effect mode. He is doggedly searching for a whodunit and his son, for *one* perpetrator and *one* victim. Ulrich, like countless crime drama protagonists before him, wants to make sure that justice is served and normalcy returns. He follows clues from 2019 to stop the young Helge Doppler (Tom Philipp), his suspect as an adult in 2019, from committing the alleged crime, when he grows up. And like network and cable-era detectives before him, he oversteps his boundaries—for good and bad—to get results. Ulrich interrogates, then beats the suspected future perpetrator Helge Doppler unconscious, and leaves him for dead.

But his act of violence instead of well-placed mentoring in a moment of trust between adult Ulrich and young Helge makes a murderer out of Helge in the first place. When Ulrich is arrested for attempting to murder Helge, his ramblings about being from the future get him committed to the mental hospital, where this version of him remains from 1953 until 1986. Intermittently, viewers get to see his 1986 teenage version through Mikkel's and Hannah's eyes, and his 2019 self, as he is trying to find his son and the culprit in that timeline.

We see Ulrich work as a detective and protective father, and while viewers understand his motivations for committing violence, even acknowledge their desire for satisfactorily doled out punishments in the past or present, they also see that he is mistaken to think and act solely in terms of linear progression. His way of thinking and solving violent crimes has "No Future"—as his jacket spells out to us in Punk meets Melania

FIGURE 2 *Ulrich and Katharina as their 1986 teenage versions in* Dark, *Season 1 (Netflix, 2017).*

Trump-style irreverence.[11] Ulrich's future is the past; he remains in "linear jail" from 1953 through 1986. He suffers slow mental decline in the psych ward of Winden's hospital, where Helene, Katharina's abusive adoptive mother and his 2019 stepmother, is his nurse Ratched. And whenever a scene portrays him in that timeline, we know where, when, and who he is (Figure 2).

In contrast to Ulrich's dogged pursuit of a series of murders that he envisions are tied to a specific perpetrator, viewers need a good memory and acceptance of a complex narrative ecosystem combined with extensive transmedia and cross-platform engagement to untangle some of the knots the writers and showrunners concocted. While Ulrich's linearly assembled dead-end forked path storyline onboards viewers to the narration system of a convergence-era crime drama, they are enticed to become better detectives than their fictional counterparts, Ulrich and Charlotte. This means that they need to appreciate the world-building energies of the fantasy elements of *Dark* that explode the confines of the crime drama while reasserting its tenacious ability for intertextual and intergeneric innovation. Since viewers' endurance and their willingness to reflect on the genres' different forms of

---

[11]Melania Trump, the first lady, wore a military-style jacket spelling out "I don't care do u?" on her visit to the Southern US border's internment camps.

delivery are a must, they have to resort to time-shifted transmedia resources for their ultimate gratification.

With this built-in fluid spectrum of identification that offers mirroring engagement modes, Netflix creates a community of active viewers that intensifies in synchronicity around the season drop date and accompanying social media activity to subsequently engage in nodal interactions around episode and seasonal story—and character arcs. Future-oriented meta-discussions about possible storylines, returning actors, fan interactions with showrunners, and the fate of renewal or cancellation keep the community involved. This time-shift from the televisual now into the future again reflects *Dark*'s time-travel structure, especially when the season one cliffhanger showed Jonas appearing in the year 2052 only to be bludgeoned by the adult Elisabeth, bearing echoes of Ulrich's assault on Helge. Transmedia engagement will help viewers discern that Jonas—and the show—will have to survive for him to return as his adult double in the first season.

Between the temporal layers of *Dark*'s narration, the unchanging, iconographic 1980s mise-en-scène of the turquoise children's room that is part of the Doppler cabin's underground complex, where Noah and Helge are experimenting with time travel on hapless preteens, continues the string walls' medium-reflexive engagement with the narration systems of network and post-network television. The following section inspects how the room's mise-en-scène with its prominently featured television set contributes to the time-shifted reworking of the crime drama genre, the medium itself, and reception practices.

Experimenting with Television: The Bunker/Children's Room

The eeriness of the turquoise bunker set up as a children's room stems from the operating chair and its occasionally depicted immobilized inhabitants, but since the act of violence is only intimated in seasons one and two, torture and resulting trauma come to live associatively in the 1980s décor and pervasively repetitive soundscape. The room prominently features a television set from the era playing a Nena music video and thus prompts viewers to engage with its media-reflexive mise en abyme.

With its children's room set design, the bunker torture chamber in *Dark* irreverently reflects on one of the most established international debates around television as a medium, namely the moral panic around television's potential for influencing impressionable children. Psychological and sociological media studies are obsessed about this topic in increments

FIGURES 3 AND 4 *Children's/bunker room*, Dark, *Season 1 (Netflix, 2017).*

throughout television history. The debate has been amplified by the proliferation of screen types, user-generated content on social media, and increased cross-platform screen time.[12]

On one level, the quickly inserted and just as quickly replaced bunker scenes are an exaggerated physical manifestation of the broadcast-era idea that children are incapacitated, passive, and empty containers strapped in front of the television set, that they are not as much interacting with the content on television as that television is programming their minds (think Drew Barrymore's character in *Poltergeist*). On a medium-specific level, the children's room scenes function like a mini-series within the serial narration system of *Dark*. This mini-series forces us to watch television like it's 1986. Since viewers get installments in specific intervals, they have to watch it in a linear fashion. They cannot binge this mini-series (unless they create their own from stills or watch user-generated content in the form of a gif or meme) (Figures 3 and 4).

The premise of *Dark* lures us with a promise of revisiting key cultural moments through the time-traveling characters. The generic hybrid pulls us back and forth between times, seeking to connect the dots between past, present, and future. Part of the attraction of this generic extension of the crime drama (e.g., similar to J. J. Abraham's *Fringe*, Fox 2008–13, or *Continuum*, Showcase, 2012–15) is that viewers crave to see an accurate representation of a historical period and place while also indulging in the fictional imagination of the future. Akin to what Andrew Higson and Lutz Koepnik attest for British and German heritage films of the 1980s and

---

[12]According to Brandon S. Centerwall, the American Medical Association House of Delegates passed Resolution 38 in 1976: "The House declares TV violence threatens the health and welfare of young Americans, commits itself to remedial actions with interested parties, and encourages opposition to TV programs containing violence and to their sponsors." "Television and Violence: The Scale of the Problem and Where to Go from Here." *JAMA* 22 (1992): 267.

1990s, our affect-laden look seeks to be met by richly textured audiovisual stimuli.[13] In the process, we get more than we bargained for in *Dark*.

The bunker room scenes confront us with our nostalgic look at the past, a look that displaces historical and psychological messiness with meticulously detail-oriented costumes, contemporary scoring, and décor. This look does not represent the past complexly as the other plotlines taking place in the 1950s and 1980s do. For example, in the 1953 subplot, a time in Germany usually associated with strict heterosexual normativity, we can witness the blossoming friendship and romance between two women, both married and mothers. By contrast, the meticulously designed death diorama recreates a German children's room from the 1980s, as one would find in a Glessner Lee homicide investigation seminar.[14] Indeed, when the scene returns, viewers are presented with minimal variations of the self-same, essentially a *tableau vivant*.

Throughout its run, the experimentation chair and the television set are at the scene's core. Their central placement both initiates and alleviates anxiety, as one uneasily scans the room and takes in the strewn about toys and other objects enshrined in material cultural history: "It's not so bad, look, there's a TV set with a Nena music video." The look and sound of the diegetic television set lures viewers into nostalgic complacency. Against the odds of the room's location below the hunting cabin and the torture chair, the wallpaper with its cute fox and rabbit pair suggests that in childhood, on Noah's ark, or in the German 1980s, there are no hunters and hunted, no perpetrators and victims. The television set with Nena's animated music video distracts the non-diegetic viewer and encourages a sideways look that avoids the torture chair. The camera obliges and zooms in on the music video. With its moving image it provides a needed contrast to the uncanny immobility the chair suggests—an Easter egg to be unraveled for viewers unfamiliar with Nena, an invitation to reminisce for viewers who are.

More than any other object, the television set makes up for the missing window, introducing a connection between the internal and the external world into the room. The diegetic television set makes us believe that the 1980s happen inside and outside. The medium that brought the Vietnam War into living rooms in the 1960s and augmented existing disenchantment and resistance to ignite one of the biggest protest movements in modern history is showing a pop-music video of a German new wave band. The window

---

[13] Andrew Higson, *English Heritage, English Cinema. Costume Drama since 1980* (Oxford: Oxford University Press, 2003) and Lutz Koepnick, "Reframing the Past: Heritage Cinema and Holocaust in the 1990s," *New German Critique* 87 (2002): 47–82.
[14] David Montgomery, "Miniature Murder Scenes," *The Washington Post*, September 14, 2017, https://www.washingtonpost.com/lifestyle/magazine/these-miniature-murder-scenes-have-shown-detectives-how-to-study-homicides-for-70-years/2017/09/13/6037b9c4-812a-11e7-902a-2a9f2d808496_story.html (accessed February 12, 2022).

into the historical world sends back into the broadcast-era scenario a form of content that heralded in the privatization era of television. And instead of showing a protest in action, such as one of the many demonstrations against nuclear power plants and the stationing of Pershing II rockets in West Germany in the early to late 1980s, the set shows us a performance. This performance intones an impatience for the future to arrive, meant to facilitate and accompany the time travel of the children, when strapped into the chair.

While viewers may suspend their disbelief about the other time-travel moments in *Dark*, this television-in-television scene makes them privy to the machination of that suspension. At the moment viewers encounter the bunker room, they are encouraged to suspend the very mode of digitally time-shifted viewership and instead revert back to the end of the broadcast era. This scene is not just producing a nostalgic look at the scene, it enforces how we look at the scene, and it reproduces that scene and the time in that very way of seeing. The televisual mise en abyme makes us adopt a way of seeing that is very much aligned with historically differentiated national, regional, and cultural but also psychological conditions. And in the process, viewers do not experience a nostalgia for the 1980s but for the 1980s way of seeing. And this "seeing" includes the diverted look, the look that absences the present and directs itself elsewhere, always-already to another time and place. The more the look desperately seeks to escape the chair—the tele-logo-phallic apparatus—the more it succumbs to its power and hold.

The mise en abyme continues, when we consider that this self-reflexivity is part of the "postmodern condition" of the 1970s and 1980s. *Dark* installs its very own network television primer, through which post-network viewers perceive the 1980s. Ingeniously, the bunker scenes pop up without prior notice. The bunker's sudden appearance delivers jump-scares straight out of the 1960s–1970s Edgar Wallace horror productions on television. These genre tricks bestow the hybrid drama with the generative power to sustain the mystery of the committed crimes and the perpetrators' motivations. Promising shocking discoveries but delaying them in perpetuity, each installment may feature a new victim or camera angle, but only the complete mini-series plus its transmedia surplus (the rest of *Dark* and ancillary content) can reveal what happens and why. By integrating the bunker scenes as a network-like mini-series, *Dark* initiates convergence television flow in its very editing structure and narration.

Interspersed into the other elements of the main narrative, the children's room scenes function in a manner that is at turns Brechtian, Benjaminian, and post-Freudian. The room falls out of the complexly layered time-travel narrative and represents a petrified version of the diverted look. The scenes momentarily freeze narrated time, become the caesura in the time-shifted narration of *Dark*. Like the return of the repressed, the dream-like alienation effect is created by a fetishistically staged West German 1980s materiality that doesn't change. Considering Lacan's concept of the mirror-stage, these scenes insert alienation at the core of the subject-constituting look. A vulnerable, terrified child looks back at adult viewers. The regression is palpable. The horror of the children's room is simultaneously the cradle and death of postwar national culture, the antithesis of longed for and attested normalization and stability.

The 1980s were a crucial time in determining how Germany dealt with its past; and no other discourse exemplifies this more urgently than the *Historikerstreit* debate around German remembrance of the Holocaust. Public intellectuals like Jürgen Habermas, Jürgen Kocka, and Hans-Ullrich Wehler publicly expressed their outrage over German historians Emil Nolte, Michael Stürmer, Andreas Hillgruber, and Joachim Fest's attempt to normalize German fascism by comparing it to Stalinist and global atrocities in official historiography. The latter group of historians wanted to achieve an exoneration of postwar German generations from the "special burden of collective guilt." In his 1986 book *Zweierlei Untergang*, Hillgruber, especially, was adamant in claiming equal right to suffering for KZ-inmates, displaced ethnic Germans (from Poland and Czechoslovakia), and German victims of Allied bombings. The debate was widened by then president Ronald Reagan's May 1985 ill-conceived visit to Bitburg, a cemetery where alongside regular Wehrmacht soldiers, officers of the Waffen-SS had been laid to rest. Subsequently, the debate percolated through official government rhetoric, when in 1988, then parliament president Phillip Jenninger seemed to give credence to Hillgruber's arguments in, of all things, his commemorative address on the anniversary of the Night of Broken Glass (November 9–10, 1938).

It is important to read *Dark*'s bunker under the Doppler hunting cabin in this troubling, culturally specific context. Similar to Hillgruber's equivalence argument, *Dark*'s representation takes German viewers back to the bunker experiences during the Allied bombing raids at the end of the Second World War; the lives of boys and girls, women, and the elderly suspended in precarious balance as minutes turned into hours and the different days of fleeing to the bunker flowed into one another. Like the Nena loop, sounds must have echoed, prayers and lullabies repeated ad nauseam, in short, the scene of trauma for urban dwellers at the time, unsure of what kind of world they would find upon their exit, or if they would emerge into a wasteland, like Jonas does when he emerges in 2052. While the space evokes collective trauma, it also conjures images of Hitler taking his own life, or the Goebbels drugging their own children and themselves in their Berlin bunker to avoid the aftermath of the lost war and being prosecuted for their crimes. The scene thus performs a normalization along Hillgruber's rationale in that it merges the narratives of those responsible for, those following along, and those suffering under the oppressive regime. Matching the scene of collective German trauma to *Dark*'s bunker inhabitants—all of them relatively innocent boys, even Erik Obendorf—glosses over the different levels of responsibilities for the war and the Holocaust but also the spectrum between fascist fanaticism to partisan opposition represented by actual bunker dwellers in 1944/5.

It gets more complicated. The torture device in the center of the room, that the diverted look is so eager to see in action *and* not see, is a medical chair. On the one hand, this might direct associations toward German and Austrian true crime cases that manage to fuse the act of remembrance with tabloid sensationalism. Of these, the Austrian Elisabeth Fritzl case from 2008 is probably the most famous internationally, but many German viewers will also remember the Oetger, Kronzucker, Schlecker, Herrmann kidnappings. On the other hand, one could argue that the central location of the chair as a recognizable torture device prevents the complete erasure of differences between perpetrators, followers, and victims of Nazi genocide where the bunker becomes the primal scene of collective trauma rather than the concentration camp. The torture chair clearly suggests a connection to the regime's systemic medical experiments on the disabled and the socially, ethnically, and politically unwanted portions of the population, but especially on Jewish concentration camp inmates. Racial hygiene experiments included mass sterilization and euthanasia. Drug testing and high-altitude experiments were conducted on Jewish, Roma, and Sinti camp inmates, including children.[15] In this context, the chair might prompt viewers to reintegrate the Holocaust into their selective individual memory processes, transferences, or denials.

As Aleida Assmann showed in her 2016 book *Shadows of Trauma. Memory and the Politics of Postwar Identity*, Germany has struggled with embracing an "active remembrance culture" in the aftermath of the Holocaust. And while the medical torture chair in *Dark* seems to compel such an active act of remembrance, the ongoing debate around memory culture within Germany takes on more of an urgency as a major shift in attitudes and support toward the Holocaust's central position in German memory culture is evidenced by a 2019 opinion poll conducted by YouGov, which found that "every fifth German thought the Holocaust played too big of a role in Germany's memory culture." The same poll established that "twenty-two percent of Germans agreed that the remembrance of the Holocaust occupied too much space in relation to other topics."[16]

---

[15] "Nazi Medical Experiments," *United States Holocaust Memorial Museum Holocaust Encyclopedia*, https://encyclopedia.ushmm.org/content/en/article/nazi-medical-experiments (December 7, 2020).
[16] "Erinnerungskultur. Umfrage zu Holocaust Gedenken," *ZDF Heute Online*, January 25, 2020, https://www.zdf.de/nachrichten/heute/ergebnis-einer-yougov-umfrage-holocaust-gedenken-zu-praesent-100.html (December 7, 2020).

To make matters worse, the young blond, red, and dark-haired boys strapped into the chair at intervals might even lead the viewers with such a populist agenda to see the bunker as a representation of their grievance against a continuous penalization of Germany for the Holocaust and crimes against humanity. Since the show's leads aim to eradicate the origin of "the fall" in different ways, viewers among the quarter percent of Germans so inclined might perceive that the latest generation of Germans, including naturalized migrants (with combined hair colors to evoke the national flag), is still, and in their opinion unfairly, punished collectively.

After following the polysemic twists and turns of the bunker room, perhaps the best that could be said about it is that its multidimensional configuration exposes and contributes to the winding turns of the *Historikerstreit* itself, and the continuing collective versus cultural memory debate since then. Following Astrid Erll's work, visual media both remediate composita of culturally specific memories and "solidify" their representational shape into a recurring receptive pattern.[17] And this occurs structurally in the case of the integrated mini-series of the bunker scenes as well as in the petrification of the televisual glance at the scene of crime(s), to which I will turn now.

Following Erll's notion of composita, a more complex representational televisual experiment emerges still. Unlike specific historical associations that move us through time in a serialized fashion, the children's room scenes function like a solidifying afterimage. Since the short scenes are sprung on viewers, they cannot avert their look quickly enough, even if they would want to do just that. As established, they can, however, divert their look from the horror at the center to the periphery, when the scenes confront them with the static 1980s German children's room. Thus, Netflix viewers assume the position of the children in the chair, who are blinded in the time-travel experiment and can henceforth only recall the shadowy imprint of the last image on their inner eye. The show makes the viewer obsessively see and return to that same image, forcing them to retain it, keeping it in mind for the duration of the season, episode after episode. When an episode has not had a bunker room segment in a while, one wonders, when it will pop up again, never sure what awaits, somewhat relieved and also perturbed, when it stays the same. The turquoise room thus functions as a self-reflexive companion to the always already mediated and intertwined timelines shown in the time-travel segments. The bunker room's frozen 1980s German tableau reveals how deeply engrained the Holocaust is in German rituals of perception and remembrance, but also what the reduction of the look to a time-stamped archetype can produce: blindness to messy complexities, a

---

[17] Astrid Erll and Ann Rigney, "Introduction: Cultural Memory and Its Dynamics," in *Mediation, Remediation, and the Dynamics of Cultural Memory*, ed. Astrid Erll and Ann Rigney (Berlin: Walter de Gruyter, 2009), 4 and 8.

childhood stasis—and the inability to deal with systems that may not look like 1930s fascism and perpetrators that may not behave like stereotypical fascists.

In addition, the static bunker room scenes embedded within a fast-paced, time-shifted open-frame narration remind viewers that systemic stasis and entropy coproduce one another. During the foundational years of television, GDR and FRG networks provided the kind of alternate German realities to West and East German viewers that *Counterpart* and *Dark* point to and fictionalize. East German propaganda programs like Karl-Eduard von Schnitzler's *Der schwarze Kanal* (DFF, 1960–89) were essentially a totalitarian version of *The Daily Show*, analyzing Western media to prove the other side's failures. But most GDR viewers could divert their eyes and watch Nena on a West German channel instead. The bunker room in *Dark* operates as such a divided screen. Within the diegesis, the kidnapped children, like the bed-bound Christiane in *Goodbye Lenin*, are standing in for the GDR's unsuccessful attempt to control media-reception. The chair also hints at the use of sonic and visual torture to submit GDR citizens accused of treason to confess or to reeducate them for reentry, horrific acts that *Dark* represents are doomed to fail from the outset. In the room, however, diegetic viewers are not exposed to communist political propaganda but instead continuously fed a carefully curated conserved reality of linear West German MTV. *Dark* thus turns MTV into *Der schwarze Kanal* and implies that privatization in the 1980s continued rather than removed television from playing its part in the ideological-technological apparatus buttressing the state powers in East and West. However, selling the democratization impulses early digital media scholars attributed to emergent media, extra-diegetic convergence-era viewers are able to leave the bunker room and change the channel as the show's inner segmentation explores other time- and storylines in *Dark*, other genres and formats, accessing a complex intersection of philosophies, politics, and perspectives.

But there is also a more general convergence-era resonance to the television in the bunker room that might foster an appreciation of *Dark*'s sociopolitical critique on a global level. Since social media first provided a parallel avenue for news coverage in the context of the 1989 Tiananmen Square protest and massacre, alternative media sources have mushroomed. The debate ranges between welcoming their democratization effect, bemoaning the 24/7 treadmill news cycle they have engineered, fostering a culture of remediation, to panning apps and web-based publication outlets for promoting disinformation. Of course, much has been written about this.[18] Suffice to say in this context that the echo chamber effect is

---

[18] See Lev Manovich, *The Language of New Media* (Cambridge, MA: MIT Press, 2001), Henry Jenkins, *Spreadable Media* (2013), Christian Fuchs, *Social Media: A Critical Introduction*

directly attributable to the way social media have re-channeled production, distribution, and reception patterns. Facebook's infamous algorithms mining posts to push and amplify content that someone is already supporting would be a key example. We can read the bunker room in *Dark* as an allegory of the echo chamber, which has arisen as one of the contributing factors to the rise of populism and disinformation campaigns across the world. Similar to QAnon on Parler, Noah's operation "kidnaps" and "incapacitates" the most sought-after target audience (teenage boys) from accessing crucial facts pertaining to global, national, and regional developments, from reaching a balanced opinion on any subject, arresting their development. Noah and Helge, as stand-ins for media influencers, seek to undo the boys' supposed mainstream media indoctrination by forcing them to endure the endless chorus of Nena's 1980s music video instead.

Dark is referencing not only Franz Kafka's critique of the colonial-era European understanding of humanistic through technological progress in *In the Penal Colony* (written during the First World War, published in 1919), but also recent global television successes dealing with the inevitable fall of smaller-scale empires (e.g., *Boardwalk Empire*, *Ozark*, *Breaking Bad*). In moments of stasis, when cooking meth in the high-security underground lab had ceased to signify exciting criminal activity and become the equivalent of watching paint dry, *Breaking Bad* resorted to music montages to show the passage of time. To jumpstart action, the "Fly" episode (Season 3, Episode 10, May 23, 2010) self-reflexively demonstrated the necessity of entropy for storytelling. Both the long-range scheming to reach elusive stasis and make it permanent (i.e., ensuring financial security for the family) and entropy make scripted television seriality successful. Bo Odar and Friese combine Vince Gilligan's and Franz Kafka's approaches in the first two seasons of *Dark*, where viewers mostly see the underground chamber empty, being prepared for experiments, or after the results of failed experiments.

Apart from snippets of Erik Obendorf in the chair, viewers don't get to see the apparatus at work, because in *Dark*, television takes the place of the apparatus at work. The afterimage produced by the television set's analog flicker extends outward from the diegesis and parallels the victims' pressure-burnt ears and eyes in an adaptation of Kafka's penal machine. Most explicit in the Internet of Things, our devices are interconnected, surveilling us, managing our needs, desires, and anxieties, and household routines. They limit or expand the world for us, run projections according to auto-generated loops or customized protocols, one of them might very well be "Sounds of the 1980s" or Nena's music video. As we are strapped to them and they to us, they co-construct and continuously rewrite and rewire

---

(London: Sage, 2017), Axel Bruns et alii, ed., *The Routledge Companion to Social Media and Politics* (New York: Routledge, 2016).

our Selves and each other. N. Katherine Hayles's describes this process that she refers to as "intermediation":

> [A] first-level emergent pattern is captured in another medium, which leads to an emergent result captured in turn by yet another medium, and so forth. The result is what researchers in artificial life call a "dynamic hierarchy," a multi-tiered system in which feedback and feedforward loops tie the system together through continuing interactions circulating throughout the hierarchy [...]. Distinguished by their degree of complexity, different levels continuously inform and mutually determine each other.[19]

Literally and figuratively emulating the process of intermediation, Noah instructs Helge to drop the dead bodies in different times, so that only "digital subjects" hooked up to the television apparatus can discern that the murders are serial crimes and part of the dynamic hierarchy. Consequently, time travel not only allows Noah to get away with murder, but it also removes both individual and systemic crimes from their immediate sociohistorical contexts on the Netflix show and facilitates their de- and recontextualization.

While the association with Holocaust iconography has become a global shorthand for German specificity, in this televisual project each unique historical context—the First World War, the Third Reich, the Second World War, the Holocaust, East German Stasi terror, the domestic terrorism of the 1970s, the 1980s with its environmental disasters—become composite micro-seasons of serialized crimes against humanity. The diverted televisual look that is engaged in a form of parapraxis,[20] a performed failure as Thomas Elsaesser reminds us, thus meets destruction, guilt, and trauma wherever and whenever it follows the internal and external televisual flow. Yet, in replaying the dawn of mass media (Kafka's story) through the emergence of privatization (mid-1980s) and its capitalist economics of desire, *Dark*'s bunker room mini-series demonstrates how the television apparatus guides viewers in diverting their looks. That in and of itself signifies not an escape from the past—the afterimage effect ensures against complete denial—but a continuous projection onto crimes happening somewhere/somewhen, just not here and now.

---

[19]N. Katherine Hayles, "Intermediation: From Page to Screen," in *Electronic Literature: New Horizons for the Literary* (Notre Dame: University of Notre Dame, 2008), 45. She developed the concept of intermediation in *My Mother Was a Computer* (Chicago: University of Chicago Press, 2005).
[20]Thomas Elsaesser, "New German Cinema and History: The Case of Alexander Kluge," in *The German CinemaBook*, ed. Tim Bergfelder, Erica Carter, Deniz Göktürk, and Claudia Sandberg (London: BFI, 2020), 408–17.

Structurally, the polysemic remix and intermediation of often ambiguous cultural historical resonances in internal mini-series segments and micro-seasons inscribe a stronger continuity between broadcast and streaming eras than is generally assumed. But the post-network German crime drama's worldwide reach and its function as an ambassador of the new Germany as well as its integration into global media rituals also alert us to the importance of reading transnationally streamed programming through local, regional, and national lenses to reveal the intersections between semiotic and semantic codes that connect for different audience demographics and geopolitical positions in different ways.

The following section will take a closer look at specific instances of material popular culture in *Dark* and how each plays its part to deliver a modular architecture for German television in the convergence era. First, the focus is on material popular culture, followed by the intersections between popular music and television. The chapter concludes by conceptualizing the time-travel tunnel as a story-engine that not only leaves but also confuses traces of cultural specificity with markers of globalization. Following some of these traces is rewarding for understanding when what is German is recoded, obscured, or emphasized and why. As a high-concept crime drama hybrid, the cave as story-engine shows the intersection at which the process of globalization of domestic content and form meets the localization effort of Netflix.

The Modular Architecture of Post-Network Original Language Crime Dramas

Material Popular Culture

The technology, color palette, fashion, or musical score of a different time period help to differentiate the 1920s from the 1950s and 2019 from 1986. But as established, often only intimate knowledge of the plotlines and historical junctures work because the place, Winden, and its featured residencies remain relatively similar between the 1950s and 2019 timelines, exuding continuity and social stability that neither the 1920s nor 2050s possess. Mikkel arrives in 1986 at what he thinks is the Nielsen residence, where he instead finds his father as a teenager. Jonas arrives at the 1986 high school (constructed in the 1970s), which looks exactly the same as it does in 2019, but students listen to music from mobile cassette players instead of air pods.

Dark's premise breaks with the well-honed time-travel rule that different temporal versions of oneself can never meet (from *Star Trek* and *Back to the Future* to *Harry Potter*). In *Dark*, Doppelgänger abound, occupy the same

FIGURES 5 AND 6 *Jonas (2052) and Jonas (2019)* in Dark, Season 1 *(Netflix, 2017); Raider/Twix Candy Bar (1986/2022).*

time and space. A "Stranger" (Jonas from the future) visits Jonas as a teenager in 2019. Jonas from the future is bearded and wears brown and black, while 2019 Jonas is clad in his iconic yellow raincoat (Figures 5 and 6).

Their doubling is matched by props and artifacts and takes the material form of the double caramel chocolate cookie sticks within the golden-red Raider/Twix wrappers. Raider makes prominent appearances in the 1986 timeline—Mikkel and Hannah share a Raider bar at the hospital, Egon is seen eating one in his car—and in 2019, when one is found in the woods and on the mutilated corpse of a young boy. Unlike a Snickers bar, the duo of cookie sticks can be shared or one eaten now and one saved for later. A network-era snack as if made for the post-network era, Raider/Twix combines instant with deferred gratification; its double sticks encourage redistribution to peers to build social capital. Known in the European market as Raider, the company decided to rebrand it by replacing the European specificity with the American Twix for global consumption in 1991. Placing the focus of the rebranding on the continuity of content, taste, and quality, the campaign in Germany used the slogan "The more things change, the more they stay the same" or in 1980s parlance: "Raider heisst jetzt Twix, sondern ändert sich nix" (Raider is now called Twix but this changes nothing). Raider/Twix can be seen as a parallel to the television crime drama, which has adapted its packaging, has multiplied and hybridized with other genres, and has gone global. Consuming different manifestations of the genre on different platforms or networks has just increased viewers' appetite for more crime dramas.

In 2017, Mars introduced the "Left" and "Right" packaging of Twix. This rebranding follows in the footsteps of one of the most successful advertising campaigns in US history, namely the Wrigley's *Doublemint* gum commercials that began utilizing a set of identical twins in 1939 ("Double your pleasure, double your fun with Wrigley's *Doublemint* Gum"). The 2017 rebranding campaign by Mars showcases the company's attempts to build on the media moment. The Left/Right campaign seeks to expand contact and recognizability with a demographics increasingly deserting network and cable television for social media and YouTube by providing a customizable experience for candy consumers, and to engage them interactively with a hashtag-based Twitter and Instagram campaign: "Twix is out to celebrate things in the real world that are the same, but different—just like Left Twix and Right Twix," said Allison Miazga-Bedrick (Twix brand director, Mars Chocolate North America).[21] Like in 1991, the 2017 rebranding is all about the image, the packaging, the brand, not the recipe or the content.

In *Dark*'s temporally layered storyworld, the message of "same but different" is substantiated by the interaction between different versions of the same character in the same place. In the final season, even the multi-verse is still Winden. Most of the characters' backstories make the development into their future selves plausible and remain on a continuum. Thus, despite the changes in their appearance and their sociohistorical, natural, and cultural environments, their core identities remain relatively stable: Jonas and Martha keep carrying a torch for each other, Elizabeth turns from tenacious and precocious preteen into a kick-ass survivalist leader, Regina remains a deeply insecure and anxious woman. And until the third season, one version of Ulrich remains locked away, slowly disintegrating in the mental ward, where he was placed on his fateful visit to 1953.

How deeply material culture, with its aesthetics of repackaging, is connected to the narrational system in *Dark* becomes apparent in the seventh and key episode from the first season: *Kreuzwege* (crossroads). When the stuck time traveler Mikkel Nielsen/Michael Kahnwald meets Hannah (his future wife, Ulrich's accuser and later lover as well as Jonas's mother in 2019) at the hospital in 1986, he shares a Raider bar with her. This moment—a disguised primal scene, if you will—prompts the conflicted teen Jonas, who had received a stern warning not to take Mikkel back to 2019 from his future self just minutes before (lest he threaten his own existence), to abandon his rescue mission and let matters run their course.

Picture this scene: a convalescing long-haired young teen on crutches puts money in a vending machine and shares a Raider bar with a sad-looking but cute brown-haired girl, both hobble/walk away from the camera together. Like Jonas, their future son, who watches them from a safe distance (so that Mikkel does not recognize him), we can't hear what the two are saying. It's the image that matters. The camera, who remained on them from Jonas's distance for this scene, pulls in for a close-up of Jonas's reaction. Tears are streaming down his face.

This vital moment in the 1986 hospital hallway takes the form of a television commercial. Like the two preteens leaning on the fence watching Cindy Crawford—in slow motion—getting a newly designed can of Pepsi

---

[21] Abbey Lewis, "Mars Releases Left and Right Twix Packs," *CSP* (March 22, 2017), https://www.cspdailynews.com/snacks-candy/mars-releases-left-right-twix-packs (October 28, 2020).

out of the vending machine in the famous 1992 Superbowl commercial, the desiring gaze is duplicated on multiple levels in *Dark*'s Raider version.[22] Jonas is our stand-in spectator in this case. He, like the two boys, is relegated to remain a spectator on the other side of the hallway/fence which functions as an uncrossable social borderline and proscenium arch. Like the boys, who transfer their taboo-breaking desire for Cindy Crawford onto the new Pepsi can, Jonas has to transfer the desire for taking his father out of the Oedipal scenario to accepting his choice to die. At this point in the season, viewers are ready to identify with Jonas's predicament, guaranteeing that they will be affected by the scene and Jonas's reaction. They are watching him witness the first romantic spark and consummate moment between his two parents-to-be. And it is the sharing of candy planting the seed of affection rather than the admonition Jonas received from his alter-ego that sells him and us on leaving the timeline intact. At the same time, the scene trains viewers through Jonas to replace the instant gratification of episode-based resolutions (e.g., as in a procedural crime series like *Law and Order*) with deferred serial consumption Netflix style, again like the boys in the Pepsi commercial (by the time they have come of age, they will have consumed a lot of Pepsi).

Stationed not at the symbolic keyhole but in a public hallway, Jonas is prompted to abandon his mission. At the same time, the scene becomes one of a strategic series of narrative twists that feed the serial enigmas of the show (e.g., in a later episode, Hannah first wants to rescue Ulrich but abandons him in the mental ward, when he professes his love for Katharina). While Netflix does not air regular commercials per se, *Dark* integrates the storytelling format and televisual aesthetics of classic television ads into its narrative. Material culture is thus strongly linked to affect here and tied to Jonas's epiphany in emotional and structural ways. For one, the moment clearly links time-traveling to spectatorship and spectatorship to consumer practice.

The interconnectedness between material culture, televisual verisimilitude and affect, character development, and narrational system is mirrored in the way the story mines publicly accepted interpretations of German history. The past is represented not for its cultural separateness but for its rich internationally resonating reservoir. For the show's resurrection of 1986, verisimilitude is ensured by an avidly shared material and popular culture on YouTube and social media. In 1991, Raider changed its name to Twix in European countries, but the tandem chocolate caramel cookies and the gold/red packaging still exist today, in Germany and most of the globe. The Raider wrapper that is found along a forest path in *Dark*'s 2019 recalls

---

[22] 1992 Superbowl Pepsi commercial: https://www.youtube.com/watch?v=AcroQsUN60s (October 28, 2020).

viewers to the 1980s and a different political and cultural era, an era that also evokes a different television experience. For German viewers, the wrapper might also call forth the breadcrumbs supposedly marking *Hänsel und Gretel*'s way home. In the Grimm Brothers' fairy tale, birds eat the crumbs, which obliterates the homeward path so that the lost children seek refuge in the gingerbread house of the witch. In mise en abyme fashion, in *Dark*, the witch's house is an underground root cellar/bunker with a 1980s-styled torture chamber, where someone is conducting time-travel experiments on male preteens (Hänsels).

The like-new plastic Raider wrapper is an archaeological find in 2019. As the sheer indestructible garbage of the industrial age, the 1980s are regurgitated by the mythologically endowed German forest. The wrapper deconstructs the myth of the ancient forest, a forest that was likely plundered for firewood in the harsh postwar winter of 1945/6 and has been managed as a material resource ever since—its trees harvested and replanted many times over. But at the same time, the wrapper also resurrects a new myth, the myth of a "better Germany," a "better world," if the comments under the YouTube Raider/Twix commercial from 1991 are any indication.[23] Karl Valentin's famous saying describes this reflexive melancholic realization of mortality, of roads not taken or unclaimed potential: "Die Zukunft war früher auch besser" (The Future was also better in the past). If one googles Raider and *Dark*, one will come across T-shirt designs, sound tracks of 1980s pop music, and other nostalgically branded fan-merchandise attaching itself to lost material objects that have been made retrievable and rescuable through the show.[24]

The libidinal object-attachment is similar to serial television fandom in that both refuse to accept closure. In this sense, Raider is a canceled project, brought back alive by a Twix rerun and a crime drama. And the nostalgic affect that ironically reattributes a Benjaminian aura to a reproduced and reproducible mass culture object stems from and in turn produces an origin story and a value hierarchy decoupling the product from its mainstream success by rebranding it as a superior product—"I was a fan of Raider before it was Twix." A highly commercialized product, such as Raider or a Netflix show like *Dark*, can thus take on the artisanal aura and illusory obscurity of an indie band or the clout of independent cinema. What is of

---

[23] https://www.youtube.com/watch?v=VvkGjlr1lg8 (April 24, 2019).

[24] This rediscoverability trend is apparent in other German TV projects like *Ku'damm 56* and *59* (ZDF) or *Deutschland '83* and *'86* (Hulu). Whereas the former dwells in the economic miracle years of West Berlin, the latter is a spy drama dealing with the years immediately preceding the fall of the Berlin Wall in the East. In the United States, *Mad Men*, *The Deuce* (HBO), *The First Lady* (SHOW), *The Americans* (FX), *Better Call Saul* (AMC), *Stranger Things* (Netflix), *The Marvelous Mrs. Maisel* (Amazon), build on the popularity of British period dramas like *Downton Abbey* (PBS).

special interest in this case is that the rebranding of Raider as Twix travels through the national discourse to better relaunch itself on the global stage.

For West German boomers, the Raider wrapper forges a connection to their youth. For East German boomers unfamiliar with the 1980s candy brand, it is not the name change but the material culture hook that triggers a familiar mnemonic practice: *Ostalgie*—the nostalgia for pre-1989 East German material culture that all but disappeared with the economic merger and market dominance of West German and global products. *Dark* thus manages to unite West and East German boomers by producing a common desire to recoup the loss of cultural, regional, and national specificity here embodied not by the iconic regional *Spreegurken* (Spree pickles) brand of *Goodbye Lenin* fame but by a globally identifiable and digestible candy bar.

For millennials and Gen Z in Germany and beyond, Raider functions as a popular culture curiosum googled in a few minutes. Its insertion plants a second screen interactivity that engages the target demographics where they reportedly live—on social media. The product placement of Raider in *Dark* thus functions along a similar line as Mars's aforementioned 2017 Left/Right hashtag-campaign. In addition, the Sony Walkman will invite memories or serve as a historical recall for most international viewers. A facile assumption would lead to the acknowledgment that any show hoping to be "picked up" by US and global viewers would rely on and circulate the most common references. The genius of *Dark* lies in the combo pack of the two items found on the time-traveling corpse in 2019: Raider and Walkman—one specific to time and place, one specific to time but born global. As a global rebranding campaign, the wrapper becomes an analogy to German television gone Netflix.

The Raider wrapper found in 2019 is only readable as indexical evidence of a specific point of origination in German history, because of the brand's globalization campaign in 1991. This means that globalization produces an instance of branded national cultural specificity that is carried forward besides or parallel to content continuity. To international viewers of the first season, the different brand name on the familiar-looking wrapper might as well have been an indication of the parallel world that *Dark* will introduce in its third season. I would argue that this is one of the key reasons why the showrunners paired the wrapper with the iconic Sony Walkman. The pairing of the two assures that both domestic and international viewers can decode the time-travel elements of the narrative at the same time that the pairing mimics (a) the double sticks of caramel cookie in each package of Raider/ Twix; (b) the German audience's long-standing straddling of domestic and global media content; and (c) Netflix's attempt at glocalization. The dialogue between Raider and Sony portrays German sociohistorical cultural specificity as a by-product of global capitalism's acculturation process.

Unlike Nena's and Kreator's German lyrics, neither Raider nor Sony were "made in Germany." The empty 1980s candy bar wrapper found in 2019 becomes an indigestible breadcrumb for Ulrich and the police in the case of the missing children. They know what and from when it is, but they are unequipped to interpret its meaning. It is as if the nationally and globally traveling parts of the narrative—the economics of scarcity and branding, 1980s nostalgia—are obstructing its local and regional spatiality. As the trailer for the first season makes clear, the central question is, "When is Mikkel," not where. And that question itself became the enticing engagement invitation to viewers. Mikkel is still in Winden. But the place is just the launchpad for the layers of past and present we are asked to keep apart and reconnect. Time supersedes place. And this is the case for the show not just thematically but also structurally for the medium on which it is exhibited.

Recombinant by Design

As established, *Dark* works with a multi-laminated system of narration and a transmedia family structure to converge with the global flow and cross-platform overflow of material popular culture. Outside of the use of the original language, any remaining national or regional specificities need to be already inscribed by or attachable to mass-circulating imagery and meaning. Raider/Twix, the yellow raincoat, and modular school architecture are authentic yet transposable, mobile in their adaptability, attachable, sharable, and memeable.

Jonas's golden rainslicker and the yellow-rimmed windows of his high school building attach themselves to the Raider/Twix wrapper in intriguing ways within *Dark*'s at first generally gloomy and later postapocalyptic mise-en-scène. Is Jonas's perpetual golden rainslicker a marker of national identity? Is the modular school building? International audiences likely recognize the slicker from Scandinavian crime shows or have come to know it as a horror trope—"the raincoat of horror."[25] Some might associate it with the 2017 film *It*, where Georgie, the first child victim, wears a yellow rainslicker as he kneels in front of the sewer. Others might connect it to the 2017 video game *Little Nightmares* (Dennis Talajic and Tarsier Studios), whose tiny avatar is clad in a hooded yellow raincoat while maneuvering through a gigantic gray ship-world of cannibalistic, masked humanoid creatures. Since the game's character is less innocent than it looks (it eats a rat and the gnome that offers it food when it gets hungry), viewers might transpose their learned skepticism to Jonas and his intentions in *Dark*.

To German audiences, the fishermen's *Ölzeug* (oil cloth) colloquially referred to as "(Ost)Friesennerz" (East Frisian mink) is also a regional

---

[25] So called by *TV Tropes*, which has added Jonas of *Dark* to its list of examples. The Wiki-based site features a link to purchase a yellow raincoat: https://tvtropes.org/pmwiki/pmwiki.php/Main/RaincoatOfHorror (December 15, 2020).

marker that signifies on the national level. The *Ostfriesland* in the moniker points to its origin in North Sea fishing. Due to its ubiquitous appearance on city streets, the name also pokes fun at the coat's and the wearer's proletarian roots. At its height of popularity in the 1980s, the raincoat was affordable across the economic spectrum and created a group-based uniformity—similar to jeans—that was in equal parts desired—by high school and university students especially—and disliked—by those attributing communist leanings to the wearers. The yellow nylon/polyester coat was also a border-crossing design. It was worn in West and East Germany (where it was produced by VEB *Jugendmode*).

The golden rainslicker is a brilliant costume choice for multiple reasons. It functions like Rick Grimes's hat in *The Walking Dead*.[26] Like the hat, that forever ties Rick—or his son and daughter, who wear it—to his duty as a community sheriff, the coat becomes a familiar image and leitmotif for Jonas's work ethics, his ceaseless dedication to stop the time loop once and for all. And it highlights Jonas and Martha, who wears his coat on occasion, in a large ensemble cast. While we might have some trouble remembering who is who and from which time as the complex narrative winds around itself, when we see Jonas in his *Friesennerz*, we know he is the "original" Jonas from 2019. That Jonas is our guide through the multi-verse.[27] Jonas's consistent costume becomes a shining beacon in the overwhelmingly rainy and gray mise-en-scène and narrative of *Dark*. And the raincoat codes Jonas as a reliable and consistent character, who is always prepared for the worst, even if it means he sometimes has to go against his own belief system. He might fear danger and suffer greatly, as he does from his father's death and in what seem like incessant thunderstorms, but he seeks the truth and goes looking for it, instead of hiding in plain sight. As a signifier that connects working class to university students, the coat also sets Jonas apart from Bartosz and his "rich boy" clothes. While Bartosz changes his outfits frequently, sells drugs, and becomes Noah's foot soldier, the 2019 Jonas remains steadfast through seasons one and two.

While the raincoat makes Jonas stand out to the television audience, it lets him blend into the time-shifting diegesis. In 1986, his raincoat covers for his

---

[26] Rick Grimes (Andrew Lincoln) keeps his sheriff hat until he is reunited with his wife and son. He passes the hat to his son, when he has to leave on a dangerous mission. In the 2019 season, the first episode takes place five years into the future from where the 2018 season left off, and the hat allows viewers to identify the grown-up Judith, Rick's daughter.

[27] In his 2020 article "From Nordic Noir to Euro Noir," which I unfortunately only discovered at the time of proofreading, Kim Toft Hansen reads the local-global resonance of the *Friesennerz* in a similar vein. He points out that "Nordic noir has become part of the international stylistic and narrative vocabulary that works side by side with references to *Twin Peaks*, Stephen King, and different global popular cultural references." (288). He adds *Stranger Things* and *Stand By Me* to the intertextual reservoir of *Dark*. In: *Nordic Noir, Adaptation, Appropriation*, ed. L. Badley, A. Nestingen, and J. Seppälä (London: Palgrave Macmillan, 2020), 275–294.

in-ear headphones dangling out of his jeans. Egon Tiedemann, the soon to be retired police officer, notices them, but luckily does not pursue the issue, when Jonas demonstrates plugging them into his ear. Egon writes them off as just one more technological marvel his generation has no knowledge of or use for, ironically wondering: "Dinge gibt's!" (the things that—but do not yet—exist).

If the raincoat signifies on multiple geopolitical levels at the same time, the color yellow forges a close relationship between Jonas and the concrete modular high school building from the 1970s with its yellow window frames. The Reinfelder Schule in Berlin and shooting location of *Dark*'s featured 2019 high school looks like many others around the country constructed for the baby boomers born in the 1960s. In *Dark*, both the raincoat and the school's architecture stand out as mass-produced, modular, prefabricated designs, ready to be adapted to any media form, any place, any personal, professional, or institutional need, when circumstances change. Due to declining birth rates in the 1980s, some of these former high schools are now used for different purposes (Figures 7 and 8).

When we translate how these analyzed design elements recode cultural specificity for the post-network era, it starts to make more sense. Our converging mediascape regularly features German with or without English subtitles and German locations on shows like *Homeland* (HBO) and in blockbuster film trilogies like the *Borne* franchise. What signifies as German has merged with the stream of globally mediated images. Culturally specific iconography has been attaching itself visually, sonically, and cybernetically in a *Bauhausian* or *Transformer*-style assemblage to a global corpus, across platforms, recycled and reinserted on Instagram, Twitter, Facebook, in video games, television, and films. In the *Transformer* film *Bumblebee* (Travis Knight, 2018), the protagonist Charlie (Hailee Steinfeld) finds the auto-bot in its yellow VW form hiding in a junkyard. Once she has repaired it, Bumblebee adapts itself to different

FIGURES 7 AND 8 *Locations: Reinfelder Schule, Berlin (2019; by permission from Felipe Tofani); Heisenberg Gymnasium (Hamburg, 2021; sourced: https://fotostrasse.com/locations-series-dark-berlin/ - accessed June 13, 2019; original image by permission from Felipe Cintra at Fotostraße, Flickr: https://flic.kr/p/24kk63j.https://hg-hh.de/profil/7-gute-gruende-fuer-das-heisenberg-gymnasium - accessed May 15, 2022).*

environments and reshapes itself for different functions. What began as Hitler's pet project and morphed into *Herbie, the Love Bug* (Robert Stevenson, 1968), itself a movie and television franchise, is reappropriated for a multi-platform media age. Its German production history is but one modular part that can go dormant for one function and environment only to be reanimated for another, depending on the medium, genre, ideology, and viewing mode.

Popular Music and Transmedia Television

Since its inception, television has functioned as the companion to radio in promoting both established and new popular music talent. As discussed, *Dark* features a 1980s themed décor to match a music video playing on a loop on a television set in its most enigmatic mise-en-scène: the bunker torture chamber styled as a child's bedroom. The 1980s was the era of cable television and MTV. Television music videos not only changed how viewers approached the medium itself, and their featured artists, songs, and performances in significant ways, but also writers' and filmmakers' concepts of narration, editing, and videography for the medium, producing specifically formatted "MTV-friendly" videos.[28] MTV supercharged the already fluid interchange between content consumption, advertisement, and media-specific production and presentation formats. And it rang in the genre-based niche-proliferation expanding across the program-spectrum with *VH-1* in the late 1980s and *The Box* in 1992 in the United States, and in Germany beginning with *MTV Central* in 1997 through cable and satellite providers.

Following Michel Foucault, the Walkman and the television set featured in *Dark* become readable through apparatus theory. As Teresa de Lauretis and Stephen Heath make clear for the cinema, the media apparatus can be understood as "a particular institution with relations and meanings (a whole machinery of effects and affects)," which include the regulatory machinations of social habitus and the spectator's "mental machinery" along with Christian Metz's notion of the "technique of the imaginary."[29] 1980s network television and MTV hailed viewers simultaneously as subjects of the state and consumers of capitalist products. Privatization was advertised as the expansion of viewer and listener choices, yet in *Dark*, this period of television history is depicted as one music video playing on a continuous loop from a VCR in the children's/torture room, the opposite of the promised variety.

---

[28] Jack Banks, *Monopoly Television: MTV's Quest to Control the Music* (Boulder: Westview, 1996), 175.
[29] De Lauretis, Teresa and Stephen Heath, eds., *Cinematic Apparatus* (Milwaukee: University of Wisconsin Press and MacMillan, 1980), ix and 2.

However, extradiegetic viewers unfamiliar with 1980s German pop music are indeed given the variety advertised, as they are taken back to a different era, similar to the wayback-machine of online television, especially YouTube, which has become the path to access audiovisual traces of a nation's and a generation's televised imaginary and its history. In creating these divergent affects through the same technology, *Dark* foregrounds television as apparatus. The nostalgia-inducing aspect of popular music and MTV is conflicting with the torture aspect, both emanating from the same machine. The technical apparatus eats and regurgitates its mutilated, fragmented children. Netflix viewers then re-consume them, and the technical-industrial recombinant seriality continues: In *Dark's* philosophy *The End is the Beginning (Das Ende ist der Anfang)*.

The dichotomy between the immobile television set and its viewer—literally strapped into the chair, figuratively strapped to the linear or looped programming—and the mobility of the Walkman clash with one another and showcase the drastic emergent changes in media technology, production, dissemination, and reception practices between the network and post-network eras. Unlike the transistor radio, the Walkman (1979–91) was the first device that delivered individual audio-mobility allowing teenagers to live in their own sonic worlds and set the external adult-dominated world to their individual and their generation's popular rhythms and lyrics. Along with the VCR and the boom box, the analog cassette-tape Walkman allowed users to record, mix, reorder, and produce a customized playlist of radio, music, and audio-sources. The Walkman freed German youth, in particular, of the uncontrollable genre-mixing on public radio stations before privatization kicked in (from rock and pop to *Schlager* and folk). While the boom box was important for creating, sharing, and broadcasting music loudly, the Walkman introduced the privacy-in-public function that first the iPod (2001) and then smartphones carried over into the new millennium.

Dark repeatedly plays with the diegetic/non-diegetic use of music mapping onto public and private soundscapes that announce and conjure different time periods and characters' storylines. One scene from the crucial seventh episode of the first season may serve as an example: Jonas has just arrived in 1986 from 2019, and he is making his way across the school courtyard past a horde of fellow teenagers in 1980s hairdos and outfits engaged in various conversations and activities. As he does so, we hear the British New Wave band *A Flock of Seagull* perform "I Ran (So Far Away)" from 1982. The song describes a hypnotized traveler who "floats on a beam of light" shining down on a girl with "auburn hair and tawny eyes."

Since the earbuds made an appearance in the scene before, what at first appears as a non-diegetic score layers over Jonas's regular habit of entering his school in 2019 listening to his customized playlist through his headphones. Thus, the source of the score ambiguously oscillates between non-diegetic and internal diegetic. Martha, Jonas's crush, has auburn hair and tawny eyes, and he remains in her thrall through time and place shifts. But the band's typical new wave sound also clearly signals the 1980s and channels the leitmotivic use of "Don't You Forget about Me" (Simple Minds) in *The Breakfast Club* (1985) and Huey Lewis and the News's "Power of Love" and "Back in Time" from *Back to the Future* (1984).

With the ambiguous scoring, the producers key Jonas's first arrival in the past as a nostalgic return for viewers, who remember their own Walkman use during high school and college, and fans of the iconic 1980s high school films. In the hallway, Jonas comes across the young Regina Tiedemann. We don't recognize her at first but are helped out by a bully, who insults her and pushes her into the wall "Regina, du alte Brillenschlange" ("old four-eyed Regina"), invoking the constant abuse George McFly, Marty's father, has to endure at the hands of Biff Tannen in *Back to the Future*. Jonas asks Regina what day and year it is, but he needs to repeat the question, when she has removed her headphones, because Regina is listening to "I Ran" on her Walkman, at which point the score merges with the diegesis, attaching it to 1980s lived reality. While this shift helps to authenticate the musical score, it also becomes its own transporter device, aiding viewers to arrive in the time period more fully rather than reveling in the retro-effect at the exclusion of paying attention to character-based story momentum. The act of bullying also makes clear why Regina, aided by her personal mobile soundscape, is keeping to herself, resentful and untrusting of the "popular kids." Whereas the soundtrack matched Jonas's time travel before, the song now represents Regina's desire to "run so far away." In his yellow raincoat and with his friendly demeanor, Jonas becomes her embodiment of the song's Aurora Borealis on a dreary gray and rainy school day.

Several fan sites as well as Netflix-affiliated websites have compiled the episode-by-episode soundtrack of *Dark* for interested viewers. And these have merged with Spotify to encourage the integration of the Netflix content, its ancillary material, and popular music cultures.[30] Viewers can access the lyrics and sounds of teenage Ulrich's favorite German trash-metal band Kreator, find Danish artist Agnes Obel's songs from her 2016 album *Citizen of Glass*, and listen to and watch Austrian Falco's *Jeanny* (1985), the song that fascinates teenage Katharina. The already assembled playlist crosses times and borders and promotes a hipster mix of known and relatively obscure artists' works. Following the transmedia para- and intertextual resonances of two titles in *Dark*—Nena's *Irgendwie, irgendwo, irgendwann* (Somehow, Somewhere, Sometime, 1984) and Falco's *Jeanny* (1985)—will reveal in more detail how culturally specific and global discourses intersect and will

---

[30]Spotify, https://open.spotify.com/playlist/19LrIvlvpwZXbpSRhkjOoq (accessed November 3, 2020).

provide the foundation why that matters for post-network transnational television.

Nena's Irgendwie, irgendwo, irgendwann (Somehow, Somewhere, Sometime, 1984)

To international audiences, Nena's voice might be more familiar from her international first hit "99 Red Balloons," but her voice in the music video of "Irgendwie, Irgendwo, Irgendwann" is recognizable, resonates as an approved sound of the 1980s from the 2019 vantage point.[31] It also experienced a rapid renaissance through *Dark* and online sharing. In a chart by *Tunefind*, due to *Dark's* season three drop and the song's reappearance in the series finale, Nena's second hit from 1985 became the top television song for two weeks in a row in July 2020.[32] The first verse and chorus:

> Im Sturz durch Zeit und Raum (Falling through time and space)
> Richtung Unendlichkeit (towards eternity)
> Fliegen Motten in das Licht (moths fly into the light)
> Genau wie du und ich (exactly like you and I)
> Irgendwie fängt irgendwann (Somehow sometime starts)
> Irgendwo die Zukunft an (Somewhere the future)
> Ich warte nicht mehr lang (I won't wait much longer)
> Liebe wird aus Mut gemacht (Love is made from courage)
> Denk nicht lange nach (Don't think too long)
> Wir fahren auf Feuerrädern (We are riding on fire wheels)
> Richtung Zukunft durch die Nacht (towards the future through the night).

The song features Nena's characteristically high-pitched nonchalant delivery. During the pop-ballad stanzas, she sings with a relatively tinny voice, she swallows her consonants and elongates her vowels, with all lines rising in pitch and left hanging in mid-air. She switches to a slightly fuller and lower register in the punk-rock chorus backed by her drummer, bass player, and guitarist. The pitch intonation of the lines is uncharacteristic for the German language, which tends to fall at the end of a statement. Instead, she intones every line as a question. This pitch inversion not only presents a significant feminization of punk-rock music, fusing it with teeny pop, but is also an Americanization of German intonation, allowing it to blend in with globally dominant US pop tunes.

---

[31] Nena's 1984 music video: https://www.youtube.com/watch?reload=9&v=oas5nAlfrwg (June 19, 2019).
[32] *Tunefind*, July 27, 2020, https://blog.tunefind.com/2020/07/top-tv-song-irgendwie-irgendwo-irgendwann-by-nena-dark/ (November 3, 2020). The article mentions that Nena contributed to a 2011 track by Kevin Costner's Band (featured in *Yellowstone*, Paramount, 2018–), which showcases the increasingly transnational cross-platform labor of musicians and composers.

The group's music video bears this out.[33] Throughout, Nena's face is featured alternately in soft-focus close-ups during the stanzas or medium long shots (situated in the middle of the band) during the chorus. Her hair tousled, she wears a black leather jacket paired with a soft, long, and voluminous pink scarf, a single silver star earring dangling to her neckline. Her outfit blends a rock-band staple with a bourgeois office look, domesticating her image in comparison to contemporary punk-rock singers like Nina Hagen or Joan Jett. Band members are wearing punk versions of glam-rock outfits with at least shoulder-length hair.

The first part of the video features supposedly futuristic looking androgynous roller skaters dressed in pink and black tights with pink umbrellas. They glide around the three band members and Nena on the sidewalk in front of a traditional German café (we can see an assortment of cakes in the display window). In the middle section, the band has moved into the street and the ground is covered in snow. The café backdrop has been replaced by what looks like a warehouse or derelict factory building. During the instrumental solo, the camera pulls into a bird's-eye perspective to catch the snow being blown upwards and then settles on eye-level for the remainder of the song. The upward blowing snow inverts the laws of physics somewhat playfully while at the same time indicating the dehumanized god's eye view descending on earth's nuclear winter. The two parts of the video are accentuated by Nena's personal attention to her blond bass player on the left in part one and the black-haired guitarist on the right in part two, hinting at the false dichotomy between two devils/angels. In 1986, this dichotomy translates to West versus East; in *Dark*, it translates to Jonas/Adam and Martha/Eva versus Noah and Elisabeth.

In part two, the traditional and sunny German city block from part one has turned into an isolated frontier town in a postapocalyptic winter. Not only the season has changed but also the look of the place. What was recognizably German has given way to a background with a decidedly postindustrial and postapocalyptic silhouette. In a conflict between East and West, Soviet Union and America, an actual Reagan/Gorbachev duel, Germany would cease to exist. It also hints at America's iconographic dominance for envisioning any future, how the Western meets Science Fiction in Cyberpunk, in particular (as expressed in William Gibson's *Neuromancer*, 1984).

Nena's video iconography spoke to *Dark*'s showrunners and set designers. The message of enduring human love expressed in spite of the dystopian world ending—from "99 Red Balloons": "Found a balloon, think of you and let it fly" or from this video: "Love is made from courage"—resonates with Jonas's and Martha's love for one another across the times and multi-

---

[33] Nena, "Irgendwie, Irgendwo, Irgendwann," music video: https://www.youtube.com/watch?v=oas5nAlfrwg (November 3, 2020).

verses. "Falling through time and space" becomes Jonas's mantra: "I think we fit together perfectly. Never believe anything else." Young love itself, its ups and downs, intensities of emotion, passion, and anxiety, becomes the motor that drives the time-traveling narratives. This romantic thread overcoming the "darkness" in the title and mise-en-scène helps viewers follow the characters winding their way through Winden's and Germany's past, present, and future, including alternate realities. And at the same time that Nena's "Irgendwie" pits romance against dystopian darkness—the nuclear Holocaust on people's mind in the mid-1980s and today—it adds an impatience to the mix ("I won't wait much longer"), egging on listeners and viewers to stop overthinking things and start living.

Within the text of *Dark*, the latter applies to Mikkel Nielsen/Michael Kahnewald, who is struck mute when stuck in 1986. Unable to return to 2019, he can only decide, when he will let his future in 1986 begin, not where. As discussed earlier, Hannah helps him make that decision sooner rather than later. The second stanza of "Im Sturz durch Raum und Zeit" embodies the experience of both Mikkel and the abducted children strapped into the time-travel experiment chair *as* Nena's band performs the music video on the diegetic television set. Psychologically, as is common with disassociation due to psychological trauma or injury, Mikkel might progressively experience his first decade in the 2000s as a dream, not his "awakening" in 1986. Since viewers haven't been privy to his childhood, for them, Mikkel, the character, is permanently associated with the 1986 timeline in season one; this is also a when, not a where. For the kidnapped children like Mads, Erik, and Yasin, individually plucked out of different time zones, the tune accompanies their last minutes of life. Ironically, except for Mads, the mise-en-scène from the 1980s is irrelevant to them and does not yield much significance outside of accompanying their fear and terror. While the bunker-inmates can understand the lyrics, they likely won't recognize this version of Germany. Instead of anchoring them spatially and temporally, the aesthetic, sonic, and performance styles of the video would seem at least grotesque if not alienating to a techno, rap, or dubstep loving kid from 2019. As far as viewers know in seasons one and two, Mads Nielsen (Ulrich's brother), who was abducted from 1986, would have been the only known victim to actually connect the when and where. The score thus misses its diegetic target and travels through space and time to find another captive audience: Netflix viewers.

Falco's Jeanny (1985)

Falco broke into popular music with his *Rock Me Amadeus* (1985) inspired by Milos Foreman's film *Amadeus* (1984). The top song from his third album *Falco 3* is thus born out of a transmedia inspiration. *Jeanny* is from the same album. While the former went on to top the charts on both sides of the Atlantic and has endured in popular music culture, the latter had a more tumultuous trajectory domestically and in Europe. It never made it onto US charts despite its partial use of English. The reason is twofold. Musically, it fuses spoken words in Falco's Austrian dialect with a pop-melody chorus and a news announcement spoken by news speaker Wilhelm Wieben. The genre mix does not translate well linguistically and musically, and thus its kind is rare in the global pop-chart system. But more importantly, *Jeanny*'s lyrics and the accompanying music video led German and European stations to boycott and blacklist the song:

> They are coming. They are coming to get you. But they won't find you. No one will find you. You are with me.
>
> Newsflash: In the last months the number of missed persons has drastically increased. The latest publication from the police reports another tragic case. It revolves around a nineteen-year-old girl, that was last seen fourteen days ago. The police do not rule out the possibility that this was a criminal act. (Falco, *Jeanny*, 1985)

While the lyrics draw a stalker portrait, the easily accessible music video on YouTube is much more ambiguous.[34] Falco walks around the rainy, foggy woods, carrying the lifeless Jeanny to an underpass. In what appears to be a flashback, we see Jeanny leaving a bar, and we see Falco watching the news report quoted earlier on a television set, then following her into a pedestrian tunnel. Throughout, his walk is crosscut with footage of Jeanny lying on a stretcher as a doll/mannequin/corpse hybrid, wearing a white corsage outfit Madonna would make famous a few years later. As the camera pulls to a close-up of her face, her eyes open. In the final chorus of the song, Falco, in a straight-jacket, cowers at the rear end of an elongated white-tiled room alternatively relishing his memories and railing at his fate. His eyes remain shut tight and don't open, even when Jeanny appears and kisses him on the cheek with freshly drawn red lipstick. As the chorus repeats and spins out of control, Jeanny appears alternately clad in a glitzy evening dress, a wedding dress, and in dominatrix leather stockings, tormenting Falco with her hair and body. Finally, Jeanny sits close to the camera on the floor wearing pants and a large sweater-hoodie with a scarf, breaks the fourth wall, and falls over laughing. Cut to a bearded guard, who looks in on Falco, who now has his eyes open. No Jeanny in sight.

---

[34] Falco, *Jeanny* (1985), https://www.youtube.com/watch?v=Urw-iutHw5E (accessed August 15, 2021).

The video weaves together the heterosexual male fantasy of unrestricted sexual access to and dominance over women with an S&M-inspired revenge fantasy. The mix milks the Madonna-whore continuum to its fullest. Yet, ultimately, Jeanny arrives in the body of an ordinary young woman laughing at and rebelling against her stylized role in this doubled male fantasy construct—in Falco's mind and in the video. Her laughter comes close to the "laugh of the Medusa" as Hélène Cixous called it in her 1975 essay. Addressed directly to the camera, Jeanny's laugh unsettles the power dynamic of the "phallologocentric discourse," brings the fantasy construct to a halt. She leaves Falco to face his Norman Bates ending in a mental ward. As the guard looks in on him, Falco's eyes open wide, signaling he has traded positions with the previous corpse/bride Jeanny.[35]

Echoes of *Jeanny* reverberate in *Dark*. In the 1986 storyline, Hannah is witness to Katharina describing Falco's song to a friend and exchanging the tape with her. The intense storyline might very well have story-boarded her shocked reaction to the "primal scene" she witnesses between Ulrich and Katharina in the storage room. Katharina also listens to *Jeanny* on her Walkman while doing homework at the kitchen table. Jeanny and she are the same age, and Katharina is about to willingly lose her virginity to Ulrich in the school's basement. Hannah, two grades below them and desperately in love with Ulrich, spies on them through the basement window. Subsequently, Hannah accuses Ulrich of rape, reporting the event directly to the police. Ulrich is apprehended until Katharina vouches for her consent.

In the kitchen, with her headphones blasting *Jeanny*, Katharina doesn't hear her mother, Helene, come in. Helene slaps her, abruptly and painfully bringing Katharina out of Jeanny's world into her own, which is just as violent: "Jeanny, quit living on dreams, the world is not what it seems." The scene effectively counters the stranger-danger violence from the song with domestic violence, a much more common occurrence. Like the song that invites listeners into a stalker's twisted rescue fantasy, *Dark* also flips the script on sources of love and loving. What should be a loving relationship is dominated by domestic abuse; what Hannah represents as sexual abuse is the closest thing to love Katharina has. Thus, Katharina's own family background and Hannah's conniving antics introduce a complexity into narratives of desire, abduction, and assault that refutes the simplicity of dividing the world into family and other, victims and perpetrators, or innocent and corrupting forces, particularly when the real culprits causing Katharina harm in *Dark* are her own husband, mother, and a fourteen-year-old girl out for revenge. This complexity highlights the diverse reception practices when it comes to popular music and music videos, why teenage

---

[35]Hélène Cixous, "The Laugh of the Medusa," trans. Keith and Paula Cohen, *Signs* 1, no. 4 (1976): 875–93.

girls in the 1980s avidly listened to and watched Falco's *Jeanny* instead of rebelling against it, for example. If they were rebelling, their ire was more likely to be directed at adults and mainstream media telling them not to listen to or record and share that song. As noted earlier, one of the few ways that songs like *Jeanny* could and did circulate was an avid tape mixing and sharing culture.

In the current age of "spreadable media" (Henry Jenkins), *Dark* resurrects the "forbidden" song, lets it time travel to 2017/18, and gives it a new audience. Viewers wrestling with the #MeToo movement have had ample practice dealing with misogynism in hip-hop as well as ambiguities in postfeminist music videos from Madonna to Lady Gaga. *Dark* not only "spreads" but also "poaches" the video's ending for its own narrative. In the second season, Hannah travels to the past and encounters Ulrich in the mental ward to which he had been committed after his attempt to take Helge's life in 1953. She wants to spring him and professes her love for him waiting him to say it back to her. Instead, he assures Hannah, he will leave Katharina, if she gets him out of there, but then can't help himself and asks about Katharina and the kids. Fed up, Hannah deserts him to his fate and concocts her own fix of the timeline, ultimately to be betrayed by Ulrich with Charlotte in the third season's alternate 2019 timeline. Mirroring Falco's end in the *Jeanny* video, Ulrich wails after her in 1953 only confirming to doctors and policeman Egon Tiedemann that he is mad indeed. Traveling from 2019 to 1986, Katharina likewise manages to find and visit a visibly grayed and hollowed-out Ulrich in the mental ward. But she never makes it back, being killed by Helene, her own mother (Ulrich's nurse), in the attempt to get at her keys.

Together with the revenge-thirsty Hannah, time-traveling Claudia, who kills her cancer-ridden daughter Regina in the third season, and Katharina's abusive mother Helene, *Dark* features three violent women who, each for entirely different reasons, primarily target other women. Combining the affective energies set loose by murderous moms with broadcast television's polysemic textualities, the show represents women who participate in and those who suffer from the systemic violence against other women, including members of their family. Murdering mothers meet abusive father figures in Noah's twisted rescue narrative. This becomes especially problematic when realizing that Falco's *Jeanny* is a Michael Jackson *Thriller* adaptation (1982). Falco's and Jackson's music videos both feature horror mise-en-scènes, complete with fog machine, and a mix of natural and urban decay. By 2017, both the 1993 and the 2005 trials accusing Jackson of pedophilia had occurred and could thus play into the showrunners' recontextualization for Noah's time-travel experiments.

The inversion of gender that occurs between Jeanny's and Katharina's storylines compared with the abduction of children by Noah and their grooming by Jackson is striking for this very reason, since Noah, like

Jackson, favors boys for his experiments. Even though the Winden coroners assure Ulrich and Charlotte that "there is no sign of sexual assault" on the found bodies, an ambiguity that sustains and feeds deep-seated societal anxieties and curiosities remains. In Western countries, official accounts of sexual assault victims overwhelmingly report girls and women as victims and men as perpetrators. Yet they also acknowledge that dominant masculinity constructs make it much more difficult for those who identify as male to publicly report, personally acknowledge, not to mention psychologically deal with abuse. In thirty-three-year intervals, *Dark* forces the Winden community to deal with the serial abduction of its young boys mirroring the Jackson trials that forced fans to reconcile their own appreciation for the King of Pop, his music, and his celebrity lifestyle, with the allegations of abuse.

The eroticized representation of the über-villain Noah in *Dark* also intersects with a trend in recent serial killer dramas. Examples include Zac Efron as Ted Bundy in the *Bundy Tapes* (Netflix), Joe Goldberg (Penn Badgley) in *You* (Netflix), Paul Spector (Jamie Dornen) in BBC's *The Fall*, Dexter Morgan (Michael C. Hall) in Showtime's *Dexter*, and Hannibal Lecter (Mads Mikkelsen) in *Hannibal* (NBC). At the end of season one, we see Noah—like Jeanny in the video—breaking the fourth wall. He does so as he is sweeping blood off the bunker room floor. Naked from the waist up, glistening with sweat, he looks directly into the camera as Helge is removing a boy's body from the bunker. Is he preventing the Falcos (stalkers/rapists) of the future or is he the Über-Stalker and Frankenstein to Helge's Igor? Is he challenging us to avert our gaze or to keep looking? Unlike Jeanny, who is fully clothed when she looks into the camera and laughs, thereby destroying the voyeuristic engagement with the scene, Noah is engaging viewers erotically and dominantly within the scopophilic realm. Like the television set within the bunker room, his returned look is opening a portal into our dimension, making us aware of our own time-bending efforts (Netflix). This look meets viewers strapped into the Panopticon for their acquiescence to systems of violence, those that aim at gaining or retaining power, at seeking to promote or stem the tide of social and political change, to preserve or reform perceptions and acts of remembrance—and those that turn representations of these attempts into cult.

As a pendant to Jonas's yellow rainslicker, Noah's costume gives him unquestioned access to most spaces and times, including the hospital in 1953 and 1986. Noah usually wears a priest's collar and black robe with a black bowler hat. And since people are trained to see the office and not the man beneath, the outfit makes Noah's self-same appearance decades apart possible without raising suspicion. The black bowler hat Noah usually wears—although pointedly not in the scene discussed earlier—

facilitates the slippage between contexts in a practice that Amy Taubin refers to as "multilaminated" encoding and decoding. She employed that term to describe the pervasive influence of Martin Scorsese's *Taxi Driver* (1976) in popular culture.[36] I borrow it from her to describe the global-local coding of convergence television. Michael Jackson in "Thriller," Falco in "Jeanny," and Noah in *Dark* wear the same kind of black bowler hats. For viewers familiar with Falco's and Jackson's videos, the hat links German language to US popular music culture. Yet additionally, for avid viewers of US television, which includes many of the former, Noah's hat further evokes associations with Walter White's Heisenberg persona from *Breaking Bad* (Bryan Cranston, AMC). *Dark* essentially evokes Heisenberg's "I am the danger" to explain why Noah's desperate and gruesome attempts to ensure that the world, his world, has a future lead to him becoming the evil that undoes it.

Noah appears in all of *Dark*'s time periods at one point or another. We catch him not only offering counseling to Greta in the 1950s timeline but also chatting up Elisabeth in the woods in 2019. One could say that Noah functions as a "memory bearer." According to Jan and Aleida Assmann, a "memory bearer" is a person who stores, organizes, and interprets memories as well as practices rituals of commemoration and remembrance.[37] Noah retrofitted the bunker as a shrine to 1986, a room engineered to function as a portal to alternate times and worlds. And even though the diegetic victims die, the integration of commercial television in the form of MTV accomplishes this for Netflix viewers. If how we watch constitutes and positions us as subjects, then his project reveals the way television is reshaping social and media rituals along with memory processes.

As shown, the hybrid crime drama is leaning on popular and material culture's ability to function as a conduit for German television's globalization and Netflix's localization. And yet, it is simultaneously invested in recharging and broadcasting the German canon. The final section of this chapter demonstrates how *Dark* situates itself in the tradition of network television and takes up the call to remind the world of the significance of German cultural contributions, to which it adds itself. The latter reveals the meteoric rise of television as an accepted cultural product since the 1990s, specifically since the golden age of "high quality" US dramas, into whose illustrious club Germany has now finally been admitted. Why *Dark* still has to prove that it belongs there is the topic of the concluding section.

---

[36] Amy Taubin, *Taxi Driver* (London: BFI Film Classics, 2012); Jan Assmann, *Das kulturelle Gedächtnis: Schrift, Erinnerung und politische Identitaät in frühen Hochkulturen* (München: C.H. Beck, 1992), 54.
[37] Assmann, *Das kulturelle Gedächtnis*.

Recharging the German Canon

As established in the preceding sections, *Dark*'s recombinant modular television architecture facilitates the convergence of the culturally specific with the global circulation of mass-produced popular culture. Its time-shifted narration recreates the family/nation in the form of a transmedia kinship structure, even though its linear and chronological dominance, including its reliance on biological reproduction, is deconstructed on the diegetic level. But it also continues with the network era's tradition of value-signaling what the bourgeois elite holds dear, what has been referred to as German *Leitkultur* in the contentious postwar debates around the meaning of national and cultural identity after the Holocaust. Questions about the definition of citizenship became acute during different phases of migration and immigration from Eastern and Southern Europe, the continent of Africa, and the Middle East, and subsequent to the establishments of the united Germany on October 3, 1990, and the European Union in 1993.

At the same time that Germany has had to redefine its borders and its national identity, it had to reconsider its relationship with ethnic and racial Others in its midst, the growing percentage of Muslim minorities and people of color. Political representatives had to build an on-ramp to citizenship, and they had to articulate the reasons for a diversity-based understanding of "German" and "Germany" to constituencies uneasy with the emerging concepts of first multiculturalism, then integration rather than assimilation. The residual ambivalences and lingering conflation of German with whiteness, Christianity, and Western culture surfaced in the first designs of citizenship interview questions, which heavily emphasized the roles of German language and dominant culture as a test for "integration willingness." The current immigration test in German stresses historical knowledge and familiarity with local, regional, and federal rules and regulations.

Abroad, the new millennium saw a deep structural decline of German-centric programs and learning goals in primary through tertiary education systems, especially in the United States, Germany's biggest postwar ally and Netflix's home base. While German intellectual culture and history, in the form of art, philosophy, sociology, literature, and film, were integrated into many other nations' educational systems, supported by Fulbright, DAAD, the Goethe Institute, and the German societies abroad (among other organizations), this pipeline has been severely truncated in the last fifteen years. Reasons are manifold, among them the de-emphasis of Europe as a center of knowledge, the decline of the Humanities at large, especially the dethroning of literature by digital media, and the splintering off of Science, Technology, and Engineering from their intellectual and cultural histories, the economic importance of Asia, weakening of postwar alliances during the Trump presidency, and so on. As a consequence, millennial and younger television audiences have not had the exposure to the generalist knowledge of German history, philosophy, and literature that their parents might have had. This is the new cultural landscape Netflix and *Dark* have to navigate. It matters if a film or television show can count on cross-cultural associations or if a name like Heisenberg will load associations to quantum mechanics along with the German context of its theoretical physicist, or whether after *Breaking Bad*, the handle primarily refers to Walter White, a fictional character bearing his name, because he has become an iconic fixture on social media and in memes. Even search engines, keeping track of the category of recent and privileged searches of their users, might suggest Werner Heisenberg lower on the results page.

That these cultural, political, and technological changes have touched a nerve is exemplified by the German embassy's well-funded initiative called *Wunderbar Together* launched in 2018.[38] The goals of the campaign stress the importance of the alliance, promote US/German relations, highlight commonalities, educate about Germany, and support conjoint projects across the disciplines and social arenas from sports to media. The German shows on Netflix have to be read as part of this bigger picture. The ability to disseminate German-language content not only to high school or college students abroad but to the broader public in trade-partner countries is seen as crucial to not only promote German culture but also uphold postwar political and economic stability at home. Raised on the strong cultural education commitments from the German networks, writers and showrunners, but also their co-funding agencies in the local, state, and national governments, have stakes in stabilizing or even reversing the decline through post-network German-language television.

As discussed, *Dark* employs a number of strategies to onboard viewers to post-network television facilitating the integration of cultural specificity with globally resonating material. But it also draws on a spectrum of literary allusions from folk and fairy tales to canonical literary works and philosophical thought. How can viewers not familiar with the sources enjoy them nonetheless, and how does *Dark* not only contribute to replenishing German cultural offerings, even if these connections remain lost to many viewers, but also wrestle with its own status as a television text from a country that has long denied television entry into *Kultur* (high art)?

Acknowledging the rapid rate of cultural citations, associations, analogies, and adaptations that the cave-labyrinth produces and puts into a dialogue between different time periods, one's viewing experience is bound to be energized. Because it is impossible to trace all possible sources and inspirations, this section will connect two examples that exemplify the cross-section of folklore and canonical literature—*Der Rattenfänger*

---

[38]The *Wunderbar Together* website lists over 2,500 events and projects funded by the initiative in the United States: https://www.wunderbar2gether.org/about (accessed January 20, 2022).

von Hameln (*The Pied Piper*) and Johann Wolfgang von Goethe's *Faust*. Allusions to Franz Kafka's *In der Strafkolonie* (*In the Penal Colony*), a canonical modernist text, were previously analyzed in relation to the bunker/children's room and its role in reflecting on television's medium-specific narration.

Der Rattenfänger von Hameln (The Pied Piper, Thirteenth Century)

The cave is a discursive machine that reinscribes not only widely accessible references (e.g., from the bible) but also more specific German folklore into postmodern globalized culture. The way the showrunners portray Elisabeth Doppler's (Charlotte's and Peter's daughter) and Mikkel's meandering subplots recoups a regionally based legend and makes it resonate on national and transnational levels. Their plotline is strikingly similar to the c. 1284 German legend of the *Pied Piper*. Once the piper has cleared the rats from the town, as promised, Hameln citizens refuse to pay. He starts playing a magic tune on his flute, and all of Hameln's children follow him. All disappear into a local mountain never to be seen or heard from again, except for two survivors with disabilities. Historians have connected the rat catcher legend's existence to emigration patterns in the thirteenth century, to the plague, to postwar trauma and disability, and even to religious cults.

In *Dark*, like in the *Pied Piper*, the murdered children are found with their eyes blinded and their eardrums punctured. In addition, Elisabeth is deaf, Mikkel is struck mute upon his arrival in 1986. In both versions of this archetypical tale, children and children's bodies manifest the sins of adults. Watching the final season of *Dark* in the summer of the worldwide Covid pandemic amid the results of draconianly enacted family separation policies at the US border to Mexico, but also the televised images of child migrants from war-torn African countries and Syria in Europe, provided viewers with a direct correlation between the *Pied Piper*'s and *Dark*'s outbreak narratives and their own historical world.

The sins of the adults are visited upon the next generation: the violence of wars, the crisis of the nation state, the defaulting on previous alliances, the exploitation of nature, the hubris of science, and interpersonal betrayal result in humanitarian and climate catastrophes that affect children and their future. Winden is a new Hameln. Hameln's stingy townspeople, reneging on their deal with the rat catcher who rid the city of its infestation, are 2019's overscheduled, egotistic, work, sex or alcohol addicted, feuding Winden citizens: parents, who betray one another, who forget to pick up their kids from school; friends, who default on promises; a society that refuses to protect its environment for the future of humankind.

In addition, *Dark*'s production context between 2016 and 2020 was a time where neuro-diverse children, teenagers, and adults were increasingly featured as lead characters on television (e.g., in Netflix's own *Atypical*). The hearing-impaired Elisabeth not only survives the encounter with Noah in the woods but assumes a larger role in the following two seasons. She falls in love with Noah's younger self after the apocalypse and begins digging out the cave tunnels with him in 2020. It is revealed that she gives birth to Charlotte, her own mother, who is then taken back by Noah to be raised by clock maker Tannhaus to begin the loop again and ensure her own birth. Elisabeth also becomes a survivalist leader in postapocalyptic Winden of 2052, where she holds Jonas's life in her hands. In the alternate world in the third season ("Eva's world"), she is no longer hard of hearing, attesting to the power of the story-engine to reveal the dominant structure of ableism as a parallel reality that is not superior.

With its connotations to the *Rattenfänger* saga, *Dark* involves itself in ongoing global disputes, reminding viewers to heed the lessons of the past and commit to existing treaties on the diplomatic and economic level, to diversity and inclusivity on the civic level, to climate action and shutting down nuclear reactors and weapons programs on the political level. With these interventions, it observes network-era protocols more reminiscent of *Tatort*'s didactic social-critical phases than of contemporary crime dramas on Netflix. At the same time, also following network television's uneasy relationship to itself and its mission, it acknowledges television's part as pied piper, luring adults into complacence and children into its imaginary worlds. The latter demonstrates what perhaps remains as one of the deepest cultural specificities of the series, namely the struggle with its own cultural status as television. *Dark* builds into its very textuality and narration a medium-reflexive mea culpa that finds few counterparts in US television history. The references to Goethe's *Faust* make this even more apparent.

Goethe's Faust (Der Tragödie erster Teil, 1808)[39]

Dark's showrunners, who like generations before them likely had to study Goethe's *Faust* in their German literature classes in high school, cite and adapt several well-known elements from the drama for their narrative. They transform this canonical text, itself an adaptation from the Faustian tales of the Middle Ages, into a crime drama, a televisual narrative for the next generation. And in doing so, they emphasize the culturally specific need to justify television as an art form singularly equipped to recharge the German canon on the world stage at this mediascape juncture. As the first-generation founder of German contributions to the Netflix catalogue, *Dark*'s investment in the German literary archive hints at a significant amount of heavy lifting

---

[39] I am thankful to my colleague Matthew D. Miller at Colgate, with whom I had the pleasure to co-teach *Dark* in a cross-institutional initiative sponsored by LACOL (Liberal Arts Consortium for Online Learning) in 2020.

to convince its domestic backers that it was not "wasting" this opportunity for moving German culture out of the shadows. The issue is thus not what references do audiences understand but why *Dark* bothers and what it says about original language convergence-era television.

Faust, the titular character of Goethe's famous tragedy, is a scholar of the sciences. He holds a self-reflexive monologue in a segment of the drama called "Wald und Höhle" (forest and cave). In the cave, he is closer to hell than to heaven, especially when Mephisto joins him there, yet also symbolically returned to the womb. While Faust hears and sees nature's furious violence outside (storm raging, trees falling), the cave protects him from the elements. Inside, however, he twists himself into a knot about his unfurling desire and his allegiance with the devil, alternately thanking the earth spirit for getting him a tryst with Gretchen, and critically reflecting on his own lust. Euphorically, he reminisces the first encounter with the young woman, only to become increasingly pensive about his dependence on Mephisto. Faust wrangles with himself whether to give into lust or let rationality (science), morality, and ethics prevail. On the one hand he is blaming Mephisto for nourishing a "raging fire" in his chest. On the other hand, he is already under the influence of the witch's brew from the previous scene in the witches' kitchen. The brew rejuvenates him, but also primed him to see a "Helen" (of Troy) in every woman. He eventually decides to get Gretchen to have sex with him, setting the tragedy in motion: Faust kills her brother Valentin, and she kills the child she conceived with Faust out of wedlock, a crime which ends with her execution.

The most obvious intertextual resonances between *Faust* and *Dark* appear in the names: Martha (Gretchen's neighbor Marthen), Gretchen (Greta Doppler and Regina's dog), Helene (Katharina's abusive mother). On the narrative level, the murder of Gretchen's brother becomes the murder of Ulrich's brother Mads in 1986. Faust's dalliance with Gretchen becomes Greta Doppler's rape by an occupying soldier in 1945, leading to the birth of Helge and her abusive behavior toward him, which in turn echoes Gretchen's murder of her child. Mephisto's jewelry boxes to tempt Gretchen to acquiesce to Faust's desire turn into Michael's, Jonas's, and Tannhaus's boxes and envelopes that, for example, contain the map to the cave and the town's family trees. These entice Jonas and Katharina to time travel in order to rectify mistakes; they tempt Hannah and Ulrich to enact revenge. The doubling of Jonas, whose older self suddenly appears to council the 2019 Jonas to do or not do what he set out to achieve (e.g., to rescue Mikkel from 1986), could be compared to Mephisto's sudden appearances to council Faust.

The cave scene is generally regarded as the turning point in the drama, a word which in German is called a *Wendepunkt*, which closely resembles the name of the fictional town *Winden*. As a noun, a *Winde* refers to a winch or pully system. As a reflexive verb "sich winden" refers to, for example, a river winding through a landscape, but also to squirming/contorting one's body and mind under internal or external pressures. The Winden cave itself becomes a relay station where fate and coincidence wind around one another and each entry/exit becomes a turning point, for characters and their storylines, for linear time. If Goethe's cave is likened to the moment before the inevitable fall, *Dark*'s cave doors stand for motivations and choices that seem to be consciously made yet appear pre-programmed and vice versa, if one believes Adam (old Jonas) and Eva (old Martha). As memories are actualized or relived in individual storylines, they layer themselves over the twists and turns in the forking path plot as a whole. Like Faust, some characters enter the cave with one objective only to change it when encountering good or bad advice (Jonas-Jonas), opportunity (Ulrich-Helge), obstacles (Hannah-Ulrich, Katharina-Helene), or desire (Jonas-Martha). In *Dark* terms, even well-intentioned time travelers, like Jonas, bear responsibility for tragic outcomes.

The process of digital reproduction as adaptation is visually conceptualized by the title sequence of each episode, where the horizontally unraveling mirrored images appear like conjoined twins or butterfly/angel wings. The unfolding images make clear that dualities emerge from the same image and place, the vaginal crease of digital reproduction from whence they sprang to rebirth ever new concatenations of 0s and 1s. With this medium-reflexive kaleidoscopic imagery, that cues viewers into its compound cross-cultural world-building energies, *Dark* offers the German canon to them as a continuously inspiring resource to grapple with the existential crises and moments of the new millennium and emergent digital technologies. Its seeds itself into that canon and reproduces it. And at its most basic, viewers abroad responded to *Dark* as continuing that "heavy" German philosophical and aesthetic tradition, even if they were not aware of that stereotype, did not remember similar arthouse labels for Weimar-era cinema and New German film productions, and could not trace all the allusions and connotations.

First-generation shows like *Dark*, *Perfume*, and *Babylon Berlin* thus paved the way for second-generation shows like *How to Sell Drugs Online (Fast)*, a comedy-crime drama hybrid that domestic cultural critics panned for its superficial approach to drug dealing and consumption, and its exaggerated sense of humor, while being lauded in industry circles for its innovative editing and style. *Die Zeit* went so far as to refer to it as the "the second German show on Netflix and the first German Netflix scandal."[40]

---

[40] Daniel Gerhardt, "Der Traum vom großen Pillendreher," *Zeit Online*, July 27, 2020, https://www.zeit.de/kultur/film/2020-07/how-to-sell-drugs-online-fast-netflix-serie-2te-staffel-pubertaet?utm_referrer=https%3A%2F%2Fwww.google.com%2F (accessed January 22, 2022).

Debates like these only emphasize once more how convergence-era German television is embroiled between the tradition of associating the medium with anti-intellectual tendencies (seen as imported from the United States) on the one side and the network-era attempt to instill German television, especially the drama, with the educational entertainment and nation-building value imparted by the German literary canon on the other. As a small yet vital industrial country, relying on an export economy that includes finessing its image as a serious contender, the stakes are felt to be high. The result is a German brand extension via global television. The next chapter on *Perfume* will explore this aspect in more detail.

3

Relational Memory

Perfume (Netflix, 2018)

What happens when a show shot in the Main/Rhein region, a location it shares with the home base of its network ZDF, moves to a global streaming platform? How do the structure and aesthetics of the television text adapt and reflect this spatial intersectionality? How does the transmedia adaptation *Perfume* revise the network crime drama format? Does it stay truer to network genre conventions than *Dark* or depart from them in different ways? How does it represent cultural specificity, and what does that indicate about German television on Netflix? These questions lead to four areas for deeper analysis in this chapter. The first one researches how differences between domestic network rivals ARD and ZDF carry over onto the global screen and what aspect of ZDF crime series, if any, remains. The second continues the investigation into regional to global discourses in relation to the streamed television text. Since this is a show targeted at an adult audience whose main enigma revolves around sexual, psychological, and physical abuse, the third focus is on the configurations and representations of power, specifically as they involve gender and sexuality. The fourth aspect investigates the concepts of relational memory and nostalgia in connection with the internal segmentation of *Perfume* and how the combination of flashback narration and a preference for transmedia micro flows contributes to historical revisionism at the very moment the ZDF crime drama aligns itself with post-network medium specificities.

Switching Channels: Domestic Rivals on Netflix

Whereas *Dark*'s edgy crime, fantasy, and horror hybridity appeals to a cross-generational section of viewers, *Perfume*, an unorthodox adaptation of the already twisted 1986 Patrick Süskind novel and Tom Tykwer's 2006 film adaptation, pitches its combination of crime and horror in televisually seductive ways to adults. The show was produced by Oliver Berben (Constantin), Gunther van Endert (ZDF), Sarah Kirkegaard and Florian Weber for ZDFneo, and acquired by Netflix for streaming around the 2018 winter holidays. Philipp Kadelbach from the much-debated 2013 ZDF mini-series *Unsere Mütter, unsere Väter* (*Generation War*) directed the six episodes of the first and only season. His approach to the representation of historical, cultural, and collective memory in the Second World War series impacts the conceptualization of history and memory in *Perfume* and will be kept in mind during closer analysis.

As a project developed by ZDF for its domestic streaming platform ZDFneo, *Perfume* sets itself apart from the previously discussed ARD projects and ARD/Netflix collaborations. The ZDF project's move to Netflix showcases the streaming platform's multisource approach to harvesting high production value crime dramas and underscores the convergence aspect of the post-network era. On Netflix, products of domestic rivals appear in the same genre categories and on the same watchlists. Station identities, institutional politics, and broadcast histories enshrined in competitive parallel scheduling and windowing are elided in favor of compelling content and televisual aesthetics. In that process, it is doubly important for television studies to pay attention to the networks' historically different approaches to the medium, to reception, to content and genre development, exhibition and distribution practices, and to the formal composition of the television text itself.

The *Zweites Deutsches Fernsehen* broadcasted its first program from a set of wooden barracks in Eschborn outside of Frankfurt am Main on April 1, 1963. The network established its *Sendezentrum* (broadcast center) in Mainz. It boasts that its location made Mainz known as "a media city across national borders."[1] In the year 2000, the ZDF opened its glossy new Berlin *Hauptstadtstudio Unter den Linden*, symbolically broadcasting from the heart of the united nation. But even today, the network brands itself in close relationship to the middle of Germany, the Mainz and the Main/Rhein region, by using the *Mainzelmännchen* as its official mascot. The name of these gnome-like characters combines Cologne's *Heinzelmännchen* folk saga with the popularity of GDR's *Sandmännchen* and Mainz, the headquarters of the ZDF. The six characters appear in animated shorts (of five to ten seconds) between content and ad blocks. In over 50,000 shorts since 1963 (plus a mini-series and ancillary merchandise), their recognizability and

---

[1] Medienstandort Mainz, https://www.zdf.de/zdfunternehmen/zdf-mitarbeiter-und-standorte-zdf-studios-100.html (accessed September 21, 2020).

humorous antics have served as palate cleansers and steady reminders that viewers were (still) watching ZDF.

Like its predecessor ARD, which was founded in 1950, the ZDF elects its chief executives. But while the ARD organizes itself through a *Mitgliedversammlung* (member conference) of its ten regional broadcast stations, which elect its own and the ARD's central leadership positions, the ZDF utilizes the structure of a *Fernsehrat* (Television Board), which is elected for a span of four years. Up to 2016, the ZDF consisted of seventy-seven members composed of party representatives proportional to their representation in the federal government, representatives of the states, delegates from the government, the three major religious denominations as well as trade organizations and so-called *Räte* (advisors) from major educational and cultural institutions.

For the early convergence period, a contentious debate between ZDF leadership and its board is of interest for the topic of this book. It revealed the pressures on the networks during a rapidly changing mediascape and exposed the unraveling status quo along with existing power dependencies between network, political parties, and industry. *Chefredakteur* (editor in chief) Nikolaus Brender's contract (2000–10) was terminated with a majority of the conservative block's votes on the ZDF board. This decision could have been a retaliation against Brender who publicly stated that he put a stop to regular "threatening phone calls" from mostly right-leaning politicians to key figures in ZDF's administration and program direction. According to his defense, the phone calls revealed a direct and unconstitutional attempt to influence the public broadcaster. One example given was the appeal to change or delete certain unflattering or oppositional coverage in its news program *Heute*.[2] A subsequent constitutional lawsuit brought by the states of Rheinland-Pfalz and Hamburg led to a 2014 *Bundesrat* decision that enforced structural changes and regulations to increase "the distance" between the state and leadership positions on the network. While the achievement, or at least obligatory observance, of this "distance" would be monitored in-house and domestically, another type of distance opened up that would allow for less scrutiny of political influence throughout the production process: coproduction arrangements for fictional television content streamed on the network's own digital channel and abroad via Netflix.

Because *Perfume* features explicit portrayals of sexual abuse, female sexual submission, and male-dominated violence, it seems imperative to

---

[2] Lisa Caspari, "Konservative Politiker gehen dreister vor als andere," *Zeit Online*, October 25, 2012, https://www.zeit.de/politik/deutschland/2012-10/csu-zdf-brender-beeinflussung? And "Eklat um Brender: Wo steht das ZDF?" *Meedia*, February 23, 2010, https://meedia.de/2010/02/23/eklat-um-brender-wo-steht-das-zdf/ (accessed September 20, 2020).

examine the gender dynamics of its home network and program direction vis-à-vis Netflix. Until 2015, the different chief managerial positions at ZDF were exclusively filled by men, who tended to stay in office between ten and twenty years (e.g., Dieter Stolte, ZDF). At the time of writing, Karin Brieden as *Stellvertretende Intendantin* was the only woman on the ZDF network's senior staff. In 2015, ARD named the first woman, Susanne Pfab, to the post of General Secretary followed by Marlene Thiem as the first woman to fill a similar role at the ZDF in 2016. In 2021, after Volker Herres's twelve-year tenure in the crucial position of ARD program director, Christine Strobl took over that post, the *first* woman in that role since the network's founding. An institutional culture of traditional male dominance was thus firmly entrenched in both networks until very recently. Despite the democratic process written into both networks' public broadcasting contracts, it is noteworthy that individual executives often stayed in power for a decade or more. This meant that they steered their network through different mediascapes and sociopolitical changes. Unlike in the United States, where the rate of job changes in that stratosphere tends to be expected and accepted, Germany prefers continuity. Lasting through the cable and satellite years well through the digital revolution, this lack of gender parity is evident on the administrative, production, and content development levels of both networks, with a quicker change registering at the ARD than the ZDF since 2015. It is important to keep this fact in mind, when thinking about the gender configurations in *Perfume*.

In combination with lopsided gender representation, a particular concern for an investigation into *Perfume* as a crime drama is the ZDF's penchant for commitments to producers and directors with the proven ability to repackage memory projects for the new mediascape, specifically those of the Hitler era. For the cable and satellite era, this is evidenced by Guido Knopp, whose 1990s fast-paced mini-series about the Third Reich garnered both viewer and critical attention for their "recalibrate[ion]" of the "original Hitler media campaign of the 1930s and 1940s." As Wulf Kansteiner insists, Knopp's case makes clear that "only the transformation of the West German television landscape into a dual system of commercial and public networks created the cultural and political basis for the radicalization of German memory after unification."[3] He expertly lays out how Knopp's *Der verdammte Krieg* ("That damned War," ZDF, 1991–5), a reenactment of the German Sixth Army in battle with the Soviet troops at Stalingrad, "translated the topics of Nazi discourse into the visual and political languages of the late twentieth century." Knopp's translation, according to Kansteiner, "offered viewers the exceptional pleasure of remaining within the political consensus of the

---

[3] Wulf Kansteiner, *In Pursuit of German Memory: History, Television, and Politics after Auschwitz* (Athens: University of Ohio Press, 2006), 162.

German democratic mainstream while playfully exploring the perspectives of the former perpetrators in a collective setting."[4] When Knopp followed the success of the Stalingrad project with *Hitler: Eine Bilanz* (Hitler: A Reckoning, ZDF 1995), which reached five million viewers or 22 percent of all television viewers during its broadcast, post-show viewer engagement reached a pinnacle.[5] Until 2014, Knopp's Hitler projects not only recreated a big tent in an era of dispersed viewership, but they managed to lay the groundwork for hybrid fictional documentary memory projects that allowed older viewers to "revisit, reorganize, and reinvent their own memories," and also "attract future German consumers who will no longer know anybody who lived in the Third Reich."[6]

Kadelbach's *Perfume* follows in Knopp's footsteps and needs to be considered as a legacy project of the ZDF's consistent approach to screen the past as "historical pornography."[7] And a crime drama, not a documentary, became the perfect vehicle to take this abiding revisionist strategy to the global stage. Publicized attempts to become more transparent, to diversify and make the network environmentally sustainable notwithstanding, the ZDF is still largely a male domain leaning to the right of the ARD. And judging from the rebranding campaign following the 2010 leadership debacle, and the higher ratings in more recent years, the ZDF has embarked on a conscious and effective campaign to pitch its projects to a more diverse audience through coproductions with Amazon and Netflix.[8]

ZDF Crime Series

The ZDF started its suite of successful crime series with *Der Kommissar* (1969–76), followed by *Derrick* (1974–98) and *Der Alte* (1977–), whose titular roles were (and still are) occupied by dominant white male investigators supported by long-term, usually also, white male assistants and a wider circle of changing and progressively more diverse team members as the years went by. Broadcast on Friday nights, they were slotted to

---

[4] Ibid., 165–6.
[5] Ibid., 169.
[6] Ibid., 178 and 175.
[7] Ibid., 180.
[8] Until recently, the ZDF's organizational make-up mirrored its network audience which trended male, older, and whiter than the ARD's. However, the 2017 study pretests revealed that the network's online content is accessed by the fourteen to forty-nine age groups in similar rates to their Netflix use and that the gender disparities among online ZDF television viewers appears less pronounced. Bernhard Engel and Eva Holtmannspötter, "Studienreihe: Medien und ihr Publikum," *Media Perspektiven* 2 (2017), https://www.ard-werbung.de/fileadmin/user_upload/media-perspektiven/pdf/2017/0217_Engel_Holtmannspoetter.pdf (accessed September 20, 2020).

accompany the German equivalent of the TGIF ritual. *Derrick*, in particular, is noteworthy for its success in syndication in over 100 countries. In 2013, after Derrick's lead actor had passed away (2008), sociologist Jörg Becker discovered archival material that revealed that Horst Tappert had joined the Waffen-SS when he was nineteen (in 1943).[9] Since then, the ZDF has suspended reruns of the series.

In 1978, the network first broadcasted what would become its format adaptation of the 1970 *Tatort* concept: *SOKO 5113* ("Special Commission"). Over the years, new regional teams were added to the early evening weekday lineup, each episode running for forty-five minutes at 6:00 p.m. Since then, ten regional teams and their cases, some in cooperation with the Austrian network ORF, have rotated into that window, except for *SOKO Leipzig* (2001–), which was moved to Friday's prime time due to high viewer demand (*c.* 5 million viewers for the earlier episodes).[10] The *SOKO* series capitalizes on and strengthens the already regionally organized frame of the early evening schedule. Because the multiregional series takes place before the regional (7:00 p.m.) and national news (8:00 p.m.), it occurs during traditional family dinner time. In this early evening slot, a commercial block breaks its broadcast into two approximate twenty-minute segments. For this reason, the series has followed a tighter internal segmentation and resulted in different reception patterns than its ninety-minute prime-time *Tatort* competitor on ARD. *SOKO* narration follows the established crime drama pattern of the "obligatory case of the week" with limited serial continuity elements.[11] Like *Tatort*, *SOKO*'s casting has also diversified significantly over the years, with many regional *SOKO* teams now featuring lead investigators from underrepresented backgrounds. UFA Fiction, Germany's biggest media-production company, started cross-media integration through a blog feature for *SOKO* in 2019. The company and its client, the network, were hoping to attract younger less-television-oriented multi-platform viewers and create a sense of community around "the brand" with a "360-degree approach" for its daily series, including *SOKO*.[12] In the following analytical segments, it will be crucial to situate *Perfume* within these institutional, media-specific, and genre-based contexts.

---

[9]*Der Spiegel*, April 26, 2013, https://www.spiegel.de/international/germany/report-reveals-derrick-actor-horst-tappert-was-an-ss-member-a-896765.html (accessed October 14, 2020).
[10]"Start der Erfolgskrimiserie 'SOKO Leipzig' am 25. Oktober im ORF2," *ORF*, October 23, 2013, https://www.ots.at/presseaussendung/OTS_20131023_OTS0121/start-der-erfolgskrimiserie-soko-leipzig-am-25-oktober-in-orf-2 (accessed October 14, 2020).
[11]Glenn Riedmeier, "Aus für SOKO München," *TV Wunschliste*, August 23, 2019, https://www.wunschliste.de/tvnews/m/aus-fuer-soko-muenchen-zdf-stellt-soko-mutterserie-ein (accessed October 14, 2020).
[12]Wilfried Urbe, "'SOKO Leipzig' gucken und surfen," *Frankfurter Rundschau*, January 30, 2019, https://www.fr.de/kultur/soko-leipzig-gucken-surfen-11602970.html (accessed October 14, 2020).

Perfume Synopsis

A group of adults from a former high school clique react to the murder of one of their own. The men relive their boarding school years as the profiler Nadja Simon (Friederike Becht) draws closer to their inner circle to find a serial killer stealing glands and intimate scents from the victims to produce a mind-control perfume. *Silence of the Lambs* meets *Twin Peaks*, and all taboos are broken. The show's innovative editing and cinematography were nominated for the *Deutsche Fernsehpreis* 2019.

The first scene shows Katharina Läufer (Siri Nase) from behind, her red hair flowing down her naked back. In the second scene, her red-haired son Felix (Jimmy Gutzeit) arrives at Roman's (Ken Duken) and Elena's (Natalia Belitski) nearby house carrying a bloodied strand of his mother's hair like a kite. Gustav Klimt's paintings of red-haired women, especially his *Nuda Veritas* (1899) and *Danae* (1907–8), but also portraits of Gertha Loew, Ria Munk, Mäda Primavesi, among others, have become identical with a specific artistic obsession but also with the globally circulated image of *Jugendstil* (Art Nouveau) art. Klimt's proclivity for red-heads and glittery gold patterns have made his style popular with perfume brands, for bottle and scent design, such as Kilian's *Woman in Gold*. *Perfume* thus not only adapts the Patrick Süskind novel but borrows Klimt's consuming passion for red-heads to construct its plot around a woman with a natural scent that has the power to kindle mind-altering obsession.

Like its predecessors, *Perfume* clearly indicts the perfumier Moritz in the crime, but unlike the novel and film, which follow the development, trial, and demise of the serial killer and perfumier Jean-Baptiste Grenouille (Ben Wishaw in the film), the television drama keeps the identity of the actual murderer a (relative) secret until the end. The transmedia adaptation thus manages to retain a level of suspense for viewers who have read or seen novel and/or film before. And it adjoins their foreknowledge to first-time viewers' entry into the basic plot by milking the forensic format's penchant for offering parallel investigative paths before identifying the definite culprit. Unlike the film, as has become customary in the streaming era of television, soap opera elements flesh out the individual backstories and motivations of suspects and investigators, paralleling their psychological profiles and resulting in more narrative complexity.

Profiler Nadja Simon, her colleague Matthias Köhler (Jürgen Maurer), and prosecutor Joachim Grünberg (Wotan Wilke Möhring) investigate the crime scene, where the local red-haired beauty Katharina Läufer, known as "K," is found floating in a private pool. Initially, they find neither evidence nor motive until Simon makes the rounds and questions K's former classmates and friends. Increasingly, fragmented memories of the group interlace with one another as they peel back in layers. Everyone knows each other and keeps secrets: Roman and his wife Elena, the pimp Butsche

(Trystan Pütter), the perfumier Moritz de Vries (August Diehl), Daniel Sluiter (Marc Hosemann, Christian Friedel), and the murder victim, Katharina Läufer.

During the investigation, the cold case of Merten, a boy who went missing from the all-male boarding school in the 1990s, is reactivated. In a desperate attempt to be loved and included in the wealthier circles of the boarding school students, where her father still works as a factotum, Elena persuaded Daniel to experiment on a dog and then kill Merten to preserve his scent. They buried the boy underneath the dog in the moorland. Elena, wearing Merten's scent, was subsequently taken in by Merten's mother, a ploy that worked while his "perfume" lasted.

In the scene introducing lead investigator Nadja Simon, she rides shotgun to the crime scene. Her authority in this case counters existing gender politics in a male-dominated work environment. In a close-up eyeline match, Simon stares at two stickers pasted over each other on the glove compartment that connect Bukkake with the warning triangle "Men at Work." The superimposed stickers produce the equivalent of a print meme and the act itself. The meme encourages multiple intertextual and inter-sexual readings of the traffic sign, a sign that by itself is usually found on the margins of roads and highways, warning of construction zones ahead. And, of course, it announces Simon's precarious position within the police hierarchy while also proffering the first clue to the case at hand: after concerts, Katharina would always take home a couple of guys. She would even drug her son's milk so he would not interrupt the sex.

Following in the footsteps of BBC's *The Fall* (2013–16), where the complexly drawn and successful lead character (Gillian Andersen) regularly prowls for men and even sleeps with an informant, *Perfume* quickly establishes that one of the construction zones is Simon herself. She has an illicit and stormy affair with her married superior, prosecutor Grünberg, and is alternately ignoring his texts or sexting with him. In what presages an unhealthy disrespect for boundaries, they have sex in the conference room, right after an official meeting. In a voice-over phone call, he wants the dark-haired Simon to go away with him for the weekend. All the while the scene shows him together with his blond wife and two blond children at the breakfast table. Director Kadelbach, who is no stranger to directing commercials for major brands, inserts a postcard German family idyll that could harken back to the height of the economic miracle. Its racial overtones become more obvious, when the fair family's happiness is contrasted with the profile shot of the dark-haired "home-wrecker," Simon. It turns out, she is pregnant with Grünberg's child. He ends the affair, when she refuses to get an abortion.

At the first crime scene, when everyone takes a dose of smelling salts to cover the stench of water-corpse decay, Simon refuses. She cannot detect or experience scents. But like the therapist and murderer Lydia, who is Katharina's underappreciated twin sister, Simon has experienced lovelessness and has suffered from parental neglect. Now Grünberg wants her to abort her unborn child, forcing her to relive her own trauma. She is motivated by a gnawing sense of abjection and begins to see the addictive scent that Moritz produces with Lydia's murderous help as a possible solution to cajole Grünberg to choose her and their baby rather than his wife and kids. The season one finale shows her deeply ethically and personally compromised as she narrowly survives a violent sexual encounter with Grünberg after she overdosed herself with the stolen perfume.

Waxing Nostalgic: *Perfume*, Postmemory, and Restorative Nostalgia

Perfume is not a family show. It delivers best, when binged on a screen up close, alone, or with a partner. Watching it on a screen far away across the room would rob it of its programmed intimacy and its provocative layering of desire, trauma, and crime. *Perfume*'s internal segmentation constructs and draws on the concept of relational memory. This section explores how the show's seemingly arbitrarily composed sequencing expresses itself in micro flows that rely on and foster relational memory processes.

Coming out of Germany's traditionally more conservative- and male-dominated network, the ZDF's contribution to Netflix's German crime drama lineup is catering to a sociopolitical shift in attitudes toward remembrance culture within its domestic audience. But *Perfume* inserts itself not only into a precarious moment in Germany's memory debate but also into the more global postmemory situation as such. According to Marianne Hirsch,

> "Postmemory" describes the relationship that the "generation after" bears to the personal, collective, and cultural trauma of those who came before-to experiences they "remember" only by means of the stories, images, and behaviors among which they grew up. But these experiences were transmitted to them so deeply and affectively as to seem to constitute memories in their own right. Postmemory's connection to the past is thus actually mediated not by recall but by imaginative investment, projection, and creation.[13]

In the context of *Perfume*, Hirsch's notion of mediation is essential. It begs to be employed as part of transmedia practices and experiences. As demonstrated in the previous chapters, television and other media

---

[13]Marianne Hirsch, "Postmemory," https://www.postmemory.net (accessed December 17, 2020).

layer themselves over the memory-based storytelling disseminated by the generation that witnessed a traumatic event (e.g., the Holocaust, Vietnam, 9/11) and received by the subsequent generations. As Hirsch notes, the hierarchical relation between storytelling sources and modes shifts for postmemory generations. As "the generation after" is stepping into vision-centric leadership positions, their approaches to the past have percolated through television formats, aesthetics, and textuality at the same time that technology, medium specificity, and globalization have encouraged significant changes in representation, style, and reception patterns. The confluences between these can be demonstrated by the working biography of the man at the helm of *Perfume*, Philip Kadelbach.

He established himself as a director deeply involved in Hirsch's process of "imaginative investment, projection, and creation." In the Berliner *taz*, Ulrich Herbert criticizes his *Generation War* about five young adults, born *c.* 1920: "Nazis are always the others (. . .) The five protagonists are all victims at the end or stand against the Nazi-state." The mini-series, he continues, depicts young adults as naïve to the political mechanisms that surround and influence them, which is at odds not only with historical evidence but also with the rise of youth activism, facilitated by social media, in the series' own production context. On the one hand, that the series was written and got produced displays the investment in thinking creatively and ongoingly about the Germans that supported or rejected fascism in the Third Reich. On the other hand, Herbert argues that the mini-series fails to show that the fictionalized young adults were of a "thoroughly ideologically and politicized generation that wanted the German victory of National Socialism because they supported it."[14] Following Svetlana Boim's definition of nostalgia, portraying the generation of "our mothers and fathers" in this way

> is also a romance with one's own phantasy. (. . .) The nostalgic desires to obliterate history and turn it into private or collective mythology, to revisit time as space, refusing to surrender to the irreversibility of time that plagues the human condition.[15]

If *Dark* veers toward reflective nostalgia, *Generation War*, and I would also argue *Perfume*, veer toward restorative nostalgia. Herbert ends his article by stating, Kadelbach's former series portrays Germans "how they would have liked to have been."[16]

---

[14] Ulrich Herbert, "Nazis sind immer die anderen," *taz*, March 21, 2013, https://taz.de/!5070893/ (accessed December 17, 2020).
[15] Svetlana Boim, "Nostalgia and Its Discontents," *The Hedgehog Review* (Summer 2007), https://hedgehogreview.com/issues/the-uses-of-the-past/articles/nostalgia-and-its-discontents (accessed January 10, 2021).
[16] Herbert, "Nazis sind immer die anderen."

Postmemory and restorative nostalgia connect with and emerge from the key ingredient that determines the plot, but also with the internal segmentation of *Perfume*. Smells are triggers for memory processes, but television cannot deliver these (yet). Cinematic experiments with scratch and sniff never took off and have remained amusing anecdotes (so far). *Perfume* seeks to emulate the mnemonic processes by mining television's episodic segmentation and seriality, cinematography, editing, and mise-en-scène. First, the step-by-step production of scents is used to construct the segmentation of the television text itself. Perfumes are produced by layering different scents over one another. And the show's six episodes layer themselves over and side by side their medium-specific production and intertextual foundations. Indicated by their titles that spell out the steps involved in the manufacturing process the episodes stand for the different sources of scents. But instead of petrochemical steps in line with contemporary perfume production, the episodes follow a more traditional process, including *Ambergris* (secretion of bile duct from sperm whales) and *Skatole*, which used to be the source for musk (urine, excrement, etc.), in this case made from human bodies, not animals.

As part of the process, scent sources are encased in wax or fat to lift and preserve their specific scents. In *Perfume*, Moritz not only coats parts of a client in fat and shaves her body after a period of saturation to manufacture her very own personal perfume, but he also preserves the scent glands of the murder victims in a similar fashion. Thus, the crime drama models its internal segmentation on the making of perfume as much as it combines the peel back of forensic discoveries with perfume's role in initiating memories.

Second, the manufacturing of perfume transmits itself to the television production and reception processes and creates a combination of consumerist and investigative desires: the desire to possess the perfume and the text in totality by binging, and the forensic desire to find closure. However, like inspector Simon, these conflicting desires have the viewer alternately identifying with the positions of investigator, perpetrator, and victim, since the murders were committed to possess the intoxicatingly arousing personal scent of the singer, Katharina, and of the older prostitute, Perle.

Perfume's forensic format seems ready-made for the post-network era because the scent-driven narrative of insatiable lust matches assumptions about binge-watching Netflix. In the narrative of the film, which serves as an important transmedia source for the series, the hunger to inhale does not stop at smelling but continues to mass-induced hysteria and ends with cannibalism. The television adaptation does not go quite as far but comes close. Similar to Katharina's countless fans and lovers, many of whom descend upon her funeral like zombies in the wrong genre, Netflix viewers may crave the next segment, the next episode, might not want to stop watching. And Netflix complies by providing a continuous, seamless narrative and reception experience.

And yet, third, the drive to straight-line the show in its entirety is paired with a just as addictive rerouting. At its most basic, rerouting strategies are built into the intertextual work of transmedia adaptation. Among them shifts in time and space, followed by gender and more recently race (e.g., Shonda Rhimes's first Netflix production *Bridgerton*, 2021), are generally the biggest targets for transformation for different reasons: to update the topic, play to the strengths of a different medium or platform, appeal to a different audience, and so on. Both the 1985 Patrick Süskind novel *Perfume* and the 2006 film adaptation are set in urban France. By contrast, the television show takes place in the somewhat unspectacular Niederrhein region adjacent to the border with the Netherlands and the area, where Germany's heavy industry is located adjacent to agricultural fields and peat moors that are cross-stitched with power lines, train tracks, and *Autobahnen*.[17] What occurred in the eighteenth century in novel and film was turned into the 1990s for the flashback scenes and the narrated time of the late 2010s in the series. The gender of the lead investigator was changed to avoid an all-male cast and to offset the passivity of Elena, the only other female character in the ensemble.

In its conflicting and codependent tele-sexual drives for total consumption and rerouted, delayed satisfaction, the arrangements of spaces and transitions between locations stand out in *Perfume*'s attempt to adapt German crime drama conventions to Netflix. The next section therefore probes how the drama constructs space. As an original German-language crime drama on Netflix and in comparison to *Tatort*'s regional concept, do viewers get a sense of *Perfume*'s location (this is happening in Germany, in the Niederrhein)? Or, put differently, how does the drama locate itself?

Peripheral Adjacencies: Welcome to Fargo, Germany

From the very first shot, a cold open of the murder scene, the show follows viewer expectations of a television crime drama. From the rear, we watch as the red-haired singer-songwriter Katharina immerses herself in the large naturalized swimming pool at her luxurious modern bungalow. The second scene follows Katharina's young son running across a field with a

---

[17]Martina Stöcker, "Parfum bei ZDFneo. Neue TV-Serie spielt am Niederrhein und selten wirkte er so trostlos," *RP Online*, November 14, 2018 (accessed September 20, 2020) *Perfume* was shot on location near Cologne and Duisburg, the Bergische Land, the Hoher Venn near Aachen, and a boarding school in Hamm. The ruin of water castle Eibach near Lindlar functions as the secret getaway for the boarding school days.

long, bloodied strand of his mother's hair, blowing behind him like a kite. The third scene captures a car with the investigators crossing over a flat landscape, mostly consisting of barren fields of grayish-brown soil. The contrast between wealth and poverty, rural and suburban lifestyles could not be starker and invites critical engagement. The scenes establish very quickly that the series is not a remake of the film or a faithful adaptation of the book but offers a new take on the story. Not only the choice of locations but also the way the first three scenes are shot and assembled code the material as a television text. Like many episodes of *Tatort*, *Perfume* is situating its crime scene in an elevated social setting. However, instead of providing iconic views of recognizable locations in transitional shots, viewers are asked to locate themselves through television genre conventions. These conventions give them access to a luxury lifestyle that they know is often a deception, hiding the horror beneath its shiny surfaces (marble, reflective pool). And the second scene proves them right. The presence of the young child and his mysterious actions trigger a social critique of this lifestyle and by association also Katharina's fitness as a mother. At this point, our identification figures for reasserting law and order are shown driving to the crime scene, emerging from and leaving their bourgeois-coded normalcy, to which viewers are expecting to be returned eventually. Instead of dislocating viewers from the beginning, *Perfume* reestablishes the genre conventions of a typical network-era crime drama without providing recognizable geopolitical markers.

In a subsequent scene, Simon's colleague Köhler is interviewing a potential witness whose messy and cluttered nondescript house is situated along the path the murderer's car could have used to get to the bungalow. From Katharina's Americanized bungalow, this scene drops us at her dilapidated residence. Denizens of the one would not be found in the other. Only the editing concocts them as a neighborhood. It adjoins two worlds and what feels like two different times. The neighbor lives with countless rescue dogs in the bottom half of a two-story building that looks like a combination of barn and garage. Unlike Katharina's elusive, elite scent, the wet dogs emit a stench many viewers can recall on the spot. Köhler tries to find out whether the woman has seen a car on the murder night, and he eventually does. With a dog on his lap, the woman prods him to try dog food "it's good for you." In her quirkiness, she is our first real informant, both about the murder and about the region. She explains that she is trying to rent the upper floor to tourists, who never arrive, even though supposedly, the "Niederrhein is an up-and-coming tourist destination." While Netflix viewers might not (yet) be the tourists the locals need to supplement their income, this scene circumscribes a specific location that is less defined as German or regional but as suffering from postindustrial decline, a place whose residents in the majority, unlike Katharina and her gang, have not managed to transition to the global hyper-media economy. When the older woman off-handedly tells Köhler that the car was not local, and he is perplexed that she has memorized the license plate, crime drama devotees take note: this is Germany's Fargo/*Fargo* (FX, 2014–). And chips start to fall into place (sorry!).

From here on out, *Perfume*'s cinematography and editing rarely make a directional connection between two locations nor do they present us with any kind of center (town or otherwise), so that it becomes impossible to distill a geographic map of the region. *Perfume*'s spatial fragments never join to form a whole. While *Dark* used a recombinant strategy to facilitate the local-global convergence, *Perfume*'s resembles a bricolage of solitary fragments akin to a ruinous aesthetics that relate to each other only tangentially. Like in the film and television versions of *Fargo*, dwellings are dispersed, with "empty" space strewn with occasional remnants of the industrial and agricultural pasts between them. A column or crumbled wall sticks out here, another smokestack is visible over there. *Perfume*'s impressionistic scenes add to a fragmentation of space, an experience that is shared by Netflix viewers around the globe. Only avid crime drama reception and recognition of iconic character types from Columbo to Marge Gunderson help to situate post-network viewers. The Niederrhein becomes a media(ted) region that merges with the aesthetics of globally migrating television and attaches itself even more consequentially to constructs of time, rather than space. *Perfume* portrays the Niederrhein region as a ruinous landscape whose value only accrues in relational transmediated memory processes.

After locating viewers through genre conventions, the drama utilizes cinematography and mise-en-scène, ensemble character profiles, a flashback-rich, mnemonically inter-laced narration, and the inherent media reflexivity of transmedia adaptation in ways that reformat it as a post-network crime drama. These aspects of *Perfume*'s design require a more extensive elaboration of its internal segmentation pattern. The series engages in a pattern of semiotic and narrative transit routes and peripheral adjacencies that morph from purely functional transition devices into carriers of meaning, meaning that derives from seemingly inadvertent side-by-side placements in the setting, parallel shot composition within the mise-en-scène, camera angles, and transitions between scenes derived by editing. In the process, some elements are abandoned, matching the empty space of the landscape, while others, left in fragments, like the ruins dotting the landscape, reassert their significance and are restored in time-shifted montages.

An example for the transitional adjacency of the setting is offered by Butsche's brothel and Simon's motel. Both are located alongside a major highway and adjacent to each other. Their side-by-side location along the highway and vis-à-vis each other underscores the parallelism of spatial configurations and how these enable relational memory processes, which carry over into the cross-editing between flashbacks and present-day scenes. Like a conference hotel, the clean, postmodern architecture of the brothel features a trendy glass façade. The only giveaway to its function is the neon outline of a nude woman at night. The motel to its left looks like it charges by the hour. During the day, the buildings could therefore trade places. This ambiguity carries over to the characters. They, too, could switch places and do. In the final episode, "Fesselung" (bondage but also captivation), detective Simon becomes the murderer everyone suspects the pimp Butsche to (already) be.

The pattern of peripheral adjacencies continues in the cinematography. *Perfume*'s cinematography operates with a recurring pattern of opening tracking shots that move inward from the sidelines or undetermined places of origin.[18] Cuts at the end of scenes likewise have a tendency to deposit viewers into different places and times rather abruptly, building an interrupted syntactical network that reveals interconnections only in retrospect. When the camera tilts upward through a mesh of gigantic power lines to the side of the four-lane highways dissecting the flat earth, *Perfume* is careful to situate the viewer not on but tangential to arteries of the industrial region. This has the effect of stressing the process of mediation itself, of drawing attention to the simultaneous existences of and competition between different technologies of transit, transportation, and communication. By extension, convergence is portrayed as a parallel system, adjacent to, not replacing network television just yet.

Now that the pattern of peripheral adjacencies for the construction of spatial relations has been established, the next section turns to the ways in which *Perfume* mobilizes this pattern within its narrational system and for viewers, and how this, in turn, activates relational memory conduits and/as transmedia practices.

Relational Memory and Micro Flows in Transmedia Television

Relational memory is the ability to remember arbitrary associations between objects or events. These memories include things related by location, order, and context. (. . .) Specifically, (. . .) the hippocampus encodes information in spatiotemporal sequences reflecting the sequences of eye movements observed in the behavior. Certain patterns of eye movements may even help the hippocampus build relational memories.

---

[18]*Perfume*'s invasive camera-eye is reminiscent of Michael Mann's *Manhunter* (1986), whose murderer is a serial voyeur, who regularly invades houses to steel fetish items before finally returning for the kill.

Memory for relations among the constituent elements of experience, providing the ability to remember names with faces, the locations of various objects or people, or the order in which various events occurred. Can be contrasted to item memory, i.e., of the individual elements themselves. The hippocampus is required for memory for arbitrary or accidentally occurring relations.[19]

Elizabeth Evans's work on transmedia television is pivotal for thinking about *Perfume*'s relational memory paths that follow peripheral adjacencies rather than a center/margin or straight content to content, screen to screen movement. She describes the interconnection between structural and narrative movements as micro flows that wind themselves through transmedia televisual storytelling and industry practices:

> "Flow," in this instance, becomes a narrative characteristic. Rather than building a single narrative "flow" from screen to screen, leading the viewer from a webisode prequel to the episode to a game in sequence, multiple "micro flows" are in place *within* individual episodes and across screens.[20]

Evans contends here that cross-screen experiences are accompanied by and reinserted into the narrative as micro flows. This structure describes how *Perfume* makes transmedia storytelling a part of its narrational system, its cinematography and editing, and how this in turn reflects on the show's post-network existence on Netflix. A closer look at the segmentation of the second episode will make this concrete. To understand the narration format and how it creates meaning, the next section studies the chronological segmentation of nine short scenes and how these construct micro flows "*within* and across screens," as Evans suggests.

Scenes 1–5: Instead of driving or walking to interview Elena's father about Merten's disappearance, the boarding school's caretaker, who is burning protest signs for admitting girls to the school on a field by the river, Simon and Köhler take a boat along a Niederrhein tributary to get there. Since it is a bleary, bluish-gray day, this choice of transportation appears unmotivated and unnecessary. Cut. They interview him. He mentions a Hendrik Ahlers. Cut. From the wooded backyard somewhere else, the camera-eye (unattached to a character) warily approaches Roman's and

---

[19]Seth D. Koenig, "Remembering What We've Seen: The Hippocampus and Relational Memory," in *Research Works Archive* (University of Washington), https://digital.lib.washington.edu/researchworks/handle/1773/40839 (accessed December 2, 2020), and Alex Konkel and Neal J. Cohen, "Relational Memory and the Hippocampus: Representations and Methods," *Frontiers in Neuroscience* 3, no. 2 (September 15, 2009): 166–74.

[20]Elizabeth Evans, "Layering Engagement: The Temporal Dynamics of Transmedia Television," *Storyworlds: A Journal of Narrative Studies* 7, no. 2 (Winter 2015): 111–28, here 123.

Elena's house, only to transition abruptly to a narrow path between two indoor tennis courts, capturing Simon and Köhler head-on as they try to interview Hendrik Ahlers. The only connection between these scenes is the mention of that name and the context of a game: Ahlers remembers a smelling game the teenagers used to play, guessing a person by the description of their smell. After the interview, the two inspectors are shown having lunch in the restaurant adjacent to the tennis courts.

The camera is unanchored in its approach to these five scenes. And each of them occurs in transitional or peripheral spaces—flowing down the river, next to the river, a wooded backlot, a hallway, a courtside restaurant—or the camera flips sides, like between two tennis partners. In the last shot of the outside of the courtside restaurant, the axis is not aligned with the net but instead with the off-court space perpendicular to the net. Instead of a transition shot, the camera disobeys the 180-degree axis, which shows the restaurant's four windows that are ensconced in a bare concrete wall. The realignment of the camera infuses the restaurant and court combination with the dialectic between interrogation and observer room, each obeying their own sets of rules and functioning within scripted hierarchies. Game aspects are carried forward as a micro flow and reflect on the conventions of the crime drama, in which the interrogation room plus one-way mirror make regular appearances to test psychological resolve and exhibit rehearsed performances from both sides. In this way, the axis break also signals the possibility of rule-breaking, by not only inverting positions (putting the police and not the accused on display) but also extending to generic ruptures within the crime drama format. The repositioning of the camera converts the editing process itself into a rematch happening on a different plane, a different screen, constructing a transmedia micro flow from diegesis to extradiegesis, between forensic narrative, competitive game, crime drama, and the medium of television.

Scenes 6–9: The next scenes begin with a flashback, switch to a collective daydream, and end with a reproduction of both in the present timeline. Without a conventional close-up, match cut, exhibition shot, or voice-over to indicate that a flashback is coming, viewers are dumped from the concrete gray of the tennis court into a vintage green-gold-saturated color scheme from the 1990s. In the park of the boarding school, Roman, Butsche, and Moritz get ready to canoe to their secret hiding place, a ruin in the woods. Retroactively, the boat trip and Ahlers's mention of the ruin—"those were the days," he intoned two scenes earlier—suffice to connect the two boat trips. The color palette of the bleary work-related motor boat trip has switched to a sunny summer canoe trip. By reproducing the scene in reverse (present first, past second), viewers become aware of what has been lost, while restoring some of the luster (of youth and potential) all the same. At the ruin in the flashback, each character sits on or leans against a differently elevated wall-remnant without looking at one another. A single question—"I wonder what K and the senior are doing?"—followed by successive close-ups of each boy's stare motivates a cutaway to K and the anonymous senior, as they are swimming and then having sex in a shed. In that dream-like scene, K is on top and the camera looks up at her, placing the viewer (and the combined stares of the boys) into the senior's position on the bottom. The "imagined" sex scene ends with a close-up of young Roman's now anxious face, just before another cut. Instead of a transition shot, the camera uses their now collective point of view to look down on a reading girl (young Elena) in the lower corner of the ruin as if conjured by their frustrated desires. One of them asks: "Who do we have here?" Cut to the present.

Not only do the three boys now inhabit K's dominant position from the sex scene, Elena occupies the anonymous senior's position at the bottom. Along with this reversal, the power dynamic changes, as it did in the axis break of the tennis room/restaurant scene. The ruin setting and the three to one dynamic make the violence of this reversal tangible. Genders have realigned with traditional sex positions; refracted male power is being consolidated and reclaimed. Out of this reversal, which is additionally imbued with younger Roman's anxiety and jealousy, the previously wary camera-eye now approaches his and Elena's present-day house in the next scene with a voyeuristic intentionality. The camera-eye has retained the boys' predatoriness and expanded it to include the audience for the adult reproduction of the ruin scene. In the adult version, Elena is not only part of the tableau but her to-be-looked-at-ness (Laura Mulvey) is quadrupled as a result (the boys' gaze, the adult men's gaze, the audience's gaze, the camera's gaze).

As the camera approaches the house, the parallel glass windows offer a direct sightline into several adjoining rooms. On the left, Butsche can be seen following Roman to the kitchen, while Moritz, Daniel, and Elena are visible in the living room to the right. The window arrangement connects back to the tennis court scene, having us approach the persons inside both as contenders in competition for K's attention and as suspects in the murders of Merten and Katharina. Even when the camera eventually arrives inside the house, the pattern of parallel scenes prevails, this time not taking place through the editing process (tennis court axis break) or between "arbitrary or accidentally occurring relations" (graphic match between restaurant and bungalow windows) or looking relations (the three gazes in the ruin conjuring up a primal scene) but in the mise-en-scène: a drunk Daniel plays with a drunk Elena's hair in the rear of the living room, as she sits on his lap. In front of them, in two armchairs, Moritz and Butsche reminisce about Katharina and pronounce their desire to be able to rewatch an "endless loop" of Katharina tossing her hair back and stretching her long legs. Butsche gets up and takes Elena's one stocking off, throwing it at Daniel—"for jerking off"—while Roman watches the show. Elena is performing Katharina: Daniel plays with her hair; she stretches her legs toward the camera. Roman is turned on and threatened—as he was in the ruin—but unwilling to admit the latter.

The inter- and intra-segmental parallelism of these scenes reproduces Moritz's desired "endless loop" before the diegetic and extradiegetic spectators' eyes, as a reproduction of a reproduction. We get to witness a transmedia moment within the diegesis. The film loop is projected for us as network television, film's first Other, on online television. The reproduction of the film loop from the cinematic moment at the ruin, and the restorative nostalgia with which Moritz imbues the moving image in the present, is inserted into the living room like a television set's screen. In the ruin, the camera converted the boys' intense scopophilic gaze into a glance at the very moment they looked at Elena. That glance inadvertently found bespectacled Elena, huddled in the corner of the ruin, reading a book, coding her from the beginning as a "poor" but "available" and "domesticatable" substitute for Katharina, in looks and class. In the present timeline, when Roman orders Elena to accompany him to bed, Moritz goads Butsche on to "watch them through the window, like back then," to which Butsche counters with "that's just boring." Elena's life consists of performing someone else for someone else (a substitute for Marten and his mother, for Katharina and the men). The cinematic version of female masquerade (Mary Ann Doane) is reproduced as transmedial in this televisual micro flow.

Watching *Perfume* has become watching television as television, delivering a serial micro flow of exhibitionist, voyeuristic episodes, as the camera approaches another set of illuminated windows from the dusky outside. Inside, Grünberg and his wife are sharing a glass of wine. The scene would appear to show a cozy evening ritual, if we did not know about his affair with Simon and if the camera did not copy the previous exterior/interior tracking shot switching from an extreme long shot to a medium close-up. The courteous but curt dialogue revolves around why Simon has his private number, and he counters with an allegory, another parallel drawn in front of her and our eyes. Even though his wife seems to enjoy the bestsellers filling the shelves, he muses that she will always return to the classics, for example, *Anna Karenina*, which she is holding in her hand. The wife is not having any of it: "You will rot in hell, Grünberg." The book allegory further develops the gendered high/low culture angle between film and television from the previous segments, when Grünberg relates his wife to a classic work of literature and Simon, his affair, to the promiscuity of popular fiction. In doing so, he also projects his adulterous sex drive onto her reading habits, reproducing the "reading frenzy" argument of worried late eighteenth- to nineteenth-century patriarchs, who equated educated women's reading habits with sexual licentiousness.

The gender/genre diatribe also points to the central enigma of the show's murder mystery, which brings the show's reflexivity on transmedia television to a head. Simon locates a well-read copy of none other than Süskind's novel, itself a classic by now. The book launched the film and the Netflix series, each of which prompted its lead characters to investigate smells. In *Perfume*, this activity led to Marten's and the dog's murders, one buried on top of the other, their glands removed. Their burial becomes a palimpsest of the technological reproduction process manifesting in trans-species/transmedia corpses. Simon's belated discovery of the book and beginning obsession with the power of scents within *Perfume* therefore parallel the alluring transmedia story-power of *Perfume* as a serial crime narrative screened on streaming platforms that encourage serial as well as time-shifted reception. The way the plot doubles back and digs up Merten's corpse beneath the first—the dog—becomes a representative expression of time-shifted viewing and viewers' cross-platform paratextual sleuthing activities. While the reveal of the main culprit might have come as a surprise, dedicated viewers going back through the dog-discovery scene and through Elena's, Daniel's, and Merten's storyline in the flashback scenes likely exhumed Merten's body before the detectives finally did. The discovery of the experimental animal sacrifice—the original corpse—leads to Merten's body—the second corpse (the first copy), unsettling the spatial and temporal relationship between original and reproduction. Like the delayed find of Süskind's text, on which the entire premise of the series is based, Elena and Daniel buried the second body (copy) underneath the original to imprint the latter with the copy's aura/smell rather than the other way around as Walter Benjamin would have it. The police disinter the first before they find the second body underneath, reverting typical archaeological sedimentation. And the reordered chronology and spatiality continue in the ancillary market, where the series incentivizes fans to (re)read Süskind's novel, (re)watch Tykwer's film, or start another crime drama to pass the time until the second season drops. Elizabeth Evans argues: "The viewer is actually free to layer 'flows' on top of each other, moving from television set to tablet and back again in potentially infinitely variable ways."[21] Thus, the burial scenario inserts itself as an allegory of transmedia television at the core of the narrative and at the same time reflects the television text's established internal segmentation into micro flows.

The layering of the corpses on the plot level also approximates the mining factor of online television, whether for distracted, interrupted, or analytical reasons. And it follows the pattern of adjacencies, the internal rerouted seriality of this post-network drama's narration, editing, mise-en-scène, and cinematography. Given the postmodern self-reflexivity on and in between each semiotic, aesthetic, narratological, diegetic, and non-diegetic level of the Netflix crime drama, and given that Moritz explicitly mentions memory functioning like a recorded and rewindable moving image, the very syntax of post-network television is in play.

---

[21] Ibid.

Abandoned Futures and Ruined Pasts

Now that the segmentation analysis has revealed important information about the structure of micro flows and how they contribute to the construction of relational memory paths in transmedia television, it is time to consider them together. Does *Perfume*'s approach pitch a different understanding of the geopolitical moment and what should be considered German to the global audience than *Tatort*, *Dark*, or *Babylon Berlin*?

Walter Benjamin traced the collapse of the authenticity of "historical testimony" and "the authority of the object" from the Baroque tragedy to modernity, the "Age of Mechanical Reproduction." Pitting the inverse palimpsestic gravesite and Moritz's meme-aesthetics (his "eternal loop" of Katharina) against Benjamin's loss of aura, it is less the reproduction of originals that are of concern in the digital production and reception of *Perfume*, and more the fetishistic personalization of audiovisual loops that come close to the spritz of a lost one's perfume. A specific looped gesture or smell "meet[s] the beholder or listener in his own particular situation, it reactivates the object reproduced."[22] Taking his cues from Benjamin, Henry Jenkins defines cultural convergence in the "Age of Digital Transformation" as

> the process by which people in their everyday life use media in relation to each other, form evaluations about which media best serve specific purposes, assemble information across multiple channels of communication, and embrace artworks that depend upon appropriation and remixing of cultural materials or upon the archiving and recirculating of previous media texts.[23]

How cultural memory, specifically in its postmemory phase, is related to medium specificity is corroborated by Walter Benjamin's association of allegory with ruins in his contemplation of the Baroque tragic drama. Since this very association revolves around death and decay, it is not a stretch to rethink Benjamin's connection in the context of the post-network crime drama. Kerstin Barndt reminds us of Benjamin's concept of allegory—"allegories are, in the realm of thoughts, what ruins are in the realm of things"—in her context of reading Germany's industrial ruins:

> Ruins are palimpsests that invite us to contemplate a layered temporality. (. . . .) Both allegories and ruins are symptoms of epistemological

---

[22] Walter Benjamin, "Das Kunstwerk im Zeitalter seiner technischen Reproduzierbarkeit" (1939).
[23] Henry Jenkins, "The Work of Theory in the Age of Digital Transformation," in *A Companion to Film Theory*, ed. Toby Miller and Robert Stam (New York: Blackwell, 1999), 349–50.

uncertainty and the collapse of time. For Benjamin, allegorical readings emerge with secularization, a historical rupture that shattered the theological paradigm of salvation and its attendant certainties. The loss of these certainties caused the temporal order to collapse into a dark history of nature, dominated by disaster, decay, and death. While Benjamin develops his theory in dialogue with the baroque tragic drama, his ideas are refracted through the lens of modernism and modernity. (...) [T]he conceptualizing of history as layered time avoids the pitfalls of linear, teleological, or circular historical narratives and accounts for the plurality and nonsimultaneity of historical times.[24]

Discussing Bernd and Hilla Becher's photographs of defunct water towers, Barndt argues that their serial presentation "[invites] an analytical gaze based on comparison and the play of form and function." The series "refracts our perception and poses a powerful counterpoint to the melancholic contemplation of any individual photograph as memento mori" (Ibid., 273). Taken together with the established editing and cinematographic patterns from the second episode of *Perfume*, Barndt's analysis of the serial display of ruin-images addresses the medium specificity of nonlinear and time-shifted television. We can read the individual segments that make up one episode and all six episodes of the first season of *Perfume* as discontinuous, broken apart, serially paralleled narrative fragments. As shown in the segment analysis of the second episode, these fragments connect across time and space without resorting to linearity or conventional medium-specific continuity devices. In fact, the process of comprehension is geared toward rewinding—not just through flashbacks but also through time-shifted parallel scenes that skip a set of chronological steps. If Brandt is correct that the serialization of ruin-images—the vertical and horizontal side-by-side representation of decaying fragments—wards off "melancholic contemplation," it follows that *Perfume*'s boarding school mini-series told in flashbacks, while providing the show's own "abandoned set of futures," might prevent viewers from dwelling in its noxious 1990s nirvana.

But as Svetlana Boim cautions, "the fantasies of the past determined by the needs of the present have a direct impact on the realities of the future."[25] The fragmented corpus of the post-network crime drama that assembles in the serial televisual *Gestalt* is itself restructuring the habitus of recollection.[26]

---

[24]Kerstin Barndt, "Memory Traces of an Abandoned Set of Futures," in *Ruins of Modernity*, ed. Nora Alter and 271–93, here 271–3.
[25]Boim, "Nostalgia and Its Discontents."
[26]Max Wertheimer founded the *Gestalt* School of Psychology in 1912 with a study of the perception of movement. Geared toward describing and explaining patterns of perception, even those based on optical delusions (e.g., the famous marquee light example), Wertheimer and his colleagues insisted the whole was greater than its individual parts.

One needs to consider how this series inserts itself in the dialogue about and within the cultural memory of Germany's fraught history with domestic violence. In 2015, the German *Bundeskriminalamt* published a case report that specified that in 82 percent of domestic violence cases, women were the victims. Of 100,000 women that had become victims of domestic violence, 331 cases were murder or attempted murder.[27] The first shelter for female victims of domestic abuse came into existence in Berlin in 1976. From there it was a long road until the overhaul of paragraph 177 in 1997, which redefined domestic sexual abuse as a criminal act, no longer simply a case of *Nötigung* (coercion). Until 1997, Germany did not officially abandon this heterosexually defined paragraph that allowed husbands to exert corporeal punishment and demand sex in marriage without giving their wives the legal recourse to defend themselves against these acts of domestic and sexual violence.[28] In 2001, finally, parliament adopted the *Gewaltschutzgesetz* (violence protection law) which was overhauled again to include stricter measures in 2016. The current law has broadened its protective mantle to include domestic partners of any sexuality or gender.

Until 1997 is a long time to officially revoke a patriarchal power clause, so much so that it initiates another close look at the second episode's segmentation amid the show's broader messaging. The demonstrated transmediality comes as a result and at the cost of violence and trauma. The sex scene between Roman and Elena cannot become the equivalent of the "boring" television-type sex, Butsche describes. *Perfume* is under pressure to deliver something else to its diegetic and extradiegetic audiences. The boys discover young Elena in the ruin after Roman and they had fantasized about Katharina having sex, a scene that viewers get to see. We only return to the young Elena surrounded by the three boys in the ruin after the scene with the Grünbergs. But before the intense gazes of the three boys that surround her turn into action, the scene switches to the present Roman and Elena in their bedroom, where he hits her, pushes her head down into the mattress, and is about to rape her. Cut. The viewer is transported to a montage of quick successive joins from a side-lit Simon in a car to the Grünbergs sleeping, to Elena's father laying out pictures of young Elena, all overlaid with a somber non-diegetic composition from a string quartet.

---

[27] "Deutschland: 100.000 Frauen erleben Gewalt in Partnerschaft," *WAZonline*, November 22, 2016, https://www.waz.de/panorama/deutschland-100-000-frauen-erleben-gewalt-in-partnerschaft-id12378938.html?displayDropdownTop=none&displayDropdownBottom=block (accessed December 15, 2020).

[28] "Lebenssituation, Sicherheit und Gesundheit von Frauen in Deutschland," *Studie im Auftrag des Bundesfamilienministeriums*, 2004, https://www.bmfsfj.de/blob/84328/0c83aab6e685eeddc01712109bcb02b0/langfassung-studie-frauen-teil-eins-data.pdf (accessed December 15, 2020).

This montage of reactions to Elena's specific and the community's broader undoing rekindles the restorative nostalgia that was largely absent in the flashback scenes. At the end of the montage, in a clear role reversal of victim and perpetrator, we rejoin a suffering Roman sitting on the edge of the bed like the violence was done unto him. A composed but bruised Elena comforts him like a mother would a repentant child. Viewers do not get to see the trauma from Katharina's or Elena's own perspectives. Instead, as demonstrated, viewers assume the perpetrators' positions, again and again. Since Elena was involved in Merten's death, the scene even gives viewers license to see the domestic abuse as her penance. Not only is the actual scene of trauma and suffering inferred, teased, and continuously deferred but perpetrators and victims also exchange places along a spectrum of culpability. How do the micro flows and the montage infer, displace, and defer trauma onto different people (Merten and the dog, Simon, Grünberg, and Elena's father) and onto different times and places, and how does this reorder cultural memory? To put it in stronger terms: together with the montage, itself an assemblage of fragments, the sequence seeks to preemptively repair the trauma and reorder the ruined/broken relationships during the time that the actual trauma occurs offscreen. The sorting of photographs from Elena's childhood, the cuddling Grünbergs, Elena's maternal gesture, these acts all imply recollection, a process of reassemblage that merges into forgiveness and resignation to the status quo.

By contrast, back in 1980, Helma Sanders-Brahms depicted a rape scene taking place in a factory ruin in 1945 in her film *Deutschland, Bleiche Mutter*. A woman and her young daughter are walking across Germany, when she gets raped by two US soldiers. In explaining the assault to her small daughter afterward, the mother states matter of fact that what the daughter saw was an example of "to the victor the spoils." This scene has alternately been interpreted as an example of women's internalization of male-dominated power hierarchies or an alienation attempt to critique the silence surrounding widespread sexual assaults during the late stages of the war and postwar occupation. Given that the rape in the film is followed by years of domestic abuse, leaving the mother with a facial paralysis and ending in a barely averted suicide attempt, the single wartime trauma is overshadowed by unremitting acts of institutionalized gendered violence during the economic miracle era.

Neither late 1990s nor present-day Elena should have to bear the continuation of this legacy, yet she does. Iconographically, Kadelbach appropriates Sander-Brahms's scene, situating young Elena's undoing into a ruinous landscape evocative of the immediate postwar period, so that the boys can see themselves as victors, and Elena's rape can be rewritten as their spoils. Worse, cross-cutting between the visibility of Katharina's passionate sex act and the invisibility of Elena's rape reproduces the one as the other, converting the viewers' visual access to Katharina's desire and the boys' illegitimate physical claim to Elena's body into the pornographic realm, performing the "historical pornography" Kansteiner proclaimed for Guido Knopp's *Hitler* series. Even in 2018, German women stay in their abusive partnerships. And Katharina joins their ranks as a readily available mental pin-up, even post-mortem.

Neither Roman nor Elena have learned anything from the past nor have Grünberg or Simon. But more importantly, gender dynamics and the gendered hierarchy of power in German society have not changed, legal progress notwithstanding. The Bukkake/Men at Work sticker in Simon's colleague's car makes clear that the top cop might be a woman, but like Fassbinder's Maria Braun before her, who despite evidence to the contrary clings to the bourgeois idea of marriage and family, Simon is made into an allegory of the ruinous postindustrial landscape under perpetual male-dominated reconstruction. The camera-eye joins the boys' projected individual and collective heterosexual male desire—in the flashback ruin's sex scene with Katharina—as well as in the living room scene, where Moritz projects a memory-loop of Katharina that Elena screens for us in the back. Of course, as the camera alternately captures the individual young men's faces in medium close-up in their respective shots, homoeroticism and the struggle to conform to the socially enforced heterosexuality mandate might have also fueled the sexual domination of Elena. Partaking in the assault, each boy could perform their (not) belonging. *Perfume* reassembles patriarchy from within its ruins. In Boim's context of restorative nostalgia, the scene "attempts a transhistorical reconstruction of the lost home," where men, together, retain power, even when they struggle as individuals. *Perfume* shows us a Germany where sexual violence has morphed with national identity construction.

In the discussed ruin scene, Katharina's poly-amorous emancipation and her absence, combined with the boys' puerile imagination, plus a sense of deflated class- and gender-based entitlement fueled by boarding school group-think trigger the abuse. Because Katharina does not let them, they put Elena in her place, in both meanings of the phrase. This transferal triggers Roman's assault, an act of spiteful displaced revenge, then as much as in the present-day bedroom scene. While, in mid-season, suspicion wrongly and ironically falls on Daniel, eventually all male perpetrators get off scot-free. The chafing against taking responsibility for inflicting and inheriting past and present trauma is normalized within a discourse that introduces an agent provocateur, whether in the shape of a perfume, a femme fatale, or a demagogue. In the season finale, the "nose-blind" Simon puts on too much perfume and is almost killed by Grünberg. Despite the diegetic and cultural evidence of increasing acts of violence against women, in the end, it is the three women who *Perfume* installs as agents of a murderous economy: Elena killed Merten with Daniel's help, Lydia murdered and mutilated Katharina and Perle to get Moritz to manufacture their scents, and Simon killed Lydia to use the perfume to secure Grünberg's affection.

The show's editing and cinematography establish micro flows that facilitate a relational memory where associations seemingly arbitrarily and voyeuristically attach themselves to deferred and displaced second and third screens of the primal scene or the scene of the original trauma. As the fragmented, ruin-like micro flows serialize avoidance they set free a relational memory-based on restorative energies. These recontextualize past and present trauma according to an "accidental discourse" that uncouples cause from effect, actions from consequences. As a result, a postfeminist nominal female agency emerges alongside a distressed hetero-masculinity that layers itself over the traumatic history of violence against women, both within and outside of the diegesis.

4

Watching National German Television on Netflix

Dogs of Berlin (Netflix, 2018–)

The original German-language crime drama *Dogs of Berlin* (2018, producer Sigi Kamml, showrunner Christian Alvart) was produced directly for Netflix by Alvart's own media-production company Syrreal Entertainment. Despite its rootedness in the private sector, of all four German Netflix crime dramas discussed here, *Dogs of Berlin* adheres most closely to German broadcast crime genre protocols while expanding narrative complexity. This chapter demonstrates how the show's cinematography, narrative format, and political topicality adapt ARD's *Tatort* concept for Netflix. *Dogs of Berlin* not only continues the former's tradition of expressing national and global discourses through a regional focus but also features its classic "odd couple" detective team format. Its representational modus retains *Tatort*'s regional focus (Berlin) and integrates up-to-date sociopolitical issues to invite a social critique of contemporary German society. I inquire how this unofficial adaptation of *Tatort* for post-network television exports national German television to a global audience.

Dogs of Berlin Synopsis and Narration

The crime drama's hook is set with the murder of soccer champion Orkan Erdem (Cino Djavid) just before the final world cup-qualifying game between Germany and Turkey. But the focus is on the uneasy partnership between two detectives. One is Kurt Grimmer (Felix Kramer), an East German former neo-Nazi and sports gambler with a double family life straddling two socioeconomic classes with different political affiliations. The other is Erol Birkan (Fahri Yardim), an upstanding gay cop with a West German-Turkish background. As their complex worlds collide, the partners have to come together, respect, and support one another, to solve the crime and save themselves.

Both Kurt and Erol live intersectional lives, their family's roots weighing heavily on both of them. Erol is a DEA agent and is out as gay. He and his husband live in a neighborhood in West Berlin. Erol has an abusive father, who has just come back from Turkey and from whom he needs to protect his mother. Having grown up in the district Kaiserwarte, he has personally experienced the long tendrils of power emanating from that district's Lebanese-run Tarik-Amir clan. Kurt, a civil servant in the LKA (*Landeskriminalamt*, state criminal investigation office), has also tried to move on and up. His effectiveness as a detective and his engaged leadership have charmed his immediate boss, but his family ties to a local National Socialist group are well known and keep thwarting his rise to power. When Kurt married Paula (Katharina Schüttler), with whom he has two kids, he not only left the East Berlin neighborhood of Marzahn, his drug addiction, and his family's neo-Nazi organization, but he also moved up the social ladder. Kurt's and Paula's new comfortable house and garden are situated in an affluent suburb. Both Erol and Kurt have uprooted their lives to some extent, and both are under the sway of their pasts. However, Kurt has reclaimed Marzahn as his home through his affair with his high school crush Bine (Anna Maria Mühe) and her two kids, one still an infant.

Dogs of Berlin's first season features ten episodes that bear soccer-related titles, for example, "Offside" and "Foul Play." The narration uses a frame narrative, beginning with a voice-over of Orkan Erdem, the victim: "I knew the day of reckoning would come eventually, but I did not know that I would set fire to the city." From there, the plot order is reversed, jumping back in time to seven days before the murder and counting down each episode as the series progresses. In the first episode, "V.I.P," the camera first tilts upward to give viewers an overview of the layout of the city, making a smoke plume visible to the west of the *Fernsehturm* (television tower). A quick succession of cuts alternates between high- and low-angle shots. These reveal the scene through the telephoto grid from a police helicopter before joining protesters, riot police, and their dogs on the ground in medium close-ups. The screen-filling transparent title *Dogs of Berlin* is superimposed over the chaos. The letter cutouts first focus on barking German Shepherds on their leashes then pull back to a high-angle view of the smoke from the direction of Marzahn, with police radio, sirens, and screams supplying the diegetic sound. Each episode follows the same general pattern starting with a present-day title sequence and then backing up to a specific day before the riot.

Dogs of Berlin—An Unofficial *Tatort* Adaptation on Netflix

While it is true that a large portion of actors and crew active in German television today have come through the *Tatort* talent factory at one point or another in their careers, *Dogs of Berlin* takes this percentage to a new level.[1] Christian Alvart (1974–), a West German from Frankfurt, "has a solid *Tatort* background and loves what Germans call *Krimis*." He studied at the University of Pittsburg and experienced the narrative television boon in the United States.[2] He thus brings a bi-continental approach to this project that combines the serial narrative complexity and cinematic aesthetics of US shows he admires with existing German crime drama conventions. Overseeing his own media-production company—Syrreal Entertainment— and casting experienced domestic crime drama actors and *Tatort* crossovers for the two leads help him to further bridge the different sets of expectations between cinema and television and between domestic network and Netflix audiences in the post-network media environment. In October 2020, the success of this combination resulted in Netflix acquiring his 2018 film *Cut Off (Abgeschnitten)* with Moritz Bleibtreu and Fahri Yardim (who plays Yalcin Gümer on *Tatort* and Erol Birkan in *Dogs*) in the lead.

Alvart directed five episodes of the Hamburg *Tatort* since 2013, in addition to the 140-minute cinema spin-off *Tschiller: Off Duty* (2016), starring Til Schweiger and Fahri Yardim as the investigative duo Nick Tschiller and Yalcin Gümer. Schweiger's efforts to steer the *Tatort* format toward action comedy, his wheelhouse, including modernizing the iconic title sequence, did not take hold. The first episode under Alvart's direction and Schweiger's dominant input garnered the highest viewer share for *Tatort* in twenty years.[3] But that bump did not survive the box-office flop of the spin-off film, resulting in the lowest viewership for a *Tatort* episode in seven years, when

---

[1] In addition to Fahri Yardim and Felix Kramer, several cast members share their *Tatort* portfolios. Just to name a few: Markus Boysen, who plays the seedy team manager Walter Laubach, started his career as the victim in *Tatort*'s canonic "Reifezeugnis" before landing roles in *SOKO* and *Derrick*. He was also cast in the series *Ku'damm*, which has become a convergent darling on the heritage side. Anna Maria Mühe (Sabine Ludar) not only appeared in five *Tatort* episodes (2004–21), but she was also cast as Beate Zschäpe in the 2016 German Netflix acquisition *NSU*. Katharina Schüttler (Paula) had a similar *Tatort* career but one that also included *Ku'damm* and the 2013 series *Generation War* (dir. Philip Kadelbach, the director of *Perfume*).
[2] Simon Kingsley, "Christian Alvart Director's Portrait: Unleashing the Dogs," *German Film Quarterly*, https://germanfilmsquarterly.de/portrait_christian_alvart_gfq.html (accessed December 22, 2020).
[3] Gernot Kramper, "Leitwolf Til und die kleinen Kläffer," *Stern*, April 9, 2012, https://www.stern.de/kultur/tv/debatte-um-den--tatort--vorspann-leitwolf-til-und-die-kleinen-klaeffer-3062314.html (accessed December 30, 2020).

it was rebroadcasted in the show's regular slot in July 2018. According to reviews, Alvart's Hamburg episodes suffered from "too much action, too much Til Schweiger, but not enough classical Krimi."[4] Critics attest that the majority of *Tatort* fans have not warmed to but instead increasingly "tschilled" to the Til Schweiger show.[5] As a result, the network let go of Alvart and hired Eoin Moore, responsible for the convincing concept of *Polizeiruf 110 Rostock*, from the sixth episode of this team's Hamburg *Tatort* forward (January 2020).

It is thus credible to surmise that *Dogs of Berlin* became Alvart's action-centric *Tatort* concept for Netflix. And knowing this history, a few continuities deserve highlighting for the analysis of format adaptation: with Felix Kramer as Kurt Grimmer, Alvart retained the Tschiller pattern of focusing on a testosterone-driven white male character contrastively paired with Fahri Yardim, who plays a calmer, more self-reflexive Erol Birkan. Having worked with Yardim since 2013, Alvart could count on an established working relationship in addition to building on Yardim's rising television celebrity (*Jerks*, ProSieben/Maxdome, 2017–). Since *Jerks* even features occasional, albeit fictional, *Tatort* shoots due to Yardim "playing himself" on the show, this demonstrates Alvart's and Yardim's willingness to modify *Tatort* and the crime drama's pivotal role in national media history for a new era of television. Due to higher production and postproduction budgets, Alvart was able to invest in action sequences in the hope that they, in combination with *Tatort*'s loyal base, would sustain world-building energies for transmedia franchising. Whereas *Off-Duty* attempted *Tatort*'s expansion to European locations by having Tschiller rescuing his daughter from the claws of the Turkish mob, *Dogs* returns to Berlin, mining its diverse demographics for tension. The locations of Alvart's attempts at *Tatort* format adaptations have to do with funding, of course, but the two projects also tell us about the lasting importance of (trans)culturally signifying situatedness for network and Netflix crime dramas.

Dogs does a better job at delivering situatedness while adapting the weekly series concept into a season-spanning serial. Which *Tatort* fan would not want to watch a season of ten episodes with their favorite regional investigative team instead of the typical ninety-minute regional grab-bag on Sunday evenings, or having to assemble the team's episodes from daserste. de or from a DVD box set? To get a sustained look at the complicated police work, see how crimes unfold from the angles of all involved parties, even from characters typically relegated to the sidelines (following the standard set by

---

[4]Lars-Christian Daniels, *Filmstarts*, 2020, http://www.filmstarts.de/kritiken/273255/kritik.html (accessed December 30, 2020).
[5]"Tschiller: Off Duty July 8, 2018," *Wie war der Tatort*, https://www.wiewardertatort.de/2018/07/tatort-tschiller-off-duty.html (December 30, 2020).

HBO's acclaimed *The Wire*), and get continuous and rewarding insights into the partners' backstories, their personal lives, relationships, neighborhoods? Which sports and crime procedural fan wouldn't want to watch the hip-hop scored investigations of a murder revolving around German *Fußball* with a wide array of suspects that include feuding members of neo-Nazi, Croatian, and Lebanese mob families? A match made in Netflix: soccer, hip-hop, Nazis, and organized crime. In 1954, the world cup win against Eastern bloc Hungary was perceived as West Germany's symbolic reentry into the postwar league of nations. In 2006, hosting the world cup in the symbolic location of the ill-fated *Olympiastadion* in Berlin signaled that unified Germany had learned from its past and could be counted on to play by the rules of the global community. In 2018, with its world cup focus, and its loan on the iconic German crime drama *Tatort*, *Dogs of Berlin* becomes the second German show to premiere on Netflix, solidifying Germany as a key player in the global mediascape.

As his projects reveal and closer textual analysis of *Dogs* will show, Alvart is not only attuned to changes in the industry but also seeks to capitalize on the opportunities converging media provide. He clearly thinks deeply about the specificity of audiovisual language and the construction of meaning:

> The most important thing is that the camera tells the story, it's the language, the story is told with pictures, so it cannot be random. I hate shooting coverage. I've always used storyboards and I don't want coincidence to play any greater role than that, coincidence. The viewer must feel the director's stance as a narrator/storyteller. [6]

His story-bible approach and central vision as writer, showrunner, director, and producer are in line with the triumvirate at *Babylon Berlin*. But in *Dogs of Berlin*, unlike Tykwer and Co., Alvart is telling intimate stories from within and across several diverse population sets situated in the present historical world.

> In Berlin you sooner or later realize that this is not just a city, but actually many very different cities in one. (...) It has a massive impact on your life, whether you are born as Mahmud in Neukölln, Siegfried in Zehlendorf or Tom in Marzahn. (...) The city is basically another main character in this series. (Interview with Christian Alvart, *Deutsche Welle*, June 12, 2018)[7]

---

[6]Kingsley, "Christian Alvart Director's Portrait": "But then a second cop arrives, a Turkish-German. He's 'good for the politicians,' Alvart continues, 'gay and Left-liberal, so not your classic Turkish cliché!'"

[7]Stuart Braun, "*Dogs of Berlin*: Capital Crime Series Debuts on Netflix," *Deutsche Welle*, June 12, 2018, https://www.dw.com/en/dogs-of-berlin-capital-crime-series-debuts-on-netflix/a-46602494

Even though Alvart acknowledges the challenges of representing these micro climates of diversity within Berlin, his approach is to represent "very different cities in one" through the contrastive racial, sexual, and political pairing of his investigative team but specifically through the double life of his lead character, the East German cop, Kurt Grimmer. In addition, the self-confidence with which he claims to do justice to the recognized diversity as a German director, especially considering his focus on violence and action in narrative and cinematography, indicates continuity rather than departure from Bernd Schadewald's direction of the 1986 "Voll auf Hass" *Tatort* episode. That Netflix greenlighted Alvart's project further needs to be seen in the context of its cancelation of the successful hip-hop drama *Skylines* after one season. Produced by a team of diverse female directors (Maren Ade and Yoleen Yusef), *Skylines* can be seen as a counter-project to *Dogs*. Its cancelation raises the important question how the diversifying nation is representing itself and being represented on the global television stage at a time when a new generation of media-makers with migrant backgrounds has been emerging on domestic and global screens (e.g., Fatih Akin, *Head On*, 2004, *Soul Kitchen*, 2009, and Bora Dagtekin, *Turkish for Beginners*, 2006–8, and *Fack Ju Göthe*, 2013).

Deniz Göktürk criticized the "culturalist stereotyping and the limitations of assigned and assumed roles within frameworks of institutionalized diversity management" in regard to paternalist projects "fostered by public broadcasting institutions" in Germany. She joined Hamid Naficy in interjecting the complexities involved in what he termed "accented cinema" into the debate about "post-migrant emancipation from invisibility—or from regulated visibility."[8] Within the context of accented films, which emerge out of personal experiences of displacement, the return to dominance of white male German directors looking at and from the position of diasporic subjects laser-focused on what Göktürk bemoaned as "problem-laden social realism" is particularly concerning. Even more so because Alvart's straddling of different environments on the meta media level as well as his crossover visualization of multiple diverse communities play a major role in the microcosm of *Dogs of Berlin*. Alvart pits cultural, ethnic, racial, socioeconomic, political, and sexual differences against one another. And his show explores the lived realities and intersectionalities between identity positions. On top of this, the drama inserts itself directly into the aftermath of Angela Merkel's decision to take in half a million Syrian refugees in 2015/16. Like *Tatort*'s foundational social relevance edict, *Dogs*' contemporariness

---

[8] Deniz Göktürk, "Paternalism Revisited: Turkish German Traffic in Cinema," in *The German Cinema Book*, ed. Tim Bergfelder, Erica Carter, and Deniz Göktürk (London: Bloomsbury/BFI, 2020), 495–512, here 495. Hamid Naficy, *Accented Cinema: Exilic and Diasporic Filmmaking* (Princeton: Princeton University Press, 2001).

elicits a different affect and involves itself more directly in public discourse than *Dark* or *Perfume*. And for these reasons alone, its first (and perhaps only) season deserves a closer textual and formal analysis.

Reproducing the East as Homeland

As Alvart himself highlights earlier, Berlin becomes "a main character." Compared to *Dark* and *Perfume*, *Dogs of Berlin* makes an effort to situate the viewer in the city and in the home-turf of its lead, Kurt Grimmer. Shooting on location in and around Berlin, both the series' cinematography and editing actively establish and maintain the connection to Berlin's specific urban and suburban environments. Furthermore, the first episode is intent on facilitating and maintaining the viewer's geographic orientation for Kurt's and Bine's home district of *Marzahn*. The careful topographical contextualization of *Marzahn* in relation to central Berlin, which is paralleled by close encounters with socioeconomic realities in Bine's and Eva Grimmer's (Kathrin Sass) storylines, is not matched for the residents inhabiting the fictional district of *Kaiserwarte*, supposedly the majority Turkish area of Berlin. The *U-Bahn* sign of *Kaiserwarte* looks like the one for *Märkisches Museum* but the area is supposed to stand in for *Kreuzberg*, often referenced as *Klein-Istanbul* because in 2019 c. 170,000 of Berlin's 3.7 million residents were of Turkish descent. According to 2019 data, districts making up the former West Berlin have a higher concentration of residents with migration background, except for the villa suburb of *Zehlendorf*. In the former East, these percentages fall below 12 percent in three districts: *Marzahn*, *Pankow*, and *Treptow*.[9]

The series approaches *Marzahn* through a documentarian lens and insists on making it visually a part of Berlin. But instead of composing *Kreuzberg* the same way, Alvart fictionalizes it, thereby moving it onto an allegorical plane rather than keeping it on an indexical level as he does with *Marzahn* and *Mitte*. This construct removes *Kaiserwarte* from Berlin's culturally specific geography with the effect of dislocating its migrant community once more. Furthermore, the area dominated by the mobster Tarik-Amir and his family is first introduced to viewers as a "no-go zone." Because the phrasing reappears whenever anyone outside of the family approaches the compound, it has the effect of reducing all of *Kreuzberg/Kaiserwarte* to the clan's compound and thus to a racially defined area functioning outside of German democracy and laws, where any nonmembers, police and other

---

[9] Amt für Statistik, Berlin-Brandenburg, https://www.statistik-berlin-brandenburg.de/regionalstatistiken/r-gesamt_neu.asp?Ptyp=410&Sageb=12025&creg=BBB&anzwer=7 (accessed December 21, 2020).

Berlin residents, are target practice. This configuration raises the threat level of territorial domination of Germany's capital by Lebanese and Croatian mobsters while lowering the danger posed by the hefty neo-Nazi contingent in *Marzahn*, despite Erdem's body found in the latter, not the former.

In addition to switching reality modes, Alvart also employs different cinematography and editing patterns for *Kaiserwarte* in contrast to *Marzahn*. Reading key sequences will allow me to explore how the change in pattern essentializes the rootedness of homeland in white *Marzahn*, reproduces uprootedness for second- and third-generation immigrants, and appropriates a migratory discourse for the East German cop with a double life. The first scene of the first episode continues the high, wide camera angle and tracking shot from the title sequence. The smoke-filled daylight title sequence gives way to a clear night-time perspective onto a blue-lit apartment high rise, behind which the iconic silhouette of Berlin's television tower is still occupying the same spot as in the title sequence. Before the mobile camera transitions into one of the upper-level apartments, it has reestablished the individual area's spatial relationship to Berlin, assuring continuity despite the time shift. The shot symbolically connects the network-era transmission of radio and television to the subscription platform, as Kurt and Bine, his girlfriend, first have audible and then visible sex. They get interrupted by Bine's school-age son, who alerts them that the baby "stinks." Kurt gets up and changes the baby's diaper. He does this without either Bine or him frantically hiding under covers or pulling on pants in the process. Displaying nudity in the family, in front of kids, makes obvious from the beginning that this is neither a network nor a US show. As Kurt is trying to soothe the baby back to sleep afterward, he happens to look out of the window to see police lights a block away. His surveilling point of view assumes the television tower's role as it gives viewers a chance to identify the recognizable semicircular *Plattenbauten* and him to respond to a crime scene. Through his eyes, we are looking at the extensive apartment complexes of *Marzahn*, a working class and overwhelmingly white neighborhood on the Eastern outskirts of Berlin.[10] His towering gaze aligns with the television tower and the police's helicopter-cam from before.

After a cut, the *verité*-style camera tracks Kurt at eye-level from behind as he walks to the crime scene with his infant daughter in his arms, in slippers. He is not on call, but this is his neighborhood: "I live right over there on Bärensteinstraße." After flashing his badge, and so that he can inspect the crime scene, he deposits the baby not in the arms of the attending young policewoman but into the arms of her young male colleague with the *nomen est omen* old-fashioned surname Wachtmeister (master of the watch). These

---

[10] In March 1975, the GDR started its typical pre-fab construction on the complex. Currently, the district has close to 103,000 inhabitants living within its 14,000 square miles.

are the first ten minutes of *Dogs of Berlin* and establish Kurt as a handsome rogue with a tendency to be self-involved, yet with progressive instincts despite his machismo swagger. But this sequence also situates him on his home beat and has him assert his claim to a dual authority—as a resident "from here" and as the first LKA detective at the scene of a crime. The mobile camera connects the police-cam, the roaming tower-eye, and Kurt's eyelines. The combination of police and media power privileges Marzahn's access to the Real (over *Kaiserwarte*) and legitimizes Kurt's position—at home in Marzahn, at his job in Berlin.

Long before we encounter him with his "actual" family in a breakfast scene in an uncontextualized house (with his wife, Paula, and his two kids) at the end of the episode, viewers have linked Kurt to Bine and both of them to *Marzahn* and/as Berlin. We have also begun caring for both of their trajectories, made easy by his charm and con-man antics, and her struggle against the state's infamous bureaucracy. As Kurt finally drives up to his and Paula's stately suburban house, the scene is shot at eye-level and stitched together with editing conventions. The camera does not tilt up for a topographical establishing shot comparable to *Marzahn*, nor does it try to locate the area in Berlin proper in any other way, withholding that situatedness from globally dispersed audiences with a broad spectrum of knowledge about Berlin. The intentionality of locating the first home scene in Marzahn raises questions about the unspecified approach in the second home scene, especially since the Erdem, Seiler, and Laubach residences are each given a similar formulaic introduction (eye-level exterior long shot, medium shot, followed by interior long shot, medium shot, medium close-up). What should define "home" just says "house" instead is isolated from its surroundings and the city as such, and thus defies the definition of "home" that was so clearly established in *Marzahn*.

The position of the white urban working class seems essentialized as *Heimat*, whereas the middle-class life is captured as a façade held together by routines and conventions, including those of the televisual kind. The "Ikea breakfast table commercial" with Paula is inauthentic not only because viewers know about Bine and the kids but also because it is filmed as an imitation of life. Paula's glossy and well-calibrated demeanor suggests a class and gender-based performance of "faked" bourgeois normalcy that Kurt and Bine had previously demonstrated as a chaotic but exciting lived reality. With its construction of *Heimat* and authenticity mapped onto a district in the former East Berlin, *Dogs of Berlin* offers a realignment of the geopolitical center of national identity.

While the series approaches the lives of Bine and Eva through a social documentarian lens from the beginning, Paula's and Erol's attempts at belonging are brutally effaced. Only after violent crimes are committed against them are their personalities and lives "authenticated." The next section investigates parallels between gender-, sexuality-, and race-based storylines, and how these redefine violence as an authenticating factor.

Violent Crime as Authentication Factor

In tracing characters' trajectories during their "rough day" episodes, it becomes obvious that the script sets up the journeys of Bine and Paula, Paula and Erol, Eva Grimmer and Hakim Tarik-Amir (Sinan Farhangmehr), as parallels. How these parallels construct meaning in relation to gender-, race-, and sexually-coded violence is only revealed upon closer analysis. While each sequence encourages viewers to empathize with the victim of abuse, viewer sympathies are unevenly distributed due to meeting characters at different stages of familiarity as violence happens to or is committed by them. In contrast to having been granted access to Kurt and Bine's emotional lives, at this stage in the series, Paula is an unknown when we follow her to her upscale home-design shop. At this point, we have also only had brief glimpses of Erol. Paula, Bine, and Erol end up getting physically and emotionally hurt. Bine is harassed by the impersonated system of the state from above; Paula is attacked by an aggressive employee on parole from below (a Bine stand-in, if you will); and Erol is badly beaten by Grimmer's men to force him into compliance.

Let's begin with Bine. Bine is not a criminal. She gets in trouble with the state because of Kurt's gambling, her drug addiction, and the children. This is how the series wants the viewer to see her. The show represents her as a benign but neglectful parent, when she serves her kids cold Döner for breakfast and when she plays video games while working a sex-phone line to make extra money off the books. These vignettes of a social welfare recipient fill us in on the real-world problems of an unemployed single mother and weighs her actions against the state's omnipotence. The camera stays on her, highlighting the connections between class, food insecurity, and gender in a battle with an uncaring bureaucracy.

Bine's sequence involves her encountering one obstacle after another. She oversleeps because of her drug habit and drops off her oldest at the local elementary school. Her car runs out of gas, and we worry with her, if it is going to make it to the nearest gas station. After her late arrival at the social welfare office, a balling infant in tow, she is confronted with a line stretching the length of the hallway. Meanwhile, diaper-changing Kurt has regressed to an uninvolved 1950s working father. He side-swipes both Bine's and Paula's frantic phone calls. His character development relies on viewers' memory of his progressive side as scenes alternate between him running the special investigation unit and his sports racket, with which he hopes to pay off his creditors. He uses his insider information of Erdem's death and Bine's savings to bet on Turkey because Germany lost its key player.

When the social worker finally sees Bine, she cuts her and her kids off from financial support, because Bine missed the timed appointment and because she did not declare the extra income from her phone sex gig. Bine gets angry and calls the social worker names. The drawn-out social documentary mode stylizes her, the working-class white German, as a double victim: of misplaced trust and of the callous state bureaucracy. In the context of 2018, the show intentionally juxtaposes the state's refusal to support Bine and her kids with coming to the aid of non-white, majority Muslim migrants from Syria. The February 2022 Russian war on Ukraine has made the difference in public opinion between the four million white majority Christian East European refugees and their 6,37,000 Syrian counterparts since 2016 apparent. The Ukraine war proved that race and ethnicity, not economic reasons, were the root causes of the intolerance and anger leveled at Chancellor Merkel's decision to accommodate Syrian refugees. Viewers who are predisposed to blame Bine—or Kurt—for their misuse of state support instead see them as an example of the collapse of traditional family values amid the Western states' higher taxpayer burden after 1989. In either case, viewer investment in Bine's storyline pays off, when she rehabilitates herself in the second half of the season and gets a job as Paula's assistant. The same cannot be said for the second- and third-generation migrants Murad, Hakim, and Kareem, whose story-arcs move in the opposite direction.

Bine's case is denied by the state, embodied by a cold absolutist female bureaucrat, who purposefully drives her car into Bine in the parking lot. In her upscale Prenzlauer Berg shop, Paula also becomes the object of abuse. Because of money missing from the register, Paula gently fires her assistant. The young parolee first hits, then kicks, and finally urinates on Paula. As she does so, she yells: "I am not your social project so you can feel good about yourself." Instead of fighting back like Bine, Paula curls herself into a ball. After the attacker leaves, she neither calls the cops nor does she preserve the evidence of destruction and physical abuse. She cleans up and gets drunk. She reluctantly calls her mother-in-law, Eva Grimmer, to pick up her kids from school.

The mirrored scenarios imply that the state runs roughshod over citizens it is supposed to support, while those relying on support abuse the system and business owners who give them a chance. Since all positions in the triangulation are embodied by women, *Dogs'* gendered allegory reworks Bertolt Brecht's 1933 poem "Oh Deutschland, bleiche Mutter" ("pale mother"), an imagery that was expanded by the directors of New German Cinema in the 1970s. With its undertones of "nurturing/being nurtured," Alvart relies on the gendered allegory to signify not only that the social contract is broken but that the system as such is seen as "unnatural." As

Bine's and Paula's violent events drive this point home, we are introduced to Eva Grimmer.

The first encounter with neo-Nazi matriarch Eva Grimmer adds a third maternal model to this duo. Eva's and Bine's traveling sequences are cinematographically matched, whereas Paula's is shot in one location. This leads one to compare parenting styles. Who is the better maternal figure: the petit-bourgeois Nazi grandmother, the spunky down-on-her luck unemployed single mother, or the lifeless, drunk shop owner with a cheating gambler of a husband? Since things can't get much bleaker, the groundwork for Eva's attempt to unite the dysfunctional (national) family has been laid. The sequence, in which Eva picks up her grandchildren in Paula's stead, carves a believable ground-level path through Berlin as it shows the three in a car, driving to the zoo, the playground, and then driving back to Nazi headquarters in *Marzahn*. Eva feeds the two dinner and supervises their homework, when Paula finally arrives to pick them up. After the abusive events, Eva's grandmotherly actions appear refreshingly normal and safe. Yet when her granddaughter reads the information tablet about the ant colony, and her younger brother protests against climate change contributing to the demise of this ant species, Eva mixes in some eugenics: "Some species are supposed to die." At the zoo playground, this ideology turns into practice, when she insists that her grandchildren should be able to use the slide first because they are "German." Despite her granddaughter's own democratic protest—"we have a rotation system"—Eva plants herself in front of the slide and shoos away not just the immigrant kids but also their grandfather.

While her racist beliefs are made clear, Eva's harassment is recontextualized by the scene in which Erol is asked to head the taskforce on Erdem's murder. Erol reminds his boss that Hakim Tarik-Amir and he went to the same school together, and that Hakim would beat Erol up at the playground for insisting on his turn at the slide. The playground scenario we just witnessed reappears to equate Hakim's bullying with Eva Grimmer's racism. Erol's nose is freshly broken by Grimmer's disguised troops the previous night and Erol admits: "I am afraid." As this memory and admission serve the dual purpose of infantilizing and feminizing Erol, Hakim's aggression is connected to Eva's racist threats. Eva's threats at the zoo playground thus join the current street violence committed between neo-Nazis and (im) migrants as an extension of the strife between different ethnic groups, coded here as interspecies survival.

Both Erol and Paula emerge bruised after the harassing crimes against them. And Erol's admission of fear only further aligns him with Paula rather than with Hakim, Kurt, or Bine. At the same time, the black leather mask he sports after the attack exudes sadomasochistic references that serve to consistently remind viewers of Erol's submissiveness and portray him as "masked," as doubled. Erol's "real" face remains hidden, which works in direct contrast to Grimmer's intact victor's visage throughout the season.

And yet, Erol's mask and Paula's scars become authenticating factors for them in the remains of the season, embodying Göktürk's notion of "regulated visibility" for Erol, while associating his intersectional life with white bourgeois femininity in its being-looked-at-ness, and vice versa. Following Frantz Fanon's *Black Skin, White Masks* (1952), in which he made a case for the psychopathology resulting from living as a Black man in a dominant white culture, Erol's elevated social status, which includes his actor's popularity on television, confers upon him a whiteness that Alvart needs to erase in order to reproduce him as racially marked. The black mask accomplishes this by foregrounding Erol's racial identity while also sexualizing him through spectacle. The mask re-produces Erol as a double outsider based on his ethnicity and sexuality. Once Erol's feminized racial identity is reestablished in its theatrical performativity, it can prop up and further naturalize Kurt's white masculinity by comparison.

The playground settings and explicit connection between Paula's and Erol's "defacing" set up a false equivalency between the motivations for and effects of violence in five different inter-social contexts: Bine being denied welfare and run over by her social worker, Eva insisting on her family's white privilege at the playground, young Hakim and Erol fighting for access to the slide on the playground, Paula being beaten at her store (her playground), Erol being beaten by Grimmer's gang (in what they consider their playground). This false equivalency makes two labor disputes look like state-sponsored crimes against private citizens and compares fascist racism with peer-to-peer bullying and interethnic friction. The parallelism removes the inherent complexities of the criminal acts and redefines intentional ideological racism as primitive territorial and sexual domination. In the path of social regression, the new generations' democratic habitus is easily brushed aside, especially when the crime itself in its brutality is turned into an authenticating factor for characters that resisted easy readability due to their negotiations of class, gender, sex, and race intersectionalities. Paula is given her own complex development only after the attack has inscribed her body with violence. The face mask guarantees Erol's racial and sexual visibility. By contrast, Bine, Kurt, and the heterosexual aggressors retain their faces and face values, thus maintaining their originary signifying powers in racial, sexual, and semiotic terms. The next two sections probe how this approach translates into the different ways the camera captures and/or criminalizes characters in motion in the city of Berlin.

"Kaiserwarte": Surveilling Bodies in Motion

Unlike the detailed transition shots that introduce the audience to the Grimmers's *Marzahn* lives, the camera likes to approach the Tarik-Amir compound from a high angle before abruptly cutting to the inside. As a result, the different cinematographic choice sets up a dialectic between inside and outside, between surveillance by state powers versus undercover access to Tarik-Amir's family. There is no scene that transitions viewers from outside to inside, which has the effect of disconnecting the residence and its inhabitants from its immediate surroundings and the city. Scenes that take place within the Croatian and the Lebanese clans' compounds often use cell phone conversations as abrupt transitions between locales. The majority of scenes focusing on Tomo Kovac (Mišel Matičević), Kareem (Kais Setti), and Hakim Tarik-Amir happen in different locations throughout the city, restaurants, bars, clubs, and in cars moving from one place to the next. Hardly ever is one place recognizable from the last time we encountered the characters. Just as Murad's (Mohammed Issa) apartment becomes familiar to viewers and begins to resemble a home, the plot has Erol move him to a friend's house for safekeeping. These cinematographic and editing patterns have the effect of detaching the characters from their identification with recognizable neighborhoods of Berlin. The surveillance pattern criminalizes Tomo, Kareem, Hakim, and Murad, and the cinematography reproduces them as migrants. *Dogs of Berlin* thus seems to repeat the approach of the 2008 *Tatort* episode introducing Cenk Batu as the new undercover cop in Hamburg. Why *Dogs* reemploys this reproduction of dislocation and migration for Netflix ten years later requires a closer look at how lead characters intersect with and move between their environments.

The pattern of surveilling brown and black bodies is pervasive. The camera first introduces us to Erol Birkan during a surveillance operation. The bare-chested Erol is dancing while undercover in one of Berlin's many techno clubs. Instead of searching for Erol's mark, the audience is looking at Erol. There is no initial establishing shot of the place within the city. Erol's, Kareem's, and Hakim's moving bodies signify for the space. Their bodies' presence turns the club into a *Kaiserwarte* club. Both Kurt and Erol are introduced "in the buff," offering their bodies as spectacles. Yet in Erol's case, the interchangeability of a doubly Other(ed) body and space reproduces an Orientalist gaze. While Kurt's nakedness anchored him "at home," Erol's nakedness is public. Both introductory scenes revel in the characters' physicality. But while Kurt is having sex with his girlfriend, Erol is undercover, keeping tabs on a drug deal. From the very beginning, Erol has to navigate different perceptions, communications, and embodiments, while Kurt is able to immerse himself in his second life.

Despite being longtime Berlin residents, Erol's, Hakim's, Kareem's, and Murad's trajectories do not differ much from star player Bou'Penga (Tyron Ricketts), who hails from Leipzig and is in town for the final game. His hair is streaked black and white to symbolize the German national team's colors, but like Erol's black mask, it also implies his identity struggles as a man of color in a white world. He drifts around Berlin between hotel rooms, bars, often alone and in hiding, eyed suspiciously, alternately accosted and praised by fans. Striving upward, he asks to be taken to the club apartment. There, he finds out from a friend that Kovac bugged the entire place for surveillance, that he uses it to get damaging video on the players, which allows the team manager and Kovac to control their every move, including forcing them to throw a game. Instead of promoting upward social mobility, their soccer-playing bodies in motion are controlled by a systemic collusion between the German state and the East European mob.

That surveillance extends beyond criminalization to systemic racism is evidenced by an intense level of suspicion and scrutiny leveled at those experiencing and performing a lived intersectionality between race and nationality. This scrutiny led the successful soccer star Mesut Özil, the real-life model for Orkan Erdem, to resign from the German national team in 2018. Prompted by the backlash after posing for a picture with Turkish president and autocrat Recep Tayyip Erdogan and the subsequent early disqualification of the German team in the world cup, he tweeted that he was tired of "being a scapegoat (. . .) I am German when we win, but I am an immigrant when we lose. (. . .) I have two hearts, one German and one Turkish."[11] Considering this context for *Dogs*, Erdem and Bou'Penga bring to light the continued relevance of race for the reigning concept of nationality in contemporary Europe.

Soccer incites both regional and nationalistic fervor and behavior in viewers and fans, which is problematic in any European country but especially in the German case. Özil's statement points to the untenable combination of a race-based understanding of nationality with the diversity that makes up not just the national soccer team but also the country's demographics at large. The tribal concept of German nationality that is resuscitated by the soccer fan community, albeit at different levels of extremism, does not transmute well into the idea of citizenship, especially not dual or global citizenship. The third episode shows fans decorated in the German colors of black, red, gold make monkey noises and gestures, when Bou'Penga walks by. Working within this confrontational discourse, players with migrant backgrounds are under intense scrutiny for their perceived and visually marked hybridity—symbolized by Bou'Penga's striped hair—always already suspected of acting on their "migratory potential," which here also insinuates him throwing the game for Kovac. While the show explores this negative stereotype with Bou'Penga in a combination of social critique and exploitation, Kurt's crisscross vertical and horizontal movements are portrayed more leniently and humorously, notwithstanding his evident shortcomings.

---

[11] Merritt Kennedy, "German Star Player with Turkish Roots Says He Quit National Team over Racism," *NPR*, July 23, 2018, https://www.npr.org/2018/07/23/631483871/german-star-player-with-turkish-roots-says-he-quit-national-team-over-racism (accessed December 28, 2020).

The way cinematography, editing, and narration situate Kurt, Bine, Paula, and Eva in Berlin is thus decisively different from how the series approaches the Berlin of Erol, Murad, and Bou'Penga. The fictionalization of Kreuzberg into *Kaiserwarte* pools with surveillance and disparate mise-en-scènes to form a pattern that criminalizes their movements through Berlin while redefining their relationship to the city and Germany as a permanently transient one. Adding onto this the video surveillance scam at the manager's club apartment, getting to the economic and social top does not remove players from this precarious association but instead adds a further transactional layer onto "arrival" and "belonging."

Because of the pattern's avoidance to validate people of color's arrival in iconic spots in Berlin, the scene on the roof of the iconic Club Lido in the *Wrangelkiez* stands out. This long take features aspiring high school rapper Murad and Tarik-Amir's driver Raif (Samy Abdel Fattah) in a place, "where Berlin is still real," as Raif intones, "as long as the Russians don't grab everything and turn it into shitty Dubai" (S1:E4). The first time, a character with migrant background pronounces a sense of historical connection to the city of Berlin, this belonging is signaled through Othering (Russians, Saudis). He remarks how Berlin's chronic cash-flow problem has amped up the globalized Disneyfication of its cultural and sociohistorical ambience through profitable real estate investments. His throwaway comment also hints at the globalized continuation of the post-1989 real estate frenzy then led by West German investors (see my analysis of *Tatort*'s "Berlin Beste Lage" for comparison). These words connect Raif's and Murad's symbolic arrival with their functions as token spokespersons for German grievances.

While this suggests one reason for the break in the pattern of surveillance and disjointed motion in the rest of the show, there is more to the choice of location. The Lido is located directly across the Spree's *Oberbaumbrücke* from East Berlin's *Rudolfkiez* and the district *Friedrichshain*. Founded in 1951, the place was a movie theater before it became a German rock venue, popular with both the *Schönhauser Straße* teenagers made famous by the DEFA film of that era and West Berliner youths frequenting *Schlesische Straße*'s "cineaste alley."[12] East Berlin cinephiles would cross the border in the 1950s until the wall went up in 1961. Then as now, it functioned as a gathering spot, where global popular culture brought and still brings East and West together. Its entrance with the 1950s cursive signage has also become an Instagram favorite of club goers. In *Dogs*, the camera is intentionally tilting up across the sign to the Lido roof top. Under a fictional poster of Orkan Erdem, Turkish-German Murad and Lebanese-German Raif wax nostalgic for the "real Berlin" as they keep their own hip-hop dreams

---

[12] See Lido website, https://www.lido-berlin.de (accessed December 29, 2020).

alive. The national team uniform Orkan wears finds an echo in Murad's spontaneous German rap and Raif's nostalgia for a Berlin before his time.

The script functionalizes these younger characters, who have bridged their ethnic divides and become friends despite their families' misgivings, for its image of the "new Berlin," when it exhibits their local and national patriotism. One could argue that this is supposed to express hope for a future in which Berlin not only becomes a present home base but also stands for a unified past. But the Lido's storied existence as a cinema and meeting hub between East and West Berlin points in another direction. It mines Raif's and Murad's families' migrant backgrounds for their connections to the East-West migration occurring prior to 1961 and after 1989. It recasts the integration process as unification. Like Erdem towering above them, Murad and Raif are supposed to become poster children for successful integration based on overcoming what history proved to be an achievable end to division in 1989. The location thereby posits a sense of tribal belonging and appropriation of the East by the West as the solutions to hybrid diasporic lives. In the same moment that the Lido forges a link between films, rock, hip-hop, and global media, it also transforms the teenagers into legacies of Germany's division, thus projecting their friendship, artistic expression, and social integration onto the global screens as the new Berlin, the new Germany.

Outside of this roof scene at the Lido, only street-level surveillance captured by Erol's team traces Murad's and Raif's erratic paths through Berlin. Even handcuffing Murad to a bike rack does not root him in place. The next time Erol looks for him, Murad is gone. If not even a police officer and compatriot can tie Murad down, the scene suggests an essential "slippery uprooted-ness" that works against Murad's own and his sister's acculturation and integration efforts. Despite its duration and geopolitical contextualization, as a social media post, the Lido Instagram does its part to remobilize Murad on the global stage. His Berlin is supposed to speak for and to the new generation of diverse and globally dispersed viewers. Yet, unlike Cenk Batu's reproduction as a migrant to accentuate post-network television flow in the 2008 *Tatort* episode, Christian Alvart is more interested in recasting Kurt Grimmer, the East German former neo-Nazi, as the successful transmedia migrant in *Dogs of Berlin*. The reasons for this are the focus of the next section.

Transmedia Migration as White Male Privilege

Given the cinematographic pattern of approaching and locating intersectional identities in surveillance mode and substantiating them through physical violence, it is significant that Alvart turns Kurt into an interzonal, interregional, cross-platform maverick. Kurt moves nimbly between his two families, his Nazi background in the former East and his liberal, bourgeois civil servant existence in the former West. He is supposed to support the state as a cop but utilizes his position for corruption. First, Kurt keeps Erdem's murder a secret to make his bet on Turkey and then he reveals his death to the German team just before the game to counter the high level of confidence attributed to the team despite Erdem's absence. One minute, Kurt knows exactly what is happening at the police president's house, texting his superior, cue by cue, what he should ask for in support of the special task force. Then, the next minute, he personally breaks into the Nazi organization headquarters, all while managing to convince his brother Ulf to fund his gambling debts with the club's money. He shows up at his bookie's place just as his counterpart Furcht is conducting an examination into his murder. And he outsmarts the suspicious Furcht—"don't let him out of your sight"—by setting fire to the storeroom to cover his tracks (after ripping Bine's and his betting receipts out of a ledger).

And even though Kurt is supposed to organize the task force, while Erol is supposed to visit Erdem's grieving family, Kurt does this in his stead. He even chastises the Turkish patriarch for not properly supporting his son's decision to play for the German team, even though Kurt personally just undercut the team's chances for success. The consequences of his constant transgressive mobility are borne out by others, as his voice-over to the half-time episode (S1:E5) teases: "The city burns—all the violence, the hate. I would have never thought that I would bring this home, to my family, to you, Paula." But because he wears a protective cup like a soccer player, he even manages to escape relatively unscathed from the groin kicking he takes at the hand of his brother's fellow Nazis as punishment for stealing club funds.

Throughout the ten episodes, Kurt is able to maintain his double private and professional lives. The script, crime drama conventions, and the actor make viewers root for his character. Felix Kramer's portrayal of a rogue detective with sex appeal recalls 1980s blue-collar star-*Tatort* detective Horst Schimanski (Götz George) from Duisburg, who also on occasion agitated against the state's bureaucracy, when he felt it inept to right wrongs, remedy social inequities, or unsuited to his own personal goals. Yet unlike Schimanski's rebellion, Kurt's corruption is not the result of democratic or social-critical principles. Both his affair and his façade of bourgeois life seem to have grown out of and aim at satisfying his impulses while sustaining his needs. Yet, despite his obvious duplicity, Kurt is and remains part of and continues to have access to all his "families," including the blue and brown fraternities. Despite Eva's "we have to reevaluate what family means," Ulf stands by his brother. At her lowest point, when a drugged-up Bine complains, "you are more there than here" referring to Paula, Kurt sits her down and intones: "Don't ever tell me to leave Paula. She was there for me, when I was like you are now. I owe her everything."

Instead of underscoring Erol's multiple precarious and ongoing navigations between cultures, the show's narration and character development transform Kurt into the successful migrant by having him repeatedly transition between moral, professional, sexual, economic, as well as political boundaries. Because viewers have witnessed the reconstruction of homeland in the first episode, Kurt's border crossings are performed with visible effort. By comparison, Erol's and Murad's are coded as ingrained. As an economic refugee, Kurt left his *Heimat* of Marzahn to succeed in his job in the West. As a down on his luck East German addict and a neo-Nazi, social-liberal Paula from West Berlin reeducated him and moved him into middle-class respectability. But instead of being emasculated by these feminized domestication efforts, he retains his masculine virility and working-class roots through the affair with Bine, which also grants him reentry to his homeland. Having been born and raised in the East prior to unification puts a further spin on the two leads' different treatments. Portraying Kurt as a migratory figure showcases a particular German grievance going back to the loss of East Prussia and Silesia, amid the redrawing of the German and Polish borders during Allied occupation after 1945.

Kurt's inner-German migration is ensconced as a reminder that "the immediate postwar years were dominated by forced migration, homelessness in a destroyed country, poverty, hunger, life in between rubble and reconstruction, freezing, death, and grief."[13] In addition, as Melanie Schiller continues, "the millions of refugees who were at times violently excluded from the societies that had to become their new homes, the *Heimat* may indeed be the loss of the eastern territories, the home that had to be left behind."[14] Karl Berbuer's 1948 infamous *Trizonesien* Schlager turns this self-inherited postwar German experience into a feeling that captures the grievance over dislocation and occupation that, I would argue, needs to be seen as a precursor to Kurt Grimmer's post-1989 portrayal.

When France joined the Bizone in 1949, Germany became a Trizone. "We are the Natives of Trizonia" expresses the roiling emotions from the German perspective at that time. According to Melanie Schiller, the title immediately hails the singers as a tribal, a colonial community instead of as citizens of a democratic state. The continued and unironic use of "blood and soil" as the constructive national element "self-naturalizes" Germany. After extolling German cultural heritage by reciting its famous dead white men, the song ends with "That's why we are proud of our country." The patriotic fervor of this last line is especially problematic given that another line—"We are indeed no cannibals but we kiss so much better"—flippantly

---

[13] Melanie Schiller, *Soundtracking Germany: Popular Music and National identity* (London: Rowman and Littlefield, 2018), 47.
[14] Ibid.

denies the Holocaust and German wartime atrocities. The popularity of the *Schlager* signals that postwar German national identity formation did not significantly depart from its fascist foundation. As Schiller shows, in this example of a carnivalesque semi-parodical mode that contradicts its anthem-function at actual sports events at that time, expressions of and support for a German nationalism were actively renegotiated despite official de-Nazification and democratization attempts.[15]

Kurt's interzonal hopping in a united Berlin taps into this postwar sentiment and connects it to the more recent social, political, economic, and demographic transformations after 1989, best encapsulated by *Ostalgie*, the East's collective sense of losing an idealized community spirit, specific rituals, and a shared material culture between 1961 and 1989. The anti-occupation aspect of the immediate postwar years has found renewed energy in the impression of East German disenfranchisement after 1989. The echoes of this anti-occupation rhetoric have found further expression in the normalization of anti-Islamic agitation against what the right wing refers to as an "invasion." Both of these instances have begun to layer themselves over the streaming era's privileged cross-platform agility in the form of refusing to be subjugated to the dominant networks' ideologies (whether liberal or right wing) and their hierarchical linear and chronological structures.

With its intentionally differentiated cinematographic approaches to establishing and situating its characters depending on their ethnicities, and by pairing Kurt's German-German relocation with Erol's intersectional life, *Dogs of Berlin* overwrites Erol's cross-cultural negotiation with Kurt's German-German transmedia migration, thereby framing Germany's entrance onto dispersed global screens as the rebirth of a nation. To unpack this, I will analyze one final sequence from the second episode that features a montage of crowd scenes watching the world cup qualifier between Turkey and Germany on different screens in different places using different technologies.

The Illusion of Liveness: Watching Soccer with Neo-Nazis

Since *Dogs of Berlin* offers itself as an unofficial adaptation of *Tatort*, how it represents the singing of the national anthem signals how the national is performed, and what is marked and marketed as German on global television. For this it is helpful to turn to Benedict Anderson, who empathizes

---

[15]Ibid., 39–84.

the importance of simultaneity in the singing and performing of the national anthem:

> There is in this singing an experience of simultaneity. At precisely such moments, people wholly unknown to each other utter the same verses to the same melody. The image: Unisonance. [National anthems] provide occasions for unisonality, for the echoed physical realization of the imagined community.[16]

Anderson's emphasis on "people wholly unknown to each other" prompts me to translate this nation-building moment for the convergent era in two ways. Remembering that the unisonality in the show occurs within the context of a soccer match and not a political rally, it has the weight of an established and normalized ritual experienced by almost anyone on the planet at one point or another, whether live or mediated. On Netflix, unisonality hails domestic or diasporic German viewers specifically. But it also hails viewers through its patriotic gesture as such and even interpellates those merely accepting or reacting to its performative speech aspect. Because of the niche-based and time-shifted programming that defines online television, the unisonal anthem sequence delivers a rare moment for an "echoed physical realization of the imagined community," which produces the illusion of a shared time and space.

In her essay on the "concept of live television," Jane Feuer studied how the ideology of liveness is achieved and sustained in a medium consistently engaged with and in the overcoming of interruptions: "The live program is thus taken as the very definition of television. In this way, television, as an ideological apparatus positions the spectator into its 'imaginary' of presence and immediacy."[17] Despite its segmented fragmentation and viewers' cursory interaction with network television, she asks why "the idea of television as essentially a live medium persists so strongly as an ideology?" This is a particularly important question for the convergence era. If overcoming fragmentation via flow is part of its medium specificity, including the "extreme spatial fragmentarization" of local, national, and global points of origin and dissemination, then streaming television continues to structure itself around the ontology of what Feuer calls a "live" glance that "can create families, where none exist."[18]

Binge-watching a specific show, especially, can recreate an intensified viewer engagement that not only "presences" time-shifted content but also

---

[16]Benedict Anderson, *Imagined Communities: Reflections on the Origin and Spread of Nationalism* (London: Verso, 1991), 145.
[17]Jane Feuer, "The Concept of Live Television," in *Regarding Television*, ed. E. Ann Kaplan (Frederick, MD: University Publications of America, 1983), 12–21, here 14.
[18]Ibid., 18–20.

"shares" characters' inclusion in and abandonment of environments within and outside of the internal flow of segmentation of a show's narration system. As Zachary Snider has pointed out, "binge-watching is actually more of a communal experience" than generally suspected. On the one hand, binge-watching itself constructs and maintains communities through cross-platform integration and habitual communal watching, whether in the same place or remotely, sharing screens or chatting on Discord. But on the other hand, as he argues, it creates intense emotions and often requires mental gymnastics that effect both small and large communities during and post-binge in significant ways.[19] Placing Anderson's, Feuer's, and Snider's observations into a dialogue, the national anthem sequence in *Dogs of Berlin* is revelatory for the intersectionality of medium specificity with regional, national, and global discourses.

In this sequence from *Dogs*, viewers are watching other viewers in a complex triangulation of diegetic and extradiegetic eyeline matches. As the teams assemble for the cup-qualifying game on the field, the sequence alternates between diegetic audiences presented on integrated television screens, stadium jumbotrons, and other forms of projection screens, and *Dogs* characters in front of these screens. Kurt watches both live and via screen at the stadium. Ulf, Eva, and fellow neo-Nazis huddle in front of club headquarters and a projection screen. Hakim and Kareem watch from a sports bar. *Dogs of Berlin* here recreates network-era television's synchroneity within its narrative and cinematography. This long sequence seeks to bestow the power of a ritual crime drama like *Tatort* onto the convergence-era television experience by engaging the event-character of a decisive soccer match. Following sport television's formal conventions, the crime drama uses transmedia representation and multiple screen-in-screen projections. The result is that as the crime narrative is recoded, viewer positionalities are also realigned. The analytical stance recedes into the background and is substituted by reception habits rehearsed in watching live, competitive sports.

Abusing his official capacity as investigative lead, Kurt has just dropped his strategic bomb on the German team: Erdem was murdered. We witness the impact his words have on individual team members and see him in the hallway afterwards, in slow motion no less, walking toward the camera, grinning from ear to ear. Sports videography meets *Rocky* and *The Right Stuff* and thus code him victorious. His crime is transformed into a winning blow; the corrupt detective has become the contender. Since the public still assumes that Erdem is missing, a sport reporter's voice-over underscores the issue of "nervousness and lack of confidence" that "might cost the German

---

[19]Zachary Snider, "The Cognitive Psychological Effect of Binge-Watching," *The Netflix Effect*, 117–28, here 124.

team the victory over Turkey today." Even if the team threw the game, Kurt's action would be exonerated by this publicized assessment.

After a cut, the teams are somberly lined up, each man holding the hand of a young boy clad in the opposite team's color (no girls here). The camera tracks sideways along the row of boys at their eye-level. First it tracks to the right along the orange-clad row on the German side, then with a graphic match to the left along the white-clad row of boys on the Turkish side. The pattern repeats with the German adults filmed at a higher angle before reframing to watch both teams leave for the stadium.

At the moment the camera zeroes in on the soccer ball, the "live" feed switches to a projected image at the outdoor gathering in front of Ulf's Nazi headquarters. On that screen within a screen, the German team members can be seen walking hand in hand with the boys. This is the first image we see on that mediated screen, a shot that is followed by the engaged but seated *Kameradschaft Marzahn* contingent. Their position places them at the lower angle, adjoining the row of boys on screen. Instead of presenting the neo-Nazis through an overt nationalist iconography, the colors are subdued blues and grays. A white bull dog draws our eyes to the front, where Ulf and Eva sit on an orange pillow, matching the Turkish colors. Props consist of Ulf's *Springerstiefel* (army parachute boots), two visible scarves in the national colors, and two smaller flags in the background, one the traditional German flag, the other a partially visible black and gold flag with *Deutschland* lettering. Only one racist slur directed at the Turkish team speaks a clearer language: "Scheißkanaken." After presenting this community of viewers, the angle reverses, and the camera focuses on the projection screen but keeps the locale in the frame. The shot reveals a stadium row in medium close-up, where at least twenty depicted fans, women and men, wear black, red, and gold coloring with two individuals signaling their support for the Turkish team with orange paraphernalia. The camera pans first left, then switches direction as it loses the external diegetic framing and full-screens what the *Marzahn* group sees. To emphasize this reframing for the analysis: the only way to tell that we are watching on a different screen than our own is by the lower resolution of the image.

First, Grimmer's intervention symbolizes the inordinate amount of power wielded in the unholy combination of state authority and fandom, a white male policeman and fan in the target demographic, in particular. He makes his own rules, breaks boundaries, gets up close and personal, he influences and demands, plays to win. Second, the custom of entering the stadium with young soccer players presents an image of the national community projected into the future, assuring its continuity, as these young boys symbolically take the adults' place and, in turn, hold hands with a new set of aspiring national players. Of course, the custom is intended to tone down the heat of the moment and to remind teams and fans alike to behave as role models for the next generation. But the by-the-rule single-gender assembly also does its part to put a patriarchal stamp on the event and that imagined community, leaving women and girls on the sidelines—literally and figuratively. Furthermore, since we don't get a parallel close-up shot of the Turkish players (only of the German players), the orange-clad kids holding hands with the German players become the Turkish team's substitutes. This puts German men into the position of hosts and caretakers vis-à-vis the infantilized Turkish community, reviving the paternalistic *Gastarbeiter* (guest worker) label from the 1970s.

Third, as the screens switch back and forth between diegetic in-stadium viewers and those in other venues, there is a noticeably uptick in national emblems and colors in the mise-en-scènes. The effect of this escalation, especially in shots of the stadium-audience, is to normalize the Nazis. In contrast to the standing and obviously riled-up crowd in the stadium, the smaller group in *Marzahn* seems visibly less nationalistic and therefore appears less threatening.[20]

Fourth, as the first image screened to the *Marzahn* group, the mirroring of engaged viewership—in the stadium, in *Marzahn*, and within Netflix's viewership (overlapping fan circles of soccer or sports, Germany, crime dramas, etc.)—reconstitutes a simultaneity of engagement often proclaimed absent from post-network television. Inserting audience shots in front of various screens and alternating between stadium and "at home" audiences create the illusion of a dichotomy between diegetic and non-diegetic viewing, one deemed a more authentic experience than the other. Utilizing established identifications with particular viewing characters in some shots—but not in others—fuels this illusion further and makes the borders between what is part of the fictional and the historical world porous. Indeed, the sequence's construction of liveness comes about precisely through the commonality of watching others watching the same thing but is also a direct effect of the differences in screen resolution.

Fifth, connecting a frameless and crisp high-end all access experience behind the scenes and in the stadium proper with the same images in varying degrees of lower resolution, some extremely pixilated and lagging projected on small and large screens, accentuates live television in its cross-platform mode. Viewer comments underneath online *Dogs of Berlin* reviews tend to pan the low-resolution green screen soccer shots as the worst cinematographic element of the series.[21] I would argue, instead, that this in and of itself contributes to the post-network televisual aesthetics. Even if we

---

[20]The dominant black and blues even bleed into the final battle scene between Tarik-Amir and neo-Nazi forces in the season finale, merging them in the rainy, gray and foggy night-time scene. The battle in *Dogs* works with a similar color-palette as the muddy Viking/Teuton battle against the Saxons/Romans in History Channels' *Vikings* or the German Netflix show *Barbarians*, opening up a transmedia television portal into the "archaic and mythical" Germanic, indeed.
[21]Braun, "*Dogs of Berlin*."

liken the game shots to watching a 1990s-era screen-captured soccer version of *Madden*, these still imbue the sequence with more verisimilitude than an HD close-up aesthetics ever would. The pixilated *Marzahn* projection makes that screen our home screen. In the Zoom era of Covid-19, this is both a screen set up in someone's backyard and a Zoom screen someone is sharing with us, watching with us. Live, in the stadium, gazes are alternatively glued to the pixilated replays on the jumbotron or to second-screens on cell phones for particular close-up shots or for contributing or scanning social media feeds, all the while viewers watch the action unfold on the field below. Engaged live sports viewing is therefore already spread out across screens, already segmented (player profiles, half-time, fouls, corners, offsides, player exchanges, etc.), time-shifted, and binge-appropriated (number of replays while game is running). It is the perfect viewing mode to represent and capitalize on post-network viewing habits.

Let's resume the sequence, which now transitions into the singing of the national anthem.

The German team members stand side by side, arms over each other's shoulders. At medium close-up, the camera tracks right across a majority of white players and blond boys in front of them until it reaches the only dark-skinned player in the group, barely visible at the edge of the frame, upon which the scene cuts to a close-up on one little brown-haired boy as the words "Einigkeit und Recht und Freiheit" (unity, justice and freedom) appear in the subtitles. As he looks sideways, the camera captures one-shots of individual players in close-up as they mouth or sing the words of the anthem with differing states of concentration and emotion, this time including a Black player looking upward, who appears to be praying but ending with another white player staring directly at the camera. Importantly, the sung words of the German anthem are not only muffled and diffused but the sound-image pairing is completely off, especially during the close-up shots of individual players. Better lip readers than I might make out that some are singing different words or another verse altogether. This asynchronicity ends with an abrupt cut to the now standing *Kameradschaft Marzahn* crowd—with a young blond woman featured in the center—just as the chorus begins. But instead of following the approved third stanza's chorus of "Blühe, blühe deutsches Vaterland" (Flourish German Fatherland), they are performing the Nazi-era chorus of the *Deutschlandlied*'s first verse: "Deutschland, Deutschland über alles, über alles in der Welt" (Germany above all in the world). As they loudly and clearly, in unison, sing that chorus, the camera tracks to the right once again. As the first chorus ends, the camera pulls back to a shot of the crowd from behind with the projection screen now showing a gigantic waving German flag, then a Turkish flag. What could have been justification for a transition instead reframes the crowd from the front as they go through the repetition of the chorus with the same words but this time, the camera tilts up, bathing the scene in the bright light of the projector, before cutting to a close-up of a crying Bou'Penga singing the correct words: "für das deutsche Vaterland." With a cut to the title, the episode ends.

First, it is only through the subtitles that non-German-speaking Netflix viewers would be able to discern the different words sung in each shot. If viewers just listen to the audio, the words *Deutschland* and *Vaterland* would probably come across as familiar, words that appear in both versions, the official and the Nazi-era chorus. Judging by the faux pas committed at sports events around the globe, where musicians have, on occasion, sung the first or all three verses by mistake,[22] it is safe to assume that the majority of globally dispersed viewers would not be familiar with the convoluted and sordid history of the *Deutschlandlied*, and how the third stanza by itself ended up as the national anthem first of West Germany and then united Germany. The actual chorus of the third stanza does not even make an appearance. It is drowned out by the *Marzahn* Nazis. Whereas domestic viewers would recognize the intentionality of the cross-cutting between Nazis and players singing the different choruses, this slippage between the verses anchored by a few words commonly associated with Germany and its past signifies along contradictory lines on the global stage. For better or worse, it suggests a spatial continuity between stadium, world cup, and *Marzahn*, the national, global, and local, and a temporal continuity between the Third Reich and contemporary Germany.

Second, the audible and syncopated asynchronicity displayed during the third stanza in the stadium makes it impossible to sing along as an audience member. Not only national but also international unity is in peril. The anthem is broken into fragments that do not assemble to form a whole as we witness individual players struggling with words or mumbling along. The team seems unable to sing the chorus together in unison. All of a sudden, there is no team. It is precisely the unpaired sound/image in the stadium shots that is re-synchronized at the exact moment, when instead of the third stanza chorus, the *Marzahn* Nazis are singing the forbidden chorus—in unison, audibly, and clearly. Viewers can suddenly sing along. And the team is reborn.

Third, the cinematography does its part to support the sonic rebirth. Instead of cutting back to the stadium at this point, it is significant that viewers are treated to a repetition of the Nazi-era chorus, as if the first had not sent the appropriate message. The extreme nature of this moment cannot be undone by televisual polysemy. Not only do viewers have to endure the chorus a second time resulting in a normalization of the chorus on the global

---

[22] For example, Will Kimble sang the first verse at the 2017 tennis world cup in Hawaii. *The Guardian*, February 12, 2017, https://www.theguardian.com/sport/2017/feb/12/us-tennis-nazi-era-anthem-germany-fed-cup-match-deutschlandlied (accessed January 1, 2021).

stage, but the camera also approximates a Riefenstahl maneuver by tilting upward. The projector light illuminates the singing Nazis with an unearthly glow as their singing additionally endows the nationalistic pride with the aura of a prayer. Even making the crying Bou'Penga intone the last line of the third stanza cannot diversify or democratize the "deutsche Vaterland" that is sonically and visually reclaimed in the process. His recitation of the phrase 'für das deutsche Vaterland" echoes after the cut to the title, falsely suggesting an inclusivity that has just been visually and audibly refuted and denied.

Furthermore, all the tracking shots in the sequence, except for the one featuring the Turkish lineup, go left to right without forming a circle. The rightward track along the interlocked chain of German players and young boys is picked up by the rightward track of the camera along the *Marzahn* viewers, framing them in the same way, symbolically making them part of the national community. This is not the case for any of the men of color. While one is appearing on the fringe, barely noticeable before the cut, as if he were inserted as a token and his presence taken as a cue to reassemble a proper Germanness with the next cut, the two others are framed by themselves, symbolically remaining outside of the national team proper. Because the tracking pattern is systematized throughout the sequence, I am tempted to assert that the camera-eye is declaring a political position with these rightward tracks that materialize as a lineage of white and blond on both sides of the screens as we look on.[23] One might counter that showing two men of color visibly upset as they are pledging their allegiance to Germany reveals their unease and sends a message of fear and persecution, especially in the diegetic context of Erdem's murder. Granted, but this alone does not negate the complicity between camera-eye, editing, and sound design, which try very hard to arrive at a "physical realization of the imagined community," as Anderson suggests. Since the sequence does not include the Turkish anthem, not even in part, it does not extend the nation-building to Europe, a move that would at least balance out the chauvinism. Combined with the cinematographic and editing choices analyzed earlier, the unisonality is increased by the intentional choice to restrict the nation-building moment to Germany, actually performing the forbidden verse "Germany over everything in the world" by exclusion.

The scene focusing on Ulf's punishment for giving the Nazi club's treasure chest to his brother, Kurt, makes this even clearer. The members put the question to a vote: for or against Ulf's expulsion from the club. The floor opens to arguments for both sides. Then members vote by hand signal. Ulf is allowed to stay by a narrow margin. Of course, this revisits the

---

[23] See Jean-Luc Godard's famous long-take tracking shot in *Tout Va Bien* (1972), which connects the track of the camera with the cash registers' conveyor belts and political discourse.

"Hitler was voted into power" argument, but it also showcases the lengths to which Alvart and his team have gone to normalize the neo-Nazis in the series, to integrate them, like their official party organ, the AFD (*Alternative für Deutschland* Party), into post-unification German democracy. On one level, showing how the group utilizes democratic means to arrive at premodern punishments—the proverbial *Eierspeise* (egg salad)—also represents the dangers of fascism in its modern guise. Yet, as I have shown in this chapter, that takeaway is reduced by viewers' substantial libidinal investment in Eva's, Ulf's, and Kurt's storylines, as a family, as individuals, and by the affect generated by the concerted effort of screen technology, cinematography, editing, and scoring to deliver the illusion of live television and in turn produce community through synchronicity.

In addition, the narration of the first season is structured in reverse. Given what was established above for live sports television conventions and community-building, the entire season of *Dogs of Berlin* is shot like a sports match with replays and player commentary in voice-over (first by Erdem Orkan, then by Kurt Grimmer). Fighting crime becomes one line of offense or defense among others (corruption, surveillance, nationalism). Even the cinematography of the culminating street battle continues that pattern. It is shot as a *Vikings*-style hand-to-hand combat pitting neo-Nazis against Lebanese family members and filmed in rain-washed grayscale. The scene includes repeat shots from different angles in slow motion. Again, the cinematography and editing pattern are governed by televisual conventions established for live sports: switching between camera perspectives and foci, live versus replay modes, overhead versus sideline shots, slow motion and fast forward, extradiegetic commentary amid diegetic sounds. Narration, cinematography, and editing collude in stylizing the fight sequence in which brother fights against brother as a replay of the soccer match—as a tribal battle, a battle that is choreographed and scored to create a nationally coded summons across multiple platforms and transmedia engagement practices.

Applying Karen Barad's and Judith Butler's theories of performativity to materialist media theory, Grant Bollmer argues that

> the material attributes of technology manage to record certain aspects while neglecting others. Emphasizing inscription, along with other repetitive techniques that are mnemonic in effect, accentuates the centrality of technology in shaping the experience of history, culture, and time itself.[24]

A coordinated and reiterative effort between technology, cinematography, editing, *mise-en-scène*, character development, narration, and cross-platform

---

[24] Grant Bollmer, *Materialist Media Theory* (New York: Bloomsbury, 2019), 50.

reception inscribes a mnemonic path toward acceptance of resurgent German nationalism. With its differing representation patterns of Kurt Grimmer and Erol Birkan, multi-platform and transmedia mobility reemploys alterity as a path to reassemble hegemony. *Dogs of Berlin* inserts itself into and impacts a mediated process in which post-unification Germany pitches its grievances about lived and imagined diasporic conditions as well as (self) censored nationalism to the global stage. The Netflix series inscribed its German brand of populism into the media flow during Trump's "America first" doctrine that reevaluated and discarded international allegiances, and as the brittle concept of the nation-state was being revived by the Brexit model and autocrats attached to the European Union (Poland, Hungary, and Turkey).

Dogs of Berlin adapts the *Tatort* format with its regional focus on Berlin and local spotlights on its *Kieze*, its contrastive and diverse casting, its contemporaneous sociopolitical climate study to make material and circulate a cultural imaginary that trends conservative and seeks to reclaim the discourse of the national through Netflix's multinational catalogue's enfranchised egalitarianism. While the format's familiarity banks on crossover viewers' continuous, ritualized reception patterns of *Tatort* and similar network crime dramas in the domestic market, it is laying mnemonic paths conceptualizing the new Germany for a global community that has had little or no previous exposure to German television prior to 2016. And it should be concerning that instead of the long tradition of *Tatort*'s social critique and self-reflection, however didactic, misguided, or problematically polysemic, the world is made to watch and accept *Perfume* and *Dogs* as "German" television.

Conclusion

I ended the last chapter on a cautionary note because Netflix and other globally operating corporate media entities have contributed to a reset of contextual, publicly debated, and continuously revised approaches to regionally and nationally coded self-representations. As demonstrated, all of the major post-network German crime dramas interweave their narration, editing, and cinematography with historical contemplations in the form of period drama (*Babylon Berlin*), time travel (*Dark*), relational memory and nostalgia (*Perfume*), or the resurgence of nationalism (*Dogs of Berlin*). In *Babylon Berlin*, creators are toying with the "what-if" scenario as each season mounts substantial progressive energies against reactionary forces that, viewers know, will eventually prevail. In *Dark*, most palpably, Jonas/Adam sets out to prevent a climate apocalypse by traveling back and forth in time. *Perfume* and *Dogs of Berlin* both feature prominent and enigma-sustaining flashback narration. *Dogs* associates the final fight between immigrants and neo-Nazis with a televised soccer game through its nonlinear narration, while *Perfume* produces side-by-side live-action reproductions of scenes lifted from collectivized boarding school memories. By sliding these German crime dramas into the genre row next to US and other domestically produced original language crime dramas, Netflix publishes them as part of a series, a series that reissues the national as part of the global in complex and sometimes disturbing ways. The arrangement in a multinational series concurs and interacts differently with the television text as such, global and domestic mediascapes, and the existing and unfolding sociopolitical landscapes in each domestic context.

In the case of Germany, the arrival of German crime dramas on Netflix feeds into the genre's reputation as a domestic crisis monitor and continuity manager of postwar stability. While its convergence with Netflix signals normalization of what signifies as German, the German crime drama also screens its self-critical tradition of media-awareness on the platform. The shapes these intertwined processes take matter. It matters how the first generation of German crime dramas on Netflix construct meaning and how resultant representational approaches intersect with, underwrite, or resist existing concepts of regional and national identity formation. And while polysemy is multiplied by more complex storytelling modes, genre hybridity, and a penchant for postmodern medium reflexivity in nonlinear television, these are not per se new developments for the crime drama, as the analysis of nine *Tatort* episodes between 1970 and 2008 revealed. Each of the nine episodes explores existing and develops emerging aspects and combinations within the televisual wheelhouse of each era for different reasons. Since the ARD references *Tatort* as a *Heimatfilm* in some of its in-house publications, even the tendency to combine the crime format with period drama elements dates back to the network era. However, by taking this tendency to the global screen, *Babylon Berlin*, *Charité*, *Dark*, and *Perfume* normalize the drive toward reclaiming the German past as heritage. Instead of departing from this specific subsector that has its roots in the networks' *Fernsehfilm* tradition and in late 1980s German heritage cinema, Netflix has amplified this element of the German mediascape above others.

Whether continuities like these or departures from the network era are applauded or denied and why has repercussions for how television texts and the platforms they appear on deal with their own medium histories and vice versa. Thus, Netflix's reliance on the crime drama format and its stamp of global approval have deeper repercussions on the domestic side than the indication "that audiences still skew local in their tastes" or "that the global does not replace the local," as Ramon Lobato contends.[1] As shown, geographically dispersed, multi-platform viewing habits and crossover appeal in genre, narration, and aesthetics are important factors in this regard, but it is also crucial to investigate how and why Netflix as a technological platform and private venture reissues what is perceived as national and local to its global and domestic audiences, especially given that this localization, when it occurs, is based on post-2016 original language shows from Germany in contrast to the much broader representation of television classics from the English-speaking media world. The public German networks have had to work within carefully calibrated federal communication guidelines that were developed during the democratization of a young republic emerging from dictatorship. These guidelines included a high degree of public transparency and commitment to a broad palette of education and entertainment. In contrast to most public broadcasters in democratic countries, Netflix can cherry-pick and develop content without any agreed-upon and transparent educational commitment. Yet, the platform's packaging of a selective German-language catalogue gives the illusion that viewers can watch German television on Netflix.

Critical assessments at this juncture are crucial because the company has expressed no interest and has no stake in resourcing and disseminating representative cultural content. As one of the results, existing systemic inequities based on gender, race, and class are transported to the convergence

---

[1] Ramon Lobato, *Netflix Nations* (New York: New York University Press, 2019), 182–3.

era just as they are changing on the domestic level. The "Netflix effect" (Kevin McDonald) has led federal funding boards that were originally designed to sponsor new talent outside of established industry pipelines to allocate public monies to support domestic production companies that overwhelmingly still rely on established white male directors as showrunners rather than support underrepresented minorities from an increasingly diverse talent pool. That practice also exports and reimports a problematic understanding of what and who counts as German, both globally and locally. Since crime dramas "that made it to Netflix" have demonstrably been privileged when reimported to the home market, they have increased competition between global streaming platforms, terrestrial domestic networks, and non-terrestrial transnational European media, thereby also engaging non-Netflix content producers in budget conflicts, while compelling them to adjust production practices along with approaches to casting, genre format, aesthetics, and storytelling. Acknowledging the co-dependencies and by-products of the convergence era for what they are requires us to pay attention to these dynamics as they unfold on and through television as technological apparatus and as culturally inflected textuality. And the best way to do that is to broaden the knowledge of German television history and its rich textual archive beyond streamable content. This book has been an effort to add to that important cross-cultural scholarly enterprise.

Cultural specificity does include not just linguistic authenticity in the televisual Now but also the ways in which a country has imagined itself throughout media history, specifically how it has organized and formatted this imaginary. While watching Netflix's German television offerings as a way to connect to that media history does reveal some intriguing ways in which post-network strategies utilize cultural specificities, how these continue network and cable-era approaches to the crime drama cannot be assessed without diachronic research. The first part of this book was therefore dedicated to *Tatort*, the longest-running German crime drama produced by the first postwar public network, ARD, to show how its regional franchise concept adjusted to each mediascape change and often anticipated strategies to survive and thrive during the next one. Working through sample episodes of three regions from *Tatort* over the span of thirty-eight years and through three mediascape changes, I situated my analytical methodology within network television practices. The prime-time flow between national news, the crime drama, and critical viewer engagement garnered some insights into how concepts of the regional, national, and global co-constructed one another at specific intersections of time and place. I concluded that its stable placement in the network's lineup primed the regionally diversified *Tatort* creators and viewers to represent, perform, and read geopolitically across and between positionalities. Instead of using television as a mirror of a dominant and naturalized idea of socially perceived and enacted reality, the combination of program flow with the individual but format-driven and regionally inflected television text has consistently initiated medium reflexivity going back to the very first episode in 1970, even integrating its own and Berlin's entwined hyper-medial existences in more recent years. Throughout, *Tatort* rarely forgot that it was television, even verging on camp at times. And gauging by the extensive reception studies for this project, neither did its viewers. But viewers took geopolitical fights to the show, used it as a public debate forum to contest its fictionalization and representation of regional, national, and global issues, and in the process, they relocated themselves in the intersections between them.

Given the knowledge differential that prevails between the widely exported US television catalogue and the rest of the globe's media histories, and given that Netflix is becoming part of the continuous process of self-projections and their revisions, makers, producers, viewers, and readers need to inform themselves about the type of national imaginary that a company who stylizes itself as a global television network is circulating. As it stands, Netflix's library leads one to assume that only the Commonwealth and the United States possess significant television histories, whereas major television-producing parts of the world like Latin America, Europe, and Asia are represented "in perpetual infancy." In turn, this artificially constructed "birth" mints the shows as foundational members of a new national imaginary.

The danger in this ahistorical and lopsided representation lies in re-nationalizing a very limited output of post-2016 original language television shows or to consider them very binarily either as reformers *or* as loyal descendants from national network television. As we saw, showrunners like Tom Tykwer of *Babylon Berlin* are contributing to this mythmaking, even though they should know better. But frontier discourse sells, especially at an American company stylizing itself as the global frontrunner on the new media frontier. This book has shown that *Tatort* on German network television was not "one" but many and that the interchange between innovation and conservation embedded crucial strategies for resisting, contributing to, or just surviving technology, industry, and reception changes. My reading of the confluences that facilitated the post-network success of *Babylon Berlin* and *Dark, Perfume*, and *Dogs of Berlin* revealed how these lessons were applied or disregarded by degree.

How Netflix-vetted global approval co-constructs domestic television and how German/y sees itself and is seen on and through online television will have to be studied going forward. Beyond making a contribution to this topic, the broader aim of this book was to inspire English-language media studies to integrate more cross-cultural television research on over seventy years' worth of original language productions, to study them within their media environments, and consult the rich library of German-language television studies. If nothing else, the rise of disinformation and outright information wars committed against other nations but also involving domestic audiences stress the urgency and need for linguistically and historically competent cross-cultural media literacy and analysis. And the book issues an appeal to German studies to incorporate more critical media studies, to go beyond reading television's medium-specific aesthetics through film theory or reducing its cultural contributions to plotlines.

Since Covid-19, even hesitant moviemakers around the globe have realized that streaming serial television and film, including original language content, with nonlinear and transmedia storytelling elements, is transforming the mediascape they grew up in and in which they rose to the top. And that this change translates into competition and opportunity. In 2020, not Tom Tykwer but Maria Schrader won an Emmy for her direction of the limited Netflix series *Unorthodox*. At the 2022 Oscars, no German film or short made an appearance. After all, as Wanda Sykes said during her bit as cohost of the 2022 Oscars: "We celebrate the movies by watching the Oscars on television!" Since partnerships between streaming platforms, pan-European media conglomerates, and domestic networks, including their online affiliates, already exist, these could work together with federal funding boards to bring domestically produced back catalogues into global view in order to close the television knowledge gap. Further, they could increase their commitment to inclusivity by supporting a more diverse set of projects and makers. It's (a) prime time.

BIBLIOGRAPHY

References to primary sources such as television episodes as well as print and online newspaper articles, reviews, publicity materials, and blogs can be found in the text and in the footnotes.

Albrecht, Richard. "Literarische Unterhaltung als politische Aufklärung. Der neue deutsche Kriminalroman in der Bundesrepublik der 70er Jahre. Ein literaturgesellschaftlicher Nekrolog." *Recherches Germaniques* 14 (1984): 119–43.
Anderson, Benedict. *Imagined Communities: Reflections on the Origin and Spread of Nationalism*. London: Verso, 1983.
Asmus, Gesine. *Hinterhof, Keller und Mansarde 1901–1920*. Hamburg: Rowohlt, 1982.
Assmann, Aleida. *Shadows of Trauma: Memory and the Politics of Postwar Identity*. New York: Fordham University Press, 2015.
Assmann, Jan. *Das kulturelle Gedächtnis: Schrift, Erinnerung und politische Identität in frühen Hochkulturen*. München: C.H. Beck, 1992.
Banks, Jack. *Monopoly Television: MTV's Quest to Control the Music*. Boulder: Westview, 1996.
Baranauskas, Andrew J. and Kevin M. Drakulich. "Media Construction of Crime Revisited: Media Types, Consumer Contexts, and Frames of Crime and Justice." *Criminology* 56, no. 4 (2018): 679–714.
Barndt, Kerstin. "Memory Traces of an Abandoned Set of Futures." In *Ruins of Modernity*, edited by Julia Hell and Andreas Schönle, 271–93. Durham: Duke University Press, 2010.
Barra, Luca and Massimo Scaglioni, eds. *A European Television Fiction Renaissance*. London: Routledge, 2020.
Barthes, Roland. *A Lover's Discourse: Fragments* (1977). New York: Hill and Wang, 2010.
Beck, Klaus. *Medien und die soziale Konstruktion von Zeit*. Wiesbaden: Springer, 1994.
Beisch, Natalie, Wolfgang Koch and Carmen Schäfer. "ARD/ZDF-Onlinestudie 2019: Mediale Internetnutzung und Video-on-Demand gewinnen weiter an Bedeutung." *Mediaperspektiven* 9 (2019): 374–88. https://www.ard-zdf-onlinestudie.de/files/2019/0919_Beisch_Koch_Schaefer.pdf
Benjamin, Walter. *Das Kunstwerk im Zeitalter seiner technischen Reproduzierbarkeit* (1939). Frankfurt am Main: Suhrkamp, 1963.
Berle, Waltraud. "Tatort Bundesrepublik." *Vorwärts* 1 (1983): 28.
Bergfelder, Tim, et al., eds. *The German Cinema Book*, 2nd ed. London: BFI, 2020.
Bleicher, Joan Kristin. *Fernsehen als Mythos*. Opladen: Westdeutscher Verlag, 1999.

Boim, Svetlana. "Nostalgia and Its Discontents." *The Hedgehog Review* (Summer 2007). https://hedgehogreview.com/issues/the-uses-of-the-past/articles/nostalgia-and-its-discontents (accessed January 10, 2021).

Bollhöfer, Björn. *Geographien des Fernsehens: Der Kölner Tatort als mediale Verortung kultureller Praktiken.* Bielefeld: Transcript, 2007.

Bollmer, Grant. *Materialist Media Theory.* New York: Bloomsbury, 2019.

Brembilla, Paola and Ilaria A. De Pascalis, eds. *Reading Contemporary Serial Television Universes: A Narrative Ecosystem Framework.* New York: Routledge, 2018.

Brooker, Will. "Living on *Dawson's Creek*: Teen Vieers, Cultural Convergence, and Television Overflow." In *The Television Studies Reader*, edited by Robert C. Allen and Annette Hill, 569-80. London: Routledge, 2014.

Brück, Ingrid, Andrea Guder, Reinhold Viehoff and Karin When. "Krimigeschichte(n). Zur Entwicklung des deutschen Fernsehkrimis." In *Fernsehforschung in Deutschland. Themen - Akteure - Methoden*, edited by Walter Klingler, Gunnar Roters, Oliver Zöllner, 401-15. Baden-Baden: Nomos, 1998. .

Brück, Ingrid, et alii, eds. *Der deutsche Fernsehkrimi: Eine Programm- und Produktionsgeschichte von den Anfängen bis heute.* Stuttgart: Metzler, 2003.

Bruns, Axel, et alii, eds. *The Routledge Companion to Social Media and Politics.* New York: Routledge, 2016.

Butler, Jeremy. *Television: Visual Storytelling and Screen Culture.* New York: Routledge, 2018.

Caldwell, John T. "Second-Shift Media Aesthetics: Programming, Interactivity, and User Flows." In *New Media: Theories and Practices of Digitextuality*, edited by Anna Everett and John T. Caldwell, 127-44. New York: Routledge, 2003.

Calloway, Colin G., Gerd Gemünden, and Suzanne Zantop, eds. *Germans and Indians: Fantasies, Encounters, Projections.* Lincoln: University of Nebraska Press, 2002.

Campbell, Bruce, Alison Guenther-Pal, and Vibeke Rützou Petersen, eds. *Detectives, Dystopias, and PopLit.* New York: Camden House, 2014.

Carey, James W. "A Cultural Approach to Communication." In *Communication as Culture: Essays on Media and Society*, edited by James W. Carey, revised ed., 11-28. New York: Routledge, 2009.

Carter, Erica, Jan Palmowski, and Katrin Schreiter, eds. *German Division as Shared Experience.* New York: Berghahn, 2019.

Centerwall, Brandon S. "Television and Violence: The Scale of the Problem and Where to Go from Here." *JAMA* 267, no. 22 (1992): 3059-63.

Chalaby, Jean K. *Transnational Television Worldwide: Towards a New Media Order.* London: Tauris, 2005.

Cixous, Hélène. "The Laugh of the Medusa." trans. Keith and Paula Cohen, *Signs* 1, no. 4 (1976): 875-93.

Cornell, Alan. "Series, Location, and Change. National Reunification as Reflected in German Television Detective Series." In *Crime Scenes: Detective Narratives in European Culture since 1945*, edited by Eimer O'Beirne and Anna Mullen, 3-14. Amsterdam: Rodopi, 2000.

De Lauretis, Teresa and Stephen Heath, eds. *Cinematic Apparatus.* Milwaukee: University of Wisconsin/MacMillan, 1980.

Edwards, Emily D. *Metaphysical Media: The Occult Experience in Popular Culture*. Carbondale: Southern Illinois University Press, 2005.
Eichner, Susanne. "Crime Scene Germany. Regionalism, Audiences, and the German Public Broadcasting System." In *European Television Crime Drama and Beyond*, edited by Kim Toft Hansen, Steven Peacock, and Sue Turnbull, 173–92. London: Routledge, 2018.
Eichner, Susanne, Lothar Mikos, and Rainer Winter, eds. *Transnationale Serienkultur: Theorie, Aesthetik, Narration und Rezeption neuer Fernsehserien*. Wiesbaden: Springer, 2013.
Ellis, John. *Visible Fictions: Cinema, Television, Video* (1992). London: Routledge, 2000.
Elsaesser, Thomas. "Tales of Sound and Fury: Observations on the Family Melodrama." In *Imitations of Life: A Reader on Film and Television Melodrama*, edited by Marcia Landy, 68–92. Detroit: Wayne State University Press, 1991.
Elsaesser, Thomas. "New German Cinema and History: The Case of Alexander Kluge." In *The German Cinema Book*, edited by Tim Bergfelder, Erica Carter, Deniz Göktürk, and Claudia Sandberg, 408–17. London: BFI, 2020.
Elsler, Monika, ed. *Die Aneignung von Medienkultur*. Wiesbaden: VS Verlag, 2011.
Engel, Bernhard and Eva Holtmannspötter. "Studienreihe: Medien und ihr Publikum." *Media Perspektiven* 7–8 (2017): 388–407. https://www.ard-media.de/fileadmin/user_upload/media-perspektiven/pdf/2017/0708-2017_Engel_Ruehle.pdf
Erll, Astrid and Ann Rigney. *Mediation, Remediation, and the Dynamics of Cultural Memory*. Berlin: Walter de Gruyter, 2009.
Evans, Elizabeth. "Layering Engagement. The Temporal Dynamics of Transmedia Television." *Storyworlds: A Journal of Narrative Studies* 7, no. 2 (Winter 2015): 111–28.
Everett, Anna and John T. Caldwell, eds. *New Media: Theories and Practices of Digitextuality*. New York: Routledge, 2003.
Fassbinder, R. W. "The Third Generation (1978)." In *German Essays on Film*, edited by Richard W. McCormick and Alison Gunether-Pal, trans. Krishna Winston, 229–34. New York: Continuum, 2004.
Fehrenbach, Heide. *Cinema in Democratizing Germany: Reconstructing National Identity after Hitler*. Chapel Hill: University of North Carolina Press, 1995.
Feuer, Jane. *Seeing through the Eighties: Television and Reaganism*. Durham: Duke University, 1995.
Feuer, Jane. "The Concept of Live Television: Ontology as Ideology." In *Regarding Television: Critical Approaches*, edited by E. Ann Kaplan, 12–22. Frederick, MD: American University Publishers, 1983.
Feyerabend, Wolfgang. *Berliner Hinterhöfe*. Berlin: Thies Schröder, 2015.
Fisher, Jaimey. "Wandering in/to the Rubble-Film: Filmic Flânerie and the Exploded Panorama after 1945." *The German Quarterly* 78, no. 4 (Fall, 2005): 461–80.
Fiske, John. *Understanding Popular Culture*, 2nd ed., New York: Routledge, 2011.
Fuchs, Christian. *Social Media: A Critical Introduction*. London: Sage, 2017.
Gerbner, George. "Toward 'Cultural Indicators': The Analysis of Mass Mediated Public Message Systems." *AVCR* 17 (1969): 137–48.

Gerhards, Sascha. "*Krimi* Quo Vadis: Literary and Televised Trends in the German Crime Genre." In *Tatort Germany: The Curious Case of German-Language Crime Fiction*, edited by Lynn M. Kutch and Todd Herzog, 41–60. Rochester and New York: Camden House, 2014.

Gibbs, Martin, et alii. "#Funeral and Instagram: Death, Social Media, and Platform Vernacular." *Information, Communication & Society* 18, no. 3 (2015): 255–68.

Göbel-Stolz, Bärbel. "Once Upon a Crime: *Tatort*, Germany's Longest Running Police Procedural." In *German Television: Historical and Theoretical Perspective*, edited by Larson Powell and Robert Shandley, 193–214. New York: Berghahn, 2016.

Göktürk, Deniz. "Paternalism Revisited: Turkish German Traffic in Cinema." In *The German Cinema Book*, edited by Tim Bergfelder, et al., 2nd ed, 495–512. London: BFI, 2020.

Gräf, Dennis. *Tatort: Ein populäres Medium als kultureller Speicher*. Marburg: Schüren, 2010.

Hake, Sabine. *German National Cinema*. 2nd edn. New York: Routledge, 2008.

Hall, Katharina, ed. *Crime Fiction in Germany: Der Krimi*. Chicago: University of Wales Press, 2016.

Halle, Randall. "German Film: Transnational." In *The German Cinema Book*, edited by Tim Bergfelder, et alii, 2nd ed., 517–26. London: BFI, 2020.

Harzenetter, Wilma. *Der Held Schimanski in den Tatort-Folgen des WDR*. Alfeld: Coppi, 1996.

Hayles, N. Katherine. *Electronic Literature: New Horizons for the Literary*. Notre Dame: University of Notre Dame, 2008.

Hayles, N. Katherine. *My Mother was a Computer*. Chicago: University of Chicago Press, 2005.

Heiduschke, Sebastian. "Film Censorship, the East German *Nouvelle Vague*, and the "Rabbit Films": *Das Kaninchen bin ich* (*The Rabbit Is Me*, Kurt Maetzig, 1965)." In *East German Cinema: DEFA and Film History*, edited by Sebastian Heiduschke, 77–83. New York: Palgrave, 2013.

Hey, Richard. "Über das langsame Verfertigen von Mördern beim Beschreiben ihrer Opfer." In *Der moderne deutsche Kriminalroman*, Vol. 2, Stuttgart: Metzler, 1982, 110. Unpublished Lecture, Regensburg Seminar "Die deutschen Schriftsteller und die Spannung." October 8–10, 1976.

Hickethier, Knut. *Filmgenres: Kriminalfilm*. Stuttgart: Reclam, 2005.

Hickethier, Knut. *Geschichte des deutschen Fernsehens*. Stuttgart: J.B. Metzler, 1998.

Higson, Andrew. *English Heritage, English Cinema: Costume Drama since 1980*. Oxford: Oxford University Press, 2003.

Hoff, Peter. *Polizeiruf 110: Filme, Fakten, Fälle*. Berlin: Das neue Berlin, 2001.

Jarausch, Konrad and Michael Geyer. *Shattered Past: Reconstructing German Histories*. Princeton: Princeton University Press, 2003.

Jenkins, Chadwick. "Engaging Flow: On Ruttmann's *Berlin, The Symphony of a Great City*." *Popmatters*, November 30, 2018. https://www.popmatters.com/berlin-walter-ruttmann-2620911194.html?rebelltitem=1#rebelltitem1 (accessed December 20, 2020).

Jenkins, Henry. *Textual Poachers: Television Fans and Participatory Culture*. New York: Routledge, 1992.

Jenkins, Henry, et al. *Participatory Culture in a Networked Era*. Cambridge: Polity, 2015.
Jenkins, Henry, et al. *Spreadable Media: Creating Value and Meaning in a Networked World*. New York: New York University Press, 2013.
Jenkins, Henry. "The Work of Theory in the Age of Digital Transformation." In *A Companion to Film Theory*, edited by Toby Miller and Robert Stam, 234–61. New York: Blackwell, 1999.
Johnson, Catherine. *Online TV*. New York: Routledge, 2019.
Johnson, Derek. *From Networks to Netflix: A Guide to Changing Channels*. New York: Routledge, 2018.
Johnson, Derek. "Spin-Offs, Crossovers, and World-building 'Energies.'" In *Reading Contemporary Serial Television Universes: A Narrative Ecosystem Framework*, edited by Paola Brembilla and Ilaria A. De Pascalis, 74–92. New York: Routledge, 2018.
Kansteiner, Wulf. *In Pursuit of German Memory: History, Television, and Politics after Auschwitz*. Athens: University of Ohio Press, 2006.
Kittler, Friedrich. *Aufschreibesysteme 1800/1900*. München: Fink, 1985.
Klingler, Walter, et al., eds. *Fernsehforschung in Deutschland: Themen - Akteure - Methoden*. Baden-Baden: Nomos, 1999.
Kniesche, Thomas W. *Contemporary German Crime Fiction: A Companion*. Berlin: de Gruyter, 2019.
Koepnick, Lutz. "Reframing the Past: Heritage Cinema and Holocaust in the 1990s." *New German Critique* 87 (2002): 47–82.
Kopp, Kristin. *Germany's Wild East: Constructing Poland as Colonial Space*. Ann Arbor: University of Michigan Press, 2012.
Kramer, Thomas, ed. *Lexikon des deutschen Films*. Hamburg: Reclam, 1995.
Kumpf, Sarah. "Die Aneignung qualitativer US-Serien." In *Die Aneignung von Medienkultur*, edited by Monika Elsler, 25–34. Wiesbaden: VS Verlag, 2011.
Kutch, Lynn M. and Todd Herzog, eds. *Tatort Germany: The Curious Case of German-Language Crime Fiction*. New York: Camden House, 2014.
Landy, Marcia, ed. *Imitations of Life: A Reader on Film and Television Melodrama*. Detroit: Wayne State University Press, 1991.
Leiperdinger, Martin. "State Legislation, Censorship, and Funding." In *The German Cinema Book*, edited by Tim Bergfelder, et alii, 2nd ed., 315–26. London: BFI, 2020.
Lobato, Ramon. *Netflix Nations: The Geography of Digital Distribution*. New York: New York University Press, 2019.
Lotz, Amanda D. *The Television Will be Revolutionized*. 2nd edn. New York: NYU Press, 2014.
Maeder, Dominik. "Das serielle Subjekt. Eine Skizze zur Poetologie des Serial Dramas." In *Transnationale Serienkultur: Theorie, Aesthetik, Narration und Rezeption neuer Fernsehserien*, edited by Susanne Eichner, Lothar Mikos, and Rainer Winter, 87–102. Wiesbaden: Springer, 2013.
Manovich, Lev. *The Language of New Media*. Cambridge, MA: MIT Press, 2001.
Marks, Laura U. and Dana Poland. *The Skin of the Film*. Durham: Duke University, 2000.

Marx, Karl and Friedrich Engels. "Theorien über den Mehrwert." In *Das Kapital*, Vol. 4.1, Berlin: Dietz, 1985.

Mattson, Michelle. "*Tatort*: The Generation of Public Identity in a German Crime Series." *New German Critique* 78 (Fall 1999): 161–81.

MacDonald, Kevin and Daniel Smith-Rowsey, eds. *The Netflix Effect*. London: Bloomsbury, 2016.

McCormick, Richard W. and Alison Gunether-Pal, eds. *German Essays on Film*. New York: Continuum, 2004.

McLellan, Josie. *Love in the Time of Communism: Intimacy and Sexuality in the GDR*. Cambridge: Cambridge University Press, 2011.

Miller, Toby and Robert Stam, eds. *A Companion to Film Theory*. New York: Blackwell, 1999.

Mittell, Jason. "A Cultural Approach to Television Genre Theory." In *Thinking Outside the Box*, edited by Gary Edgerton and Brian Rose, 37–64. Lexington: University of Kentucky, 2005.

Mittell, Jason. "Narrative Complexity in Contemporary American Television." *The Velvet Light Trap* 58 (2006): 29–40.

Mittell, Jason. *Complex TV: The Poetics of Contemporary Television Storytelling*. New York: NYU Press, 2015.

Molsner, Michael. "Die Obszönität der Fakten. Möglichkeiten des deutschen Kriminalromans." *Kürbiskern* 4 (1978): 64–72.

Moltke, Johannes von. *No Place like Home: Locations of Heimat in German Cinema*. Berkeley: University of California Press, 1995.

Morley, David. "At Home with TV." In *Television after TV*, edited by Lynn Spigel and Jan Olsson, 303–23. Raleigh: Duke University Press, 2004.

Morley, David. *Family Television: Cultural Power and Domestic Leisure*. Reprint. London: Routledge, 2005.

Mously, Sara. *Heimat im Fernsehen*. Saarbrücken: VDM Verlag, 2007.

Mueller, Agnes, ed. *German Pop Culture: How "American" Is It?* Ann Arbor: University of Michigan Press, 2004.

Mulvey, Laura. "Visual Pleasure and Narrative Cinema." *Screen* 16, no. 3 (1975): 6–18.

Mummert, Ingo. "Der deutsche Sonntagskrimi: Warum die neue Fernsehserie "Tatort" so erfolgreich ist." *Konkret*, February 25, 1971.

Naficy, Hamid. *Accented Cinema: Exilic and Diasporic Filmmaking*. Princeton: Princeton University Press, 2001.

Nordenstreng, Kaarle and Tapio Varis. *Television Traffic – A One-Way Street? A Survey and Analysis of the International Flow of Television Programme Material*. Paris: UNESCO Reports and Papers on Mass Communication, 1974.

Parker, James. "The Meaning of *Slaughterhouse-Five*: 50 Years Later." *The Atlantic*, March 31, 2019. https://www.theatlantic.com/entertainment/archive/2019/03/why-slaughterhouse-five-resonates-50-years-later/586180/ (accessed November 13, 2020).

Penny, H. Glenn. *Kindred by Choice: German and American Indians since 1800*. Chapel Hill: University of North Carolina Press, 2015.

Peter, Jürgen. *Der Nürnberger Ärzteprozeß im Spiegel seiner Aufarbeitung anhand der drei Dokumentensammlungen von Alexander Mitscherlich und Fred Mielke*. Münster: LIT, 2014.

Poiger, Uta. *Jazz, Rock and Rebels: Cold War Politics and American Culture in a Divided Germany*. Los Angeles: University of California Press, 2000.

Powell, Larson and Robert Shandley, eds. *German Television: Historical and Theoretical Perspective*. New York: Berghahn, 2016.

Powrie, Phil. "On the Threshold between Past and Present: Alternative Heritage." In *British Cinema, Past and Present*, edited by Justine Ashby and Andrew Higson, 316–26. London: Routledge, 2000.

Pundt, Christian. *Mord beim NDR: Tatort mit Manfred Krug und Charles Brauer*. Münster: LIT, 2002.

Radewagen, Thomas. *Ein deutscher Fernsehbulle: Trimmel – der "Tatort"-Star und seine Mediengenese; eine vergleichende Untersuchung von Werremeiers Kriminal-Romanen und "Tatort"-Drehbüchern*. Berlin: Preprints zur Medienwissenschaft, 1985.

Rentschler, Eric. "The Place of Rubble in the *Trümmerfilm*." In *Ruins of Modernity*, edited by Julia Hell and Andreas Schönle, 418–38. Durham: Duke University Press, 2010.

Sandberg, Claudia. "*Das kleine Fernsehspiel*: Model of a TV Avant Garde." In *The German Cinema Book*, edited by Tim Bergfelder, et alii, 331–3, London: BFI, 2020.

Schiller, Melanie. *Soundtracking Germany: Popular Music and National Identity*. London: Rowman and Littlefield, 2018.

Schindler, Nina, ed. *Flimmerkiste*. Hildesheim: Gerstenberg, 1999.

Schreiter, Katrin. "The *Schrebergarten* as a Political Space in Postwar German Literature." In *German Division as Shared Experience*, edited by Erica Carter, et alii, 199–218. New York: Berghahn, 2019.

Schütz, Erhard, ed. *Zur Aktualität des Kriminalromans*. München: Fink, 1978.

Simmel, Georg. "Philosophie der Mode." *Moderne Zeitfragen* 11 (1905): 5–41.

Simon, Sunka. "Weimar Project(ion)s in Post-Unification Cinema." In *Berlin: The Symphony Continues*, edited by Anne Costabile-Heming, et alii, 301–20. Berlin: Walter de Gruyter, 2004.

Snider, Zachary. "The Cognitive Psychological Effect of Binge-Watching." In *The Netflix Effect*, edited by Kevin MacDonald and Daniel Smith-Rowsey, 117–28. London: Bloomsbury, 2016.

Spigel, Lynn. *Making Room for TV: Television and the Family Ideal in Postwar America*. Chicago: University of Chicago Press, 1992.

Spigel, Lynn and Jan Olsson, eds. *Television after TV*. Raleigh: Duke University Press, 2004.

Stiegler, Christian. "Invading Europe: Netflix's Expansion to the European Market and the Example of Germany." In *The Netflix Effect*, edited by Kevin MacDonald and Daniel Smith-Rowsey, 235–46. London: Bloomsbury, 2016.

Süss, Daniel. *Der Fernsehkrimi, sein Autor und der jugendliche Zuschauer*. Bern: Huber, 1994.

Tanner, Tony. *Adultery in the Novel*. Baltimore: Johns Hopkins University Press, 1979.

Taubin, Amy. *Taxi Driver*. London: BFI Film Classics, 2012.

Terkessidis, Mark. "Die Heimatflüsterer." *Tatort: Der Mord zum Sonntag, DU Kulturmedien* 779, no. 8 (2007).

Thomas, Tanja. *Deutschstunden: Zur Konstruktion nationaler Identität im Fernsehtalk*. Frankfurt: Campus, 2003.

Toft Hansen, Kim, Steven Peacock, and Sue Turnbull, eds. *European Television Crime Drama and Beyond*. London: Routledge, 2018.

Toft Hansen, Kim. "From Nordic Noir to Euro Noir." In *Nordic Noir, Adaptation, Appropriation*, edited by L. Badley, A. Nestingen, and J. Seppälä, 275–94. London: Palgrave Macmillan, 2020.

Torner, Evan. "The DEFA Indianerfilm as Artifact of Resistance." *Frames Cinema Journal* 4 (2013). http://framescinemajournal.com/article/the-defa-indianerfilm-as-artifact-of-resistance/ (accessed November 10, 2020).

Turnbull, Sue. *The TV Crime Drama*. Edinburgh: Edinburgh University Press, 2014.

Unger, Karl. "Kritisch-liberale Bullen am Tatort Gesellschaft," *Konkret*, February 1982: 34–7.

Vogt, Jochen, ed. *Medien Morde: Krimis intermedial*. München: Fink, 2005.

Wacker, Holger and Almut Oetjen, eds. *Tatort: Das grosse Buch für Fans*. Berlin: Schwarzkopf und Schwarzkopf, 2002.

Wenzel, Eike, ed. *Ermittlungen in Sachen Tatort*. Berlin: Bertz, 2000.

Williams, Raymond. *Television: Technology and Cultural Form*. London: Routledge, 1974.

Wolf, Fritz. "Die Tagesschau." In *Flimmerkiste*, edited by Nina Schindler, 52–3. Hildesheim: Gerstenberg, 1999.

Young, Robert C. *Colonial Desires: Hybridity in Theory, Culture and Race*. New York: Routledge, 1995.

INDEX

"99 Red Balloons" (song) 242, 243
2001: A Space Odyssey (1968) 61

ABC 81, 122, 167
Abel, Marco 86
Abendzeitung (Evening Paper) 67
Abraham, J. J. 221
Abu Ghraib torture and prison abuse scandal (2003) 116
accented cinema 288
action films 94, 96, 152
Ade, Maren 203, 288
Adenauer, Konrad 103–4
adultery 211, 212
aesthetics 5, 25, 40, 46, 55, 56, 81, 88, 89, 121, 122, 158, 162, 169, 178, 180, 184, 185, 193, 205, 214, 232, 257, 266, 313
"Age of Digital Transformation" (Jenkins) 277
Aimee und Jaguar (1999) 199
Akin, Fatih 33, 202, 288
Aktenzeichen XY Ungelöst (1968–2002) 186
Albrecht, Richard 16
Alfred Hitchcock Presents (1955–65) 133
Alice in the Cities (1974) 169
alienation 37, 117, 122, 137
Ali-Fear Eats the Soul (1974) 79
Aljinovic, Boris 115
allegory 157, 277, 278
Allgemeiner Deutscher Arbeiterverein (General German Worker's Association) 162
allotment gardens 98
Alternative für Deutschland (AFD) 71, 73, 129, 310

alternative heritage film 141
Alvart, Christian 24, 33, 188, 203, 283, 285–90, 293, 295, 299, 310
Amadeus (1984) 244
Amazon 2, 190, 195, 213, 261
"Am Brunnen vor dem Tore" ("At the Well before the City Gate," song) 172
AMC 1, 2, 23, 185, 187, 198, 249
American crime genre 75, 113
Americanization 95
Andersen, Gillian 264
Anderson, Benedict 38, 302–4, 309
anticommunism 61, 204
antifascism 111
anti-Islamic racism 68
anti-Jewish racism 68
anti-Semitism 38, 50, 173, 204
ARD 3, 5, 10, 17, 20, 23, 28–30, 32, 33, 35, 39, 42, 43, 46, 51, 64, 75, 88, 90, 94–6, 99, 103, 112, 115, 116, 117, 123, 124, 127, 132, 133, 135, 140, 150–3, 163, 165, 177, 183, 188, 191, 193, 194, 197, 199, 200, 209, 257–62, 313, 314
ARD Mediathek 10, 80, 163, 179
ARD/ZDF-Onlinestudie 191
Arndt, Stefan 201
Art Nouveau 263
Ärztekammer (Chamber of Physicians) 50, 52
Ärzteprozess (Medical Tribunal) 50
Arztroman (Doctor/Hospital Romance) 51
al-Assad, Hafiz 148
Assmann, Aleida 225
audial iconicity 32

audiovisual gap 128
audiovisual language 287
Auerbachskeller 172
Auf Achse (*On the Road*, 1977–86) 64
"Auf der Sonnenseite" (On the Sunny Side) 73–85
  critical and viewer engagement 75–8
  diaspora real(i)ties and imagined communities 81–5
  reproducing migrant as television trope (Batu episodes) 78–81
  Tagesschau synopsis 73–4
  Tatort synopsis 74–5
Austria 49, 50
authenticity 34, 35, 37, 72, 136, 155, 277, 291
avant-garde experiment 118
Avci, Ramazan 63

Baader, Andreas 61
Baader Meinhof Complex (2008) 194
Babylon Berlin (2017–) 6, 23, 183, 187–9, 191–9, 201–5, 207, 255, 277, 287, 312, 313, 315
Bachmann, Lutz 129
"Back in Time" (song) 241
Back to the Future (1984) 241
Bademsoy, Tayfun 63
Badgley, Penn 248
Barad, Karen 310
Baranauskas, Andrew J. 42
Barndt, Kerstin 277, 278
Baroque tragic drama 277, 278
Barrymore, Drew 221
Barschel, Uwe 71, 72
Barthes, Roland 84
Bates, Norman 246
"Baum der Erlösung" (Tree of Absolution) 39
Bavaria Film GMBH 194
Bayernkurier (Bavarian Courier) 67, 90, 92
Bayrischer Rundfunk (BR, Bavarian Broadcast Station) 29, 33
BBC 209, 248, 264

Becher, Bernd 278
Becher, Hilla 278
Becht, Friederike 263
Beck, Klaus 43
Becker, Jörg 262
Becker, Jurek 64
Becker, Meret 103
Becker, Wolfgang 86, 112, 127
Bierhallen Putsch (beerhall coup) 59
Beinersdorfer, Fred 16
Belitski, Natalia 263
Bella Block (1994–2018) 2, 17, 30
Benjamin, Walter 14, 146, 147, 276–8
Bents, Iris 78
Berben, Oliver 258
Berbuer, Karl 301
Berg, Rainer 105, 107
Berger, Edward 187, 203
Berger, John 108
Berlin 38, 86–9, 93–5, 97, 102–4, 106, 107, 109, 111, 112, 116, 136, 158, 180, 287–9, 291, 296, 298, 315
"Berlin, beste Lage" ("Berlin, Top Location,") 103–14
  Doppelgänger geography and aesthetics 106–11
  Tagesschau synopsis 103–4
  Tatort synopsis 105
  Topography of Terror as film noir 111–14
  viewer and critical engagement 105–6
Berlin Alexanderplatz (1931, film) 12
Berlin Alexanderplatz (1980, TV series) 193–8, 200, 203
Berlin Alexanderplatz (Döblin) 13, 23, 105
Berlin Berlin (2002–5) 112
Berliner Morgenpost (Berlin Morning Paper) 46, 67, 88, 105
Berliner Zeitung (Berlin Daily Paper) 78, 117
Berlin Mitte 112, 114
Berlin Republic 89, 115, 116, 118, 119, 121

INDEX

Berlin Republic 89
Berlin Wall 87, 111, 133
Besson, Benno 118
Bettin, Sabine 67
Betz, Malte 117
Beverly Hills 90210 (1990–2000) 153
Beyer, Frank 64
Biberkopf, Franz 13
Biedermann, Karl 112
Bild 61, 105, 117
Bild am Sonntag (Bild Sunday Paper) 77, 117
Bild und Funk (Bild Broadcast Guide) 54, 55, 92
Bild Zeitung (Bild Daily Paper) 61, 116
Black Mirror: Bandersnatch (2018) 200, 215
Black Skin, White Masks (1952) 295
Bleibtreu, Moritz 285
Bleicher, Joan K. 7
blockbusters 33, 238
blogosphere 179
Bloodline (2015–16) 208
Bochco, Steven 81
Bock, Ullrich von 58
body politic 142–4
Böhlich, Bernd 148–62
Bohm, Hark 63
Bohn, Ralph 114–26
Bohse, Sven 203
Boim, Svetlana 266, 278, 281
Böll, Heinrich 116
Bollhöfer, Björn 13, 34, 36, 59, 124
Bollmer, Grant 310
bombing raids (1945) 112
bo Odar, Baran 188, 203, 228
Borgmann, Sandra 207
Borne franchise (2002–) 238
Bornemann, Gerd-Roger 63
Born in '45 (Jahrgang '45, 1966) 158
Bosetzky, Horst 14, 15, 16
Böttcher, Wolfgang 158
Böttiger, Helmut 134, 135, 137
The Box 239
Brambach, Martin 128
brand recognition 31, 185

Brandt, Willy 43, 49, 50, 86, 114, 130, 131, 133, 134, 143, 147
Brauer, Charles 48, 79
BRD Trilogy (1978–81) 194, 210
Breakfast Club, The (1985) 241
Breaking Bad (2008–13) 23, 188, 198, 228, 249, 251
Breathless (1960) 158
Brecht, Bertolt 143, 145–6, 223, 293
Brender, Nikolaus 259
Brenner, Matthias 164
Bridgerton (2020–) 268
Brieden, Karin 260
British films 140
British heritage films 83, 221
broadcasting 20, 29, 93, 150, 169, 183, 260
Bröcker, Oliver 155
Brooker, Will 215
Bruch, Volker 199
Brück, Ingrid 16
Bumblebee (2018) 238
Bundeskriminalamt (BKA, German Federal Bureau of Investigation) 279
Bundschuh, Joseph 164
Bundy Tapes (2019) 248
Burma hurricane disaster 162
Butler, Jeremy 44
Butler, Judith 11, 58, 310

cable/satellite era 93–7, 116, 183, 186, 198, 260
cable/satellite networks 42, 96, 133, 189, 191, 192, 194
Caldwell, John 215
canonical literature 251
capitalism 53, 185, 204
Carey, James 43
Carpentier, Nico 40
Carrière, Mathieu 33
Carstens, Christiane 91
Caruso, David 81
Castorf, Frank 118
Caucasian Chalk Circle, The (Brecht) 143
Caucasus Conflict 74

CBS   5, 62, 77, 92
Cenk Batu   79
censorship   67, 118, 194
Chalaby, Jean K.   184, 186, 200
Channel 4   79
character(s)   31–5, 40, 51, 66, 72, 78, 81, 85, 209
  development   147, 185, 193, 301
  types   133, 169, 189, 270
Charité (2017–21)   187, 207, 313
Cheyenne Social Club, The (1970)   94
Chingachgook, die große Schlange (Chingachgook, the Great Snake, 1967)   155
Christian Democrats (CDU)   49, 74, 104, 120, 122, 143, 149, 162
Christiansen, Sabine   116–22, 124
Christian Social Union (CSU)   49, 74, 120, 122, 143, 149, 162
cinematic aesthetics   112, 147, 285
cinematic delay   127
cinematography   82, 83, 95, 102, 124, 152, 155, 180, 263, 267, 270–2, 276, 278, 282, 289, 290, 296, 298, 299, 302, 304, 306, 308–10, 312
Citizen of Glass (2016, album)   241
citizenship   250, 297
civil rights   71
Cixous, Hélène   246
class   49, 52, 80, 91, 96–103
Clinton, Bill   122
close-up shots   56, 69, 82, 96, 102, 126, 144, 145, 157, 172, 174, 192, 194, 305–8
Cold War   130, 148, 158, 177
collective memory   173
Collet-Serra, Jaume   86
Cologne   38
colonial identity   107
colonization   152, 157
Columbo (1968–2003)   133
Comedian Harmonists (1997)   199
communism   111
"The Concept of Live Television" (Feuer)   121
conservativism   79, 98

Constantin Film   185
Contergan (2007)   194
Continuum (2012–15)   221
convergence era   78–81, 89, 185, 230
  technologies   192
  television   80, 205, 304
Cooper, James Fenimore   129, 155
coproduction   30, 185, 190, 194, 198, 261
  international   192
  transmedia   197
  transnational   193, 197
Cornell, Alan   29
Couldry, Nick   123
Counterpart (2017–18)   144, 185, 202, 227
Covid-19 pandemic   36, 46, 128, 307, 316
Cranston, Bryan   23, 249
Crawford, Cindy   232, 233
crime dramas   8, 9, 12, 17, 27–30, 32, 33, 42, 43, 47, 48, 54, 62, 76–9, 81, 93, 103, 115, 121, 123, 124, 126, 131, 138, 141, 147, 148, 161–3, 176–80, 183, 184, 186, 188, 191, 203–5, 208, 216, 253, 258, 286, 312, 314
crime fiction   17, 56
crime genre   27, 35, 184, 186, 214
Criminal Germany/UK/Spain (2018–)   6, 185, 200, 201
criminal organ trade   52
cross-channel surfing   96
cross-culture   22, 40, 69, 79, 188, 205, 251, 315, 316
cross-cut montage   167
cross-fertilization model   195
crossover effect   193
crossover episode   30, 133, 137, 140, 178
cross-platform engagement   4, 5, 176, 189, 214, 215, 218, 221, 236
CSI (2000–15)   5, 62, 77
CSI SVU (1999–)   186
culture
  appropriation   21, 200, 201
  authenticity   200–2
  convergence   277

identity 250
imperialism 28
memories 112, 114, 173, 277, 279
responsibility 151
specificity 3, 152, 158, 183, 186, 205, 230, 235, 238, 251, 253, 257, 314
Cut Off (*Abgeschnitten*, 2018) 285
CW 209
Cyrano de Bergerac (1897) 170

Dagtekin, Bora 288
Daily Show, The (1996–) 227
Dallas (1978–91) 172
Danae (1907–8) 263
Danes, Claire 202
Dark (2017–20) 2, 6, 8, 23, 24, 183, 185, 187–91, 195, 203–56, 277, 289, 312, 313, 315
   bunker/children's room 220–30
   Falco's "Jeanny" 244–9
   material popular culture 230–6
   popular music 239–44
   recharging German canon 250–2
   recombinant by design 236–9
   synopsis 206–7
   time-shifting as post-network formal and narrative device 213–20
   transmedia families 207–12
   transmedia television 239–44
Das Boot (1981) 194
Das Erste (*Deutsche Fernsehen*) 28, 191
Das Kaninchen bin ich (The rabbit/ guinea pig is me, 1965) 118
Das kleine Fernsehspiel 194
Das kunstseidene Mädchen (The Artificial Silk Girl, 1932) 13
Das Mädchen Rosemarie (The Girl Rosemarie, 1958) 210
data-gathering and mining 55
Dawson's Creek (1998–2003) 200, 215
de Burg, Chris 82
decoding process 125, 186
decolonization 85

DEFA studio 64, 118, 127, 154, 155, 159, 298
de-industrialization 129, 149
de Lauretis, Teresa 239
democratization 51, 79, 227, 302, 313
Demos, Moira 208
Der Alte (The Old Guy, 1977–) 30, 261
Der Dicke/Die Kanzlei (Fatso/The Office, 2005–12) 17
Der junge Törless (Young Törless, 1966) 203
Der Kommissar (The Inspector, 1969–76) 17, 30, 133, 261
Der Landarzt (The Country Doctor, 1987–) 51
Der letzte Mann (The Last Laugh, 1924) 147, 185
Der Rattenfänger von Hameln (*The Pied Piper*, Thirteenth Century) 252–3
Derrick (1974–98) 2, 17, 30, 93, 261, 262
Derrida, Jacques 45, 207
Der schwarze Kanal (1960–89) 227
Der Spiegel 18, 78
Der Student von Prag (The Student of Prague, 1913) 147
Der Tagesspiegel (Daily Mirror) 116, 117
Der Untergang (Downfall, 2004)
Der verdammte Krieg (That damned War, 1991–5) 260
"Der verlassene Raum" (1988, Biedermann) 112
Deutsche Arbeiterfront (DAF, German Workers' Front) 71
Deutscher Fernsehpreis (2019) 263
Deutscher Fernsehfunk (DFF) 17, 21, 133, 227
Deutsche Welle 287
Deutschland, Bleiche Mutter (1945) 280
Deutschland schafft sich ab (Sarrazin) 34
Deutschland sequels (2015–21) 1, 128, 185, 187, 199, 203, 207

Deutschmann, Heikko 115
"Deutsch" search engine 189
Dexter (2006–13) 248
Die Ehe der Maria Braun (Marriage of Maria Braun, 1978) 172
diegesis 176, 192, 207, 212, 227, 228, 237, 241, 273, 275, 282
Diehl, August 264
Die Linke (Party of the Socialist Left) 162
Die Rheinpfalz 93
Die Schwarzwaldklinik (Black Forest Clinic, 1985–9) 51
Die Sünderin (The Sinner, 1951) 210
Die Tagesschau (Daily Evening News, TV program) 42, 43
die tageszeitung (The Daily Paper, Berlin) 105, 106
Die Toten Hosen (The Dead Pants, band) 64
Die Welt (The World, weekly paper) 54, 92, 105
Die Zeit (Time, weekly paper) 43, 255
digital hypertextual storytelling 218
digital media 47, 62
digital reproduction 255
digital revolution 183, 260
digital technologies 255
Disney Plus 2, 10
Djavid, Cino 283
Döblin, Alfred 13, 105, 193, 197
docudramas 198–200
docudrama series 198
Dogs of Berlin (2018–) 6, 8, 24, 33, 73, 183, 187, 188, 191, 203, 283–312, 315
   illusion of liveness 302–11
   Kaiserwarte 295–9
   reproducing East as homeland 289–92
   synopsis and narration 283–4
   transmedia migration as white male privilege 299–302
   unofficial *Tatort* adaptation 285–9
   violent crime as authentication factor 292–5

Dölle, Robert 75
domestic politics 162
domestic racism 104
domestic sexual abuse 279
domestic television 17, 189, 198, 315
domestic tourism 36, 38
domestic violence 279
"Don't You Forget about Me" (song) 241
Doppelgänger 58, 105–11, 144, 214, 230–1
Dornen, Jamie 248
Dörrie, Doris 13, 108
Doublemint gum 231
Drache, Heinz 91–3
Drakulich, Kevin M. 42
Dresden 128–30, 153–5, 158
Dr. Who (2005–) 209
dubbed versions 192, 201
Duisburg Mosque 75
"Duisburg: Ruhrort" 75
Duken, Ken 263
Dutschke, Rudi 61
DVR 80, 170
Dwyer, Alice 75

Eastern Europe 129
East German films 155
East Germans 21, 87, 135, 136, 139, 141, 142, 149, 156, 159
East German television 140, 142
East Germany 89, 90, 104, 111, 129, 135, 138, 142, 148, 158, 173, 175, 180
East-West treaty 50
Economic Liberal Party (FDP) 74, 162
editing 95, 124, 180, 192, 214, 239, 263, 267, 270, 272, 274, 276, 278, 282, 289, 290, 296, 298, 309, 310, 312
Edwards, Emily 10
Efron, Zac 248
Eichhorn, Karoline 207
Eichinger, Bernd 24
Eichner, Susanne 19, 21, 78, 83
Einbrodt, Günther 57

INDEX 331

"Eine ehrliche Haut" ("An Honest
   Skin/Man")   114–26
   blue and tan tones   119–23
   critical and viewer
      engagement   116–17
   post-1989 reorientation   117–19
   Tatort synopsis   115–16
   watching television in Istanbul
      Grill   123–6
Ellis, John   11, 28, 39, 80
Elsaesser, Thomas   14, 15, 17, 53,
   200, 229
Emigholz, Erich   105
Emil und die Detektive (1931)   13
Emma   101
employment   149, 151
Engels, Friedrich   136
entertainment ecosystem   190
episodic linearity   93–7, 103
Erinnerungskultur (culture of
   remembrance)   205
Erll, Astrid   226
Esche, Matthias   66
ethical guidance system   60
ethnic cleansing   70, 104, 115
ethnicity   11, 32, 49, 84, 105, 121,
   124, 293, 295, 302
ethnographic approach   155
Europe   28, 47, 189
European cinema   202
European colonialism   99
European-Netflix coproduction   184
European Parliament   190
European television   190, 202
Evans, Elizabeth   213, 272, 276
experimentation   32, 177, 220–30

Faber, Heike   63
Facebook   228, 238
Fack Ju Göthe (2013)   288
Falco   241, 244–9
Falco 3 (1985, album)   245
Fall, The (2013–16)   248, 264
fan culture   178
Fanon, Frantz   295
fan practice   125, 216
fantasy   72, 153, 155, 156, 159, 217
Färberböck, Max   199

Fargo   268–71
Fargo (2014–)   270
Farhangmehr, Sinan   292
fascism   53, 59, 106, 204, 224, 227
Fassbinder, R. W.   23, 79, 105, 169,
   172, 193, 197, 198, 200, 203,
   210, 281
Fattah, Samy Abdel   298
Faust (Der Tragödie erster Teil,
   Goethe)   252–6
Faust (Goethe)   172, 252–6
FAZ   67, 116
federalism   29, 62
Federal Republic of Germany
   (FRG)   30, 49, 50, 63, 74, 90,
   107, 134, 137, 149, 227
Fehlleistungen (performed
   failures)   210
Fehrenbach, Heide   210
femininity   60, 119, 153, 295
Fernseh-Dienst (TV Today)   134
Fernsehfilm (television film)   2, 94,
   151, 185, 192, 193, 197–201,
   203, 313
*Fernsehpreis für die Verständigung
   mit Ausländern* (Television
   prize for interethnic
   communication)   65
Fernsehrat (Television Board)   259
Fernsehturm (TV tower)   126, 284
Fernsehwoche (Weekly TV Guide)   66
Fest, Joachim   224
Feuer, Jane   41, 121, 303, 304
fictional crime show   117, 121
Film Funding Act (1967)   194
film market   194, 195
film noir   111–14, 180
fire-bombing (1945)   128
First World War   229
Fischer, Joschka   122
Fisher, Jaimey   158
Fiske, John   13
Flock of Seagull, A (band)   240
folklore   251, 252
folk song   173
Following, The (2013–15)   186
Fontane, Theodor   107
Foreman, Milos   244

INDEX

format structure   29–31, 39, 44, 47, 96, 178, 266
Forst, Willy   210
Foucault, Michel   239
Fox   153, 221
Frankfurter Allgemeine Zeitung (FAZ)   67, 77, 78, 116
Frankfurter Rundschau (FR)   132, 135, 164
Frauenkirche   128
Free German Youth organization (FDJ)   140
free market revolution   99
freeze-frame   146
Freiheitlich Direktdemokratische Volkspartei (FDDV, Liberal Direct Democratic People's Party)   129
Freiwillige Selbstkontrolle der Filmwirtschaft (FSK)   194
Fremantle Media International   187
Fremde (foreign and foreign land)   172
French Connection, The (1971)   160
Friedel, Christian   264
Friedkin, William   160
Friedler, Eric   78
Fries, Liv Lisa   199, 202
Friese, Jantje   188, 203, 228
Fringe (2008–13)   221
Fritzl, Elisabeth   225
Fuller, Samuel   33
funding   195, 197, 202
Funk-Korrespondenz (Broadcast Journal)   65, 78
Funkuhr (Radio and TV Guide)   55
Funk und Fernsehen (Radio and Television Journal)   105
Fußball (Soccer)   287
Futuresource   190
FX   270

Game of Thrones (2011–19)   33, 192, 198, 202
gangster genre   95
garden colony   97–103
garden plots   97–8
Gardinen (translucent window treatments)   102
gaze   24, 45, 80, 89, 100, 102, 103, 274, 279
gender   24, 35, 38, 60, 61, 84, 96–103, 257, 268
    dynamics   260
    equality/inequality   90, 101
    fluidity   62
    norms   176
    performance   58, 68
    presentation   58, 62
Generation War (2013)   199, 266
genocide   115, 143, 157, 177, 205, 225
genre   51, 94
    characteristics   123
    diversification   96
    driven television structure   95
    narratives   96
Genscher, Hans-Dietrich   89
geopolitics   8, 38, 62, 144–8, 150, 183, 184, 190
George, Götz   33, 64, 92, 300
Gerbner, George   7
Gerhards, Sascha   78
German *Catholic Day*   162
German cinema   17, 33, 147, 185, 187, 192, 193, 203, 210
German culture   14, 17, 28, 179, 251
German democracy   70, 71, 90
GDR   134, 154, 157, 158, 161, 165, 175, 178, 227, 258
German Democratic Republic (GDR)   29, 30, 43, 49, 50, 64, 90, 97, 104, 107, 129, 130, 132, 134–7, 142, 145, 146, 150, 151, 154, 155, 156–158, 161, 162, 164, 165, 175, 178, 199, 227, 258
German dramas   187, 188
German fascism   166
German-German border   103, 148
German history   173, 177, 205
German literature   6, 172, 253, 254
German Motion Picture Fund (GMPF)   195
Germanness   120, 137

INDEX

German Sixth Army 260
German society 57, 84, 85
German television 1, 3, 4, 6, 27, 30, 43, 107, 135, 140–2, 145, 183, 184, 187, 192, 196, 202, 203, 205, 230, 249, 251, 256, 257, 260, 314, 315
Germany 3, 27, 28, 33, 34, 36, 43, 47, 60–3, 68, 70, 71, 89, 97, 102, 104, 108, 121, 129–31, 141, 143, 150, 151, 155, 162, 163, 168, 171, 180, 183, 184, 187, 189, 191, 192, 195–7, 201, 203, 204, 224–6, 244, 249, 250, 260, 265, 279, 287, 293, 308, 309, 313
  divided 89, 141, 143, 177
  unification (*Vereinigung*) 87, 89, 112, 114, 116, 122, 127, 130, 134, 149, 151, 152, 156, 157, 169, 173, 175
Geschonneck, Matti 103–14
Gestalt 278
Getaway, The (1972) 160
Gewaltschutzgesetz (violence protection law) 279
Gilligan, Vince 228
Giordano, Mario 174
Glatzeder, Winfried 151
global capitalism 111, 235
globalization 83, 185, 197, 230, 235, 249, 266
Globe Studio 122
glocalization 235
Godard, Jean-Luc 158
Goebbels, Joseph 171
Goethe, Johann Wolfgang von 172, 252, 254, 255
Goffman, Erving 42
Gökgöl, Demir 74
Göktürk, Deniz 288, 295
Goma refugee camp 148
Good, the Bad, and the Ugly, The (1966) 153
Good Bye, Lenin! (2003) 112, 127, 184, 227, 235
Görtz, Franz Josef 78
Go Trabi Go (1991) 127

Graf, Dominik 33
Gray, Linda 172
Gröschel, Cornelia 128
Grundversorgungsauftrag (Basic Service Mandate) 194
Guess Who's Coming to Dinner? (1967) 76
Gümer, Yalcin 83
Gumpert, Ulrich 105
Gute Zeiten, Schlechte Zeiten (Good Times, Bad Times, 1992–) 17
Gutzeit, Jimmy 263

Haase, Jella 128
Habermas, Jürgen 46, 124, 224
Hackerville (2018) 202, 203
Hafenkrankenhaus (Harbor Hospital, 1968) 51
Hagedorn, Erwin 164, 165
Hagen, Nina 243
Hake, Sabine 200
Hall, Michael C. 248
Hall, Stuart 7, 9, 21
Halle, Randall 194
Hallwachs, Hans-Peter 134
Hamburg 38, 43, 58–60, 78
Hamburger Abendblatt (Hamburg Evening Paper) 55
Hamburger University Hospital 54
Hanczewski, Karin 128
Handloegten, Hendrik 203
Handlungsraum (action space) 82
Hannibal (2013–15) 248
Hannoversche Allgemeine Zeitung (Hannover General Paper) 106
Hansen, Rolf 50
Härtsch, Diethard 65
Hauptstadtstudio Unter den Linden 258
Hausschild, Joachim 92, 93
Haußmann, Leander 127
Hayles, N. Katherine 229
HBO 33, 62, 184, 198, 202, 208, 238, 287
HDTV 125
Head-On (Gegen die Wand, 2004) 33, 202, 288

Heath, Stephen 239
Heim, Uta-Maria 88
Heimat (home and homeland) 14, 38, 51, 61, 76, 172, 179, 192, 291, 301
Heimat: Eine deutsche Chronik (1984) 198
Heimatfilme 75, 80, 191, 313
Heinzelmännchen 258
Heinze, Doris J. 78
Heissenbüttel, Helmut 12, 14
heist films 152
Heller, E. 93
Hellig, Th. 92
Hellinger, Bert 175
Henckel von Donnersmarck, Florian 86
Herbert, Ulrich 266
Herbie, the Love Bug (1968) 239
heritage cinemas 83, 84, 140, 141, 221, 313
heritage dramas 197, 199, 204
Herres, Volker 260
Herwartz-Emden, Leonie 171
Herzog, Roman 149
Hess, Annette 203
Hessischer Rundfunk (HR) 29
hetero masculinity 79, 282
heterosexuality 79, 281
Heute (Evening News) 259
Hey, Richard 16
Heyer, Luisa 210
Hickethier, Knut 17, 27, 28, 105
Hieber, Jochen 164
high-angle shots 69, 95, 126, 284
high-contrast low-key lighting 112
Higson, Andrew 83, 84, 140, 221
Hillgruber, Andreas 224
Hill Street Blues (1981–7) 81, 94
hip-hop 247, 287
Hirsch, Marianne 265, 266
Hirschbiegel, Oliver 33, 185
historical pornography 261, 281
Historikerstreit (German historians' debate) 224, 226
Hitchcock, Alfred 96
Hitler: Eine Bilanz (Hitler: A Reckoning, 1995) 261

Hitler, Adolf 53, 59, 173, 185, 200, 239, 260, 261
Hitler series (Knopp) 281
Hockenheim Ring (German Grand Prix car race) 149
Höfels, Alwara 128
Hofer, Jens 162
Hoffmann, Michael 171
Hofmann, Louis 206
Holland, Agnieszka 202
Hollywood 86, 152, 159, 187, 202
Hollywood Reporter, The 199, 201
Holocaust 10, 14, 15, 50, 59, 111, 113–15, 131, 177, 224–6, 229, 250, 302
Holocaust (1978/9) 198, 209
home entertainment consumption 190
Homeland (Season 5, 2015) 86, 202, 238
Homicide: Life on the Streets (1993–9) 186
homosexuality 156, 165, 166
Honecker, Erich 104, 130
horror 52, 54, 96–103
Hörzu (Weekly Radio and TV Guide) 78, 92
Hosemann, Marc 264
Hotel Adlon (2013) 209
House of Cards (2013–18) 192
How to Sell Drugs Online (Fast) (2019–20) 22, 185–7, 192, 255
Hoyerswerder (Saxony) migrants 114
Hübchen, Henry 151
Huber, Richard 73–85, 82
Huey Lewis and the News (band) 241
Hulk, Sebastian 210
Hulu 213
humanity, crimes against 50, 104, 110, 226, 229, 294, 295
human trafficking (*Mädchenhandel*) 151, 157
Hungary 89
Hungary-East German border 93
hybrid genre approach 169, 189, 211
hybridity 60, 84, 85, 96, 121, 178, 312

hypermediation 116, 118, 123, 166, 179

"Ich bin ein Berliner" speech (1963) 86, 131
identity 48. *See also specific entries*
　formation 38, 42, 43, 52, 130, 155
　morphing 85
　regional 89
image-text relationship 192
imagined community 38, 81–5, 179, 303, 306, 309
imagined identity 156
"immersive secondary world" 155
immigration policies 129
import theory 156, 157
Independent, The 187
In der Strafkolonie (*In the Penal Colony*, Kafka) 252
Indianerfilme 107, 129, 152, 155–60
indigenous people 152
inner-German conflict 111
innovation 31, 32, 86, 176, 194, 197, 214, 219, 315
Instagram 238
interactive television experiment 215
inter-medial integration 152–7, 162
intermediation 229, 230
internal segmentation 32, 45, 96, 123, 126, 227, 262, 265, 267, 270, 276, 304
international cinema 33, 184
international tourism 37, 179
Intershops 139–40
intertextual associative mode 42
intertextual resonances 178, 184, 241, 254
intertextual segmentation 41
In the Penal Colony (Kafka) 228
iPod 240
"I Ran (So Far Away)" (song) 240
"Irgendwie, irgendwo, irgendwann (Somehow, Somewhere, Sometime, song)" 241, 242
Islamophobia 72, 177
Israeli Olympians 50, 52
Issa, Mohammed 296

Istanbul Grill 122–6
Italian Spaghetti Westerns 107
Italo-Westerns 130

Jack (2014) 203
Jackson, Michael 247, 249
Jahn, Moritz 206
Jarausch, Konrad 16
"Jeanny" (song) 241, 244–9
Jelinkova, Lenka 151
Jenkins, Henry 46, 47, 208, 215, 247, 277
Jenninger, Phillip 224
Jerks (2017–) 286
Jett, Joan 243
"Jetzt und Alles" ("Now and Everything," 1994) 148–62
　inter-medial integration 152–7
　mobility at standstill 158–62
　post-1989 media integration 150–1
　Tagesschau synopsis 148–50
　Tatort synopsis 151–2
Jews 67, 68, 114, 173
Johnson, Catherine 9
Johnson, Derek 31
Jordan, Peter 74
journalism 116
Jugend Forscht 163
Jugendstil art 263
jus sanguinis 68, 205
Jutzi, Phil 12

Kadelbach, Philip 199, 258, 261, 264, 266, 280
Kafka, Franz 228, 252
Kaiser, Andrea 76, 77
Kamml, Sigi 283
Kansteiner, Wulf 4, 260
Karl May Museum 129
Kayacik, Aykut 74
Kaymakci, Mehmet 63
"Keine Tricks, Herr Bülow" ("No Tricks," Mr. Bülow) 89–103
　broadcasting "*Tatort* Average" 93–7
　critical and viewer engagement 91–3

horror of gender and class 97–103
Tagesschau synopsis 89–91
Tatort synopsis 91
Kekilli, Sibel 33, 35, 202
Keller/Kaninchenfilme (basement/
  rabbit films) 118
Kellermeier, Jürgen 151
Kelly, Gene 94
Kennedy, John F. 86, 131
Kepler, Johannes 168
Keun, Irmgard 13
KfW Verwaltungsrat (Board of
  Supervisory Directors) 73
Kino International 118
Kinski, Nastassja 33, 133, 202
Kirchlechner, Dieter 91, 93
Kirkegaard, Sarah 258
Kistenmacher, Gert 132
Klaus, Wilfried 30
Klimt, Gustav 263
Klosterhalfen, Herbert 54, 55
Kluth, Jörn 92
Knauer, Sebastian 62, 65
Knight, Travis 238
Knizka, Roman 174
Knopp, Guido 260, 261, 281
Koch, Sebastian 202
Kocka, Jürgen 224
Koepnik, Lutz 221
Kohl, Helmut 89, 90, 104, 153
Köln 38
Kölnische Rundschau (Cologne Daily
  Paper) 65, 67, 106
Konkret 132
Kopp, Kristin 107
Kozloff, Sarah 31
Kracauer, Siegfried 112
Kramer, Felix 283, 286, 300
Kramer, Stanley 76
Kreator (band) 241
Kriewitz, Günther 132
Krimis (Crime Fiction) 12, 14–16, 56, 197, 205, 286
Kristallnacht (Night of Broken
  Glass) 63, 67, 113, 224
Krössner, Renate 151
Krug, Manfred 33, 35, 48, 64, 67, 79, 178

Krüger, Karen 77, 78
Krumm, Paul Albert 134
Kubrick, Stanley 61
Ku'damm (2016–21) 199, 203, 207, 209
Kühne, Frau 166
Kurtulus, Mehmet 35, 48, 74, 76–8, 83
Küster, Renate 112
Kutscher, Volker 197, 205

Lacan, Jacques 144, 224
Laclau, Ernesto 40
Lade, Bernd Michael 127
Lady Gaga 247
"Lady in Red" (song) 82
Lamprecht, Gerhard 13, 113
Lamprecht, Günther 91, 105
Lang, Fritz 12, 16, 57, 86, 100, 102, 147
Langer, Martin 82
Laubenpieper (plot gardener) 98
Law and Order (1990–2010, 2022–) 185, 233
"law of genre" 207
Lazarescu, Anca Miruna 202
Leatherstocking novels 155
Lebanon 163
Lehman Brothers 74
Leiperdinger, Martin 194
Leipzig 38, 130, 139, 162–5, 169, 172, 176
Leipziger Volkszeitung (Leipzig
  Newspaper) 106
Leitkultur concept 34, 250
Leitkulturträger 34
Leone, Sergio 153
Lewis, Damien 202
liberalization 195
Liebling Kreuzberg (Darling
  Kreuzberg, 1985–98) 64
Liebrentz, Daan Lennard 206
Liefers, Jan Josef 178
Lilyhammer (2012–) 184
limited fictional series 197–201
Linden, Thomas 106
Lindenstraße (1985–2020) 17
Lindner, Sandra 159

INDEX

linearity 82, 93–7, 213, 278
Little Nightmares (2017 video game) 236
Lives of Others, The (Das Leben der Anderen, 2007) 127, 184, 194
live sports television 310
live television 87, 121, 122, 303, 306
Lobato, Ramon 8, 184, 188, 313
Löfgren, Ovar 42
Lola (1981) 169
long shots 81, 102, 107, 145, 161, 168, 243, 275, 291
Lorre, Peter 99
Lost Honor of Katharina Blum (Die verlorene Ehre der Katharina Blum, 1975, film) 116
Lost Honor of Katharina Blum (Die verlorene Ehre der Katharina Blum, Böll, book) 116
Lotz, Amanda 213
Lover's Discourse, A (Barthes) 84
low-angle shots 136, 154, 158, 284
Lübecker Nachrichten (Lübeck Daily Paper) 133
Luckow, Alexander 92
Lüke, Reinhard 78
Lusher, Adam 187
Lynch, David 62

M (1931) 16, 57, 100, 102, 147, 185
McCain, John 74
McCann, Madeleine 163
Maccarone, Angelina 33
McDonald, Kevin 314
Mack, Max 12
McLuhan, Marshall 81
Mad Men (2007–15) 198, 199
Madonna 247
Maeder, Dominik 11
Maetzig, Kurt 118
Magdeburger Volksstimme (Magdeburg People's Voice, Paper) 106
Mainzelmännchen 258
Making a Murderer (2015–18) 186, 208
Making Room for TV (1992) 7
Mandelorian, The (2021) 2

Mannheimer Morgen (Mannheim Morning Paper) 93
Mannkopff, Andreas 91
Mark, Laura U. 173
Marlon, Joshua 210
Marriage of Maria Braun, The (1978) 210
Mars 231, 232, 235
Marvelous Mrs. Maisel (2017–) 2
Marx, Karl 14, 16
masculinity 153, 160
mass media 229
Masucci, Oliver 206
material popular culture 230–6, 249
Matičević, Mišel 296
Mattausch, Dietrich 115
Mattson, Michelle 19, 40, 71
Maurer, Jürgen 263
May, Karl 113, 129, 155, 159
MDR 162–76, 172
media-archaeological approach 41
media consumers 42, 155, 208
media consumption 42, 45
media content 44, 201
media forms 80, 118, 159, 179, 191, 193
media market 150, 187
media power 123, 126
media practices 43, 94, 157, 184, 192
    post-network 176
    Turkish-German 43
media reflexivity 5, 21, 72, 80, 85, 93, 121, 176, 178, 205, 208, 211, 212, 220, 313, 315
mediascape 3, 80, 95, 99, 102, 125, 179–80, 183–93, 201, 238, 260, 313
medium specificity 37, 39, 40, 87, 132, 178, 180, 205, 257, 266, 277, 278, 303
Mehmet, Maxim 168
Meichsner, Dieter 66
M-eine Stadt sucht einen Mörder (1931) 12
Meinhof, Ulrike 61
melodrama 53, 54, 96, 97, 128, 153, 169, 194, 201, 214

memory culture 114, 205, 212, 225, 226
Men (1988) 108
Merkel, Angela 120, 122, 288
Messestadt Leipzig (trade fair city) 130
Messter, Oskar 109
#MeToo movement 101, 247
Metropolis (1927) 102
Metz, Christian 239
Meyer-Barg, Angela 78
Miazga-Bedrick, Allison 232
Michelle's murder (2008) 164–6
micro flows 257, 265, 271–6, 282
Mielke, Fred 50
Mikkelsen, Mads 248
Mira, Brigitte 79
mirror-stage 224
mise-en-scènes 55, 69, 83, 95, 102, 119, 152, 185, 192, 199, 204, 210, 220, 244, 267, 270, 274, 276, 306
Mitgliederversammlung (General Assembly) 259
Mitic, Gojko 154–5
Mitja case (2007) 164
Mitscherlich, Alexander 50
Mitteldeutscher Rundfunk (MDR, Middle German Broadcast Station) 29, 127–76, 153
Mittell, Jason 2, 3, 198
Mitterer, Felix 39
Mladeck, Kyra 53
MMM 148
mnemonic practice 235
mnemonic processes 267
modernity 46, 86, 277, 278
modernization 68, 86, 89, 141, 147
Möhring, Wotan Wilke 83, 263
Möllemann, Jürgen 117
Molsner, Michael 15
Momper, Walter 89
montage 42, 121–4, 133, 280
Moonlighting (1985–9) 167
Moore, Eoin 286
Morgenpost 66
Morgenthau Plan 104
Morley, David 4, 6–8, 42–3

Mouffe, Chantal 40
Mously, Sara 34
MTV 153, 227, 239, 240, 249
Mubarek, Hosni 148
Mühe, Anna Maria 284
Müller, Heiner 118
Müller, Wilhelm 172
multiculturalism 34, 35, 250
multi-genre 103
"multilaminated" encoding and decoding 248
multiple screen-in-screen projections 304
Mulvey, Laura 274
München 38
Mundsburg 82, 84
Mundt, Maximilian 22–3
Munich 38, 51, 52, 58–60
Munich Olympic Village terrorist attack 49
Murderers Are among Us, The (Die Mörder sind unter uns, 1948) 50
Murnau, F. W. 86, 102, 147
music montage 153, 162
music videos 153, 239
Muslim migrants 129
My Name Is Nobody (1973) 153

narrative/narration 5, 55, 121, 133, 147, 152, 180, 185, 189, 193, 205, 208, 216, 236, 239, 253, 276, 298, 301, 310, 312, 313
 crime 205, 217
 ecosystem 43, 219
 models 32
 segments 82
 structure 85, 211
 system 232, 233, 271, 272, 304
 types 32
Nase, Siri 263
National Atlantic Treaty Organization (NATO) 89, 90, 115
national identity 104, 139, 205, 212, 250, 302
nationalism 62, 98, 172, 173, 177, 302, 311

National Organization of German
   Garden Friends (*Bundesverband
   deutscher Gartenfreunde e.V.*,
   BDG) 97
national politics 143, 144
National Socialism 171, 266
National Socialist 106
national trauma 164, 176
Native American cultures 155
Nay, Jonas 1
Nazi-era crimes 110
Nazification 50
Nazi ideology 173
Nazis 53, 173, 266
NBC 81, 94, 248
NDR 83, 130–48, 150
Nemec, Miroslav 35
Nena 220, 222, 227, 228, 235, 241–4
neo-Nazi movement 65, 114
neo-Nazis 166, 173, 302–12
Netflix 1, 2, 4, 6, 8, 9, 17, 21–4, 27, 33, 47, 73, 177, 178, 183–93, 195–8, 200–61, 265, 267, 268, 272, 276, 283, 285–9, 296, 303, 306, 308, 311–16
Neue Presse (New Paper, Hannover) 65, 66
Neue Revue (New Review, Illustrated Magazine) 132
Neues Deutschland (New Germany, GDR Paper) 136
New German Cinema 15, 86, 167–72, 186, 187, 193, 195, 203, 255, 293
New Hollywood 169
news agencies 116
New Wave aesthetics 180
Niederrhein region 270
Niedersächsisches Tagesblatt (Lower Saxony Daily Paper) 67, 92
Nolte, Emil 224
nonfiction 42
nonfiction crime 208
nonlinear programming 191
nonlinear viewing 213
Norddeutscher Rundfunk (NDR, North German Broadcast Station) 29, 32, 48–85, 127–76, 185
Nordwest Zeitung (Northwest German Daily Paper) 67
Nosbusch, Désirée 79
Nosferatu (1922) 102
nostalgia 83, 84, 141, 223, 235, 236, 240, 257, 298–9
NSU: German History X (2016) 200, 201
Nuda Veritas (1899) 263
nudity 81
Nürnberger Prozesse (Nuremberg Trials) 50
NYPD Blue (1993–2005) 81, 82, 122

Obama, Barack 74
Obel, Agnes 241
Obendorf, Erik 225, 228
Oberschlesier Landsmannschaft 149
Obitz, Günther 92
Ode, Erik 133
Oetjen, Almut 27
"Oh Deutschland, bleiche Mutter" ("pale mother") 293
One Fine Day (1996) 171
online journalism 46
online media 47
online television 240, 276, 303, 315
ÖRF 33, 40, 262
Oscar 186
Ostalgie (Nostalgia for East Germany) 235, 302
Ostfriesland (East Frisia) 237
Ostpolitik (West German foreign policy regarding the Eastern bloc especially East Germany and East Berlin) 130, 134, 137, 143
Ostverträge (political, social and economic agreements made between West Germany and some Eastern bloc countries in the early 1970s) 43, 49
Otherness 71, 77, 80, 111
Ozark (2017–22) 208, 228
Özil, Mesut 297

Pabst, G. W. 86

panoramic gaze 158, 159
panoramic memory 158
Party for a Rule of Law Offensive (Schill Party) 117
Paternoster 108–9
Peckinpah, Sam 160
pedophilia 165, 166, 173, 174, 247
Pegida (Patriotic Europeans against the Islamization of the West) 129
Perfume (2018, TV series) 6, 8, 24, 183, 187, 191, 203, 207, 255–82, 289, 311–13, 315
  abandoned futures and ruined pasts 277–82
  peripheral adjacencies 268–71
  post-memory and restorative nostalgia 265–8
  relational memory and micro flows 271–6
  switching channels 257–61
  synopsis 263–5
  ZDF crime series 261–2
Perfume (Süskind, novel) 268
period dramas 197–201, 205, 207, 209, 312
peripheral adjacencies 268–71
Perry Mason (1957–66) 133
Petersen, Wolfgang 33
Pfab, Susanne 260
Pfeiffer, Rainer 62
phallologocentric discourse 246
Philipp, Tom 218
Piscator, Erwin 118
Pleitgen, Oliver 63
Pleitgen, Ulrich 66
Poe, E. A. 14
point-of-view shot 102, 125
Poland 43, 104, 106, 107, 109, 149
Polish Warsaw Uprising 148
Politbüro (principal policy making committee of the GDR) 87
political identity 72
political talk show 115, 117, 121, 123
Polizeiruf 110 (DFF, 1971–89; ARD, 1990–) 17, 29, 30, 133, 178, 286

Polterabend (Mischievous Evening) 68
polysemy 39, 69, 72, 73, 123, 174, 178, 216, 226, 230, 247, 308, 311, 312
pop music 141, 222, 234, 240
popular culture 199, 201, 249, 250
popular music 230, 239–45
populism 73, 189, 200, 205, 228, 311
post-feminism 204
post-memory 265–8
post-network crime dramas 6, 167–72, 185, 192, 211, 230, 276–8, 312
post-network era 6, 169, 213, 231, 238, 258, 267
post-network original language crime dramas 200, 230–44
post-network television 12–18, 220, 251, 276, 283, 306
postwar Germany 50, 60, 69, 90, 143
"Power of Love" (song) 241
Powrie, Phil 141
Prahl, Axel 33, 178
Presseclub (TV show) 90
print media 46, 47
privatization 22, 44, 47, 89, 93, 96, 99, 177, 194, 223, 227, 229, 239, 240
Pro7 93, 94, 103
professional ethics 55
proletarianism 103
ProSieben/Maxdome 286
psychological interventions 147, 175
public broadcast networks 99, 150, 151, 192
Pundt, Christian 48, 49
punk music 64
punk-rock music 242
Pütter, Trystan 264

Quaas, Tom 163
"Quartett in Leipzig" 36

Raab, Klaus 168
Raacke, Dominic 115
Rabin, Yitzhak 148
race 35, 38, 68, 84, 98, 99, 103, 104

crimes 50, 68
  identity 72, 295
  motivated attacks 114
  riots 65, 104
racism 53, 65, 84, 104, 177, 295
Radebeul 129
Radewagen, Thomas 48, 54
radioactive memory 173
Radio Bremen (RB) 29
Radsi, Samira 187, 203
RAI 194
Raider/Twix 231–6
Rainer Barschel Affäre 62, 65
Raketenstreit (rocket fight) 89
Ramcke, Kerstin 48
RBB 103–26
Reagan, Ronald 86, 224
realism 48, 127, 134, 137, 157, 168
rebound effect 48, 54
rebranding campaign 231, 232, 234, 235
reception patterns 42, 130, 228, 262, 266, 311
"Rechnen Sie mit dem Schlimmsten!" (Worst-Case Scenario) 49–62
  cop out of place 58–60
  crime out of time 55–8
  critical and viewer engagement 54–5
  doctor figure in German history and culture 50–1
  Tagesschau synopsis 49–50
  Tatort synopsis 51–4
  untethered culprit 60–2
Recznicek, S. 155
regional concept 132, 140, 141
regional garden plot clubs (*Kleingartenverbände*) 97
regional identity 36, 45, 51, 89, 130, 139
regionalism 28, 29, 95
re-industrialization 129
Reinhardt, Max 118
Reinl, Harald 129
Reitz, Edgar 198
relational memory 257, 265, 270–7, 282
Remembrance Day bombings 63

Rentschler, Eric 158
representational aesthetics 79
restorative nostalgia 265–8, 280, 281
reunification (*Wiedervereinigung*) 156
reverse shot 102, 154
Rheinische Merkur (Rhineland Newspaper) 67
Rhimes, Shonda 268
rhythmic editing 121, 122
Ricciardi, Laura 208
Richter, Julia 164
Richter, Walter 48, 76, 131, 133
Ricketts, Tyron 296
Riepe, Manfred 106
ritual viewers 43, 44
Riverdale (2017–22) 209
Robins, Kevin 43
rock ballad 153
"Rock Me Amadeus" (song) 244
Rohr, Peter-Schulze 130–48
Roland, Jürgen 89–103
romantic comedies 171
Rostand, Edmond 170
Rote Armee Fraktion (RAF) 61
Roth, Claudia 122
RTL 1, 17, 93, 94, 99, 103, 185, 187
RTL/Sundance TV 1, 128
rubble films (*Trümmerfilme*) 158, 159
"Rückspiel" 36
Rudolph, Sebastian 206
Runde Ecke (Round Corner) 130
Run Lola Run (1999) 112, 184, 188, 201
Russia 44
Russian government 149
Russia-Ukraine war (2022) 293
Ruttmann, Walter 122
Rwandan refugee crisis 148, 149
Rye, Stellan 147

Sabine Christiansen (1998–2007, TV show) 115, 121–3
Sächsisch (Dialect spoken in Saxony) 138, 140
Salem, El Hedi Ben 79
Saler, Michael 155

Sanders-Brahms, Helma   280
Sarrazin, Thilo   34
Sass, Kathrin   289
Sat1   93, 94, 103, 112
Sauerbruch, Ferdinand   50
Sauerbruch-That Was My Life (1954)   50
Sax, Uta   91
Schabowski, Günter   87
Schadewald, Bernd   62–73, 288
Scheel, Walter   131
Schelsky, Helmut   102
Scheunenviertel   105, 108, 111–13
Schill, Ronald   117
Schiller, Karl   49
Schiller, Melanie   301, 302
Schlager   240, 301, 302
Schlingensief, Christoph   118
Schlöndorff, Volker   116, 203
Schlüter, Andreas   174
Schmidt, Niels Bruno   155
Schmidt-Schaller, Petra   83
Schneider, Thomas   93
Scholten, Michael   76
Schrader, Maria   200, 316
Schreber, Moritz   98
Schrebergarten culture   97, 99, 102
Schreiter, Katrin   97
Schröder, Thies   120
Schroeter, Renate   134
Schubert, Franz   172
Schulungsabend (evening training session)   136, 137
Schulze-Rohr, Peter   49–62, 137
Schüttler, Katharina   284
Schwarzer, Alice   101
Schwarzkopf, Dietrich   54, 150, 152
Schweiger, Til   33, 83, 285, 286
Schygulla, Hannah   172
science fiction   55, 205, 214
scopophilia   103
Scorsese, Martin   72, 249
Second World War   114, 154, 158, 224, 229, 258
Self-Other   111
self-reflexive scene   71, 116, 121, 125
semiotic code   41

Sender Freies Berlin/Rundfunk Berlin-Brandenburg (SFB/RBB)   28, 88, 92, 105, 150
Sendezentrum (Broadcast Center)   258
seriality   11, 96, 110, 144–8, 185, 186, 267
Setti, Kais   296
sexism   62
sexuality   24, 35, 56, 60, 61, 101, 257
sexual violence   211, 212, 281
SF   33
SFB-Rundfunkrat (Station Free Berlin Broadcasting Council)   88
Shadows of Trauma: Memory and the Politics of Postwar Identity (Assmann)   225
Shepherd, Crystal   167
Showcase   221
Showtime   86, 202, 248
Silber, Christoph   82
silent cinema   50
Silesian autonomy   149
Simmons, J. K.   202
Simple Minds (band)   241
Sinjen, Sabine   33, 51
Sky   177, 193
Sky1   183
Sky Deutschland   1, 197
Skylines (2019)   203, 288
Slaughterhouse-Five (Vonnegut)   128
smartphones   240
smart TV   186, 191
Snétberger, Toni   115
Snider, Zachary   304
soap opera   128, 167–72, 176
social democratization   79
Social Democrats (SPD)   62, 74, 103, 104
social identity   44
socialism   106, 162
Socialist Unity Party (SED)   90, 130
socialization   189
socially critical films   118
social media   47, 178, 179, 189, 196, 208, 220, 221, 227, 228, 232, 233, 235
social realism   166

sociopolitical issues   39, 40
Sodann, Peter   127
SOKO (Special Investigation Unit, 1978–2020)   30, 202, 203
SOKO 5113 (*Special Commission*, 1978)   262
SOKO Leipzig (2001–)   262
SOKO Munich (1978–2020)   17
Somewhere in Berlin (1946)   113
Sonnenallee (1999)   127
Sony Walkman   235, 239, 240
Sopranos, The (1999–2007)   184, 198, 208
Soul Kitchen (2009)   288
soundscape   82, 199, 220, 240, 241
SPD   49, 103, 120, 162
Spiering, Katharina   212
Spigel, Lynn   7, 8
sports videography   304
Spotify   241
Spur der Steine (Trace of Stones, 1966)   64, 127
Stader Tagesblatt (Stade Daily Paper)   133
Stahlnetz (Steelnet, German Dragnet, 1958–68, 1999–2003)   17
Stairway to Heaven (song)   153
"Stalingrad of German politics"   43
Stappenbeck, Stefanie   115
Star Wars politics   86
Starz   144, 185
Stasi (*Staatssicherheitsdienst*)   130, 132, 175, 229
Staude, Sylvia   164, 169
Staudte, Wolfgang   50
Steinbrecher, Kurt   166, 172–4
Steinfeld, Hailee   238
Stellvertretende Intendantin (Acting Chief Administrator)   260
Stenzel, Monika   91
stereotyping   54, 69, 71, 83, 99, 132, 168
Stern (Star, Weekly Illustrated Magazine)   62, 65, 72, 165
Sternberg, Josef von   86
Sternenfänger (*Star Catchers*, 2002)   200
Stevenson, Robert   239

Stewart, Jimmy   94
Steyerl, Hito   112
Stiegler, Christian   189
Stolte, Dieter   260
Stoph, Willy   131
storytelling   198, 203, 214, 216, 233, 266, 272, 312, 316
Stosch, Stefan   106
streaming   189, 303
  networks   192
  platforms   2, 9, 179, 183, 194, 195, 314, 316
  service   196
street-film aesthetics   112
street violence   93
Strobl, Christine   260
student movement   137
Studio Babelsberg   86, 202
Studio Hamburg   48
Stürmer, Michael   224
Stuttgarter Zeitung (Stuttgart Daily Paper)   132
subscription   2, 189, 190, 194, 197
subsidy   195
Süddeutscher Rundfunk (SR, South German Broadcast Station)   29
Süddeutsche Zeitung (SZ, South German Daily Paper)   65, 77, 92, 93, 117, 132
Südwestrundfunk (SWR, Southwest German Broadcast Station)   29
Suleiman, Muhammad   163
Sundance   185, 187, 203
superimposed scene   81
surveillance pattern   138, 296–9
Süskind, Patrick   24, 258, 263, 268, 275, 276
Süssmuth, Rita   149
Sykes, Wanda   316
Syrreal Entertainment   283, 285
systemic racism   53, 70, 84, 297

Tagesschau (Daily Evening News, TV program)   20, 39, 44–7, 49–50, 67, 89, 178
Tagesspiegel (Daily Mirror, Paper)   54, 67, 78, 88, 105

INDEX

Tageszeitung (Daily Paper) 93
Talajic, Dennis 236
Talentschmiede (talent factory) 194
Tanner, Tony 211
Tappert, Horst 262
Tarsier Studios 236
Tatort (1970–) 2, 3, 5, 6, 10, 11, 12, 14, 17–21, 27–33, 41–7, 177, 185, 188, 191, 193, 202–4, 213, 268, 269, 277, 287, 302, 311, 313–15
   intersections of national, regional, and local viewing 34–5
   stories "close to reality" 39–40
   tourism 36–9
Tatort Berlin 86–126, 179
   "Berlin, beste Lage" ("Berlin, Top Location," 1993) 103–14
   "Eine ehrliche Haut" ("An Honest Skin/Man," 2004) 114–26
   "Keine Tricks, Herr Bülow" ("No Tricks," Mr. Bülow, 1989) 89–103
Tatort Dresden and Leipzig 127–76, 180
   "Jetzt und Alles" ("Now and Everything," 1994) 148–62
   "Taxi nach Leipzig" ("Taxi to Leipzig," 1970) 130–48
   "Todesstrafe" ("Death Penalty," 2008) 162–76
Tatort Hamburg 48–85, 179, 285, 286, 296
   "Auf der Sonnenseite" (On the Sunny Side, 2008) 73–85
   "Rechnen Sie mit dem Schlimmsten!" (Worst-Case Scenario, 1972) 49–62
   "Voll auf Hass" (Committed to Hate, 1987) 62–73, 288
Tatort Kieler (2010–17) 202
Tatortreiniger/Crime Scene Cleaner (2011–18) 32
Tatort Sommerpause (production pause) 46
"*Tatort*-Tourismus" 36
Taubin, Amy 248
Taxi Driver (1976) 249

"Taxi nach Leipzig" ("Taxi to Leipzig," 1970) 30, 39, 76, 130–48
   body politic 142–4
   critical and viewer engagement 131–4
   one nation under network television 134–42
   seriality and geopolitics 144–8
   Tagesschau year-end synopsis 130–1
   Tatort synopsis 134
televised fiction 136
Television and Reaganism (Feuer) 41
television apparatus 125, 229, 239, 240
television fans 46
Television Framework Agreement 194
television genres 126, 161, 269, 270
television-in-television shot 122, 126
television medium 86, 96, 138, 213
television news 42, 43
television reception 30, 41, 42, 44, 76, 79
televisual aesthetics 6, 125, 194, 233, 258, 306
televisual codes 178
televisual flow 11, 103, 115, 116, 121, 163, 165, 169, 229
televisuality 44, 47, 125, 148, 172, 226, 308
televisual practice 7
Terkessidis, Mark 37, 75, 83
textuality 6, 40, 42, 46, 205, 253, 266
Thiele, Rolf 210
Thiem, Marlene 260
Third Reich 29, 50, 53, 86, 131, 143, 164, 165, 171, 173, 177, 199, 205, 212, 229, 260, 261, 266
Thomalla, Simone 33, 163, 171
Thompson, Ethan 2
three-dimensional graphics 136
Thriller (1982, album) 247, 249
"Thriller" (song) 249
Tiananmen Square protest and massacre (1989) 227
TikTok 42

time-travel genre   205, 217, 220
Timm, Peter   127
"Todesstrafe" ("Death
    Penalty")   162–76
  critical and viewer
    engagement   164–7
  family therapy   175–6
  german unification   172–5
  post-network crime
    drama   167–72
  Tagesschau synopsis   162–3
  Tatort synopsis   163–4
Töpfer, Kurt   149
Torner, Evan   155, 156
totalitarian systems   136, 142
"Tote Taube in der Beethovenstraße"
    (Dead Dove in Beethoven
    Street)   33
tourism   36, 38, 178, 179
traditional masculinity   58
traditional windowing   121
transgressive sexualities   211
trans/homophobia   62
transitional adjacency   270
transitory scenes   31, 81, 85
transmedia   80, 178, 186, 219, 220,
    236, 257, 304
  migration   299–302
  practices   208, 265, 271
  source   267
  television   205, 239–44, 271–7
transnational casting and
    production   202–3
transnational television   132, 184,
    188, 193, 203, 242
Traue, Antje   210
Treaty of Moscow   131
Tremé (2010–13)   202
Treyz, Catherine   190
tribal identity   156
Tribel, Jördis   206
"Trizonesien" (song)   293
Trümmerfilm (Rubble Film)   152
Trump, Donald J.   2, 250, 311
Tschiller: Off Duty (2016)   285, 286
Tukur, Ulrich   33
Tunefind   242
Turkish culture   124

Turkish for Beginners (2006–8)   288
Turkish minority   67, 68
Tutti Frutti (1990–3)   99
TV Hören und Sehen (TV and Radio
    Guide)   55, 66, 67
Twin Peaks (1990–91, 2017)   62
Twitter   12, 238
Tykwer, Tom   24, 86, 112, 188, 197,
    198, 200, 201, 203, 258, 276,
    315, 316

UFA Fiction   262
UK Hammer Studios   52
undercover concept   78, 85
UNESCO   128
Unger, Karl   15
United Kingdom   93–4
United Nations   103
United Nations Security Council   148
United States   22, 44, 89, 93, 116,
    121, 128, 186, 189, 192, 196,
    202, 250
Unknown (2011)   86
Unorthodox (2020)   200, 201, 316
Unsere Mütter, unsere Väter
    (*Generation War*, 2013)   258
Unser Sandmännchen (1959)   135,
    150, 258
"Unter Brüdern" ("Among
    Brothers")   30, 133
upper-class lifestyle   139
urbanization   97
urban modernity   12
US crime dramas   133
US dramas   189, 249
US Marshall Plan   104
US popular culture   3, 169
US popular music   169
US streaming services   190
US television   2, 3, 159, 184, 186–7,
    198, 253, 315
US television formats   200–2
US Westerns   107, 155

Valentin, Karl   234
Valerii, Tonino   153
van Endert, Gunther   258
van Zandt, Steven   184

VEB Jugendmode 237
Verbotene Liebe (1995–2015) 203
Verein Freie Volksbühne (Association for a Free People's Theatre) 118
Vereinsmeierei (club fanaticism) 98
verité-style camera 290
Verkehrsvertrag 49
Verliebt in Berlin (2005–6) 112
VH-1 239
VHF 135
Vicari, Lisa 206
videogame 159, 160
videography 55, 80, 127, 153, 164, 192, 239
Vietnam War 49, 76, 222
Vilsmaier, Josef 199
visual culture 6, 147, 178
visual media 46, 191, 226
visual style 178
Vogler, Rüdiger 169
Vogt, J. 37
völkisch ideology 29
Volksbühne 118
Volkslied 172
Volkspolizei 131, 161
"Voll auf Hass" (Committed to Hate) 62–73, 288
   critical and viewer engagement 64–7
   father-figure failures 70–3
   racism and racist crimes 67–9
   Tagesschau synopsis 62–3
   Tatort synopsis 63–4
von Beust, Ole 117
von Borries, Achim 203
von Borsody, Eduard 29
von der Leyen, Ursula 122
von Donnersmarck, Florian Henckel 127
von Festenberg, Nikolaus 78
von Lojewski, Günther 92
Vonnegut, Kurt 128
von Saure, Hans Wilhelm 117
von Schnitzler, Karl-Eduard 227
von Trotta, Margarete 116
von Weizsäcker, Richard 90
von Wick, Klaudia 78

Wacker, Holger 27
Waffen-SS 224, 262
Wahl, Thorsten 117
Wahl, Wolfgang 52
Waldschlösschenbrücke 128
Walesa, Lech 149
Wallace, Edgar 92, 223
Walulis, Philip 31
Warsaw Ghetto Uprising 131
Warsaw Treaty 131
Waschke, Mark 206
Waterkant-Gate corruption scandal 62
WAZ 92, 132
WB 200
We Are the Wave (2019) 202
web-based fan 46
Weber, Florian 258
web services 116
Wegner, Matthias 53
Wehler, Hans-Ullrich 224
Weimar cinema 86, 112, 180, 255
Weimar era 199, 205
Weisgerber, Eleonore 91
Weissensee (2010–) 127, 199, 209
Weisz, Franziska 83
Weizsäcker, Richard 101
Weltkrimi 78
Wendepunkt 255
Wenders, Wim 86, 169
Wende-theme 64, 127
Werner, Axel 207
Werremeier, Friedhelm 58, 132, 133, 136, 137, 142, 147
Weser Kurier 92, 106
Westdeutscher Rundfunk (WDR) 28, 30, 185, 193, 194
Westfälische Rundschau 66
West German films 155
West Germans 87, 135, 136, 141
West German television 107, 135, 141, 145
West Germany 22, 48, 68, 87, 104, 111, 129–31, 138, 148, 152, 157, 165, 173, 180, 223, 287, 308
Wettcke, Thorsten 82
wide-angle landscape panorama 158

Wieben, Wilhelm   245
Wild West novels   159
Wilhelmsburg   82–4
Wilhelmshavener Zeitung
   (Willhelmshaven Daily
   Paper)   67, 93
Williams, Raymond   20, 41, 216
Willis, Bruce   167
Winczewski, Patrick   162–76
Winger, Anna   187, 203
Winger, Jörg   187, 203
Winkler, Angela   206
Winnetou novels   129, 155
Wire, The (2002–8)   62, 202, 287
Wir im NDR   78
Wir sind auch nur ein Volk (We are
   also only a people, 1994–5)   64
Wishaw, Ben   263
Witte, Günther   39, 45, 132, 151, 163
Wittenborn, Michael   74
Wo ist Coletti (1913)   12
Wolf, Fritz   46
Wowereit, Klaus   122
Wrigley   231
Wunderbar Together   251
Wunschkonzert (Request Concert,
   1940)   29

Wutke, Martin   163

xenophobia   38, 176

Yardim, Fahri   33, 83, 284–6
Yasemin (1988)   63
Yeats, William Butler   96
Yigit, Burat   74
YouGov   225
Young, Robert C.   99
You (2018–21)   248
YouTube   31, 42, 125, 179, 192, 232,
   233, 240, 245
Yugoslav conflict   115
Yugoslavia   103, 104
Yusef, Soleen   203
Yusef, Yoleen   288

ZDF   17, 24, 30, 51, 90, 99, 103, 131,
   133, 191, 194, 198–200, 203,
   209, 257–62, 265
ZDFneo   24, 258
Zeitgeschichte   127
Ziolkowska, Patrycia   74
Zweierlei Untergang (Hillgruber)   224
Zweites Deutsches Fernsehen
   (ZDF)   258

www.ingramcontent.com/pod-product-compliance
Lightning Source LLC
Chambersburg PA
CBHW052142300426
44115CB00011B/1483